THE HISTORY OF PRESTON GUILD

THE PRESTON GUILD MERCHANT OF 1862.

(From our Special Correspondent.)

FOR full five hundred years the Guild or Corporate Fraternity of Preston has existed to conserve the liberties of her freemen. Since 1562 it has been the custom of resident and non-resident burgesses to meet, once in twenty years, for the purposes of renewing their freedom and sanctioning such laws as from time to time might be deemed beneficial to the fraternity. This occasion from time immemorial has been known as a "Guild Merchant," and has been a period of unusual festivity. Twenty-two of these Guild Merchants have already passed away and marked the progress of the town, and now for the twenty-third time, under the mayoralty of R. Townley Parker, Esq., a gentleman of ancient lineage and high social position, the Guild books are open for the transaction of business, and the citizens are met to commemorate the conservation of municipal liberties by a week's festivity.

It may, perhaps, be thought that during a period of such deep and wide-spread distress it would have been better to postpone this event. Such a feeling did, to some extent, prevail in the town, but it was overruled by the Corporation, who, while they admitted some seeming inconsistency in coupling together feasting and starvation, considered that the occasion would, by bringing multitudes of strangers to the town, lead to the expenditure of money. Had they thought it likely to produce a wrong impression on the country at large as to the necessity which exists for charitable relief at this period, the Guild would not now be held. In other years there has been a surplus of receipt over expenditure, and we believe it is designed on this occasion to swell the relief fund with the sum thus expected. With this understanding we chronicle the events of the week with the greater pleasure, and indulge a hope that this effort to banish sadness may not be without its good and permanent result upon a people who, under sufferings so nobly endured, enjoy the sympathy and admiration of Britain, from the august Duchess of Lancaster to the humblest of their fellow-workmen.

Guilds Merchant are by antiquaries believed to have originated in the days of Alfred. Probably they may be of older date even, for it seems that when patriarchal rule in the family was somewhat weakened by reason of the growth of population, and there was need of some other bond of association, this was substituted. When all the dwellers in a place were no longer kinsmen it became convenient for neighbours to group themselves by tens for the purposes of social government, and hence tythings or gylds. In process of time various kinds of guilds arose, all of which had the common features of equal pledge or suretyship of any nine members for the tenth, in cases where the *borh* or pledge was necessary. "Hence, nigh-borhs or neighbours," says Mr. Harland, an authority in these matters. "These little confederations of ten men or heads of families took various forms consistent with the objects for which they were instituted. Thus, "the citizens of London formed themselves into 'frith-guilds' or associations for the maintenance of the public peace, ten of them going to form a hundred," a term which is estranged from its former application to population; we are told, too, of religious guilds "for mutual comfort and support in life, Christian burial after death, and masses for the soul of a deceased member in purgatory;" of knightly guilds and trading guilds, of which the one now in course of commemoration is the last remaining specimen in the country.

Considering how important a part these guilds have played as the basis of the municipal and political constitution of our country, this commemoration has its special significance and value. Those who have no reverence for the past, and see nothing in their present position to remind them of their obligation to previous workers on the social system, may be anxious to sweep away a record which is an impediment to business; but those who rejoice in that sagacious admixture of popular elements for the government of the country, King, Lords, and Commons, tracing back to these initial municipal institutions, with their head man or alderman and council of associates, the model upon which it was formed, will bow with profound feeling before the derivable source of British freedom.

During the reign of Henry II. guilds are spoken of as common institutions. They were, in fact, taken under the protection of the King, who granted charters to guilds mercatory, confirming them in certain privileges. Such was a charter granted by this Monarch to Preston, A.D. 1173, wherein "my burgesses of Preston" are commanded "to have and hold, well and in peace, freely and quietly, fully and entirely, &c., both within and without the borough, all those liberties and free customs (saving my right of administering justice) which the burgesses of Newcastle-under-Lyne have, as I have granted." By this, which was the first of fourteen charters granted by Monarchs of this realm to the ancient borough of Preston, and another, known as the ancient custumal of Preston, the freemen were released from certain taxes and customs throughout the realm, such as tolls, in the town or elsewhere, passage across sea or river, and stallage in the market-place; and were permitted to levy certain tolls and customs upon those traders less privileged than themselves. It will be seen from one section of the oath of the burgesses that the inhabitants enrolled were secured a complete monopoly of the commerce of the place: it runs thus:—"You shall know noe foreiner (i.e. non-resident) to buy or sell merchandise with any other foreiner within this town or the franchises thereof, except at Faire Time, but you shall warn the Mayor and Bailiffs thereof." The protective law of apprenticeship is shown to have been most strictly enforced; and we obtain, on examining the documents, a very clear picture of the men and women in that day in their several relations, together with the exclusive character of the code by which the commercial element of the borough's progress, which contrasts but quaintly with our free-trade notions of commercial competition.

The exclusive privileges of free burgesses are now things of the past. Preston was, in 1835, placed under the provisions of the Corporation Reform Bill. But, though the alteration of municipal law rendered the legal portion of the ceremony unnecessary, it was determined to celebrate the Guilds Merchant as usual, with certain limits as to duration.

There is a very quaint account found in Kuerden's MS. of the manner in which these municipal carnivals were conducted about two hundred years ago. There seems to have been at that time a formal procession from the Mayor's residence to the High-cross, where the Guild was opened, and thence to church, followed by another procession, with a considerable number of taps running here and there, concluded by a grand banquet, for the proper arrangement of which directions are issued for the guidance of all officials, from the high stewards to the chief cook, the yeoman of the wine-cellar, the gentlemen of the napery, and the groom-porters. The companies of trades were dined at their respective halls, from the windows of which floated their banners. There was then a banquet given by a "Mrs. Mayoress" to two hundred ladies who danced the night out till "morning and weariness" surprised them. The second, third, and fourth days the Mayor went again to pray and then to dine, and after dinner attended to the enrolment of burgesses and the reception of fines. Sunday passed over pretty quietly. The trades companies appear to have done the hospitable to each other over a period of six weeks; and when the time came for the conclusion of the festivities the Mayor went to court and reported the business of the Guild for the confirmation of the burgesses. These transactions having received the seal of the Corporation, the clerk announced the Guild adjourned for twenty years.

The Guild Merchant of 1762 is rendered memorable by the three hundred splendidly-attired ladies who accompanied the Mayoress to church, and from thence, to gratify the crowd of spectators, proceeded to parade the market-place. Some writers mention the effect of this unparalleled display of beauty with the keenest enthusiasm:—

> But I cannot describe or sufficiently praise
> The beauties that beamed with astonishing blaze;
> They were rich constellations, a galaxy bright,
> * * * *
> A host of pure angels—too much for the sight.
> Amidst their parading such glances were sent
> That sighs were excited wherever they went.

This Guild lasted a month; two grand balls were given every week, and theatrical entertainments and all sorts of shows and amusements were provided for the populace. Robert Parker, grandfather of the present Mayor, was then in office, and is reported to have been singularly studious to please and to inspire mirth and festivity into every individual. His daughter and Miss Hulton were the principal beauties of the succeeding Guild Merchant. The same dazzling display of female beauty has been attempted at more recent periods, but the practice now has entirely fallen into desuetude.

We must now, however, proceed to depict the celebration of this the twenty-third Guild Merchant, opened on Monday, the 1st inst.; and, in doing so, beg to acknowledge the obligations under which we lie to R. Ashcroft, Esq., the town clerk, and Mr. Dearden, the hallkeeper. The initial proceeding took place in the hall of the Grammar School, the old Townhall having been removed to make way for the stately edifice shortly to rise under the wand of Mr. Scott. The Mayor, in his robes of office, occupied a dais at the further end of the room, and there received the company as they arrived. The attendance was as great as the room could accommodate. Amongst the notabilities were observed the Mayors of Blackburn, Bolton, Wigan, Warrington, and Burnley, in their robes; Sir Thomas Hesketh, Bart., M.P.; Major-General the Hon. Sir J. Yorke Scarlett; C. Jacson, R. Newsham, T. B. Crosse, T. Green, Esqrs.; Sir T. H. Maxwell, together with the Rev. Canon Parr (Guild Chaplain) and the clergy of the district, conformist and nonconformist. The procession formed outside the building, and proceeded by the main thoroughfare to the parish church through a dense throng of spectators. The sun was merry in the sky, and shone upon the display of banners with a kindly greeting. The shops and balconies, gaily decorated, were filled with well-dressed ladies and gentlemen; the roofs of the houses even afforded a precarious standpoint for the more determined sightseers. We could not look at the dense mass of humanity which, as it were, formed the foundation of this living wall on either side without detecting in eye and feature, in air and dress, the evidence of the intense conflict here daily waged with want. The sun, although it heightened the effect of the decorations, did but reveal the dark shadows that were lying beyond. After full cathedral service the Vicar delivered a discourse, which, though exhaustive as an apology for commemorations, was deficient in that varied and felicitous application for which such an occasion affords special opportunity. We were glad, however, to remark a bold denunciation of men who refuse to contribute to the relief of those by whose labours they have risen to affluence. After the service the procession, having accompanied the Mayor back to the hall, was there dismissed. The Roman Catholics, a body of considerable importance in Preston, held High Mass at the Church of St. Augustine, the Bishop of Liverpool being present.

During the afternoon a great volunteer review and sham fight came off on Preston Moor. The rain and the confined limits of the field appropriated to the troops afforded two obstacles to the success of the evolutions. The ground was kept by Major-General the Hon. J. Yorke Scarlett, the reviewing officer, on whose staff were observed Colonel Wilson Patten, M.P., and Colonel Manners. The reception of the Major-General by the entire body of 3000 volunteers in line presented a fine spectacle, and evidently excited the enthusiasm of the 30,000 spectators asserted to have been upon the neighbouring ground. Unfortunately, an accident occurred at this period of the proceedings which resulted in bodily injuries to several and great alarm to all who occupied one of the stands, for that structure gave way suddenly and precipitated its occupants with disordered dresses and fractured limbs to the ground. In his subsequent address to the corps the Major-General did not deal in flattering speeches; while he bestowed a general commendation on those who had engaged, he evidently wished to impress upon the officers the necessity of intense application before they could make themselves equal to their important duties.

The athletic sports peculiar to the district were carried on at the same time within an inclosed space on the Marsh, and drew great crowds. One hundred guineas, inclusive of leather and silver belts, were awarded in prizes on this and the following day. The combatants were divided into heavy and light weights. Fifty-four wrestlers tested the power of their sinewy limbs on Monday. The light weights followed on Tuesday. These men are about 9½ stone each. Foot-races and high-pole jumping at various times engaged the energies of competitors. "Soon as the evening shades prevailed" Blondin attracted some 20,000 to another part of the Marsh, where he performed his wonderful feats with the usual success.

The mayoral banquet on Monday evening was attended by about 400 gentlemen. The Mayor was surrounded with the nobility and gentry of the county, and the municipal, civil, and ecclesiastical dignitaries of the town. The Earl of Derby and Lord Stanley were both present, and several distinguished representatives of both services. From the banqueting-chamber to the ballroom was but a step. Both apartments are comprised in the Corn Exchange. The Corn Exchange proper, a large court with glazed roof, has been wonderfully transmogrified. Inventive fingers have been at work to deck the prosaic Chamber of Commerce for the Queen of Beauty. The troughed ceiling is hidden by painted centrepieces, bordered with bannerets and festooned. Music, Science, Literature, and Art have each an emblematic representation. The walls above the galleries are covered with heraldic blazonry, and the walls beneath, on a level with the lounges, reflect the graceful forms which float upon the floor improvised for the occasion. Blue, green, and red are the prevailing colours, spangled with gold fleurs-de-lis. The gaspipe laid above the gallery circles the area, and produces a charming effect. The transformation has been effected by native genius, Mr. Horn, together with Messrs. Brewster and Burrows, having been intrusted with the decoration.

The company included nearly all the wealth, fashion, and beauty of the county, and the Guild Mayor's ball of 1862 has been pronounced by competent authority to have been an immense success. For those who were not at the ball the Theatre Royal was open. Verdi's opera "Il Travatore" was produced there with great effect, Mdme. Rudersdorff, Miss Reeves, Mr. E. St. Aubyn, and Mr. Eliott Galer being among the principals. Crowds of people were flocking into the town during the day. The public walks and thoroughfares of the place were full of strangers, and the river Ribble was alive with pleasure-boats. All classes of the people were bent upon enjoyment, and the relief committees had been careful that the poor operatives should not feel the distress of their position more than could be avoided.

On Tuesday the sun rose jubilant, and waked a multitude of expectant eyes to the gaieties of a second day. One great benefit due to these Guild Merchants we have not noticed. In the history of Preston they have proved so many start-points along the centuries. They have usually given birth to some important improvements, moral, social, legal, or architectural. For instance, after the Guild Merchant of 1702 the Blue-coat School is established; after that of 1742 the fire-engine is first introduced and the waterworks are commenced; after that of 1742 another school is founded; after 1802 the Theatre Royal is built and the Ribble Navigation Act is obtained; after 1822 several churches and chapels are erected, together with the Corn Exchange, and so on. The great event which is to follow upon this Guild Merchant is the erection of a Townhall (designed by G. G. Scott) which will vie with those much-admired civic palaces of Belgium. The ground floor will, according to plan, comprise a large exchange-room, with suitable offices for the discharge of municipal business. On the upper floor will be a large room fitted for public meetings, with gallery, orchestra, and council-room. Along the principal front is a bold arcade carried by coupled columns, and at the end a lofty clock-tower. According to the *Builder*, "the walls are to be built of local stone. Granite and marble columns are interspersed among others of stone, so as to relieve the colours constructively. Sculptured decorations, too, will be extensively introduced in numerous foliated capitals, panels, and statues." The estimated cost is £30,000. The ceremony of laying the first stone was, consequently, performed by the Guild Mayor. That gentleman being a member of the Freemasons, it was laid with masonic honours. The brethren of this ancient order mustered from all parts of the county. Some 800 assembled in the Bairstow Congregational School, a commodious building, and thence the procession proceeded, being joined at another point by the clergy and corporation, who, deprived of their chief, had been very unceremoniously kept waiting under a fierce sun some hour and a half. Accompanied by soldiers and military bands, the cortége presented a very imposing appearance as it wound its way along by a circuitous route to the Market-place, the site of the proposed building. All Preston seemed to have emptied itself into this arterial thoroughfare, and not only Preston but the neighbouring towns and villages, besides the thousands of people who came from more distant localities. The houses were more decorated than the day before, and certainly, to judge by the banners which floated in the breeze from every available window and balcony or triumphal arch, of which there are many, it would not do to say that true enthusiasm never *flags*. The thought of distress seemed banished for a time, the eye kindled, the voice rose in tones of animated converse, and the heart pulsated to the martial music that poured on the air. After a fatiguing walk in heavy robes, the Mayor mounted a platform erected around the stone, together with the Deputy Grand Master of the order, Sir Thomas Hesketh, Bart., M.P., Mr. Scott, R.A., and others, and, having announced to the spectators the object of the meeting, the Provincial Chaplain of the order read a most appropriate prayer for the Divine assistance and blessing on the undertaking in hand. The Mayor then went on his knees to deposit various bottles in the cavity of the stone and spread the mortar. An ode was sung by the brethren while the block was lowered, libations of oil and wine, with corn and salt, were poured out from various gold and silver vessels upon the stone, and then followed a spirited speech from the Mayor to those assembled, in the course of which he took occasion to laud the ancient order to which he belongs. An impressive prayer by the Provincial Chaplain then followed, at the close of which there arose upon the impressed air the grand strains of the "Hallelujah Chorus," the choir being supported by the band of the Preston volunteers. During this climacteric and appropriate performance the whole assemblage stood uncovered. Cheers then arose for the Queen and the Mayoress, Lord Derby and Lord Stanley—who were present. May a building so devoutly and solemnly founded arise in beauty as the augury of better times to Preston—purer, nobler times, when civic corruption shall no more debase, when religious discord shall no more hinder, the Divine work of human redemption, but when all classes shall combine to develop their noblest powers to the glory of God!

Before the procession, which again formed, could make the appointed progress, a thunderstorm burst upon the town, the crowd collapsed, the Mayor's tail gradually diminished, and that good-humoured and hard-worked gentleman, after bowing to the constant few who attended him, dismissed them at last, and retired, dripping, to his apartments. After some hours, however, he shone out with renewed refulgence at the grand masonic banquet, from which he passed with an illustrious company to the ballroom, then arranged for a concert, where a select but large audience dwelt with rapt and favoured ears upon the sweet voices of Mdlle. Titiens, Mdme. Sherrington, Miss Palmer, and the melodious tones of Mr. Sims Reeves and Mr. Santley. The rain threatened in vain upon the glass above; no terror of spoiled dresses could destroy the equanimity of the pleased assemblage, which listened also with breathless attention to Weber's "Concert-stück," performed by Mr. Charles Hallé, the conductor for the occasion.

Nor must we omit to mention other matters of interest to the town generally which occurred during the afternoon and evening of Tuesday. A balloon ascent had been announced for one o'clock. Full 20,000 people assembled in Avenham Park to see what might turn up; but, alas! nothing did turn up. They were dismissed by the apology that the balloon had gone on, by mistake, to Edinburgh. We have been assured, however, that the little package lay stowed quietly away in the parcels booking-office, the attendant being on the look-out for something more nearly resembling the dome of St. Paul's. On Wednesday, however, the balloon was inflated, and went up, to the surprise of wondering masses, amongst torrents of rain. The Orchard, with its whirligigs, shooting-galleries, menageries, dramatic palaces, marionette establishments, hopping-shops, and drinking-booths, increased in popularity throughout the day.

On Wednesday there was an immense amount of convivial business to be done. The procession of the Friendly Societies, the Lancashire Agricultural Society's Annual Show of Cattle, the Walton-le-Dale Floral and Horticultural Society's Show, and the Procession of the Temperance Society and Bands of Hope, each presented claims to public favour. But dismay was general, as from out the window of the bedchamber the eye rested on the dank ground, and ascended by the stolid streams to the dark, leaden, drear sky, and sought in vain for the "silver lining." Still, making our way to Fishergate, we found, not an "army with banners," but an army lifting above its head that defence against the anger of the skies which civilisation has given to man. We heard the splashing tread of men, and the liquid strains of music struggling upwards, but saw nothing save a moving, varicoloured carpet of gingham, under which Preston sought refuge. The friendly societies had need of all their co-operative warmth to destroy the effect of this wet blanket. Surely nothing presents a more miserable picture than a flooded carnival!

There was no falling away, however; the Order of Foresters, Free Gardeners, Independent Order of Mechanics, Ancient Shepherds, Druids, Catholic Brethren, United Order of Oddfellows, and Independent Order of Oddfellows, were supported by their members. Some 2700 took part in the which reached a mile and a quarter, and occupied an hour and a hal any one point. When the dun-coloured cloud which obscured the folded up and allowed us to catch a sight of the winding stream, s of it struck us as very amusing. The Free Gardeners walked beh bearing a section of the Garden of Paradise, with the antediluvian g flesh-coloured tights, seated therein. Seen between the intervals they produced a wild sensation amongst the Prestonians, who re gracious bows with infinite delight. The Shepherds appeared with lambs, and emblematical banners, and were brought up by th persons in brown bearskins, each followed by a dog. Wolfskins v been more appropriate. The Catholic Order was preceded by a ban the Papal arms. Each department appeared in proper costume, and w by bands of music.

One might make merry with the procession of water-drinkers w off in the afternoon of this day. Surely they had "beautiful *nauseam*. The rain was incessant, and the proceedings but a r those of the morning. Struggling through the umbrellas, it was p and then to catch a glimpse of the flags, bearing a variety of most and defiant mottoes, such as "The Pump and the Teapot," "Dru not enter Heaven," "The Bar, the Barrel, the Grave!" with the o barrel staved in at both ends, indicating that it has been seen Much to the credit of these societies, which mustered some 2600 r form this procession, is the fact that drunkenness at a period like Preston kept high wassail, and was driven by the very inclemency of into the public-house, was so little visible.

The North Lancashire Agricultural Society, which opened its pro Tuesday by a trial of grass and grain mowing machines at Lea a summoned the farmers of the county to its showyard on Wedne visitor, however, came unbidden and unwelcomed. The rain ut what would otherwise have proved a most successful meeting. there such a show before. The contrast between the entries of 184 of 1862 exhibits a surprising progress. Take only the 126 pedigre cattle against the 44 ordinary cattle of 1848, and this will sample of the change which has been effected in fourteen ye who are acquainted with Preston will know the Holme w society had pitched its tent. It is a plot of pasture-ground the Ribble. Some thirty acres of this were inclosed, and the H and Florticultural Society obtained a portion of it for their ma show of implements was very strong; but the great featu shorthorns, which surpassed what we have often seen at meetings of the Royal Society. The "Butterflies" from Townele most distinguished members of the class. This blood was not onl by Colonel Towneley, but by Mr. Baxter, who, by means of it, t first prizes. The Colonel's "Royal Butterfly" is a grand bull, pe his points save the slightest dip in the rump. Several of his prize-takers in other classes. He took the prize as the best mal the yard; and Lady Pigott, also a very successful exhibitor, obta roan heifer, "Rosedale," the Guild Mayor's cup. Messrs. Jon Naylor, of Fulwood; Atherton, of Speke; L. C. Wood, of Eastwood, of Burnley Woodhouse, Lancaster; R. Booth, Dickinson, of Ulverston; and Patterson, of Ulverston, were a prize-takers. The horses, sheep, and pigs were unusually good. which won Mr. M'Culloch, of Wigan, the special Guild prize, l flights of hurdles 4ft. 6in. high. The attendance on Wednesda paratively small, and on Thursday it was smaller. During the freshes had carried away the temporary bridge erected by the obliged visitors to get across by boat or to make a circuito Penwortham-bridge. The ground lying in ridge and furrow was the previous day, but on Thursday it was frightful. The critic was fain to make literally flying visits from shed to s furrows lay full of water. The sheep and pigs, which had passe night of exposure, pent up within a small space, presented picture, and the attendants, who had been doing their best them comfortable, looked drenched to the skin. The dinner on afternoon was a grand success, so far as attendance was The congregation of 1700 people to satisfy the pangs of hunger impressive scene, but when this force is seen to bivouac under becomes highly amusing. There is something unique in the sight sheltered performing gastronomic duets. What the rain could mak was rendered so; but, as soon as the remainder had been disc Derby—who had been conveyed from the Mayor's official resid president's chair by a procession of butchers in blue coats and c in company with Lord Stanley and Sir J. Yorke Scarlett, K.C.B. upon the troubled waters and raised the spirits of the meeting to his own. Winning, courteous, and practical, his apt speeches diffu around. He retrieved the occasion, and dismissed the large mee feeling of having been amply repaid.

Wednesday finished with a grand Masonic banquet.

Everybody, however, was on the qui vive for Thursday. T supply the great feature of the Guild Merchant of 1862. Visit quarters poured into the town to witness the trades' processi actually been advertised in New York as an event of primary in the exhibition! The population of Preston was suddenly multipli Some 600,000 people that day were thrown into the public thorou struggled with one another for the best view. Those who could window pane, or a balcony seat, or a resting-place amongst the tile were fain to endure the streets, where they were wedged in like b pavement. Still all was conducted with the greatest order and c The total number of trades was twenty. Some of these occupied a and some of 300 yards. In all they included 2400 men, 120 horses, an The procession, which stretched over 2½ miles of ground, occupied ful in passing any given point, yet the arrangements of the marshals secretary, Mr. Baddeley, were so good that no confusion arose. in Fishergate, paraded various other parts of the town, and, r Friargate, were dismissed in the Market-place. Each trade enga band, arranged for its own devices, and paid its own expenses. Th whole is estimated at something like £700.

The cotton managers and overlookers, as representing the sta the town, might be expected to make a great display. They muster There were six lurries: on these were carried a lap-machine, card drawing, slubbing, and roving frame; throstle and spinning fra ning-mule, and a warping-mill. Save one, these were all silent, a tators appreciated the painful significance of the picture. The were plying their trade with the most graphic vigour, and the popu to endure the baptism of mud which fell around with the greatest Some twenty of the saddlers rode in a carriage drawn by six horses, in harness made for the Earl of Eglinton when Lord Lieutenant and other specimens of their work and emblazoned emblems of The smiths were actually forging horseshoes, and shoeing a horse w evil hour had been tempted to ascend a lurry. Two other lurries men otherwise engaged, and before each on horseback rode a Vulca armour. The printers had mounted a printing-press on a lurry working away with good earnest. The tailors could not resis representation of "the grand old gardener and his wife," with a were naked and we clothed you." The occasion was a fine one for makers, who, as may be imagined, improved it in the best ma painters mustered 200 strong, and were very picturesque in dres pation. About ninety butchers walked in procession, clad in blue, bu with white aprons and steels pendent, and were followed by their so attired, on horseback. The joiners were numerous. They had engage and illustrated, under elegant structures raised upon them, their daily The steam-engine-makers were very ambitious. They dealt in e representations and *tableaux vivans* to a great extent, and showed working engines. The amalgamated engineers filled five l machinery in all its stages. One lurry contained a fixed boiler and engines and lathes, all in operation; another contained millwrigh a third contained shaping and fitting shops; and another an engin boiler arrangement. The bricklayers kept to their legs and satisfied with carrying devices on banners and their trade emblems and tools supplied for the occasion. The perambulator-makers occupied two one the workshop was represented; in the other the showroom, women and children occupying the highly-finished carriages. The made a good show. The procession of the fishmongers attracted attention. A boat was hoisted on a lurry: it was seen floating upon a through which it was supposed to be impelled by the oars of the stro A net was cast over the stern, in the folds of which was entangled a hu millers, bakers, and stonemasons also plied their trades on lurries f occasion, and were impressive with banners and music. The costu and appointments in all cases were of the best possible descriptio *ensemble* was splendid and unique. The only conditions wanting fect success were the sunshine and blue sky.

At the tail of this procession came the Catholic guilds, with a really magnificent banners and furniture from the various altarpie formed an impressive religious demonstration, but were certainly of place at this time as schools of the Established Church would There were female guilds of St. Ignatius, St. Augustine, St. Wa boys and men's guilds of the same. The girls numbered 1058, th and the men 600. What was intended by such a display of sacr of the flag of Austria, with "Austria" in the centre of it, of th with the Papal arms in the centre of it, on such an occasion, we mu Catholics to explain.

During this procession Mendelssohn's "Elijah" was being p the Exchange Guild Assembly Room; and a grand miscellan took place in the evening in the same building, the principal p each being Mdlle. Titiens, Mdme. Sherrington, Miss Palmer Reeves, Mr. Santley, and Mr. Charles Hallé, the conductor. The temporary structure renders it ill-adapted for the conveyanc The next day the same artistes performed "The Messiah," at large audience.

Thousands of young hearts awoke on Friday to the consciousn made, as it were, for them,

> *For, after the rain, with never a stain*
> *The pavilion of Heaven was bare.*

It was the children's day. A procession of the Sunday Schools Park, and a massed meeting there at two o'clock, were annou Guild programme. The Sunday School is a great institution In the capacity of teachers or scholars, it includes a t population. Early in the morning, therefore, the town

(Continued on page 288.)

The History of Preston Guild

England's greatest carnival

ALAN CROSBY

The History of Preston Guild: England's Greatest Carnival

Copyright © Alan Crosby, 2012

An earlier version of this book was published by
Lancashire County Books in 1991

This revised and updated edition published in 2012 by
Carnegie Publishing Ltd
Chatsworth Road,
Lancaster LA1 4SL
www.carnegiepublishing.com

British Library Cataloguing-in-Publication data
A catalogue record for this book is available from the British Library

ISBN 978-1-85936-212-9

Designed, typeset and originated by Carnegie Publishing
Printed and bound in the UK by Henry Ling Ltd, Dorchester

Contents

The first edition of this book was dedicated to my daughter Anna, who was described as 'a new citizen of Preston'. She was born just while I was writing the book, a year before the 1992 Guild. Now, a year before the 2012, I rededicate the book to her—and also to her brother James, who has not yet experienced 'England's greatest carnival'.

Acknowledgements
to the first edition

Thirty years ago, living in the south of England, my mother—an exiled Lancastrian—would use the phrase 'Once every Preston Guild'. It intrigued me, and I learned that the Preston Guild was a great celebration held once every twenty years, and that it was famed far and wide. Time passed, I became a local historian, and to my great pleasure I came to live in Preston. There, as a non-Prestonian, it was a very great honour to be asked to research and write the history of the Guild—an honour which I have valued and appreciated. The work has been fascinating and challenging: there is enough material to fill several volumes, and there were many avenues and byways to explore.

Writing the history of such a remarkable institution as the Preston Guild has been immensely enjoyable, and I have been given invaluable assistance and encouragement by many people. My wife Jacquie read and re-read the text and made countless suggestions for improvements in style and content: her help, as always, was essential but—also as always—any remaining errors are likely to be the result of my own wilfulness, not of her oversight.

I would like to acknowledge with thanks the help of everybody who has discussed ideas, passed on information and given references, and in particular David Hunt, Edna Cattermole, Marian Roberts, Marie Warburton, Edwina and Jim Starkie, John Brandwood, E.H. Booth & Sons Ltd, and Alistair Hodge and Anna Goddard of Carnegie Publishing. The assistance of the staffs of the Lancashire Record Office, the Harris Museum, the Harris Library, and Preston Borough Council has been very important in the work, and my thanks are due to all of them. Preston Borough Council generously allowed me free access to the Corporation and other records in its custody, and its permission to use and quote from this material is gratefully acknowledged.

I acknowledge with gratitude the permission of the following to quote from copyright material in their ownership which is housed in the Lancashire Record Office: the County Archivist, Lancashire Record Office (DDX 88/4; DDX 398/47; DP 376/8); W. & J. Foster Ltd, Preston (DDX 438/4); the General, Municipal, Boilermakers and Allied

Trades Union (Preston branch) (DDX 1089); the Finch Family Forum, Albuquerque, New Mexico (DDX 1471/1); Mr Henry Shaw of Frodsham (DDX 1554/1); the District Education Officer, Preston (SMPr 4/1, 4); the Headteacher, St Augustine's R.C. Primary School, Preston (SMPr 47/13); the proprietors of the Lancashire Evening Post, Preston (DDPr); the Browsholme Hall Company (DDB 72/356); Mrs B.M. Whitlock Blundell of Little Crosby (DDBi 12/146, 53/3 1); Messrs. Shuttleworths, solicitors, Preston (DDCm 11/3).

This book is the result of the enlightened policy of two bodies: the Lancashire County Council and the Hams Free Public Library and Museum Endowment Trust (the Harris Trustees). The Lancashire County Council, through its library service and its imprint, Lancashire County Books, agreed to publish the work as one of its official contributions to the celebration of the Preston Guild of 1992. I am indebted to the County Librarian, Michael Dolan, for his encouragement, and to the County Council itself for supporting the project. Diana Winterbotham, the County Local Studies Librarian, read the first draft and helped in many ways. It is to the Harris Trustees that my warmest thanks are due. The Harris Trustees are: Leslie Howarth JP, FRICS (chairman); Lady Milena Grenfell-Baines; David Graham Booth; John Brandwood TD, JP; Harry Wyndham Lister Cumming BSc, MRIC; Arthur William Dawson FCA, Edward Chambre Dickson TD, DL; Lesley Antony Pickston JP; Charles Gordon Washington MBE, FCIB; and Peter Robert Metcalf FCA (Secretary). The Trust was formed by a High Court of Justice scheme at the behest of the will of Edmund Robert Harris on 24 July 1882. The Trustees most generously agreed to fund the research and writing of the book as their contribution to the forthcoming Guild, and they also allowed me complete freedom to pursue the project as I wished, making no constraints upon the approach I adopted or the detailed content of the book. This faith in my work and trust in the quality of the final product was something which I valued very highly. It is because of the Harris Trustees that this book has been researched, written and published, but any views expressed in this book are my own, and are not necessarily shared by the Trustees, collectively or individually. To them, as individuals and as a Trust, may I express my special thanks and appreciation.

Alan Crosby,

June 1991

Acknowledgments to the second edition (2012)

The first time I heard the phrase 'Once every Preston Guild' was now fifty years ago, because time has continued to pass on, all too rapidly. My mother still lives in the south of England, but I've now lived in Preston for well over a quarter of a century, my children are born and bred Prestonians, and we're all proud of it. Now another Guild has come round, the book I wrote twenty years ago has been updated, and the acknowledgments can be reviewed. It's sad to record that some of the people mentioned are no longer with us—I think particularly of Marian Roberts—and intriguing to note how organisations have changed their names or disappeared: the Borough Council is now the City Council, the Lancashire Record Office is now Lancashire Archives, the County Archivist is now called the Archive Services Manager (and she is my wife!), and Lancashire County Books (which published the original edition) has gone. All of those acknowledged twenty years ago receive my grateful thanks and recognition once more, but there are also others to thank for their help and encouragement. Special mention must be made of Andrew Mather, Linda Barton and all those who are so active in Preston Historical Society, which is now wonderfully rejuvenated and going from strength to strength; Rosemary Jolly, Christopher Ratcliff and the other members of the Select Vestry of Preston (a venerable and historically fascinating institution in its own right); Andrew Southworth for his very generous gift of Guild photographs and memorabilia; Emma Heslewood of the Harris Museum for her invaluable help and encouragement; the staff of the City Council who have been planning the Guild of 2012; and the many people who, at the numerous talks about the Guild which I have given over the past twenty years, spoke to me about their memories and shared their experiences of past Guilds.

Alan Crosby
February 2012

Introduction

T HE P RESTON G UILD is a unique and remarkable institution: the Guild Merchant was granted to the town in 1179, little more than a century after the Norman Conquest, and it still exists more than 830 years later. That is an outstanding achievement, and an exceptional example of resilience and adaptability, but perhaps even more remarkable is that the core of the Guild celebrations, the ceremony in which burgess rights are renewed, is directly derived from medieval forms and procedures. These have altered little over the centuries, and those who attended the Guilds six hundred years ago would undoubtedly be familiar with the ceremonial practised today, even though almost everything else would leave them dazed and speechless.

The ancient celebration has grown and evolved with the centuries. Its heart is still the renewal ceremony, but around that has evolved a host of other events and activities, which result in a uniquely varied and large-scale festival. Until recent years, indeed, the Guild was one of the few true English carnivals—'Venice may have its Water Carnival, New Orleans its *Mardi Gras*, but Preston has its GUILD'. It is far more than a quaint historical survivor.

As long as detailed eye-witness accounts are available, back to the mid-seventeenth century, the formal renewal ceremony has been accompanied by an extraordinary outburst of festivity, with processions, entertainments, feasts, balls and dances, sporting events, sideshows, circuses, concerts, theatrical performances, firework displays and spectacular attractions. Preston has been overwhelmed at every Guild by hundreds of thousands of visitors, pouring in from all points of the compass, thronging its streets, cramming into its public buildings, and filling every bed in the town. The Guild has attracted reporters, diarists and commentators, astonished by what they found and amazed by the scale, the colour, the excitement and the sensation of it all.

Underlying all this was the medieval guild, the Guild Merchant, with its power to restrict and regulate the trading and commercial activity that went on in Preston. Anybody who wished to conduct a trade or business in the town had to be a member of the Guild, and it was the renewal ceremony which formally acknowledged that membership. By the middle of the eighteenth century the powers of the Guild over trading were largely ineffectual, and long before the end of the century they had ceased to be applied. But the Guild remained, an organisation which, though powerless to restrict commercial freedom, was ever more influential and prestigious in its social role. The medieval forms were maintained, but the Guild celebrations were, by 1802, overtly for enjoyment, not business. And so the Guild has developed—its fame growing, its attractions increasing, its participants ever more numerous—until today it is by far the largest event of its kind in England ... though can it really be said that there is any other event 'of its kind' with which to compare it? Truly, the Preston Guild is unique.

Throughout, its special fame rested on its rarity—the fact that it was only held once every twenty years. This gave to the Guild its particular distinction, and to the English language a phrase. Its infrequency ensured that there were always sufficient resources to stage a magnificent show, while its impact was not diluted by too frequent repetition.

The antiquity of the Guild, its important place in the history of Preston, and its unique scale and popularity, meant that from early times it drew the attention of historians and antiquarians. When outside observers, such as county historians, commented on the town they usually made particular reference to the peculiar phenomenon of the Guild and its character, sometimes almost to the exclusion of any other information on the town. In Preston itself local historians have produced a multitude of books and papers of varying merit about the Guild and its history. The earliest was Dr Richard Kuerden, who in 1682 produced an invaluable account of the previous Guilds, combining it with an historical survey of the borough and town. Unfortunately, the tendency thereafter was to treat the history of the Guild in a repetitive and all too often very tedious fashion. Many writers resorted to standardised descriptions, listing each Guild in turn and giving excessive attention to legal and ceremonial procedures and the names of officials, burgesses and prominent guests.

When I wrote the first edition of this book twenty years ago, I avoided that approach. To condense a subject of this size, which has given rise to countless descriptive accounts and an enormous volume of detailed records, into the scope of a single book meant that a lot had, of necessity, to be omitted. This was especially so with the Guilds since 1842, for which so many very lengthy and often fascinating newspaper reports exist, and in which the scale and variety of the events were extraordinary. For lists of Guild officers and transcriptions of the formal proclamations and pronouncements made at the Guild, these press accounts and the works of historians such as Abram are invaluable sources and are widely available. I made no attempt to supersede them and, indeed, I made good use of them myself.

In this book I approached the history of the Guild from a different perspective. It was inevitable that there should be some element of chronological sequence, but rather than taking all 26 Guilds one by one, I grouped them into periods which reflect the main phases in the evolution and development of the Guild. Although it was impossible to avoid the occasional overlap, I think that this chronological division worked very well, and I have not sought to change it in this new edition.

The first phase is the medieval period (to 1542) in which the Guild had its origins, but during which little is known of its activities or how it was celebrated, apart from purely formal records such as the rolls and orders. For the next period, 1562–1742, there is a greatly increased volume of information about the Guild, from official and, increasingly, unofficial sources. It was in this period that the Guild enjoyed its heyday as an organisation which restricted commercial freedom, and it also began to develop as a major social event.

That social role became pre-eminent between 1762 and 1822, when the Guild was at its most exclusive, attended by all the leaders of local and county society. During this period, though, the element of popular participation was growing, and the processions and fringe attractions show signs of developing towards their modern form. In 1842 there was a strong possibility that the Guild would not be held, because municipal reform in 1835 had abolished all the ancient (albeit nominal) privileges of the Guild Merchant. It went ahead only after intense pressure from influential commercial interests and from many townspeople. This Guild, and that of 1862, accelerated the transition from the old to the new, as schools, churches and other organisations within the town were included in the celebrations.

Between 1882 and 1922 this new role, as a festival of and for Preston as a whole, developed and matured, and the Guild attracted national, even international, attention. The Second World War again threatened the Guild, and in 1942 no celebration was possible. Once again, local enthusiasm and sentiment ensured that it would be resumed, and the 1952 and 1972 Guilds were larger and more diverse than ever before.

A few points made in the book could have seemed controversial to some readers. In particular, the strong doubts which I expressed about the holding of a Guild in 1328 went against the conventional view—though those doubts were first, and very cogently, expressed by William Clemesha as long ago as 1912. It is some consolation to point out that there had unquestionably been Guild celebrations earlier than that date, well before the start of the fourteenth century.

The legal and ceremonial aspects of the Guild, so extensively covered by its previous historians, are of great interest and significance, but they are only part of the story. The processions, entertainments, balls and banquets have always been fundamental to the character and success of the celebration, and since 1762 have occupied much more of the Guild proceedings than the renewal ceremony. Most previous histories have either neglected or given too little coverage to these aspects of the Guild, or have done nothing to draw material on these subjects into a coherent narrative form. Instead, they have relied on long lists of guests at banquets and descriptions of the costumes at fancy dress balls. I therefore gave special attention to themes such as the development of the processions, the organisation of feasts and social events, and the role of the fringe entertainments.

The history of the Guild which I wrote, looking at the carnival as well as the ceremonial, was more rounded and complete than those that had gone before; when it appeared the response was very favourable and reviews were good. I was particularly pleased that Preston's most eminent historian, Dr David Hunt, not only liked the book (as he very kindly told me in person) but also observed in print that it was a 'magisterial analysis'. But no less important was that the Borough Council then commissioned me to compile and write the *Official Record* of the 1992 Guild, which was published in 1993. This provided a unique opportunity to review and document an entire Guild from beginning to end, and has proved to be of inestimable value in the writing of the last chapter of this new edition of the Guild history, which covers the Guild of 1992.

CHAPTER ONE

The medieval Guild Merchant

T HE ORIGINS of the guilds of medieval England are not fully understood and, despite a great deal of historical research into the question, may never be clearly known.[1] In many cases guilds appear to have evolved gradually and haphazardly, emerging slowly rather than being created fully formed at the outset. This means that identifying a clear starting point for their formation is often impossible. Furthermore, they differed in detail in every case, and in no two towns was their development the same. Local circumstances—social, commercial, political—were a crucial factor. The date of their origin is often unclear and, to make matters worse, historians have sometimes assumed that the first documentary record of a guild marks the date of its establishment. In reality, it is may have been no more than the date of the earliest chance survival of a piece of parchment referring to an *existing* guild.

Many communities had more than one guild; some (especially the major regional trading centres) had a large number. Sometimes there were rival guilds within the same town, while in larger places, with a more complex economic structure, different trades often had separate craft or trade organisations. These, too, were often called guilds or sometimes companies, as in the case of the highly influential London livery and trade companies. It was common for traders such as leather-workers, masons, and grocers to be organised into companies, which operated as guilds in their own right, with their own rules of admission and regulations for the conduct of trade, and with internal systems of courts, assemblies, fines and punishments.

But in most towns where such multiple companies operated there were also 'umbrella' bodies—the guilds merchant—which represented the trading interests of the town as a whole. There was no uniformity about this: some places with guilds merchant do not appear to have had significant numbers of companies, while some which had trade companies did not have an overall body, but the two often went together. Guilds existed throughout medieval England and in most countries of Europe, and not all guilds were in urban communities, for many rural communities had them.[2] They were as diverse and as endlessly various as the places within which they were found but, despite all the local variations in their character, customs and purpose, some general patterns and features can be traced.

Most guilds had an important economic role. This can be summarised quite simply. They were made up of tradesmen and craftsmen who used the guild and its legally binding regulations to try to prevent competition from outsiders, by forbidding them from carrying on trades within the town. This was not simply a matter of residential qualification. It did not always exclude people living outside a town, since some of those might be granted guild membership. Nor did it include all those living within the town, as many of them might not have been deemed eligible for such privileges. But for those traders and craftsmen who *were* members the guild was a means of protecting their own interests. Its effect was that of a powerful restrictive practice: only guild members, or those specifically authorised by the guild, could conduct a trade. Competition was reduced; prices and profits could be kept high (by a form of cartel arrangement involving price-fixing); there was no jostling for position or custom within a particular craft; and the guild members enjoyed a special and privileged position in the town and its economic life.

This position might also be granted to outsiders who served a useful role: selected and favoured traders and craftsmen of the 'right sort', rich patrons, wealthy contacts, and local gentry and aristocracy who might give prestige to guild events and activities and provide useful services to the guild members. There might also be trading links with other guild communities within the area, or even as far afield as continental Europe.[3] Such alliances and connections provided an important means by which goods might be traded, and gave the advantages of mutually beneficial contacts and of hospitality and support for merchants travelling further afield. Guilds also acted as 'pressure groups' in dealings with government, local lords, the Church, and communities in other towns. As far as trade was concerned they were therefore doubly beneficial to their members, protecting their position within the town and increasing their power and influence beyond, in the wider world.

Guilds were also social organisations. Some could be regarded as the medieval equivalent of bodies such as chambers of commerce. They represented a coming together of traders and craftsmen who met to discuss and exchange ideas, review the state of the town and the world, enjoy communal feasting and drinking, plan policies for acting against threats of competition, gossip and consider the eligibility of potential members. Unlike the formal legal and political business the social side has tended to leave little reliable documentary evidence—gatherings at taverns and halls to debate, eat, drink and be merry have rarely been recorded, but their importance was considerable. Members naturally congregated for such purposes, and it was perhaps at such gatherings that a large proportion of their real work was done—the behind-the-scenes activities which were concealed by the more elaborate and impressive ceremonial and by the formal judgments of courts and assemblies. Such gatherings would have been enjoyable and entertaining occasions for convivial relaxation while some serious and important business was conducted.

Many guilds also had a religious function. In medieval England this was natural, since religion and the observance of religious practice, whether genuinely felt or as a matter of form, permeated all facets and levels of society. Guilds often had patron saints whose names they adopted, and had close links with their parish church or a particularly favoured town church, although some had their own chapels.[4] The guild might endow the church with rich furnishings and statuary or help to pay for refurbishment or rebuilding. Sometimes it would assist with charitable work, another aspect of its role which is shared by comparable modern organisations. The church would thus benefit from the association, while the guild would have a base for its own religious services, acquire additional respectability and prestige from the connection, and be able to give public displays of its own wealth, importance and worthiness.

The political role of guilds, and their place in the development of local government, has attracted a great deal of attention from historians. Guilds generally included the leading figures in the economic life of the town and, as far as they were able, exercised a tight control over the trading which went on in their community. That, after all, was their primary purpose. They were often powerful and influential in their relationships with outside magnates and leading local landowners and, in the case of the greatest guilds, might have national significance and the ear even of the king. In many towns, though by no means all, the guild developed alongside the town council or its medieval equivalent. Both were made up of the chief men of the town—the richest ratepayers and merchants—although the guild usually included many smaller and middle-ranking traders as well. In consequence, the guild and the council were more or less similar in their composition, and although technically different were in practice indistinguishable. Elsewhere, however, they might be recognisably different bodies, and even come into conflict.

Historians researching the medieval period have been particularly interested in those towns where the guild seems to have *preceded* the town council. In these cases the guild, in origin a social and trading organisation, gradually turned into a political body, since it was the natural, and usually the only, institution to represent the interests of the town against the Crown or a potentially obstructive and interfering outsider. The guild thus became, *de facto*, the council, and the two were intimately and inextricably linked. To a considerable extent they were in fact the same. In such towns the beginnings of true local government and local representation can be traced in the evolution of the guild, and even where, as in Preston, specific evidence no longer exists, it is possible to hypothesise that this was the case. In other words, Preston's infant borough council grew out of the town's older Guild some eight or seven centuries ago.

Every local guild had its own particular history and characteristics. The documentary evidence for many medieval English guilds is poor, sometimes non-existent. In quite a few cases we only know of the existence of a guild because of a solitary casual reference in a document concerning something completely different. In others we have only the bare bones of the medieval story, through scanty collections of official and formal documents, and the richness and variety of the yearly round of guild life is lost to us. Comparatively few guilds have abundant written records which allow a full reconstruction of the life of the guild and its place in the life of the medieval town. Unfortunately, Preston does not come into this category, but nonetheless it does have important surviving medieval Guild records—more than for any town in the North West apart from Chester—and these allow us to reconstruct crucial elements of its story.

Membership of guilds

The regulation of trade was the crucial role of almost every guild but, as already noted, members would also have been attracted by their social function. Status and place in society were as important in medieval England as they are today: to be a guild member would imply that a person had reached the higher levels of town society and had become one of the elite. In some guilds there are indications that membership originally transcended class divisions—to use our modern term, it had 'inclusivity'—but in many it appears to have become more elitist as the years have passed. Those already 'in' were increasingly reluctant to allow others to join them, and ensured that real power lay in the hands of a minority of key people.

Over thirty years ago Susan Reynolds argued persuasively that guilds perhaps originated in the common ground of sociability and shared interests among new urban residents—those people who, around the time of the Norman Conquest or during the period of urban growth in the twelfth and thirteenth centuries, came from rural areas to a new and very different society. Uprooted country dwellers might well have found congenial and comforting company within an organisation offering fellowship and mutual support in a seemingly hostile environment. She suggested that these newcomers may have participated in guild activities to ease the adjustment to their changed circumstances. It is an unprovable but inherently plausible explanation.

Her conclusion is that the trade and political associations of many guilds perhaps came later, as these social groupings matured and became more influential in town society. In some ways, therefore, guilds may have been a response to the very development of towns. Once they were established, though, this element of common fellowship among a new group of town dwellers probably began to diminish. These people, as soon as they were well placed within town society, would have wished to exclude those still outside from competing with their trades. It is known that guilds in many towns were a great deal more exclusive and elitist by the fifteenth century.

It was often the case that membership of guilds was dependent upon obtaining burgess rights. Technically, a burgess was somebody who held land by burgage tenure. This was a particular urban form of tenure whereby a person could own freehold property, and could buy, sell, lease, rent, inherit or bequeath it, without reference to the lord of the manor or a local court. It contrasted with the restrictive and irksome controls imposed by the feudal landholding system in rural communities and in towns without burgage rights, and was thus regarded as a particularly valuable liberty, eagerly sought and jealously guarded. Burgage tenure in early medieval England was inextricably associated, as its name implies, with the acquisition of borough status. Indeed, some modern historians of the medieval English borough use the presence of burgage tenure as the chief criterion for the existence of a borough.[5]

Burgage tenure was not only a right: it also had a physical impact upon the shape of the places where it existed. In such towns land in the centre was divided into plots, long and narrow in shape, with the narrow edge along the street. These plots, usually deliberately and carefully laid out on a planned basis, were called burgages. For many towns the references in medieval deeds to the existence of burgages are the only surviving indication in documentary sources that a borough existed. Often, the holding of land by such tenure determined whether a man could exercise full civic rights.

Time after time, when such rights came to be granted by royal or other charter, it was the burgesses to whom the rights applied. They were the individuals singled out to exercise civic authority—to serve on councils, to vote in elections, to be members of guilds, to hold municipal office. Ordinary residents—those who did not own freehold burgage plots or had no long-term lease on them—either had no civic rights, or occupied a much more lowly position. Urban society was thus based on a hierarchy, with burgesses as the elite of the townsmen and the landless labourers at the very bottom. It should be noted that, with very rare exceptions, these rights applied only to men. Women, even spinsters or widows, were excluded from the exercise of formal rights, although if wealthy they may have had other means of bringing influence and power to bear.

This, then, was the origin of the term *burgess* but, as with so much else in medieval England, local custom varied from place to place. The word came to have several meanings and usages which differed from town to town. For example, it was often used merely to describe the owner of a burgage plot, but more generally to suggest somebody who had been admitted to a privileged place in town society and was permitted to exercise civic or municipal rights. This is how the term was employed in medieval Preston. The members of the Guild had to be burgesses, but they did not have to own burgage plots, and indeed did not have to live in Preston. Instead, they had been granted burgess status, and the Guild membership which went with it, for trading reasons or, increasingly, on social and political grounds as a mark of favour and esteem.

Furthermore, since membership was almost always hereditary it was clear that the possession of a burgage plot or the practice of a particular trade were no longer the only effective criteria for membership. A non-resident, non-trading individual could still be a burgess and guild member by reason of descent. What had originated as a term to describe a specialised form of land tenure eventually came to be a general term for a citizen of a borough who enjoyed full privileges, or even for someone who lived outside the borough but held some civic and guild rights.

The members of guilds could thus be drawn from a variety of sources, depending on local custom and tradition and on the regulations of specific guilds. There might be a small group of dominant and influential traders. Reynolds notes how in some towns the guilds were 'captured' by business interests, so that guild membership and its associated privileges were confined to merchants or to wholesalers, who carefully and deliberately excluded the craftsmen, such as weavers or carpenters, or the small retail traders. Alternatively, there might be a broad cross-section of tradesmen and craftsmen. Members might include influential people invited for social and diplomatic reasons, or they might be the descendants of the guildmen of earlier generations. Every town and every guild was different, and most changed over the centuries.

Authority—and especially the royal government based in London—was often suspicious of guilds and their members. In the eleventh and twelfth centuries, before the development of coherent local government in English towns, the Crown administered local communities directly, through the sheriffs, portreeves and other officials which it appointed. It frequently viewed guilds with concern, seeing them as troublesome manifestations of local identity and local desire for self-government. As many guilds were closely associated with the nascent urban councils which challenged the power of the Crown to run local affairs, this suspicion was certainly not unwarranted. At certain periods, therefore, medieval monarchs were in conflict with guild interests: guilds 'oscillated between official recognition and disapproval, according to whether they seemed subversive or helpful to established authority'. The Church, too, was often doubtful of their merits, even though it had close links with so many guilds. Real or imaginary, the subversive character of the guilds as groupings of independent-minded townspeople was perceived by some in authority as a challenge to the State or Church establishment. Eventually, though, the guilds and their role in town society became generally accepted. By the fifteenth century the guilds were themselves part of the establishment and were trying to suppress new and radical challenges to their own authority.

The organisation of guilds

The gradual evolution of guilds from informal social gatherings of individuals into the trade organisations which then, in some instances, acquired political, administrative and local government functions, means that usually there is no precise point at which it is possible to say 'the guild began'. Nobody arranged a public meeting, took minutes, and made formal resolutions to start a guild: medieval society did not work like that, and it would be highly misleading to imagine that modern notions of constitutions, record-keeping and the appointment of officers were in the minds of those who participated in early guilds. Only later, as they became more complex formal bodies, did ideas of structured organisation emerge, and it was only when guilds matured into fully fledged trade or political groupings that significant quantities of records were produced—many of which have long since perished.

In some towns the keeping of formal guild rolls had started by the end of the twelfth century. These recorded the membership of the guild and sometimes the trades and place of residence of those named. The reason is clear. Since a guild functioned as a means of restricting trade to its own members, it was essential that there should be a record of its membership. How else could it be categorically stated that a certain trader was, or was not, a guild member? Such guild rolls are often our earliest official records for a particular town. Because of their importance in the life of the community and because of the need to establish past membership to determine claims to hereditary participation, the rolls were carefully preserved. This was clearly the case in Preston, where the guild rolls date back to the fourteenth century, but the earliest surviving record of the town council itself is as late as 1608.

Once a guild became more organised, and had begun to establish for itself a leading position in the life of the town, it was necessary for formal meetings and ceremonies to be held regularly. These served three main purposes. First, they made possible the orderly administration of the guild and its affairs, with efficient keeping and updating of records and the transaction of business. Second, they allowed the guild to show off its prestige, power and wealth and that of its individual members—a matter of increasing significance. And third, they made possible the development of a 'guild spirit'. The members of the guild would have enjoyed participating in the ceremonial of the guild, showing the world that they belonged to such an important body, and feeling a sense of common identity with other members and of pride in their place in the community. The guild protected and fostered the interests of its members and its town against threats of competition from neighbouring communities and outside traders, and this formal and public ceremonial role reinforced its feeling of identity.

From the reign of Henry II (1154–89) onwards it was usual for the Crown, when it granted a town a royal charter, to include among its new liberties the right to have a guild merchant. This was so in the first Preston charter of 1179. Such a grant might well have been a formal and official recognition of what in any case existed—an acceptance of the inevitable since it was by no means easy to suppress an already vigorous body—but it may also have been the case that, by including formal recognition in a charter, the Crown hoped to be able to influence the development of the guild. The privileges and liberties might, in changed circumstances and if it was expedient, be more readily withdrawn or amended if it could be shown that the Crown had granted them originally. Rather than allowing the uncontrolled flourishing of independent-minded organisations, the Crown could expect to exercise an ultimate authority over them.

In some early instances it appears that the term 'guild' was used as a synonym for the idea of 'community' in general, and perhaps in such cases the Crown was not in fact intending to grant specific guild rights, but rather to recognise a community, or 'commune'. If that was so, the citizens quickly interpreted the meaning to the advantage of the guild. Royal recognition of guilds was in other cases associated with specific craft and trade organisations, rather than with any idea of approving new urban privileges. It is clear, for example, that sometimes guilds were given royal recognition by charter *before* the recognition of the town community and its self-government. In such instances the town might later have to struggle to assert its supremacy and authority over the guild which claimed independence by virtue of its earlier official origins.

Elsewhere the town councils of the fourteenth and fifteenth centuries, in the face of guild opposition, tried to impose their own regulations about trading standards, conditions and admission to membership, to prevent the sectional interests of the guild from becoming the dominant force in the town. In yet others, the councils at an early date absorbed the guilds entirely within their own apparatus, so that (as happened in Preston) the guild as a distinct body completely disappeared, having been entirely subsumed within the borough council. This is why after 1608 Preston Corporation passed Guild rules and ordinances and entered them in the minutes of its own proceedings.

Guilds ultimately faded away in most communities. The maturing of local government meant that other bodies were involved in town administration, and the guilds often lost their separate identity. In the case of religious guilds, and those with a strong religious element, the Reformation had a very damaging impact. In the sweeping away of 'Popishness' the observances of many guilds, with their veneration of the Virgin and the saints, disappeared almost overnight, while the dissolution of chantries and chantry chapels in 1548–49 resulted in the abolition of many guild chapels in parish churches and cathedrals. The post-Reformation Anglican Church had little place for guilds, with their essentially medieval character and local exclusiveness as well as their potential role as strongholds of religious conservatism.

In the sixteenth century, too, there were profound changes in the social and economic life of towns. The vigour of political and administrative development which had been seen in the fourteenth and fifteenth centuries gave way to increasing elitism and conservatism, while attempts were made to circumvent the restrictions that guilds and councils placed on trade. In some quarters guilds were increasingly seen as irrelevant and anachronistic, and in most towns the seventeenth century saw the authorities engaged in an uphill struggle to prevent trading by outsiders and to maintain the monopoly of local trade exercised by guild members or burgesses. By the mid-eighteenth century there was much greater freedom of trading and retailing, and it was possible for traders to move in and out of towns and to buy and sell as they wished. The restrictions remained in theory, but in reality the local authorities and guilds were increasingly powerless to enforce the rules. This is apparent in Preston, where prosecutions and fines for unauthorised trading had almost ceased to be levied by the middle of the eighteenth century.

In some cases—Preston being by far the best of all examples—the medieval guilds changed their character or function, while remaining nominally the same. They shed their religious trappings, and became purely secular: although special services in parish churches were continued, there was no longer identification with special saints or the Virgin. As their power to restrict trade waned and they gradually lost their economic role, their function was increasingly that of a club or society representing trading interests and exercising influence behind the scenes rather than with direct action. The ceremonial aspects were maintained but real power was lost. The institution became simply a historical survival rather than an active force. The social side of the guild was correspondingly more important and more pronounced, with entertainments and festivities increasingly dominant at guild ceremonials. By the nineteenth century such guilds as did survive were often, as in Preston, regarded with affection as examples of historic traditions and as manifestations of civic pride, and even as a means of bringing publicity and trade to the town. Their power had long since been lost, but antiquarian feelings and the sense of history which the guilds represented meant that they acquired a new role.

The Guilds Merchant in Preston

The earliest reference to the existence of the Guild Merchant in Preston appears indirectly in the charter granted by Henry II in 1179.[6] This gave to the burgesses of Preston the same liberties and rights which had already been given by the king to the burgesses of Newcastle under Lyme (Staffordshire). The original charter does not in fact survive, but its provisions are reiterated in detail in a successor charter of 1199. The date of the Henry II charter is only approximate, for no year is given (dating by year was very rare in this period) and it can be established only from the names of those who witnessed it. They included bishops and other important figures and, by referring to the known dates of their terms of office, it is possible to fix 1179 as the most likely year. Among the rights already granted to Newcastle under Lyme was one whereby the burgesses might 'have a Guild Merchant in the said Borough, with all liberties and free customs to such Guild Merchant in any wise belonging'.[7] It was frequently the case that one borough or town would be granted *en bloc* the rights enjoyed by another, to avoid the need for each to be separately recited in the charter. It was, in effect, the grant of a set of 'model' rights or liberties.

It has often been stated, quite incorrectly, that the 1179 charter made Preston the second oldest chartered borough in the kingdom. Another persistent story is that Preston had at least one earlier charter, granted by Henry II's grandfather, Henry I, at the beginning of the twelfth century. This belief is based on a sworn statement by Sir Thomas Walmesley, recorder (or chief law officer) of Preston in the late sixteenth century, that he had seen a charter of Henry I granted in 1100. Other sources, including evidence in a lawsuit of 1571, also imply that there was such a charter. However, these sources do not seem reliable. It is known that charters were being granted to other towns well before 1179 and, to take one example, the charter granted by Henry I to Beverley (in the East Riding of Yorkshire) sometime between 1127 and 1135 refers to the grant of a guild merchant But the Preston charter of 1179 definitely grants the rights exercised by Newcastle under Lyme, and this very strongly implies that Preston had no existing rights. Had the town already had a charter, with its own rights and liberties, it seems unquestionable that Henry II would simply have reiterated the grant of those rights. It was customary for successive monarchs to make such confirmations, and if such rights existed Henry II would have done so.

In 1199 King John, the son of Henry II, by a confirmatory charter, reiterated and extended the charter of 1179. His charter follows the customary pattern by stating that the king granted 'to the Burgesses of Preston, all the liberties and free customs which the Lord Henry our Father, gave, granted, and by his Charter confirmed to the same Burgesses'.[8] That pattern of wording would have been used by Henry II himself, had there been an earlier Preston charter than that of 1179. Moreover, later kings followed the same style: Henry III, in his charter of 1227, referred to the grant by 'the Lord Henry our Grandfather' and 'King John our Father', while the charter of Edward III makes specific reference to those of Henry II, John and Henry III. In none of these cases is there any reference to a charter of Henry I, and it is inconceivable that such a charter would have been ignored in these recitations if it had been in existence. It therefore seems certain that there was no such charter.[9]

In 1179, therefore, Henry II granted to the burgesses of Preston the right to have and enjoy the benefits of a Guild Merchant. This does not mean that the Preston Guild Merchant was actually created or officially came into being at that time. The grant made it possible for there to be a Guild Merchant, but there is no certainty that this right was exercised immediately. Equally, it is possible (though probably unlikely) that there was already a similar body in the town, which was merely given formal recognition by the 1179 charter. Each of the later medieval charters makes grants of further rights and privileges to Preston, adding to those which had been held since the original grant of 1179. None refers again specifically to the Guild Merchant. That is because those rights had been granted in 1179 so there was no need to recite them specifically once again. After 1179, therefore, the right to a Guild Merchant was continued by successive confirmations of the original charter of Henry II.[10]

The first record which is often claimed to relate to the celebration of a Guild dates from the year 1328. However, there is another very important, and earlier, document— the Custumal of Preston, which is undated but must have been written between 1179 and 1328.[11] The evidence of the handwriting suggests that it was compiled in the early fourteenth century (about 1300), perhaps from earlier sources. The Custumal (sometimes spelt *Costumal*) is, as its name suggests, a list of the customs, or regulations, of the town of Preston. It has 47 clauses, each one dealing with administration or with liberties exercised by the burgesses. The document concludes with the statement that these customs were derived from the Laws of Breteuil. Breteuil is a small town in Normandy, whose byelaws were used as a model for those of many English boroughs and towns in the twelfth and thirteenth centuries. Until the end of the nineteenth century writers on the history of Preston invariably mistook *Breteuil* for *Breton*, and described the Preston Custumal as deriving from the Breton Law, but it is now known that this is an error derived from a misreading of the Latin in the original document.[12]

It is impossible to say exactly when Preston adopted the basic Law of Breteuil, or when amendments and additions were made to the original code to suit local circumstances and requirements, but its provisions formed the basis of the medieval administration of the town. As far as the Guild was concerned the initial clauses were the most important. The first states that 'they shall have a Guild Merchant, with Hanse, and other customs and liberties belonging to such Guild; and ... no one who is not of that guild shall make any merchandize in the said town, unless with the will of the burgesses'. The second states that 'if any born bondsman [*nativus*] dwell anywhere in the same town, and hold any land, and be in the forenamed Guild and Hanse, and pay lot and scot [rates] with the same burgesses for one year and one day, then he shall be not reclaimed by his lord, but shall remain free in the said town'.

These clauses had two important effects. First, the right to hold a Guild or 'Hanse' (a term which means almost the same as guild: from the Old High German *hansa*, a band of men) was confirmed and was regarded as the chief liberty of the town. By the Custumal and by the royal charters which gave it legal force, the Guild was permitted to control trading and selling in the town, and to restrict this right to its own members only, unless the burgesses—the Guild members—accepted the application of an outsider for Guild membership. The second point was that if membership of the Guild was enjoyed by somebody who had been born in bondage, but who had paid rates in the manner of a free burgess for a year and a day, that person gained his freedom. In other words, somebody who was not born free but who became a member of the Preston Guild Merchant thus acquired liberty, and his lord could no longer reclaim him and force him to return to his previous dwelling place. This second clause emphasised the special rights and freedoms of the Guild Merchant.

The possible Guild of 1328

A document of 1328, which apparently no longer exists, is often said to be the first which gives evidence of the holding of a Guild ceremony. The original source, which must formerly have been among the records of the Corporation of Preston, appears to have been borrowed in the mid-seventeenth century by Richard Kuerden, the noted antiquary who was the author of the first eye-witness account of a Guild and was also involved in drawing the first detailed plans of Preston. He copied it into his manuscript notes but at some point he, or someone else, managed to lose the original.[13] His record is of great importance, but not without its problems. It is a seventeenth-century translation of what must have been a Latin original, and it may have been lost or altered in the process: we cannot be sure, since nothing can be used to cross-check.

The document is a list of Guild orders governing the procedure by which the Guild and the administration of the town were to be regulated. It was dated on the Monday after the Feast of the Decollation [beheading] of St John the Baptist. All Guilds since that of 1602 have begun on that Monday, the first after 29 August, and so have occupied the first week in September. Before then, however, the Guild usually began on 'the morrow of the Feast of the Decollation' (that is, the day after 29 August). A list of starting dates is given in appendix 1. In 1582, for example, the Guild began on a Thursday. Looking at the document, Kuerden assumed that because it referred to Guilds and Guild orders, it was actually written at the holding of a Guild. However, later Corporation records show that 'Guild orders' were issued extensively during the long intervals between Guilds and were not confined to the time of their celebration. It is very likely that such a procedure was also part of the normal business of the nascent borough council of medieval Preston.

In 1912 the Preston historian William Clemesha pointed out that the title of the document does not state specifically that it was promulgated at a Guild.[14] The phrase used is 'Maire Court' (Great Court, rather than Mayor's Court), and this was used in later documents to describe the annual mayor-making assembly, which took place at the beginning of September. There is therefore no guarantee that a Guild was being held, even though Guild orders were promulgated. Thus, although there might perhaps have been a Guild in 1328, there is certainly no incontrovertible proof, and Clemesha was very wise to be cautious on this point. Most earlier Guild historians accepted the 1328 date without sufficient checking of the precise phrasing of the document reproduced by Kuerden and first published in 1818.

The orders have a seventeenth-century flavour, because of Kuerden's translation into English, but it is likely that they represent the sentiment, even if not the exact wording, of the fourteenth-century originals. Those which relate to the Guild Merchant are given, with spelling modernised, below:

1. It is ordered by the assent and consent of the mayor, bailiffs and burgesses with the whole commonalty of the town of Preston, divers points and ordinances for the profit and welfare of the same town, to all manner of burgesses in our Guild Merchant, to have and to use them and their successors as it is after written;

2. The same mayor, bailiffs and burgesses, with all the commonalty, by whole assent and consent have ordered that it shall be lawful ... to set a Guild Merchant at every 20-year end, or if ever they have need to confirm charters or other [matters] that belong to our franchise;

3. The same mayor, bailiffs and burgesses by assent and consent have ordered that no mayor for the year being in the time of our Guild Merchant holding no other office, shall have no manner of fees, but they go whole to the mayor at the renewing of the Guild, and refreshing of our town;

4. The same mayor, bailiffs and burgesses ... have ordained for ever that there shall [be] no burgess' son the which his father is made burgess by our court roll and out of our Guild Merchant, that it be not lawful to none born to be free in other freedoms or liberties that belongs to the franchise of our town, nor his oath to be received in none of our court till the time be that he has purchased his freedom at our Mayoral Court as his father did before, and if he be sworn his freedom to be of no value;

5. All manner of burgesses which is made burgess by court roll and out of the Guild Merchant shall never be mayor, or bailiff, or serjeant, but only the burgesses whose names be in the Guild Merchant last made before; for the King gives the freedom to the burgesses which are in the Guild and to no other;

6. [it is] ordered in the time of our last Guild Merchant that all those who have no freedom by Guild Merchant, are to be fined by the mayor and twelve of the commonalty whose names are in the Guild Merchant before.[15]

These ordinances had two main purposes: the first was the regulation of admission to the Guild Merchant and the offices of the Guild, and the second the regulation of the trading aspects of the Guild. It is immediately clear that the relationship between Guild and Borough was exceptionally close. The orders of the Guild were made at the mayoral court and promulgated from that court; the officers regulating the Guild were the mayor, bailiffs and others who were officials of the town; and the rules put forward as part of the Guild ordinances governed the conduct of the borough administration. Already, by 1328, the Guild Merchant of Preston and the Borough Council were effectively the same.

The 1328 ordinances are important in other respects. Assuming that the translation or transcript which Kuerden has left to us is accurate in essentials, although perhaps somewhat unreliable in detail, they contain the first reference to the twenty-year interval for the holding of Guilds, a matter considered in more detail in the following chapter. The ordinances also make it plain that there had been Guilds before 1328. The sixth states that 'the same Mayre, Baliffes and Burges be assent and consent have ordert in the tyme of our last Gyld Marchand', which makes it plain that there had been a previous Guild, a view confirmed by Kuerden's title for the translation which includes the phrase 'Orders of a Precedent Guild'. It is entirely feasible that a Guild should have been held before 1328. The record of the document which lists orders made in that year 1328 is only a chance survival, and there is no reason to suppose that this was the only one of its kind: other records might easily have been lost or destroyed in the seventeenth century or even before. There could well have been other celebrations of the Guild Merchant after 1179 and before 1328.

If a Guild *was* held in the late 1320s it could perhaps be explained by events in the wider world. It was customary, as the evidence of the Preston charters shows and as the second of the 1328 ordinances specifically notes, for charters to be confirmed from time to time. One of the most important occasions for such renewal or confirmation was the accession of a new monarch. A new king could ignore or remove rights which had been granted by his predecessor or predecessors, so that, early in a new reign, towns would ask for their earlier charters to be confirmed as a recognition of existing rights and liberties. In this respect 1328 was significant, for Edward III succeeded to the throne in 1327. Although the new King was only fifteen, and did not assume personal rule until 1330, charters were issued in his name from 1327 onwards. It would therefore not be unreasonable to imagine that the burgesses of Preston might have held a Guild Merchant early in the new reign to give formal authority to a request for the renewal of the charter.

Although we have no record of this charter it is certain that one *was* issued by Edward III, for the next king (his grandson, Richard II) when confirming the charter of Preston in 1379, stated that 'we, allowing and approving the donations, grants and confirmations aforesaid, and all and everything in the said Charter of our Grandfather aforesaid'.[16] The 1328 orders do not refer specifically to the holding of a Guild but, as they make it clear that one had been held before they were issued, it is possible to argue that they might be a record of the formal adoption of orders of a Guild which had not long ended. Although it is quite impossible to prove, my speculation is that there could have been a Guild in

1327, the first year of the new reign, or *early* in 1328 (since of course the exact date was not yet fixed), and that the September 1328 orders represent a confirmation by the mayor and council of the decisions of that Guild.

There is no record of the holding of a Guild Merchant between 1328 and that of 1397, the first for which *contemporary* documentary evidence survives. Abram, in *Memorials of the Preston Guilds* (published in 1882), points out that the period of 69 years from 1328 to 1397 is far too long to have allowed the Guild Merchant to perform one of the crucial elements in its administration—the renewal of membership and the admission of new burgesses by hereditary right.[17] The interval is equal to at least two full generations, and in a time when life expectancy was so much less than it is today this would have represented a quite unacceptable break in the continuity of Guild government. He suggests that the twenty-year interval may have been followed approximately, giving a second Guild Merchant in the reign of Edward III, in about 1348–50. The accession of Richard II was in 1377, and a new charter was granted to Preston in 1379, so the holding of a Guild Merchant at some time in the first two years of his reign, c.1377–79, is quite possible. That would fit into the twenty-year interval for 'normal' celebrations of the Guild and thus the 1397 celebration, which is known with certainty to have taken place, would be in accordance with that pattern.

Abram's arguments are, as he freely admits, based entirely on hypothesis, but they do seem reasonable. However, there is absolutely no documentary record of any Guild during that period—no contemporary record and no later copies of documents—so inevitably the existence of Guilds in the late 1340s and late 1370s must remain entirely a matter for conjecture, unless there is a remarkable new discovery of written evidence.[18]

The 1397 Guild Merchant and its successors

With the 1397 Guild Merchant more certain ground is reached, and the Guilds which follow are, with very few exceptions, well documented. The 1397 Guild is the first for which the Guild Rolls—the lists of burgesses—survive, and it is this series, continuing to the present day, which is one of the most important records of the Preston Guild Merchant. The names of the burgesses were written, as the name suggests, on parchment rolls until the 1662 Guild, after which time they were entered into bound volumes beautifully illuminated with ever more elaborate decoration.[19]

The 1397 Guild was followed by another in 1415, an interval of only eighteen years. The twenty-year cycle was clearly not yet invariable, and it may be that the holding of this Guild was, like that of 1328, associated with the start of a new reign. There had been no Guild during the reign of Henry IV (1399–1413) and so it was perhaps felt that the beginning of the reign of Henry V was an appropriate time to hold another. After that, there was no further Guild until 1459.

Kuerden, and some writers in the nineteenth century who used him unquestioningly as a source, described a Guild held in 1429: some of the writers even miscopied Kuerden and state that the Guild was in 1439. Abram exposed the error by pointing out that the supposed Guild of 1429 results from a misreading of the date on the Guild Roll of 1459. He noted that the supposed 1429 Guild Roll includes officers with the same names as those known to have served in 1459, and rightly observes that 'it is inconceivable that fifteen personages living and filling certain civic offices in 1429 should still have been living and holding exactly the same offices thirty years afterwards'.[20]

The Guild Roll of 1459 in fact specifically refers to the two previous Guilds, in 1415 and 1397, making it clear that no other Guild had been celebrated in the interim. Why there should have been this interval of 44 years is not entirely clear. The first half of the fifteenth century was a period of severe economic decline and depression in many English towns, and these problems were probably shared by Preston. Perhaps as a result of such troubles the holding of a Guild may not have been seen as a priority. However, we have no firm evidence from local sources about the period in question, so this, too, must remain hypothetical.

The next Guild Merchant, the last of the medieval Guilds, was in 1500. No contemporary record survives from this Guild, and its rolls have been lost, but it is specifically referred to in documents relating to the Guild Merchant held in 1542. Among these is a 'prescription' of the procedures for the proclaiming of the Guild held at 'that Gyld Marchaunt, oppen the Mondaye in the fest of the decolason of Saynte John Baptist the sixteenth year of King Henry VIIth [1500]'.[21]

There is no evidence to show that any other Guild was celebrated between 1459 and 1500, so in this instance a period of 41 years elapsed between Guilds. While it is tempting to postulate that an unrecorded Guild might have been held in about 1480, after an interval of almost exactly twenty years, it is safer to view the gap as unbroken. It has been argued that in this case the serious political disruption which resulted from the sporadic fighting during the Wars of the Roses (1459–87) may have been at least partly responsible for this lapse, but this does not seem a satisfactory explanation since the town was not directly involved. It is more plausible that Preston and its Guild were still going through difficult economic times. Possibly the Guild itself was experiencing a sluggish phase, losing its medieval vitality and becoming inactive and introspective. The real answer will never be known.

The Guild Rolls

Throughout the medieval period the Guild Rolls and orders are the only documentary evidence available. We can only guess at what the Guild Merchant did in the long periods between the holding of the Guild ceremonies. It undoubtedly functioned between those times in order to exercise control over trade and, because of its significance in the administration of the town, the Borough Council and the Guild would have been more or less inseparable. Guild Rolls constitute by far the largest body of information about the medieval Guild and, indeed, about medieval Preston itself. They are of immense value as a source for the history of the town itself, giving details of its inhabitants, trades and administration.[22]

The purpose of the Rolls was to record the membership information which was the key to the work of the Guild. Those whose names appeared on the Guild Rolls were entitled to trade in the town or to carry on businesses and crafts, and they could enjoy all the privileges of Guild membership. In due course, it was they who would pass on their rights to succeeding generations. It was essential that the Guild should possess accurate, detailed and reliable lists of the people who had these privileges, and so the Guild Rolls were updated at each Guild celebration by the registration of the hereditary claims to membership. At each ceremony, families would renew their rights, with sons and brothers and fathers all ensuring that their names were separately enrolled. Gifts of membership (the granting of which was within the power of the Guild officers), and purchases of membership were also enrolled.

Each of the Guild Rolls has a formal preamble written in heavily abbreviated Latin, giving the date of the celebration and the names of the leading participants. The first to survive, that of 1397,[23] begins:

Gilda Mercatoria Burgentius Ville de Preston in Amondernes tent. ibm. die lune px.
post festu. Ascencois. Dni. Anno regni Regis Rici. se'di post conquestu. Angli. vicesimo
p. Willm. de Ergh'm tunc maiorem dicte Gilde et p. Galfm. de Meles Thomam de More
Johem. de Haconshowe senescall. dicte Gilde.

This can be translated and expanded as follows:

The Guild Merchant of the Burgesses of the Town of Preston in Amounderness held on the Monday next after the Feast of the Ascension of Our Lord in the year of the reign of King Richard the Second after the Conquest, the twentieth, before William de Ergham, then mayor of the said Guild and before Geoffrey de Meols, Thomas de More, John de Haconshowe, stewards of the said Guild[24]

The preamble was followed by a list of other officers and then by the statement that the named individuals had paid the appropriate fees and fines. Below this are the names of those enrolled or who renewed their membership at this Guild. The medieval form of the preamble to the Guild Roll was followed, with only small variations, in all later Guilds, so that a direct link with the medieval form has been retained to the present day.

The arrangement of the Rolls themselves also remained relatively standard, with a basic division between in-burgesses and out-burgesses. In 1397 the heading of the first column, again in very abbreviated Latin, was *Hec sunt noi'a eor'qui sunt in p'fata Gilda et eor' quor' patres fuerunt in p'fata Gilda* [these are the names of those who are in the aforesaid Guild and of those whose fathers were in the aforesaid Guild]. This column names those who enrolled at the Guild by virtue of being the sons of existing Guild members, and those who renewed their own existing membership: these were the in-burgesses. The next section is simply headed *Burgens' Forins'* or 'foreign burgesses' (that is, the out-burgesses). The third column has a damaged heading. Abram interprets it as a list of those admitted for the first time at this Guild. It is in fact the second part of the list of those admitted by birthright as in-burgesses: Abram made an error in his interpretation of the Latin text.[25]

The final category is headed *Hec sunt noi'a eor. quorum patres non fuerunt in p'fata Gilda et ideo fecerunt finem* [the names of those whose fathers were not in the aforesaid Guild, and they made fines]. It is therefore the list of those admitted not by hereditary right but by purchase. Those who paid fines had sureties, or pledges as to their good character, provided by two existing burgesses, and their names, together with the amount which was paid as a fine (in other words, an admission fee), are also recorded.

The 1415 Guild Roll also has three categories: enrolment by patrimony, enrolment by payment of fine, and out-burgesses. This pattern was followed in 1459, and again in 1542, except that in that Guild the names of those paying by fine seem unaccountably to have been omitted from the Roll.[26] Since that category or variations on it was also used in Guilds from 1562 onwards it would appear that its absence in 1542 was either an oversight or the result of the loss of a section of the original.[27]

All the Guild Rolls give information about the right by which membership was granted. In the case of those claiming by virtue of parentage the name of the father is given. Occupations are listed in some instances and, in the case of out-burgesses who lived beyond the boundaries of the borough, place of residence is also usually included. The in-burgesses were originally those who, when they were admitted to the Guild, lived and traded in the town, while the out-burgesses were those who when admitted were living outside the boundaries. This was the theoretical origin of the division, in the early days of the Guild, but in reality its operation was always very complicated and confused. Burgess rights were hereditary—succeeding generations inherited burgess-ships in the male line irrespective of their own immediate circumstances. Thus, the descendants of an in-burgess might move outside Preston but they would still be able to claim, as part of their birthright, in-burgess-ship. Conversely, the descendants of an out-burgess might move into the town and trade there, but their hereditary burgess-ship remained in the out-burgess category.

Because of the loss of the 1500 Guild Roll and damage to some of the others it is impossible to obtain complete statistics concerning the numbers enrolled at each medieval and early sixteenth-century Guild, and the categories of membership which they occupied. Nevertheless, approximate figures may be derived from the surviving Rolls, and these are shown in the following table:[28]

Admissions at late medieval and early sixteenth-century Guilds

Guild year	1397	1415	1459	1542
in-burgesses	197	181+	75+	219
out-burgesses	25	21	45	122
new admissions by fine	105	52	93	—
total	327	254+	213+	341

The 1397 Guild Roll is slightly damaged, so that some of the names are partly illegible or have been lost completely, but even so much of importance can be deduced. There were also at least 197 in-burgesses enrolled in 1397 whose fathers were already in the Guild. These people acquired freedom by hereditary right, and the large number who did so reinforces the supposition that a Guild had been held, with renewal of freedom, at some stage in the middle of the century, and certainly after 1328. Had the interval been the full 61 years many of the fathers would themselves surely have been born since the previous Guild. Over a hundred new purchases of freedom were made, which perhaps implies that there had been a substantial increase in the trading activity of the town since the last Guild. There must have been many inhabitants new to the town, with no claim to hereditary membership but wishing to become Guild members and thereby to obtain a privileged trading position.

It is perhaps significant in this context that after a putative Guild at mid-century the population of the town, like that of the country as a whole, would have been savagely reduced because of the Black Death. The large number of admissions by fine in 1397 could therefore represent incomers who, since the 1350s, had moved to Preston to take advantage of the 'vacancies' thus created.[29] The numbers of burgesses obtaining freedom at the Guilds Merchant dropped sharply during the first half of the fifteenth century, falling by some 23 per cent between 1397 and 1459. The effect of the fall in the number of new admissions in the 1415 Guild, which may be a consequence of the short interval since the 1397 Guild, is reflected in 1459 by a reduction in overall membership. The numbers were diminishing, and the Guild was evidently not self-sustaining.

If, as seems possible, the sharp decline in numbers during the fifteenth century is a reflection of the economic troubles of the town itself, it may be that the equally rapid increase during the first half of the sixteenth century reflects the recovery of its fortunes. This recovery is especially apparent if it is borne in mind that the 1542 Rolls apparently omit another large category—new admissions by fine—which would have increased the numbers beyond the 341 known enrolments at that Guild. The Guild Rolls from 1562 onwards seem to be complete, clear and well preserved so that thereafter it is possible to have a much more accurate picture of the numbers involved and of the trades and other details of the participants. The balance of the different categories also altered: in 1397 only 25 out-burgesses were enrolled, a mere 7.5 per cent of the total; but by 1459 the proportion had risen to 21 per cent, and by 1542 to 36 per cent. This change reflects the growing importance of the out-burgess category, with the development of the hereditary membership within this group (which meant that the more out-burgesses there were, the more potential burgesses there were in the next generation), but more particularly with the granting of admission to increasing numbers of outsiders, including important dignitaries and gentry from the county as a mark of esteem.

Initially the intention of the Guild was primarily to restrict trading rights to those within the town, so few people living outside would be admitted. Out-burgesses enjoyed fewer privileges and were not normally allowed to trade in the town, only to claim exemption from its tolls and dues. To be an out-burgess was therefore regarded mainly as an honorary status, with only limited rights, and it could therefore be granted without prejudicing the interests of the town's traders.

The 25 individuals listed in the out-burgess category in 1397 came from only eight families, and in several cases all the adult males in a particular family must have been enrolled as burgesses. The families listed are the de Hoghtons of Hoghton; the de Ethelstons of Ethelston (Elston, a small township next to Grimsargh); the Banasters of Walton-le-Dale; the de Bartons of Barton; the Botillers or Butlers of Rawcliffe; and three individuals—Thomas, son of Henry Gyveson; John, son of Thomas of the parish of Wyre (St Michael on Wyre); and Christopher, son of Robert de Preston. John of Wyre is the sole representative of a family which never again appears in the Rolls, but all the other families are regularly found in Guild Rolls for centuries after this—in the case of the Hoghton, Butler and Banaster families they proliferated so much that by the end of the seventeenth century there are numerous entries for these names in the out-burgess lists for each Guild.

The 1415 and 1459 Guilds introduced a number of other illustrious local land-owning families: Farington, Fleetwood, Clifton, Balderstone, Molyneux and Hesketh, for example. But still, in 1459, there were only 45 individuals, from fourteen families. The next surviving Guild Roll, that of 1542, shows a major change. On the one hand the Guild Merchant had admitted many new, and in some cases extremely important, families; on the other, the interval of almost a century had evidently seen the extension and ramification of existing out-burgess families. The total of out-burgesses was 122, the total number of surnames 34. In some cases there were several distinct branches of what had once been single families: thus there were eighteen Singletons (a name which first appears in the 1459 out-burgess list), including the families of William of Brockholes, William of

Ingolhead, Thomas of Brockholes, Robert of Broughton, John of Chingle Hall, Henry of Broughton, and three others whose residence is not noted.

The most important family appearing in the 1542 lists for the first time is that of the Earl of Derby, the Stanleys, who were for several centuries the leading resident family in the county, and who had an intimate and (usually) mutually beneficial association with Preston. The 1542 out-burgess list is headed by *Edwardus Comes Derbie* (Edward, Earl of Derby), and also includes Henry, Lord Strange (his heir), and the Earl's younger sons, Thomas Stanley and Edward Stanley. Second in rank at the 1542 Guild was the Hoghton family, headed by Sir Richard Hoghton, with no fewer than nine others of his family, together with junior branches such as the Hoghtons of Kirkham.[30]

A particularly distinctive feature of these medieval and early Tudor Guild Rolls is that the names of women are sometimes included. The 1397 Roll records the names of eighteen (probably the original total despite the damage to the document). Three appear to be 'ladies of repute', as Abram quaintly phrases it: that is, ladies of social standing who had the same status as the invited gentry burgesses. There are eleven widows of burgesses, one is the wife of a burgess, and three are daughters of burgesses. In the Guild Roll of 1415 only seven women are recorded, of whom five are widows of burgesses and only two, Agnes de Fysschewyk and Cecilia Roos (who also appears in 1397), are there apparently in their own right as 'ladies of repute'. One woman, Johanna del' Brex, is named in the 1459 Roll, but this probably represents a misreading of Johannes, the masculine form of the name. In 1542, the next Guild for which a burgess roll survives, one woman, Elizabeth, widow of John Clayton, gentleman, is named. This appears to be a courtesy rather than a freedom of real trading significance, and it the last entry for a woman traceable in the Guild Rolls for the next four and a half centuries.[31]

Nobody seriously thought that women should enjoy full burgess and Guild rights as active members, but of course they could and did trade—particularly in the cases of widows and daughters who inherited the businesses of husbands or fathers. The Guild Merchant could not ignore them since they were legitimate traders within the town, but it did not wish to admit them on equal terms. Its policy seems to have been to accept them (in the cases of widows and daughters) as traders and 'honorary' Guild members. In 1562 this was codified in a Guild order which stated that widows of burgesses had hitherto attempted, and even been allowed, to exercise burgess rights to the detriment of the town. In future, it said, the widows of burgesses could 'enjoy such liberties and freedomes during their Widowheade as their husbandes in lyff tyme had and enjoyed by reason of their burgesshippe'.[32]

This meant that the custom was accepted, but that widows did not in their own right become burgesses. Rather, they exercised similar rights in respect of their deceased husbands. That was of crucial importance, for it prevented their second husbands from acquiring burgess rights if the women remarried to non-burgesses.

The Guild otherwise remained entirely a male preserve until the 1920s, when the extension of the franchise and the election of female members of Preston Borough Council meant that such women were inevitably involved in the Guild as officers by virtue of their role as councillors. But women were still ineligible for Guild membership in their own right. The 1972 Guild was the last in which this rule applied: at the 1992 Guild women were, for the first time, entitled to admission on the same basis as men— though certain limitations were imposed to ensure that the anticipated increase in new admissions was kept within manageable proportions. Essentially, women could apply to be admitted in 1992 only if their father had been enrolled at the 1972 Guild. Hereditary claims predating 1972 (for example, a grandfather enrolled in the 1952 Guild) were not allowed.[33]

Evidence for occupations and residence

Some trades and occupations are referred to in the Guild Rolls before 1542, although recording of this information seems to have been much less systematic than it was later to be. In some cases it is likely that trades were only recorded in order to distinguish between people of the same surname. The 1397 Guild Roll refers to a few individuals by their trades. For example: Thomas Trigs, draper; Thomas le Bouker, coaler; John de Sylversyd, saddler; John de Leylond, tailor; and Radulphus (Ralph) Coke, flesh-hewer. In addition there are some entries where an occupation is given but only as part of the surname, which means that the person named was not necessarily practising that trade—a good example is William, son of James the Barber. These examples are from the comparatively few entries which do name trades. Out of about 290 legible and complete entries only 42 unambiguously give the trade or occupation of the freeman, with about the same number giving a surname that includes a trade.

In 1415 only 28 entries refer to trades. Ten relate to *corvisers*, or shoemakers, while another three were *cappellae* (hatters) and one a glover. These trades were closely associated with each other, because all used leather, and the fact they accounted for no less than 55 per cent of those who had their trade entered might perhaps suggest that at this Guild the various leatherworkers had become freemen *en masse*, possibly while establishing their own subsidiary craft guild. In 1415, although it was less than twenty years since the previous Guild, the use of the form 'le' in a surname, as in 'le Tailor', had almost disappeared. Instead these names had become surnames in their present form: Tailor, Barbour, Chapman.

Occupation details are almost absent from the 1459 Roll: only three are definitely recorded, a mercer, a pasturer and a saddler. The next surviving Roll (1542) is similarly uninformative, especially since it omits new admissions by fine. A weaver, John Hogekynson, is the only person whose occupation is given. Thus for over a century there

Trades named in the Guild Rolls, 1397 and 1415 [34]

1397	wright (3)	miller (l)	draper (l)
	mercer (12)[a]	tailor (5)	shoemaker (4)
	jeweller (1)	spicer (1)[b]	mason (1)
	coaler (1)[c]	glover (1)	wattler (1)[d]
	saddler (1)	webster (1)[e]	hatter (1)
	flesh-hewer (1)[f]		
1415	glover (1)	mercer (3)	draper (2)
	shoemaker (10)	tailor (1)	hatter (3)
	cutler (1)	schoolmaster (1)	barker (2)[g]
	stringer (1)[h]		

Notes: This table excludes all trades which were (or might have been) part of the surname of the individual: it also excludes clergy.

a   *mercer*: general merchant or textile dealer

b   *spicer*: apothecary

c   *coaler*: charcoal-dealer

d   *wattler*: maker of wattles (for wattle and daub buildings)

e   *webster*: weaver

f   *flesh-hewer*: butcher

g   *barker*: tanner

h   *stringer*: maker of strings for bows or musical instruments

is no information comparable with that in the Rolls of 1397 and 1415. This emphasises that the methods and styles of compiling the Guild Rolls were still not fixed. There was a good deal of use of precedent, but each successive Guild employed some new forms or dropped older ones: only in the eighteenth century did the information become more rigidly standardised.

The same variations apply to the inclusion of details concerning place of residence. Although it might be expected that out-burgesses, in particular, would be enrolled with the addition of this information, that was not always so. In the first three Rolls (1397, 1415 and 1459) there is another problem: a large number of surnames are in the form *de Barton* or *de Ribbleton*, 'of Barton' or 'of Ribbleton'. A man called 'John of Ribbleton' might come from Ribbleton, but inevitably such names very quickly became historic. John of Ribbleton, when he moved to Preston, might keep his surname, but it could then be passed on to his children, born and bred in Preston. It is therefore often difficult to distinguish clearly between a locative surname and a place of residence.[35]

If allowance is made for the difficulties outlined above, interesting patterns emerge from these surnames which give useful information about the town of Preston in the fourteenth century. When the out-burgess category is excluded (because many of these did not live in the town) there are no fewer than 67 locative surnames. Some of these refer to very local places—people with surnames such as *del More* ('of the Moor')—but there are about 58 places outside Preston which appear in the surnames of the in-burgesses of 1397.

Many of these places are close to Preston and show clearly that during the period of growth from about 1200 to 1350 the town drew many of its inhabitants from the adjacent rural areas. Names such as Alston, Howick, Ingol, Cottam, Leyland, Singleton, Ribbleton and Walton fall into this category. Some names, such as Wigan, Meols, Blackburn, Horwich, Tockholes and Haydock, show that people came from further afield in the county, while a few others reveal even more far-flung connections: there were families in Preston in 1397 with the surnames *de York*, *de Darlyngton*, *de London* and even, in three instances, *de Ireland*.[36] The Guild Roll thus reflects the growing status and wide trading connections of the town.

CHAPTER TWO

The Guild
from 1542 to 1742

I N T H E mid-sixteenth century a regular twenty-year cycle was adopted for the celebration of the Guild, in belated accordance with the early fourteenth-century orders. Thus its particular distinction was born, and a phrase was given to the English language. The interval was irregular until 1542, but thereafter the rule was faithfully observed for 380 years, until the Second World War prevented the holding of a Guild in 1942. From 1952 the pattern was readopted, and the 2012 Guild and those which follow therefore conform to the traditional cycle.

The interval between Preston Guilds is exceptionally long. Although Preston was not quite unique, very few other towns had Guild celebrations with such a pattern and none has retained it to the present. The only other major example in northern England seems to have been Kendal, where comparable celebrations were held every 21 years until 1759. The reason for the choice of a twenty-year interval is nowhere explicitly stated, since its origins lie in the period before surviving written records. There is, however, a likely explanation. The working of the Guild had two elements, one of which was the routine day-by-day and year-by-year regulation of trade within the borough. For such purposes all that was needed was an administrative body (the Corporation, or Borough Council) and accurate lists of those entitled to trade and the regulations by which they were governed, information which was provided by the Guild Rolls.

The other element was the formal ceremonial event in which membership of the Guild was publicly renewed. That was not needed every year, since it was possible to make on-the-spot admissions in between times. Formal renewal was required only once in each generation, when members of families already represented in the Guild would renew hereditary membership, at the same time as newcomers were publicly admitted for the first time. Those who had been given admittance between Guilds would be enrolled officially, even though they were already trading.

New hereditary members were almost always the sons of existing Guild members and could be of any age, from babes in arms to young men of twenty, or even older men who had failed to renew at a previous Guild but were still eligible. The only requirement was that once in a generation there should be as complete a revision of the Guild lists as possible. Hence, at an early date, a twenty-year interval must have seemed the most suitable. A further factor, which cannot be ignored, is that the Preston Guild is manifestly an extremely costly and elaborate affair, and always seems to have been so. To have held it more frequently would have placed a considerable financial burden both on the membership and on the town, as well as watering down the special impact and prestige of the event.

The medieval traditions were retained and observed into the seventeenth century because they continued to serve a real practical purpose, but by 1682 Dr Richard Kuerden, when he wrote the first eye-witness account of the celebrations, fully realised that the Preston Guild was already of great antiquarian interest. As the years passed the medieval traditions of the Guild, and its evident antiquity, became revered for their own sakes. Although the character of the celebration itself changed, becoming more elaborate and more directed towards socialising and entertainment (and, many have long and rightly argued, ever more commercialised), the heart of the Guild—the renewal and admission ceremony—has survived. Moreover, an important feature of its survival is that this is not a sentimental Victorian or twentieth-century recreation of an old custom. The tradition has never lapsed and its history is continuous, so that despite the many changes the Preston Guild is at its heart a genuine survival of the distant past. Yet it would be foolish to suppose that, could they see a modern Guild, our medieval ancestors, the tradesmen and the craftsmen, would be shocked by the commercialism. The origin of the Guild is inextricably bound up with commercial activity, and undoubtedly the fourteenth- and fifteenth-century entrepreneurs did their utmost to capitalise on the Guild celebration just as their successors have done and will do in our lifetimes and long afterwards. Indeed, they might well regard with envy and admiration the scale of modern Guilds, and their financial potential.

Information about the Guild is much more abundant from the sixteenth century onwards, since contemporary records have survived in increasing quantities. As well as the Guild Rolls there are, from the early seventeenth century, the records of the Corporation and other local government bodies. From 1682 onwards we have contemporary descriptions, and from the mid-eighteenth century printed accounts, souvenirs, ephemera, diary entries and letters. From the late eighteenth century, too, the build-up to the Guilds, their daily progress, and the views of contemporaries, are also amply recorded in the pages of local and national newspapers. It is therefore possible to develop a much more rounded picture of the Guild, a picture which by 1800 is no longer confined to a short collection of formal orders and regulations and a long list of names, but instead shines through the pages and papers of history as a lively, colourful, exciting and often controversial event.

The Guild and the Corporation, 1542–1835

The relationship between the Guild Merchant and the Council has already been considered. Despite the absence of medieval administrative records for the borough it is clear that they were always identical. The administration of the borough was conducted in the name of the mayor, aldermen and burgesses, but in reality most burgesses did not participate directly in government. Instead, they were represented by an elected group of common councilmen drawn from among their number. At the same time the mayor, aldermen and burgesses also formed the Guild Merchant, which functioned for them and was administered by them.

This became clearer after 1566, when Elizabeth I granted Preston a charter of incorporation. Until then the mayor, aldermen and common councilmen had had no corporate identity at law. They governed as a group of individuals and if, for example, a person wished to sue the Council, it was technically necessary to take out separate injunctions against each individual. There was no legally defined 'Preston Borough Council' which could be sued. Similarly, and again technically (because these distinctions were generally ignored), the Council as a body could not own or lease property, but instead had to do so as a group of individuals. This lack of legal identity gave no security, for the councillors were individually liable for debts, charges and prosecutions, and there was no concept of corporate liability.

Incorporation was a device adopted from the fourteenth century onwards to overcome this problem. It meant, literally and in practice, 'the setting up of a body'. The administration of a town was vested in an entity, called a corporation or a council, which had a legal identity separate and independent from that of its members, and which existed in perpetuity. The death, resignation or removal of individual members did not affect the existence of the body corporate. A corporation could, in its own right, own, buy, sell and lease property, be sued or sue, and make decisions. In short, it became a council in the modern form and shed those vestiges of informal organic development which it had retained from its medieval past.

All of this was achieved in Preston by the stroke of Elizabeth I's pen, when she signed the detailed, lengthy and impressive charter granted to the town in the sixth year of her reign, 1566. The title given to the new body was similarly lengthy and impressive: 'We ordain, appoint, grant and declare that our borough aforesaid of Preston shall be and remain for ever hereafter a free corporated borough in deed, fact and name, of one Mayor, two Bailiffs, and the Burgesses, by the name of the Mayor, Bailiffs, and Burgesses of the Borough of Preston in the County of Lancaster [and that it shall for ever after] be one body corporate and one perpetual commonalty.'[1]

The charter confirmed and extended the privileges, rights and liberties granted to the town by previous sovereigns. It is worth noting here that although every charter back to that of Henry II (1179) was faithfully listed and recited, there is no reference to any earlier charter. This may be considered as further confirmation that the alleged charter of Henry I dating from 1100 was a myth. The charter of 1566 also confirmed the right of the borough to have a Guild Merchant:

> We have granted, and by these presents for ourselves, our heirs and successors, we have confirmed to the aforesaid Mayor, Bailiffs, and Burgesses of the said Borough of Preston, and their successors ... a *Gild Merchant* in the aforesaid Borough, with all the liberties and free-customs appertaining to such a Guild as they have heretofore enjoyed.

It is therefore quite certain that Preston Corporation had a Guild Merchant in *its* right, and that the Guild did not exist independently. This position was maintained until 1835, when the Municipal Corporations Act reformed the constitution and legal basis of municipal government in Preston and in most other corporate boroughs. The 1835 Act superseded the earlier charters, and the whole basis of the Guild Merchant—its purpose and the desirability or otherwise of its continuation—were called into question. Ultimately, after much local pressure, the new Borough Council decided in 1842 that, despite the change in the constitution, the Guild Merchant celebrations should continue. These events are considered in more detail in chapter 6.

The oldest surviving minutes of the Corporation date from 1608, and thereafter it is possible to obtain an increasingly clear picture of the planning of Guilds and the decision-making that lay behind the celebration. In 1608 the town clerk began writing in the 'White Book' of Preston, the great minute book of the assemblies which were the council meetings of the time. The book (formally headed with the inscription *This is the Booke of Orders for the Towne of Preston [in] Amondernes in the Countie of Lancaster*) includes not only council minutes but also, from the 1640s onwards, numerous entries for the admission of burgesses by payment of fines or by gift.[2] These admissions were described as 'by copy of Court Roll', a term also used in manorial courts when tenancies were similarly enrolled. The court roll admissions were subsequently ratified and entered in the Guild Rolls every twenty years at the Guilds Merchant. It was unrealistic for men to have to wait for up to twenty years before being allowed to trade legally or to enjoy the other privileges of a burgess, and therefore the admissions at assembly meetings were those which counted. In these cases the admissions at Guild celebrations themselves were purely a formality—though the members had to pay a second time.

The relationship between the Guild, its burgesses, and the Corporation had important implications for the franchise of the town. In the sixteenth century the right to vote in elections for the two MPs representing the Borough of Preston may nominally have been vested in the in-burgesses, but in practice it seems to have been the custom that only the members of the Corporation actually exercised the right to vote. The effective franchise was thus restricted to the mayor and the 24 aldermen and common councilmen.

At the general election of 1661 the in-burgesses challenged the right of the Corporation to restrict the franchise to its 25 members. The Corporation, as was its custom, chose two members, but the burgesses refused to accept these and elected two others. The dispute was referred to the House of Commons, which had the power of adjudication. It eventually determined that the right to vote was to be enjoyed by the *inhabitants* of the town, and that the Corporation had no legal power to limit the franchise in the customary way. The word 'inhabitants' was not defined in the judgement, but it was interpreted by the Corporation as meaning that those eligible to vote must be in-burgesses living within the borough bounds. Thus from 1661 the resident in-burgesses were entitled to vote, a major extension of the franchise from the previous position of just 25 voters but one which did not satisfy non-resident in-burgesses or any of the out-burgesses.[3] It is perhaps unnecessary to add that the franchise remained exclusively male for the next 257 years.

The number of out-burgesses grew rapidly between 1660 and 1700 and, since many were powerful and influential people who felt themselves entitled to participate in Preston politics, the pressure for them to be allowed to vote was considerable. Significant numbers of out-burgesses were now living *within* the boundary of the borough, and wished to have the right to vote in the same way as resident in-burgesses. The non-burgess inhabitants were likewise seeking greater involvement and influence in the affairs of the town and began to challenge the right of the Corporation to limit the vote to burgesses alone. These challenges and pressures were steadfastly resisted by the Corporation which, in a succession of Guild orders, decreed that only the in-burgesses would be allowed to vote. In the 1760s some legal opinions held that the Guild orders themselves had no legal force and could not be used to justify the restriction of voting, but others pointed to them as a formal and enrolled expression both of tradition and of the acts of the Corporation.

The Guild orders became increasingly detailed where the franchise was concerned, in response to constant attempts to evade their conditions. In 1662, for example, it was stated that 'no foreign Burgess shall have any Vote in any Court of Election within this Town concerning the Election of any Officers ... or any Burgess to serve in Parliament for this Corporation'. This did not satisfy the opposition, and the wrangle over the extent of the franchise continued. In the 1682 Guild orders it was repeated at greater and more forceful length:

> some disputes have of late times arisen touching the right of Election of Parliament Men for this Borough And who ought to have Votes in such Election. It is now declared that no Foreign Burgess (altho he lives within this Corporation) hath or ought to have any Vote in such said election Nor that any Burgess (Inhabiting

forth of the said Borough at the time of such said Election) ought to have any Vote therein But that the Sole right of such said Elections have constantly appertained and do belong to the Inn Burgesses of this Incorporation either of the Guild Merchant or by Copy of Court Roll that do or shall Inhabit within the said Borough at the time of such said Election And that the usage of this Incorporation hath time out of Mind been accordingly.[4]

The Guild of 1722 was further troubled by this question, and it is apparent that out-burgesses had continued to make concerted efforts to evade the restrictions. An order of this Guild noted that

to evade and make void the Good intention and design of the said order [1682] and to encroach upon and destroy the ancient Rights and priviledges of the Inn Burgesses of this Incorporation at several late elections of Members of Parliament for this Borough divers persons (altho Inn Burgesses) yet not Inhabiting within this Town have come a very short time before the day of such Election and have Claimed and insisted upon giving their Votes ... upon Pretence of being at that time Inhabitants.[5]

To overcome this problem, whereby in-burgesses who lived outside Preston quite legitimately voted in elections having resided in the town only a few days, the Corporation passed a new order at the 1722 Guild to require that

for the future no person or persons altho' Inn Burgesses of this Incorporation hath or ought to have any votes or vote in Electing Members to Parliament ... unless such person or persons has or have been residents and Inhabiting within this Town three Months before the Test of the Writ of Summons to parliament.[6]

The restriction of voting to the in-burgesses who lived within the borough boundary continued, frequently challenged but never overturned, until 1768. At the remarkable and dramatic Preston election of that year the Corporation, strongly Tory and Anglican in its politics and beliefs, was challenged by the Whig faction headed by Lord Derby, who sought to have his own candidates elected for the borough seats. As part of their challenge the Whigs looked again at the 1661 judgement of the House of Commons and chose to interpret the word 'inhabitants' as meaning all adult males (apart from paupers, lunatics and other categories deemed unworthy of the vote). They therefore determined that all resident men, in-burgesses, out-burgesses and non-burgesses alike, might vote. Again a parallel poll was held, and the two factions submitted their claims to the adjudication of the Commons, with the result that the Whig case was victorious. The loose interpretation of the 1661 judgement was upheld, and until 1835 Preston enjoyed almost universal adult male suffrage—the most generous franchise in England at that time. The resident in-burgesses thus lost one of the most valuable of their privileges: they were no longer exclusively entitled to vote in Preston elections.[7]

Among the features of the burgess lists from 1562 to 1702 is a continued growth in the proportion of out-burgesses. As has been seen, their numbers in the medieval Guilds were small in relation to the numbers of in-burgesses, but the balance altered during the sixteenth and seventeenth centuries. The number of out-burgesses rose rapidly, and in 1602 they achieved a majority. Although this position was not maintained, their relative strength remained high throughout the seventeenth century, and it was not until the early 1700s that in-burgess enrolment began to increase again. Whereas in 1682 there had been about 1,400 in-burgesses and 1,200 out-burgesses, by the 1722 Guild there had been a dramatic change, with 2,655 in-burgesses and only 900 out-burgesses.

Thereafter the numbers of out-burgesses fell steadily as the value and prestige of this status vanished, and as more of the representatives of county families were granted the superior status of in-burgess. Essentially, because by then trading rights were irrelevant, it no longer really mattered if 'outsiders' became in-burgesses. By the 1822 Guild almost all the well-known and influential gentry families had been thus elevated. At the same time the numbers of in-burgesses rose correspondingly, through new admissions and the continued multiplying of the existing families, all the sons of which were entitled to hereditary Guild membership. There was a small decrease in overall numbers between 1742 and 1782, but after that time numbers rose again. By 1802 the Guild had a membership of almost 3,500.[8]

The Guild Merchant and trade in Preston

The comparative lack of information about the trading activities of the Guild and its members has already been noted. It is perhaps surprising that a body which originated as a grouping of traders and craftsmen, and which had as one of its main aims the regulation of trade, should have produced so little detailed documentary evidence of that aspect of its role. The reasons for this are various. First, the extant records of the medieval and sixteenth-century Guilds are limited to the Guild Rolls, in which occupational details were not systematically entered. From 1562 there are more frequent references to trades, but the recording of them is still far from regular. Second, the Guild itself was inseparable from the Borough Council and many of the documents which it probably produced were held among the borough records, which have not survived from before 1608. Third, the operation of restrictive trading practices was in considerable measure 'behind the scenes', and may well never have produced significant quantities of written records. It is therefore necessary to glean fragments of information from a miscellany of sources to try to determine what the Guild did and what were the practical consequences of its work in the economy and trade of the town.

The medieval Guild Rolls suggest that the Guild was not dominated by a single group of traders. In some towns a particular trade or craft 'captured' the guild, but in Preston that was not the case. No single group predominated, for in the Middle Ages (as at most times since) the economic base of the town has been wide, and no single industry has achieved a total dominance. That state of affairs can be seen in the Guild Rolls of 1397 and 1415, with their diversity of trades: leather workers of all sorts, merchants, drapers and tailors, as well as specialist craftsmen. Later Rolls include further evidence of the diversity within the Guild and thus within the town itself. The table in Appendix 2 shows occupation information from the rolls of 1562–1642, excluding clergymen and those designated by rank or title rather than by occupation.[9]

The table does not show the numbers actually working in each trade or occupation in Preston, but simply the numbers recorded on the Guild Rolls. The statistics are dependent to some extent on the genealogy of the families concerned, and on the degree of systematic recording, and do not, of course, include those who were not enrolled in the Guild. It is clear also that the Guild Roll of 1602, which has only 47 entries giving occupations (compared with 121 in 1582 and 158 in 1622) is unrepresentative. Whoever was responsible for recording the names at that Guild chose to note occupations only in special cases. Even so, it gives valuable information about the economic structure of the town.

The membership of the Guild included a very wide range of trades. For example, in the Rolls from 1562 to 1642 some 75 different occupations are listed. This reflects its prominent role in the government and society of the town, as well as its significance in controlling trade. Membership of the Guild was necessary for anyone who wished to succeed in town society, even for those who were unlikely to experience trading competition from outside and so did not need the commercial protection afforded by the Guild. For example William Charnock, a gunsmith who was enrolled in 1642, was not likely to experience serious competition from outsiders, since his was a specialised minor trade. Instead, he probably joined the Guild more for its social and political advantages.

Perhaps the most striking feature shown by the table is the importance of the leather-related trades: cordwainers; curriers; feltmakers (using the fur and bristle from hides); glovers; hatters and capmakers; saddlers; shoemakers and cobblers; skinners; and tanners. There was a sizeable group of these, as shown in the table below. Considering the unsystematic nature of the original statistics, the proportions are very similar, and it is clear that this group retained its importance from the medieval period into the late seventeenth century.

Leather-related trades in the Guild Rolls, 1562–1642

Guild year	1562	1582	1602	1622	1642
no. of burgesses with occupation details	89	121	47	158	119
no. in leather trades	23	36	15	42	27
percentage of total	25.8	29.7	31.9	25.6	22.9

Preston had close links with the adjacent countryside and was the market and commercial centre for a great rural area extending across the Fylde and the northern part of the Lancashire plain and eastwards into the fells and the Pennine valleys. There were no raw materials for early industrial development, of the sort which was already beginning to transform towns such as Wigan, and the craft trades of Preston were essentially those which depended on the processing of agricultural products.

The connection with agriculture is revealed by the presence of farmers in the Guild Rolls. These were not usually people from outside the Preston area, out-burgesses who happened to be farmers, but rather were farming within the borough boundary or in the townships immediately adjacent, such as Fulwood, Ribbleton and Fishwick. Sizeable tracts of land within the borough were still open fields, and the farmers and husbandmen who worked them were fully entitled to join the Guild as burgesses although, inevitably, the concept of restrictive trade practices had less relevance to them. Many would, however, sell their produce in Preston, and the exclusion of outside traders who might compete in the market place could only be to their advantage.

Some of the occupations which are recorded for the first time in the Guilds of 1622 and 1642 are of the sort which indicate that Preston was developing from a market town, albeit an important one, into a more complex and influential centre of commerce and business. Occupations such as gunsmith, locksmith, spurrier, vintner and musician point to a high level of sophistication in society and to the existence of specialised crafts and skills not found in ordinary market towns. That evidence is in keeping with the implications of the growing and ever more illustrious list of out-burgesses, which suggests that Preston was widely seen as the focus of county society. It also reflects other features of Lancashire life, notably the tendency to regard Preston as the centre for county government and administration—the county town in all but name.

The control of trading rights and the exclusion of outsiders were of great importance, especially in the more traditional trades, throughout the seventeenth century and into the eighteenth. Such controls were always unpopular with those who were excluded, and many must have viewed the Guild as an oppressive and elitist body, able to exert an excessive influence over the commercial life of the town.

It is clear, from notes in the Guild Rolls and from entries in the White Book and other

Corporation records, that until the early eighteenth century considerable care was taken to assess each application for admission to the Guild, in an attempt to prevent interlopers from competing effectively with the established traders and craftsmen. In some instances conditions were placed upon membership to ensure that the town would have the benefit of the trader but not suffer excessive competition. At the Guild of 1622, for example, it was agreed that

> Alexandrus Chisnall de Copple ... is this present daie admitted to buy sheepe skines in this Towne and to sell the same againe in lether by whole saile and in grosse but not by retail v^{li}.[10]

For the payment of £5 Chisnall was permitted to buy skins on the market in Preston and to take them back to Coppull to make them into leather. He could then sell the leather wholesale in Preston, but was forbidden to make retail sales in the town, since that would compete with Preston's smaller leather-dealers. The restriction was evidently acceptable to both parties since at the 1642 Guild, when he was living at Welch Whittle, he is noted as renewing his membership 'upon ye same conditions of the last Guild and not otherwise'.[11] A comparable restriction was placed upon another skinner, Evan Gerrard, who was admitted at the same Guild 'onlie for Buyinge of greene skines and sellinge them wholesaile'.[12]

The figures of occupations perhaps imply that the leather trades were particularly well placed to influence admissions of competitors, and the examples quoted above show how they were able to use the system to their advantage, increasing trade for their own businesses and reducing competition at the same time. A very clear instance of this power, and one with additional historical interest, occurs in the 1642 Guild Roll, when it was noted that John Hilton, Governor of the House of Correction, and Richard his son, were to be admitted only upon condition that they did not 'use the trade of a skinner nor whitawer in this Towne'. Hilton, a skinner by trade, had presumably taken on the job of governor as a commercial venture, but the other leather-workers (and, no doubt, the skinners in particular) were anxious to prevent him from carrying on his normal trade while resident in the town.[13] Another restraint upon the activities of outside traders is recorded in the same Guild Roll:

> Eduardus Hoghton de Euxton iroonmonger ... admitted onelie for uttering and sellinge made Iron ware and for buying Corne and Catle for his own use.[14]

Permission was granted for Hoghton to sell his ironmongery in Preston. To judge from the absence of references to the trade apart from this particular entry it may well be that the town was short of iron goods. At the same time he was authorised to buy cattle and oxen in the town and take them to Euxton but only for his own use. He was not permitted to buy on Preston market and resell at higher prices in his home village, which would have deprived the Preston cattle-traders of business.

There were other reasons for accepting burgesses only upon certain conditions. From 1622 onwards, apprentices were frequently enrolled as Guild members, but only very rarely before that date. The change in policy was the result of lengthy discussions in 1609–11 about the rights of apprentices and their role in the economic and political life of the town. Apprentices, inevitably, were not yet established as traders or craftsmen, and it was thought that potentially they could gain the privilege of membership of the Guild and then take their trade elsewhere. That would be contrary to the purpose of the Guild. Yet, it could be argued, it was in the interests of Preston to retain its own apprentices by giving them Guild membership, to prevent their being poached by other towns or traders. The question therefore centred on whether apprentices should be given Guild membership in advance of setting up their own trades.

This question was linked to another issue. In the late sixteenth and early seventeenth centuries there had been serious problems resulting from an over-casual attitude to the admission of outsiders and the inadequacy of controls over their trading and qualifications. In 1609 a resolution of the Corporation stated that

> heretofore divers of the inhabitantes of this towne of Preston as well at the Guild Merchante laitlie holden [1602] and keeped by Copie of Court Rowle have bene admitted and allowed free Burgesses within this towne, whoe before that [admission] eyther were of now Traydes nor served as Apprentices eyther in this towne or eles where at anie Trade … or occupation and after their admittance have taken upon [themselves] the use of anie traide used wthin this towne as beste pleased, to the great prejudice damage losse & hinderance of divers Auncyente artificers & Traides men within this Towne who have not onelie served their apprintishippes … But have alsoe paide great Fines to thuse [i.e. the use] of this towne for their freedomes.[15]

People were coming to Preston without specific trades and without serving apprenticeships. Having been granted freedom, they were setting up in any trade of their choice and undermining the business of existing freemen, who had served long apprenticeships and paid substantial fines (that is, admission fees) to become burgesses.

The unfairness of this competition (and it was a complaint which was repeated frequently until the nineteenth century) was such that it was held to damage and prejudice the existing 'auncyente artificers and traders'. It was therefore decided by the Corporation that in future nobody should be admitted a burgess, either at the Guild or by enrolment in the court books, without entering into a bond for the payment of a sizeable sum for the use of the town. Those who were made burgesses were to be allowed to trade only in the business which they specified at the time of enrolment: a man could not be admitted as, say, a skinner, and then change trades and work as a grocer, for this would be unfair competition. Apprenticeships were to be served in a particular trade: if apprentices were admitted to that trade, they were not normally to change to another after their full admission as burgesses. Any changes that did take place were to be with the prior approval of the mayor and Council.

After 1609 the admission of apprentices as burgesses and members of the Guild was therefore regularised and made more systematic. To protect existing traders admissions had to depend upon the completion of the indentures—and if apprentices left before their time their admissions were void. Below are some typical examples from the 1622 and 1642 Guild Rolls:

> Radulphus [*Ralph*] Hyndley an apprentice with James Whalley sadler is admitted Free upon this condicion that hee shall serve his Terme out, else not.[16]

> Item Jacobus [*James*] Longton apprentice to William Jolly nevertheles hee must serve his aprentishippe xxx^s.[17]

> Item Ricardus [*Richard*] Kinge apprentice to Lawrence Haworth if hee serve out his apprentishippe ij^{li}.[18]

Some apprentices who were nearing the completion of their terms were admitted on the expectation that they would before long establish themselves in trade, and so were given a form of associate membership of the Guild Merchant. These examples are both from the 1642 Guild:

> Item Robertus Strickland apprentice with William Bragger is admitted a Burgess for the some of xx^s in hand and xx^s more to bee paid within one year next after hee sette upp for himselfe.[19]

> Item Ricardus Jamieson apprentice to William Wharton admitted a free Burgesse if hee serve out his apprentishippe and is to pay xx^s in hand and xx^s more within one yeare next after hee sett up for himselfe.[20]

Such partial admittance could remain valid more or less indefinitely, as a form of surety for eventual admittance in full when the individual chose or was able to establish himself as a Preston trader. In the 1642 Guild Roll is the following illustration of this point:

> Item Geffrey Stephenson de Stoke in Cheshire Taylor who had been apprentice

in this Towne and paid xx^s in hand and is to pay xx^s more when hee comes to inhabite and dwell in this towne.[21]

Admissions of non-residents who were planning to come to Preston are also relatively numerous from the 1622 Guild onwards. Obviously some traders would, for a variety of genuine and honourable reasons, wish to move into the town. After the deliberations of 1609–11 the existing Guild members vetted such applications carefully and in some cases imposed conditions of the type seen above. In other instances the intending residents were admitted to the Guild in advance of their move to Preston, and immediately became licensed to trade. The standard method was for a down payment of half the admission fee to be made, the remainder to be paid on arrival in Preston. Examples from the 1642 Guild Roll include:

Item Thurstanus ffogg de Blackburn admitted a Townes Burgesse but not to trade until hee come to inhabite and live within the Towne iij^{li} x^s.[22]

Item Jacobus Gorton is admitted a free Burgesse of this Incorporation and if hee come to inhabite within the Towne then to receive the priviledge and benefitt of a townes borne Burgesse but if hee doo not come to inhabite within the Towne then to receive nor further or other Libertie and benefitt than of a forreigne Burgesse onlie xx^{li}.[23]

Item Mr Thomas Calvert v^{li} more to be paid by Mr Calvert the some of v^{li} upon his setting upp in anie Trade within this Towne.[24]

Guild members were not just traders in Preston. They recognised their place within the wider economic system and maintained contacts with other towns and similar guilds or trading companies. This was of mutual benefit, for traders could hope to gain reciprocal favours and, provided that no direct and harmful competition resulted, membership of a similar body in another town was undoubtedly a favourable feature of any application to become a member of the Preston Guild. An excellent illustration of such contacts between the Preston Guild Merchant and outside bodies is an episode in October 1666, when the following was enrolled in the White Book of the Corporation, signed by Lawrence Wall, the mayor, and fifteen of his fellow councillors:

Wheras William Cadman of the Citty of London Stationer hath this day made his application to this Councell to bee admitted to inhabit & trade in his profession of Stationer within the Incorporacon (hee having served his apprentishipp in London) And in regard of the late sadd accident of fire which hath at present prevented trading there [the Great Fire of London] ... and upon Consideracon of his Majesties gracious proclamacon on behalfe of the Tradesmen of London Ordered that the said William Cadman bee & is hereby admitted to inhabitt & trade in his profession of a Stationer in the said Borough for the terme of two yeares next coming Hee the said William Cadman first giveinge Security in no wise to be burdensone to this Incorporacon[25]

Admissions for services rendered

Admission to the Guild could be granted for services rendered to the town or to the Guild itself, and it became traditional for a limited number of freedoms to be so given when the Guild was celebrated. Sometimes all fees were waived, at other times they were reduced, and sometimes the admission was of a person who might not otherwise qualify but was thought likely to be of benefit to the town. These services might be of an eminently practical and down-to-earth variety. The 1662 Guild Roll includes the admission of John Crookes, for a fine of £2,

> upon condition that the Towne Butchers have previlhidge to empty their Bellys paunches puddings and other offall on his backside they paying him six pence a peece per annum[26]

The disposal of trade waste was evidently a serious problem in seventeenth-century Preston, and John Crookes obtained membership in return for the use of his 'backside', or croft, for the communal good. In the Guild of 1602 Thomas Woodruff was admitted free of charge as a burgess,

> for Ringinge the daie Bell and Coulefewe [curfew] for the Somer season duringe his liffe, and for making all the Seates in the Church for the townes men, Both againste the Sabaoth daies and Festival daies sweete and cleane everie of the said daies, for the said termes.[27]

An earlier instance of this practice occurs among the orders for the 1582 Guild. It was stated that Henry, son of Thomas Walmesley deceased, 'earnestlie desireth to be a Burges of the Towne of Preston'. His admission was agreed, but he had to make a payment of sorts to the town for his free admission as a burgess: it was decided that he should accept the 'keping and wynteryng of the Townes Bull yerely during the terme of twentye yeres'.[28] Robert Oldfield, a bellfounder, was admitted at the 1622 Guild for 40s. payable in two parts: one half was to be paid at once, and the other was on the condition 'that hee shall att anie tyme when the Towne shall have occasion to use his worke to pay the other xx^s'.[29] In 1582 William Sandes, joiner, was admitted in return for repairing the 'Seeling whiche standeth abowte the Checquer' (the exchequer or accounting table in the Guildhall) and his sons were admitted if he agreed to undertake the 'Bording of the said Checquer before the feaste of the Nativytie of St John Baptist ... in such manner and sorte as shall be thought decent and well by the said Maior and his brethren'.[30] At the same Guild Richard Stirrop, paver, was admitted provided that he would, each year, make and mend the postholes dug in 'the payvment of the market stidde [place] at two faires' (these were postholes erected for tethering beasts), and if he would mend the broken pavements leading eastwards from the town to the 'wyndie mylne' or windmill. The pavements were in Church Street; the windmill stood close to the junction of Ribbleton Lane and Deepdale Road.[31]

Also in 1582, a cook with the appropriate name of John Meate applied to be a burgess. It was decided to admit him upon condition that he served 'every Mayor of the said Towne of Preston for the dressing of meate and drynck at any Feaste that any Mayor ... shall call him the said John Meate unto, during his life, upon reasonable warnyng'.[32] Likewise, in 1602 the official baker and brewer to the Guild Merchant was given his freedom as a gift in return for services already given:

> John Houghton of the Lea yoman is admitted a Burgess of this towne of Preston
> in respecte of suche Service as hee hath alreadie done this guyld, and for bakinge
> of Breade and brueinge of Beare att all such Guyldes as shall happen to be kepte,
> within the saide Towne of Preston duringe his lyffe, as also, att all such Feasts,
> as the Major of the said Towne shall att anie tyme keepe.[33]

A similar assistance for life was to be rendered by Ralph Radcliffe, slater, who in 1622 was admitted on condition that he kept the Guildhall roof in good repair: 'hee shall att all tymes needfull mosse and dresse the Rooffe of the hall duringe his lyffe haveinge Slaite mosse Lyme and heare [hair] found hyme upon the costs and chardge of hym selffe'. Moss was used to pack the roof under the slates, and horsehair was mixed with the mortar to bind and strengthen it. In later years Ralph may perhaps have wondered whether the bargain was worth while, since he not only had to do the work whenever it was required, but also to pay for the materials and give his labour free.[34]

Other services might be specifically connected with the celebration of the Guild Merchant itself. Such grants were a reward to the individuals who had assisted at the Guild and had helped the Mayor and officers with the arrangements. At the 1642 Guild there were several admissions by gift of burgesses who had given such help. In each case this is carefully noted: the purpose of admission is made clear, so that if there was any argument about the trades and crafts carried on by these individuals the record could be checked. These admissions give glimpses of the sorts of celebrations which were held.

Bell-ringing, brewing and baking have already been mentioned; here are feasting and music:

> Petrus [*Peter*] Walmisley Cooke for his paines taken this present Guild and to bee hereafter readie to doo service to the Major.

> Johannes [*John*] Eastham Cooke admitted gratis for his paines takinge this Guild and to bee readie to serve the Major for the tyme beinge hereafter.

> Robertus Hindle admitted a free Burgesse for his paines taken at the Guild.

> Johannes Hodgson musician admitted a free Burgesse for his paines taken this Guild.[35]

The trading companies within the Guild

There is little evidence for the existence of formally constituted craft or trade companies within the Guild Merchant in the medieval period. Informal groupings almost certainly existed, but it is unclear how many there were, and although various writers have attempted to show the existence of such companies in medieval Preston their evidence is scanty in the extreme and does not stand up to close analysis. Whittle, writing in the 1820s, gives the names of the heads of a large number of companies who, he says, were present at the 1397 Guild. He also gives dates of incorporation of the companies, but it is clear that these were an invention or had been derived from sources that did not relate to Preston, since they conflict with what little specific evidence we do have.[36] The evidence from towns with more detailed and extensive medieval records shows that some companies had registered constitutions but that many others did not have any formal existence. The latter are often found in smaller towns with a less elaborate guild organisation. It is likely that this was the case in Preston, and that most—if not all—of the Preston companies had no charter or ordinances.

There is no reliable reference to the existence of a formal company within the Guild until 14 October 1628, when an order of the Corporation created 'a Companie or Fraternitie called Wardens and Companie of Drapers, Mercers, Grocers, Salters, Ironmongers, and Haberdashers' within the Town and Borough of Preston (salters were flax and hemp sellers). This company was thus a grouping of the shopkeepers and related traders, and the reasons for its establishment were given in the preamble to the order. It was said that contrary to Statutes of the Realm of 1554 and 1563 (which were intended to prevent outsiders trading in boroughs and to require that all those who traded or carried on a craft should have served an apprenticeship) people had been trading without such authority. 'Divers handicraftsmen and servants at husbandry [are] leaving their own occupations, seeking not only to live easily but rather idly [and have] taken upon them within this town of Preston to set up and live by trade of buying and selling of divers wares and merchandise contrary to the law.' The creation of the Company was therefore a response to what was evidently an increasing disregard for the regulations of the Guild.[37]

The Company was regulated by orders made by the Corporation. There was to be a meeting each October which would elect two members of the Company to be its wardens. Members of the Company were not to take anybody as an apprentice for less than the customary seven years and no child of a burgess was to be a trader in the Company unless he had served a full apprenticeship (although the mayor and the Council might agree to his being admitted early). This was intended to reinforce the apprenticeship system and to prevent the admission of traders who were unqualified or inexperienced. The sons of burgesses would automatically acquire their freedom by hereditary right, but it was presumably felt that, in theory at least, they ought not to trade before they had gained experience in their fathers' businesses.

It was also laid down that no person might be enrolled in the Guild Merchant in the trades within the Company of Drapers, Mercers, Grocers, Salters, Ironmongers and Haberdashers unless he was also one of the Company. This was almost inevitable in any case, but the order reinforced the role of the Company. As a further precaution against competition from outside traders, it was required that people coming into the town without freedom or burgessship might only trade freely at fair times, when it was in the town's interest to have as many people as possible trading in order to increase the tolls, dues and charges levied. Anybody caught trading outside those times would forfeit his wares and goods unless they were 'of their own making'. Half of the forfeited goods were to go to the use of the town of Preston and half to the use of the Company, perhaps to be shared out among the members of the Company for *their* own use.

The elevation of the group of shopkeepers and sellers of commodities to the status of a separate company indicates that they held a special position within the Guild and among the townsmen. It is also true that the shopkeepers were the most open to competition, since it was comparatively easy for those selling cloth, finished cloth goods, and other transportable commodities to come to the town, offer their wares for sale (thereby taking trade from the residents) and then depart. Pedlars, chapmen and itinerant vendors were particularly free to come and go and evade prosecution or punishment. Those working as craftsmen were less mobile, with their need for workshops, equipment and stocks of raw materials or unfinished work. They were more settled and thus more easily regulated, and the need for a separate company was perhaps less pressing.

That other companies *did* exist in the seventeenth century is indicated by references in the minutes of the Corporation. In 1665 a mistake was made in the enrolling of a burgess and his son, and the minute, entered in the White Book for 10 May, which records the correcting of the mistake, also reveals the existence of another company:

> Wheras at the last Guild-merchant holden within this Borough John Kay of Fullwood, webster & John Kay his Sonn were admitted burgesses of this Incorporacon And in Consideracon thereof paid the sume of three poundes, as a Composicon ... and whereas there names are entred & recorded amongst ye Forreigne Burgesses of this towne & shold have been entred and Recorded amongst the Innburgesses of the same as manifestly hath beene made appeare unto us and as is knowne to severall of us [and as he has] compounded with the company of his profession to bee admitted into there fraternity & hath paid a considerable Sume for the same [he is to be readmitted as an in-burgess and the mistake rectified].[38]

Thus there is evidence in the 1660s for the existence of a company or fraternity of weavers, with a sufficiently organised structure to be able to make charges for admittance and to allow formal entry. This company does not, however, appear in any other records. Just how many companies there were will never be known, though there may have been others apart from the drapers and mercers, and the weavers. Most of them were casual informal groupings, perhaps coming together only at the times of Guild celebrations, with little formal organisation and identity.

There is much clearer evidence of the existence of companies, at least in Guild years, by the end of the eighteenth century, when it became usual for participants in trade processions to organise on that basis. The 1762 Guild, for example, was described in a short publication by Thomas Anderson, in which he lists twelve different companies organised according to distinct trades. As they walked in procession their members wore special regalia and costumes, carried symbols of their trade, and were headed by 'Wardens' of the trades or companies (see chapter 4). All of this implied the formal and structured organisation which typified trade companies in larger cities—but in reality it seems probable that these arrangements were made simply for the Guild celebrations, and had no real substance in between times.

The end of trade regulation

The significance of the Guild in regulating trade began to diminish in the early eighteenth century. The orders promulgated at the 1722 Guild list 32 trades which were followed in Preston, and reiterated the crucial regulation which affected these: that no person could practise or carry on one of these trades unless he was a freeman burgess of the Guild Merchant. The orders laid down that fines of £1 per day might be imposed on those who traded without that qualification.[39] Such restrictions could only work in a town with a stable economic and social structure, and a relatively slow-growing population. Any change in those conditions would mean that administering the trade restrictions necessarily became more difficult, and during the mid-eighteenth century Preston did indeed begin to change. Its political affairs underwent an upheaval, its economy moved towards the factory system, its population began to grow, and its social structure altered.

Borsay shows how the Guild Rolls (which he admits are unsystematic and perhaps not fully representative) reveal a rapid increase between 1702 and 1762 in the numbers of professional men and those employed in service occupations. This increase, which can be related to the town's growing importance as a centre for county society and administration, can also be linked with the decreasing power of the Guild. The professions and services were harder to regulate, and those involved in them would have been less amenable to regulation.[40] In these circumstances the Guild became an irrelevance as a trade-regulating organisation, but of increasing importance for political and social reasons. Avoidance and evasion of the trading regulations was widespread by the middle of the eighteenth century, and the old function of the Guild Merchant had become largely nominal.

The minutes of the Corporation show, too, that official concern over breaches of the regulations had largely evaporated by the mid-eighteenth century. In practice, if not technically in law, there was virtual freedom of trade in the town by the 1760s, and many had long been able to evade the restrictions without hindrance from the authorities. Since most people likely to trade in the town were already Guild members, this was not at first too significant, but once the great expansion of Preston began and industrialisation proceeded, there was a proliferation in traders who were neither burgesses nor Guild members. The growth of population made it much more difficult to carry out systematic checks upon such people, and the mobility of the population, with constant comings and goings, added to that difficulty. The changing character of the economy made the old Guild organisation, rooted in pre-industrial England, anachronistic.

The last recorded prosecutions for trading without Guild membership occurred in 1770, 1778 and 1784. The 1770 case involved Richard Baines, the father of the Lancashire historian Edward Baines: 'an indictment was preferred against him at the borough sessions for having carried on a business as a grocer in Preston for one month in the year 1770. He resisted the vexatious interferences [but] was obliged to leave the town, and he removed to the village of Walton-le-Dale, where he carried on his business.'[41]

The last two cases concerned the sale of linen goods. On 16 June 1778 the Corporation minutes record the case of a man called Maclean and his wife, who were accused of taking a room at the house of Thomas Topping, innkeeper, and there 'Exposing to Sale ... by Retail Linnen & other Goods which [was] a Prejudice to the Traders residing within the Borough and contrary to the Bye-laws made at several Guilds Merchant'. They were hauled before the Mayor and reprimanded, being threatened with formal prosecution for their 'presumption in exposing to Sale by Retail within this Borough any Goods Wares or Merchandizes without ... having first obtained the Freedom of the same Borough or served an Apprenticeship within the same'. It was reported that they promised 'That all their Goods should be packed up that Day & that they would leave this Borough on Monday next'.[42]

The final exercise of the medieval trading restrictions was on 31 October 1784, when the Corporation dealt with the case of 'Messrs. Clarke and Brown, who have lately opened a Linen Draper's Shop within this Borough'. They were to be 'stallenged according to antient Custom' (that is, charged a due or payment, originally intended as a stall-rent for market traders, but in this case conveniently transferred to a permanent shop), and a fine of one shilling per day was levied 'during such time as they carry on business'.[43] Out of the many dozens of people who were by the mid-1780s trading without the authorisation of the Corporation and Guild, these unfortunates were singled out for punishment, but thereafter anybody could trade in Preston unhindered.

The social role of the Guild Merchant, 1550–1835

Although during the first half of the eighteenth century the Guild gradually lost its economic role, it remained, perhaps surprisingly, a powerful and influential force within Preston society. As its direct commercial power diminished, its social and political prestige grew. The Guild, albeit only once every twenty years, became a magnet for county society, and its celebration was one of the greatest of all social occasions in the North West. The growth in this role coincided with, and was encouraged by, the growth in the importance of Preston itself. From the early seventeenth century the town was generally recognised as the administrative and social centre of the county. It was not the largest town nor the town with the greatest commercial, economic or financial significance, for Manchester already occupied both of those positions. Neither was it the ancient centre of administration, for the assizes, the county gaol and the offices of the Duchy of Lancaster and its estates were all at Lancaster.

But Preston was in a very favourable position at the geographical centre of the county, where the great north–south road met the main routes from the Fylde, south-west Lancashire and, via the Ribble and Calder valleys, east Lancashire. Nowhere else enjoyed such a convenient and accessible location, and as county administration expanded and became more complex it was increasingly centred upon Preston. That meant, in turn, that the leaders of county society—gentry, magistrates, solicitors and lawyers—began to base their social lives around Preston, where they met for quarter sessions meetings, informal business discussions, and the attendant leisure and pleasure pursuits.

By the early eighteenth century the town had developed a social life and a season which were widely regarded as equal to those of other fashionable and highly respectable county centres: the Preston season was even compared with that of such resorts as Harrogate and Cheltenham. While it is doubtful if many went to Preston in preference to Bath, it is unquestionable that the wealthy and powerful leaders of Lancashire viewed Preston as a centre for their annual round of entertainment, business and pleasure.

The part played by the Guild in this process is shown by the Guild Rolls, which in the eighteenth century formed a catalogue of Lancashire gentry and nobility. Membership of the Guild was regarded as an honour and privilege. The town bestowed the honour in part to win the favour of powerful patrons because of the benefits which they brought, but admission to the Guild was seen by the gentry themselves as of value and significance. Their attendance at Guild events confirms the importance which they attached to the Preston Guild Merchant.

The admission of Lord Derby and members of his family at the Guild of 1542 marked the beginnings of this change. Previously the members of the county gentry families admitted were those who lived near Preston, not least because they had close business and social links with the town. But from 1542 onwards membership of the Guild was clearly an honour acceptable to the greatest of the magnates in the county, and thereafter the social circle from which out-burgesses were drawn widened considerably. The influence of the Guild spread, so that leading families throughout the county and beyond applied for, or were granted as a gift, membership of the Preston Guild Merchant. During the seventeenth century it became increasingly common for membership of the Guild to be granted as a gift whenever potential patrons appeared.

The older families, those honoured by membership at earlier Guilds, had ramified and extended as younger sons founded their own branches. Each son was in turn eligible for hereditary membership and eventually many different branches of one family might appear in the Guild Rolls. In the case of the families, such as the Hoghtons of Hoghton, which had been members since the fourteenth century, the numbers could be large indeed.

Such admissions had little to do with economic or trading matters since these people were not engaged in trade. Instead, the town acquired a wide range of patrons, who would help and support it when it needed assistance and who could provide advice and counsel to the mayor and the Corporation. These links were especially important in times of political crisis, such as the Glorious Revolution of 1688–89, when the mayor of Preston sought advice from the patrons of the borough as to what he should do.

The out-burgess lists for the sixteenth and seventeenth centuries show evidence of an ever-widening geographical distribution, as members of families moved elsewhere while retaining their hereditary burgess rights and Guild membership. The younger sons of gentry families often moved outside Lancashire, for trade or family reasons: the effect of this can be seen in, for example, the 1662 Roll. Members in the out-burgess category included, among many others, Ralph Assheton of Lombard Street, London; Thomas

Coulthurst of Chester; John Gardner of the City of London; Thomas Elston of Leeds; Robert Williamson of Manby in Lincolnshire; and John Woodruff of Bolton Abbey in Yorkshire.

The same process also took place among the in-burgesses. Although at first they lived and traded within the borough, the hereditary principle meant that people who were still entitled to membership might move far way from Preston. Places of residence of in-burgesses in the 1682 Guild included the City of London, Ireland, Salisbury, Ware in Hertfordshire and St Michael, Cornwall. In both Rolls numerous other Lancashire townships were represented, and significant numbers of burgesses lived in other important commercial centres, such as Manchester, Blackburn, Lancaster and Ormskirk.[44]

Perhaps the most remarkable instance of distant geographical connections, and of the importance of the hereditary descent of burgess rights, occurred in 1709, when the Corporation considered the case of the Hodgkinson family. The minute in the White Book of Corporation proceedings records that

> George Hodgkinson of Holmes Slack within Preston Gent is an Inn Burgess of this Corporation And that at the last Guild Merchant held within this Borrough [he] by some friend renued his Freedom and was enrolled an Inn Burgess in the last Guild Book ... But by reason the said Mr Hodgkinson was then abroad beyond Sea and had so been for a great many years before, It was not known that he had any Sons So that they could not be entered and enrolled at the said Guild and whereas the said Mr Hodgkinson being now come over from beyond Sea and he having (as he represents) four Sons viz John, Thomas, William, & Josiah in the Island of St. Hellena.

It was agreed that the four sons should be admitted as in-burgesses, and that at the next Guild (in 1722), they would, 'if alive' be admitted as Guild burgesses upon payment of usual fees.[45]

Many of the gentry and nobility who were admitted as burgesses and freemen were accepted as a result of a request from another patron, another means of giving favour to those who might eventually help the town. At the bottom of the 1622 Guild Roll is the following entry relating to an admission made on 6 August 1630:

> Thomas Peryon of Actowne [Acton] in the Countye of Midlesex Knight att the instance & request of himselfe and Sir Gilbert Houghton Knight was admitted gratis a Free Burgesse of the Borrough of Preston by John Hynde gent. Maior William Preston Thomas Banister William Lemon gent. Aldermen of the said Towne.[46]

Also at the 1622 Guild, Henry Taylor, son of Richard Taylor of Penwortham, was admitted as an out-burgess 'att the instance of Henry Fletwood gentleman', for a payment of sixpence only.[47] By the early eighteenth century the idea of 'honorary' burgess admittances had been accepted, although technically this category did not exist and it was quite unclear what rights, if any, it gave. An example occurs in the White Book for 10 August 1733, when the Honourable Charles Stourton Walmesley of Dunkenhalgh, esquire, was admitted by the Mayor as an 'honorary' in-burgess.[48]

During the first half of the seventeenth century it also became common for important or influential figures within the town to request that their servants should be admitted as burgesses. There is little evidence of this practice in the sixteenth century, but the number of members described as servants increased sharply at the 1622 Guild and remained high thereafter. The admission of servants was another indication of the changing nature of the Guild, for in no way could they be considered as traders or craftsmen. Honouring the servants was another way of honouring the masters, and such admissions provided the masters with extra influence in the Guild and the affairs of the town. The servants who were admitted were not of menial status, but were the stewards, estate managers and heads of household staff and, perhaps, the men who on behalf of their masters ran the day-to-day workings of various trades and crafts. Many, by virtue of their place in great households, were undoubtedly powerful people in their own right. In a number of instances it is clear from the wording of the admittance that *servant* has the sense of 'apprentice', but in others the modern meaning of the word is intended. In 1732 the White Book records the admission of Thomas Allen of Preston, servant to Thomas Hesketh, gentleman, while in the 1622 Guild Roll,[49] following the admission of Sir Thomas Peryon, is the entry:

> And att the same tyme Samuell Knott Serviens &c to the said Sir Gilbert Houghton Knight was likewyse admitted gratis a Free Burgesse of the said Towne by the said Major and Aldermen and the said Edmund Worden in manner and form aforesaid.

As already noted, during the 1620s there was growing concern that people were being admitted as burgesses in an irregular fashion, especially in the long intervals between Guilds. These anxieties lay behind a decision of 1632 that the names of all burgesses who were admitted by copy of court roll, the amounts they paid, and the securities and guarantors put forward, were to be notified to the mayor and written in the White Book. This would prevent individuals coming to a Guild and claiming, without any written proof, that they had been admitted as burgesses since the last Guild.[50] The regulation seems to have been adhered to, and in several periods records of 'copy of court roll' admissions represent by far the largest single category of entries in the

White Book. Typical entries so enrolled, and later confirmed by enrolment and renewal at the following Guilds, include

> John Greenwood of Preston milner [miller] admitted a Burgesse of the Burrough of Preston aforesaid and was sworne the xi[th] day of October 1651 and paid his fyne of v[li] [£5][51]

> Thomas Hodgson of Farington skinner admitted Burgess (for himself alone) by Copy of Court roll & Sworne the last day of February 1652 who paid his fyne of v[li] & gave security according to the Orders[52]

Note that Thomas was admitted by the Corporation without commitment to giving hereditary admittance to his children—hence 'himself alone'. He gave security as a guarantee of his good behaviour in observing the rules, and especially the trading rules, of the Guild.

In the early eighteenth century the question of irregular admittances again arose. It had been traditional for each mayor of Preston to have the privilege of admitting three people as burgesses during his term of office, by his own choice and without payment. This was additional to any bestowals of freedom upon the 'nobility or other persons of honour and distincion', gifts which had to be with the approval of the Corporation. In 1724 it was claimed that lately there had been attempts to infringe or violate this 'imemorial custom tending to introduce very great disorder & confusion into the said Comunity', by making more than three such gifts of freedom. The matter was eventually decided by a formal confirmation of the traditional practice, which was enrolled in the constitution of the Borough.[53] But the abuse of the system continued unabated. The Guild of 1742 was preceded by the enrolment of no fewer than 112 in-burgesses in the one year of the mayoralty of John Ravald (1740–41). This was an extraordinarily high number, in comparison with at most a couple of dozen admissions in a single year during the earlier part of the century.

The admission of very large numbers of new burgesses in the early 1740s was inspired by special circumstances. One possible explanation is that in-burgesses, if resident, could vote in elections, so that by admitting new in-burgesses the Corporation might hope to change the balance of electoral prospects. But many of those admitted were non-resident: while the franchise may have been significant in some cases, it is more likely that social reasons lay behind most of the admissions. The mass enrolment of burgesses in 1740–41 is a very clear indication of the collapse of the trading role of the Guild, for most of those admitted were from the gentry and land-owning classes, and had no connections with commerce or trade. The table below analyses the admissions of the mayoral year 1740–41:[54]

Occupation or status of 1740–41 admissions

gentleman/esquire/knight	88	organmaker	1
attorney at law	1	husbandman	1
clergyman	6	mariner	1
merchant	3	yeoman	3
doctor	1	butcher	1
draper	1	fisherman	1
grocer	2	weaver	1
watchmaker	1		

Thus of the total of 112 admittances no fewer than 88 were of people described as 'gentlemen' or by other titles of status, and another 11 were of professional men, a total of 99, or 88 per cent. The traders and craftsmen, who had been the mainstay of the Guild in the sixteenth and seventeenth centuries, accounted for only 12 per cent of admittances in this exceptional year. The Guild was being packed with gentry and the upper middle-class moneyed groups at the expense of the ordinary traders of the town. The same is clear when the geographical origins of the two groups are considered:

Place of residence of 1740–41 admissions

	Preston	elsewhere
gentlemen	4	84
clergy	0	6
other professionals	2	3
traders, craftsmen, farmers	10	3

If a particular date were to be selected at which the regulation of trade by the Preston Guild collapsed, 1741 would be the most plausible. Thereafter the Guild largely abandoned any pretence of enforcing the economic restrictions, and apart from the isolated prosecutions quoted earlier, there was now free trade in the town. The Guild Merchant was being transformed into a body quite different in character and with a quite different purpose. It was fast becoming a socially exclusive and elevated group.

CHAPTER THREE

Celebrating the
Guild up to 1762

T HE WAY in which the Guild was celebrated, and its procedures for election and
administration, become clearer in the seventeenth century. The first detailed
account of a Guild Merchant, giving the formal orders and a description of the celebration
itself, is Richard Kuerden's memoir of the 1682 Guild. It is an invaluable source, not least
because the next comprehensive account of a Guild did not appear until 1762.

Guild officers and Guild Mayors

The officers of the Guild were always the leaders of Preston society, people of standing and
authority within the town. This was the case with all the major Corporation appointments—
mayors, bailiffs and other officers of the borough administration—but from an early date
it was considered a special honour to serve the town during a Guild year. The borough
officials, including the mayor, were chosen at the Great Court of Election, held in the
early autumn. The role of the mayor is a subject of some interest, but one outside the scope
of this book. Nonetheless, it is perhaps useful to point out that the mayor was the chief
spokesman for the town and its inhabitants in their dealings with outsiders: local gentry
and landowners, officials and clerks of other towns or of the Crown, or, indeed, the Crown
itself. He was the chief magistrate within the town, the ultimate local decision-maker in
disputes and differences between the townspeople, and the man with overall responsibility
for good government and for seeing that the byelaws were upheld and observed. In his
description of the town, borough and Guild, Kuerden explained the procedures for these
elections, and then noted that when a Guild was due to be held

> a speciall care is to bee taken that Burgesses of good presence and complacency
> bee elected for Bailiffs, for the ensuing yeare, who, with greater credit and
> reputation, may attend the Gyld Mayor, in all his publicke Assemblys, and
> especially in the time of the Gyld, when many persons of Honour and Gentry,

are to bee treated in an extraordinary manner, for the greater Applause and Glory to the Burrough of Preston.[1]

It would have been most inappropriate for a person to be chosen as mayor, steward or alderman for the Guild who was inferior in status or character. The entertainment of the 'persons of honour and gentry' required someone who was able to rise to a high social occasion, and had the personal financial resources to do so. By the end of the seventeenth century it was generally considered that to be Guild Mayor was the highest local office to which a Preston politician could aspire, and the greatest honour that the town could bestow. Such was the status of this position, and the esteem in which it was held, that in the eighteenth and nineteenth centuries it was awarded to outside dignitaries to show the particular regard which the town had for them. The Guild Mayoralty of the Earl of Derby, in 1902, is an instance of this practice even in the twentieth century, and it was seriously suggested in advance of the 1992 Guild that a worthy outside figure should be chosen as Guild Mayor—though that idea was firmly rejected.

The 1328 orders reveal something of how the officers of the town were chosen.[2] The mayor had to be a burgess from the previous Guild: it was not possible to admit a burgess and immediately make him mayor. This was intended as a safeguard against a takeover by outsiders of the town's administration, as no newcomer could be elevated. The burgesses formed the basis of the medieval town government, but it was impossible for them all to be directly involved so, as already explained, a 'council' soon developed, comprising the aldermen (the leading and most senior burgesses) and the commonalty, or common councillors, a group of junior burgesses. These three groups—the mayor, the aldermen and the commonalty—were soon regarded as the government of the borough, and although their precise status was not formally defined until the charter of incorporation of 1566, they had for a couple of hundred years before then been generally accepted as the 'borough council' (though that term was not employed at the time).

Medieval mayors were in normal times assisted by bailiffs, whereas at Guilds special stewards were appointed. The fragmentary record of what is said to have been a Guild in or about 1328, surviving only in Kuerden's transcript, names several officers. The mayor was Aubert, son of Robert, and he was assisted by two bailiffs, William, son of Paulin, and Roger del' Wich. The absence of stewards in the 1328 record, and the presence of bailiffs, tends to support the view that this was not a list of Guild officers but of those appointed for a normal year. The 1397 Guild Roll, which is definitely the record of the holding of a Guild, names a larger number of officers: William de Ergham, the mayor; Geoffrey de Meles, Thomas de More, and John de Haconshowe, the three stewards of the Guild; Richard Blundell, Henry le Somner, Simon de Preston, John Marshall, Richard of Bretherton, William de Cane, John Alston, William of Walton [le Dale], and William Grimbaldeston, the nine aldermen; and John Lambard, the clerk of the Guild.[3]

The roles which each played were probably similar to those in later Guilds. The mayor oversaw the proceedings and acted as the ceremonial head of the celebration. He was assisted by the aldermen, who helped in the decision-making, choosing the Guild orders and deciding on the admissions and the way business should be conducted. The stewards conducted the business of the Guild itself, seeing that everything went smoothly, and receiving the sums of money which were paid in fines or fees for renewals and new admissions. Clerks to the Guild did the medieval equivalent of the paperwork, checking the names on the Rolls, confirming them from other records, issuing any invitations which might be sent and, eventually, dealing with the writing-up of the names in the new Guild Roll.

Not a great deal is known about William de Ergham, the Guild Mayor in 1397 (see Appendix 1), although it is recorded that he was also mayor on ten other occasions between 1388 and 1425, an exceptional total of eleven terms served in the highest office in the town. His surname indicates that he—or a recent forebear—came to Preston from Arkholme, in the Lune valley near Kirkby Lonsdale.[4] In the 1415 Guild the mayor was Henry Johnson; the stewards William de Clifton, William Wynter, senior, and Robert de Meles. The aldermen are named as William de Ergham, John Blundell, Roger de Wyche, John de Walton, John de Alston, William de Grenehils, John de More, Thomas de Bretherton, Robert Albyn, John Lambart, William Grymbald, John Breton and Adam Marshall; William Blundell was the clerk. There was evidently a degree of continuity between this Guild and the previous one, since only 18 years had elapsed. Although many individuals named in 1397 had either died or retired from public life, others were still active: of the seventeen people named in 1415, four had been prominent in the 1397 Guild.[5]

In 1459 Robert de Hoghton was chosen as Guild Mayor, the first time that a member of a prominent gentry family from outside the town had been so honoured. In the fifteenth century the de Hoghtons were arguably the most important local family, with substantial interests in Preston, and their patronage and support were undoubtedly beneficial to the town. Not only was Robert chosen as mayor, but one of the stewards of the Guild was John de Hoghton. For the Guild of 1500 there is no burgess roll, but there is a record of the Guild orders which give the names of the mayor, Henry Preston, four stewards, ten aldermen and the clerk. Guild membership was hereditary, so it is not surprising to find family names from earlier Guilds in this list, and it is apparent that comparatively few families provided the main officers in a succession of Guilds. The table below shows this.

Families filling Guild offices, 1397–1542[6]

	1397	1415	1459	1500	1542
mayor	Ergham	Johnson	Hoghton	Marshall	Tippling
stewards	Meols	Clifton	Hoghton	Preston	Haydock
	More	Winter	Preston	Ergham	Wall
	Hacconsall	Meols	Whalley	Hoghton	Dawson
				Ainsworth	Breres
aldermen	Blundell	Ergham	Botiller	Tipping	Walton
	Somner	Blundell	Blundell	Whalley	Clayton
	Preston	Wyche	Hirdson	Tipping	Ergham
	Marshall	Walton	Blundell	Sadler	Preston
	Bretherton	Alston	Tailor	Arrowsmith	Walton
	Ganys	Greenhills	Johnson	Allcock	Cumberal
	Alston	More	Coke	Darel	Sadler
	Walton	Bretherton	Whalley	Arrowsmith	
	Grymbalds	Albyn	Coke	Bonk	
		Lambert	Halliwell	Wainwright	
		Grimbalds			
		Breton			
		Marshall			
clerk	Lambard	Blundell	Walton	Walton	Walton

Some families (such as the Waltons, the Blundells, the Erghams and the Prestons) were particularly prominent and influential. This pattern was repeated during following centuries, as leading families inherited burgessships and passed offices down from generation to generation. After the 1542 Guild the pattern of Guild officers settled down to the regular appointment of a mayor, three stewards, ten aldermen and the clerk of the Guild. Just occasionally, though, there were deviations from this: in 1662, for example, only six aldermen were named at the head of the Guild Roll.

In the seventeenth century the mayors and other officers often called themselves 'gentlemen', even though in previous generations their families had been craftsmen or traders. The self-attributed elevation was characteristic of such families which, once established in their trade and accepted in the governing group of the town, were able to extend their influence and status so that they reached the upper echelons of Preston, and even of county, society. The Sudell family exemplifies this process. Roger Sudell, who was Guild Mayor in 1682, called himself a gentleman, as did his grandfather, William Sudell, who was a guild steward in 1642 and 1662, mayor in 1634, 1651 and 1659, and an alderman for over forty years continuously. The family was deeply involved in the politics and government of the town, but although they used the title of 'gentleman' they were in fact woollen drapers. The county gentry, living outside the town and owning extensive lands, would probably not (initially at least) have recognised any social equality. But the family's subsequent advance in status is shown by the career of Roger's brother Christopher, who became a prebend of Chester Cathedral and chaplain to the Earl of Derby, and whose daughter married into a junior branch of the Stanley family.[7]

The process could operate in the other direction. The younger sons of gentry families might, in the absence of any other obvious opportunity for their advancement, enter trade. The Assheton family of Cuerdale Hall, for example, had close links with Preston, and members of the family appear in the Guild Rolls for several centuries. The Guild Mayor in 1722 was Edmund Assheton. Although from a gentry family he himself was a mercer by trade. He settled in Preston in the early years of the eighteenth century, was elected as a common councillor in 1712, alderman in 1713, and mayor in 1714. His very rapid ascent through the ranks was no doubt the result of his influential family connections and those of his wife, the daughter of Josias Gregson, Guild Mayor in 1702.[8]

Among the leading families of the town and the Guild there were close ties of blood and marriage. Preston, like many other towns, had a relatively small close-knit group of political dynasties which enjoyed power and privilege within the community. Because they were of more or less equal social and financial status, members of these dynasties married within their own group. There was minimal popular participation in the Corporation and its affairs, and vacancies were filled by invitation, which meant that most of the leading burgesses, mayors and aldermen could find many siblings, cousins and in-laws among their fellow members of the Corporation.

For example, James Hodgkinson, Guild Mayor in 1662, was a descendant of John Hodgkinson, a burgess in the 1459 Guild. Another member of the family, William Hodgkinson, was an alderman at the Guild of 1542, and his son, another William, a burgess at the Guilds of 1542, 1562 and 1582, was mayor of Preston in 1566 and 1569. In turn, William's son Henry was mayor in 1599 and 1607 and a guild steward in 1602 (at which Guild his younger sons, James and Richard, were aldermen). James, the Guild Mayor of 1662, was the grandson of that James. He married Elizabeth, the daughter of Henry Blundell, alderman and mayor in 1629, 1636 and 1647. Her first husband had been Henry Lemon of Preston, whose father and brother were both mayors.[9] This intricate tangle of relationships, and the reserving of offices to members of relatively few families, ensured a strong and powerful ruling group within the town.

During the eighteenth century the Guild membership was increasingly dominated by gentry families from outside the town, a trend which was reflected in the choice of Guild Mayors. In 1742 the Corporation chose Henry Farington, one of the Faringtons of Worden in Leyland, who were among the most influential gentry families in the district.

Being a younger son, he was not usually resident at Worden but instead kept a house in Preston, where he was first elected mayor in 1736. The next Guild Mayor, Robert Parker of Cuerden Hall, stood even higher on the ladder of society. His family had been in the Guild for generations and he was closely related to many ancient Lancashire families including the Banastres of Banke in Walton-le-Dale. His mother was the daughter of William Clayton of Fulwood, MP for Liverpool, and Robert himself married the daughter and heiress of Thomas Towneley of Royle near Burnley. His children, including Anne, the wife of Thomas Crosse of Crosse Hall and Shawe Hill, married into other leading gentry families. Such connections undoubtedly graced the Preston Guild, and at the balls and entertainments of 1762 Robert Parker would have seen dozens of his relatives by blood or marriage. His grandson, Robert Townley Parker, was MP for Preston.[10] In 1862, a century after his grandfather, he too served as Guild Mayor.

The status of the Guild officers thus became increasingly symbolic of the change in the Guild itself. From being ordinary, though influential, traders and craftsmen in the fifteenth and early sixteenth centuries, they were drawn from the ruling elite of the town in the seventeenth century, and in the eighteenth century tended to be from neighbouring gentry families. That is not to suggest that they did not have Preston's interests at heart, or that they were remote from or detached from the town, but rather that their superior social status made inevitable the distancing of the Guild from the ordinary craftsmen and workers. They had no personal interest in the regulation or restriction of trade, and no wish to become involved in the minutiae of the administration of the town. Instead, they, like the Corporation, became concerned primarily with the political and social opportunities which the Guild had to offer.

The Guild and the Town Hall

Most of the formal Guild celebrations were conducted in the Town Hall and Guildhall, which were within the same building. The Town Hall and its predecessors occupied the same site for several hundred years, until the disastrous fire in 1947 which partly destroyed the Victorian Gothic Town Hall and led to the demolition and clearance of the site. That decision, sadly misguided on grounds of sentiment, history and civic dignity alike, has been lamented by most people ever since, for the replacement building, the Crystal House office block, was an architectural and aesthetic disaster, and remains so despite a superficial improvement and a new name.

The earliest definite references to the Town Hall occur in the charter of 1566, in which it is called the moot hall (a *moot* being a meeting or assembly) or tollbooth (the place where market tolls and dues were paid and collected).[11] Its focal position in the market place at the very centre of the town, opposite the parish church, makes it certain that there had been such a building on that site long before that date, and its predecessors had been there since the early medieval period. The Town Hall of the sixteenth century is probably that described by Kuerden in the 1680s: 'an ample antient yet well beautifyed gylde or town hall or toll bothe, to which is annexed, at the end thereof, a counsell chamber for the capital burgesses or jurors at their court days, to retire for consultation, or secretly to retire themselves from the comon burgesses or the publiq root [crowd] of people, as occasion shall require.' He records that the 'publiq hall' in the Town Hall—the great hall in which the public ceremonies and courts were held—had a raised bench or dais on which the magistrates sat during court sessions.[12]

The Town Hall was the scene of a variety of activities. Apart from being the place where Corporation business was transacted it was the seat of the quarter sessions for the hundreds of Amounderness and Blackburn (and, from 1817, Leyland). There the court of chancery of the County Palatine of Lancaster met, and borough and parliamentary elections were conducted. Underneath the hall were two rows of butchers' shops, or stalls, and a row of stalls at either end of the building where foodstuffs were sold. Although Kuerden does not give a detailed description of the appearance of the Town Hall, it is likely from his evidence that the building was two-storeyed and half-timbered, like most buildings in Preston town centre in the sixteenth century.

The building was the only one in Preston large enough to accommodate the Guild Court, so it was in the hall that the formal business of the Guild Merchant was transacted every twenty years. Afterwards the feastings and merry-making also took place there, but as the scale of the entertainments grew the accommodation was increasingly unsuitable—the old Town Hall was regarded as outdated and inadequate long before the middle of the eighteenth century. A reconstruction proposed in 1727, to be paid for by public subscription, did not materialise.[13] But in 1760 plans were prepared for the building of a new Guildhall next to it, ready for the celebration of the 1762 Guild, when the social events were to be on an unprecedented scale. The Corporation minutes for 2 May 1760 record that a report had been commissioned from Mr Johnson, an architect, and that he had been shown the 'plott or piece of Ground near the Centre of the Town where the Corporation had an Intention of Erecting some new buildings'. The purpose was very clearly explained in the minute:

> so as to be convenient both for the Entertainment of Company at the approaching Guild as so as the same may be after the Solemnity of the Guild is over be with not much Expence Converted into Dwelling Houses fit for Tenants.[14]

Such thrift was not one of the usual characteristics of the Corporation, though doubtless very commendable. The idea of a temporary Guildhall which could then become rented housing seems somewhat surprising, but between Guild celebrations there was little real need for additional permanent accommodation, as the existing Town Hall was adequate for most normal purposes. No doubt the strange commission taxed the ingenuity of the architect: a building which required, for ceremonial and entertainment purposes, a large open hall was far from suitable for instant transformation to housing for tenant families. But Mr Johnson produced a plan, and at its meeting of 2 May 1760 the Corporation accepted the tender of Richard Butler and William Woodcock of Preston to build the new Guildhall for the sum of £1,445.

Work began the same month, but changes were required as construction proceeded. The relatively limited time available had made an early decision necessary, but the Corporation soon found that the hastily prepared original scheme could be improved. On 20 June 1760 the minutes record that the original plan had involved a two-storey building with garret rooms in the roof space, but that 'Experienced workmen' had subsequently advised that it would be possible to add another storey to the building, instead of garrets. This would 'afford much more room and be of much greater use and convenience for Tenants and of much greater advantage and benefit to the Corporation'. When the hall was being used for the Guild there would be more space, and when it had been converted to houses the rents could be higher because of the additional rooms.

The Corporation therefore agreed to the change, which was to cost a further £150. It also determined to approach the trustees of Miss Stanley, the owners of an adjacent building at the back of the proposed site, with a view to buying the land and property for £63 3s., 'as the Ground and Foundation of the said Building will be so very advantageous to the new Buildings'. This brought the total cost of the project to £1,658 3s. There was insufficient money to hand, and it was decided to raise £1,000 by mortgaging the tolls of the town, the toll income from market trade and other sources being used as the security for the mortgage. The sum was later increased to £1,200, and a private mortgage was obtained from Pierce Starkey of Huntroyd near Burnley.[15]

The work was complete by the spring of 1761. It seems to have been well regarded by the Corporation and at the meeting of 23 April 1761 there was consideration of a further proposal, this time to improve and enhance the existing Town Hall to make it fit in better with the new Guildhall. The mayor produced a plan drawn up by another architect, the celebrated John Carr of York, involving alterations to the end of the Town Hall fronting Church Street, by taking down the south wall of the building and rebuilding it in line with the front of the Guildhall. This, it was said, would be 'a means of widening and Enlargeing the Street there and be a great beauty and Ornament to the Town'.[16] The plan was agreed but nothing more was heard of it, and so the somewhat inconvenient and (if we are to judge from this minute of the Corporation) aesthetically less than perfect division into two adjacent but separate buildings, in very different architectural styles, remained.[17]

The 1762 Guild was the first at which special accommodation was purpose-built for the celebrations. Since entertainment and social events were then becoming dominant this was just as well, because the great balls and dances could not have been held in the existing accommodation. But in fact the 1760 arrangement was not to last long. In 1780 the old Town Hall became structurally unsafe; parts of it actually collapsed, and the Corporation was compelled at short notice to take further steps to provide better facilities for its own business and for the Guild of 1782.

Guild orders: the rules of the Guild

From the earliest surviving records in the medieval period, and for centuries thereafter, the Guild orders tell us a great deal about the formal conduct of Guild celebrations, but not until the 1682 Guild is there any substantial account of the Guild as a whole. The formal business proceedings were the crux of the whole ceremony but were relatively short, and it is more than likely that the rest of the celebration was taken up with feasting, entertainment and socialising. Just as in later Guilds, the infrequency of the event and its primary importance to the life of Preston ensured that it was a great spectacle. The officials in their best robes, the colourful ceremonial, the presence of leading local dignitaries, and the significance of what was happening would have attracted the crowds. The participants must have been treated to dinners and superior amusements, while the masses were enjoying the lively carnival atmosphere in the streets of the town. But central to the whole celebration of the Guild was the renewal ceremony itself.

The Guild orders for this ceremony were written down from the late fourteenth century onwards, and amended and augmented in subsequent centuries as occasion required. They governed the conduct and formal business of the Guild and, since there was an intimate relationship between the Guild Merchant and the administration of the town, the Guild orders also included rules for the good government of Preston and the behaviour of its citizens. The use of the Guild and Guild orders to reiterate and reinforce the normal decisions of the Council was very important, because the orders were publicly and prominently announced, and were thus invested with special authority. This was even though in practical terms the infrequency of the Guild meant that such authority was largely symbolic. At most Guilds the officers took the opportunity to add further orders, so that by the eighteenth century they constituted a lengthy set of bye-laws covering many aspects of Preston life.

The procedures for celebrating the Guild in the sixteenth and seventeenth centuries were in essence those which have been followed ever since. The forthcoming Guild Merchant was several times proclaimed publicly by the mayor, and all burgesses were instructed to renew their membership of the Guild on the appointed days. Traders and craftsmen who wanted to be enrolled for the first time had to pay a fine for doing so, and they were required to inform the officials in advance so that their credentials could be checked, and sureties or pledges of good character obtained. Although the formal proceedings took place during the Guild itself the real business (including searches in previous Guild Rolls) had already been conducted.

The original Guild orders for 1500 are lost but they were, at some stage, written out on the reverse of the Guild Roll of 1562. Most of them concern the government of the town, but of special significance is the third order, which states that 'the Gild Merchaunt shall be kept and holden within the said Town att th'end of Twentie yeres next after this Gilde and so to be kept from tyme to tyme from thenceforth for ever'.[18] This in part reiterates the order of 1328 which itself stipulated a twenty-year interval for the holding of the Guild, but a crucial difference is that whereas the 1328 order also allowed additional Guilds to be held or the interval to be varied as was thought fit, the 1500 order makes no reference to flexibility and requires that the Guild should be held at a regular interval. In fact, the next Guild was in 1542, and there is no reference in any document to a Guild in 1520 or 1521. It seems virtually certain that no such Guild was held, but from 1542 onwards the twenty-year interval was faithfully observed until the Second World War.

The first comprehensive list of Guild orders relating to the procedure for the ceremony itself, rather than to more general conduct, is given on the Guild Roll of 1542. These orders had been prepared for the 1500 Guild and were reissued for 1542. Their detail means that they give a more precise, although not complete, picture of the different ceremonies which took place during the celebration of these two Guilds Merchant. The second part of the list concerns the general behaviour of the burgesses, but the first part is headed *Theis byn the articles & poyntes that apperteyneth to the Gyld Marchauntt att Preston.*[19]

The celebration began with a procession through the town. It was ordered that 'all Burgesses dwellyng withyn the Towne of Preston shall be redy att the Gyld Marchaunt for to goo with the procession from the Mawdelondes throughout the towne as the procession is wont to be of olde tyme that is to saye the Firste daye of the Forsaid Gyld'. The processions which, at Guilds in our time, assemble outside the town and walk through the streets are thus a custom at least five centuries old, and in fact must long predate 1500. The land at Maudlands was a large area of fields and common waste between the sites of the present University of Central Lancashire and St Walburge's church, in the vicinity of Pedder Street and Maudland Bank. The procession passed along Friargate and into the market place, ending at the parish church where a civic service was held. Although there must always have been a religious element in medieval Guilds, the orders of 1542 hint that the official or civic church service may have been introduced by the mayor and burgesses at the previous Guild, perhaps to give extra dignity to the proceedings:

after the Forsaid procession a Masse with solempnytie of the holye goyste solempny to be herd with the Major & Aldermen Forasmuch as that was advysed by the Major of the Gyld Marchaunt and Burgesses of the same Gyuld before

thys tyme Holding that Gyld Marchaunt oppon the Monday in the Fest of the
decollacion of Saynt John Baptyst the xvi° yere of the raigne of Kyng Henry the
vij°.

The Guild itself had already been proclaimed three times in the open market, 'that
the poyntes and the rights of the Gyld Marchaunt myght be known to all burges'. It
was announced that all men 'clamyng Fraunchies or Fredome withyn oure Burghe of
Preston whether they that clayme by descent or by purchas' should appear at the Guild
Merchant before the mayor and burgesses, to be told details of the liberties and other
rules pertaining to the Guild Merchant. These, it was said, were had 'by letters patentes
by oure liege Lord the Kynge and of hys most nobil progenitours to us graunted befor
thys tyme': they were the rights and liberties granted to the town and its Guild Merchant
by successive royal charters.

The first point was that all liberties and burgess rights, whether held by descent or by
purchase, and all other rights relating to the Guild, were taken back by the mayor until
the holders had fulfilled the necessary requirements of the Guild Merchant concerning
renewal of membership. This was a crucial point, for it meant that 'renewal' was literally
that. The rights of each burgess were, in theory, terminated on the first day, and each
had to renew and reclaim his burgess rights. The renewal was—again technically—at
the discretion of the Guild Mayor and burgesses, so each man put himself at the mercy of
the mayor and his officers by requesting readmission. Nobody could be a member of the
Guild and a burgess without accepting its authority and control. This made his nominal
status quite clear even if, in reality, readmission was invariably a foregone conclusion,
and even though those who failed to renew at the Guild could send proxies or sue for
renewal at a later date.

Submission to mayoral authority was re-emphasised by the next order, which stated
that any man who claimed burgess rights and freedom would be 'utterlye ... put owte and
lose Fraunchies and rights' should he be held to be 'rebell or contrarius to the Mayor' at
any time, and break any of the regulations and orders of the Guild. Anybody who was
deemed to be 'drawyng helpyng or Fandryng [trying] against the welfar and Fraunchies
of Preston and the statutes of the Gyld marchaunt' was to lose his freedom and rights
for ever. If a person broke these orders he was to be brought before the mayor and guild
officers and reprimanded.

A further regulation stated that if such a transgressor 'wull not be correct nor
justified by the Maior and hys Counsell' (that is, would not accept the reprimand) he was
forbidden either to buy or to sell within the town, and to be a freeman, 'tyll that he wull
gladly make amendes for hys defaulte at the sight of the Maior ... and hys Counsell'.
These rules, which at first sight might appear to give the mayor and officers unusual
power, were essential to good government, although their misuse was undoubtedly

widespread. The operation of effective administration within the town depended upon the mayor and his officers having the power to make and enforce decisions, and to punish those who failed to observe the bye-laws and ordinances.

One of the privileges granted to towns such as Preston by medieval royal charters was that any minor complaint or lawsuit against an inhabitant, and particularly a burgess, should be heard only in a court within the borough. Nobody could take such a complaint against a Preston citizen to an outside court where it might be given an unfavourable hearing—though naturally a Preston court might tend to err on the side of generosity. That right was guarded jealously as both a symbol and a practical demonstration of the independence of the town, and the next Guild order confirms this point. To be 'utterlye ... put owt and lose ther fraunchies by the right of the Gyld' would be the fate of any man who made 'playnte or suyt in anye other courte for anye trespas, or dett withyn the forsaid burghe [Preston]'. The Mayor was to 'discharge hym of hys fraunchies & burgesshippe till tyme be that he be reconsyled by the Maior ... and hys Counsell'.

Attendance at the Guild was compulsory for existing burgesses and for those who claimed burgess rights by descent or by purchase. There was no choice in the matter, but one of the orders promulgated in 1500 and reiterated in 1542 laid down the conditions whereby exemption might be granted and what penalty would befall those who refused to come without reason. It stated that 'all and iche on [each one] by hym selfe claymyng any Fraunchies of auncestrye or of purchas withyn the said burghe' must 'come to the said Gyld to doe those thynges that to the said Gyld appertenynt has the custome is'. Any who did not were to forfeit their freedom, 'savyng allonely to theym that he be in Fer contrye [far country] at the tyme of the Gyld holden'. Reasonably enough, it was accepted that absence in a distant place might preclude attendance at the Guild, and this order recognised that some would always be unable to reach Preston—a problem which was lessened only by the development of the railway network three centuries later.

There were severe penalties for those who were living in Preston but did not attend. The names of those required to renew were proclaimed on three successive days. If, after the third day, 'anye man be dwellyng withyn the said burghe knowyng of the Gyld and com not to itt to worshipp his Maior and th'eldermen of the said Gyld', he was to be stripped of his burgess rights and Guild membership: 'sekenes of bodye or febleness of povertie hym onely maye excuse'. Doubtless there were not inconsiderable numbers who pleaded sickness or poverty as an excuse for non-attendance, finding this a convenient way of evading an irksome duty.

Several of the Guild orders concerned the behaviour of members of the Council. Because of their prominent position in the affairs of the town their conduct was of particular importance. They were required to speak well of the town, to uphold the decisions of the Council, to support the mayor and Council and not act against them or their interests, and to attend the mayor and the Council whenever required, unless sickness prevented them or the mayor licensed their absence. The penalties for failing to observe this conduct were expulsion from the Council and loss of rights: 'if it soe fortune that he be revell and wull not come [when summoned] he shalbe put owt of the right of the Gyld and the Felleshippe of the Counsell tyll the tyme be that he have made amends to the Major.'

It was ordered that any burgess who assisted in breaking the king's peace or would not come to the assistance of the mayor in keeping the peace should be discharged of his freedom for ever. He was also to be fined as 'an untrewe man & fals forsworne' until he made amends to the mayor for his offence. All burgesses had to swear an oath of loyalty to the mayor and the town, and anybody who broke or went against his oath, and could be 'provyd by credible wytnesses' to have done so, would forever lose his freedom. Another order concerned the conduct of elections. It was forbidden for any burgess to meddle with (that is, to try to influence) the 24 councillors at the time of elections, or to disrupt their proceedings. The penalty for this was loss of freedom or payment of twenty shillings 'to the comyn box'.

At the end of the Guild orders of 1542 is another concerning the Guild itself: it required that any 'Mayor of the said Towne whiche shall hereafter be choysen or made and that shall kepe any Gild Merchaunt hereafter, and any other Officer of the said Town for that beyng shall giff his and their Fees whiche they ought to have by reason of the same Gild Merchaunt towards the maynteynyng of the said Town'. The Guild Mayor and officers were to give up the fees and expenses which they would in normal circumstances receive, and instead to contribute the money to the common purse for the good of the town.

These many orders, promulgated at the Guild, clearly had a wider significance. They formed the basic code for the behaviour of all burgesses at all times, whether or not a Guild was being held, but their place in the Guild ceremony shows that this was seen as a suitable occasion for the reaffirmation and renewal of these rules. Between Guilds the Council made additional regulations, which were often added to the Guild orders, so that by the end of the seventeenth century the Guild orders dealt with a wide range of matters of daily relevance, rather than simply the greater issues of law and order, mayoral authority and the good name of the town. Such offences as allowing animals to wander, the disposal of refuse, and even smoking in public, were thus included.

The Guild ceremonial of 1682

In the autumn of 1682 or early in 1683 Richard Kuerden of Leyland wrote a detailed memorandum of the Guild which had just finished. It is a document of unique interest and importance which gives the first eye-witness account of how the ceremonies and celebrations were conducted. The time allowed for preparation was far less than in today's Guilds. Now, because of the very much larger scale and complexity of the Guild, planning begins several years ahead. In the seventeenth and eighteenth centuries work began only about five months or so beforehand, although doubtless there had been some less formal preparation before then, and there is no doubt that excitement at the prospect of the forthcoming Guild was already growing.

The initial work was undertaken during the early spring of Guild year. The town clerk prepared a complete list of the people who would be eligible for renewal of membership as out-burgesses. Kuerden writes that

> Imediatly after the Easter Court, before such Gyld, att a Mayors Counsell, the Town Clerke shall read over the Catalogue of Forraign Burgesses, and transcribe the principall Burgesse in each distinct family, that liveth out of the County, that notice, by ticket, may be sent to them, or to some of their near relations, that by proxy may represent them, and in behalfe appeare at the succeeding Gyld.[20]

The division into 'distinct families' was essential, in order that claims of heredity might be decided, and that all those eligible might be informed. The previous Guild Roll was used in order to contact the head of each branch of every family. It was impossible, and still is, for the Guild authorities to be aware of every individual in advance, since there were many births of new sons and deaths of previous burgesses in the twenty years since the previous Guild. Therefore each man receiving an invitation had to ensure that all those eligible within his particular family came in person or renewed their freedom by proxy. In most instances, of course, the recipients were well aware of the forthcoming Guild and no doubt had it marked on their calendar years ahead.

During the same meeting of the Council at the Easter before the Guild, the Guild officials were chosen. The three stewards were appointed from among the aldermen, their particular task being to collect the fines for admissions. According to Kuerden, the clerk to the Guild was also known as the 'Grand Senescal to the Gyld': the word 'senescal' means steward, so he was in effect the high steward. His job, dealing with the paperwork, centred upon the recording of the names of those who took the oath and were admitted, and he was also the man who administered the oath itself. The remainder of the aldermen were then elected, as a formality, as 'Aldermen of the Guild', and they and the mayor sat as the bench which oversaw the proceedings of the Guild Court. Kuerden explains how, at this stage in the planning, a number of burgesses were selected by the mayor and the full Council as 'fitting persons' to be providers of victuals for the Guild if insufficient quantities of food were received from other sources.

These preliminaries having been accomplished, the forthcoming Guild was publicly announced. The Guild Mayor, his brethren of the Council, and the resident gentry and burgesses, dressed in their formal robes, went in procession to the high cross in the market place on a market day a month before the Guild was due, and the mayor's sergeant proclaimed the Guild. The proclamation stated that all the free burgesses were summoned to attend on the appointed day, for the 'Feast heretofore a Gyld Merchant [which] within this Town, hath useally, for divers ages last past, been solemnly kept, every twenty years'. The proclamation also announced the arrangements for the processions.

The route of the processions must have changed some time between 1500, when they went from Maudlands and along Friargate, and 1682, when they went from the Town Hall to the parish church and then around the streets of the town centre.

Kuerden's account of the procession in 1682 deserves to be quoted at length. On the first day of the Guild, the Monday after the Feast of the Decollation of St John the Baptist, the trade participants were to group in 'their distinct Companyes ... with their Master or Wardens, well ordered and disposed, for that purpose; and all those that cannot well be reduced into such Companys or Fraternitys, there to attend, in such Order as at that time shall be assigned to them'.[21] Once gathered,

> all the Companys of Trades, with the Wardens of each Company in their Gowns and long white Rods [of office], each Company ranged into 2 fyles, the flags of each Company displayed, and variety of musick attending each Company, march regularly up and down the streets, wayteing for the Gild Mayor's attendance. And the young men within the Town, not being as yet free to Trade of themselves, have a Captain and Leftenant of their own, their ensign being the Towns Arms, a Flagg with the Holy Lamb; and they march and attend in the like order, as aforesaid, with their drums and musiq.[22]

The Guild Mayor and his attendants then joined the procession, which formed with, at the front, a great banner bearing the royal arms and then, in ranks, the mayor's guard, the sergeants of the borough carrying the civic regalia, the bailiffs with their white rods of office, and the aldermen in their robes. After the aldermen walked the mayor himself, attended by the nobility and gentry of the town and county. They all went to the Town Hall, and then to the high cross in the market place where the opening of the Guild was officially declared, to the accompaniment of a peal of bells from the parish church.

They then progressed towards the church, 'drums beating, musick of al sorts playing'. While the Guild Mayor, Corporation, gentry and nobility were inside for the service, the trades companies and others remained outside as a guard of honour. Afterwards both parties toured the town 'from barr to barr' (these were the strong gates across the main roads leading into the centre). First, to Churchgate Barr, in what is now Church Street, where a scholar of the grammar school made a speech honouring the mayor, and a 'Barrel or Hogshead of nappy Ale standing close by the Barrs is broached' ('nappy' was strong ale, with a head on it). The Guild Mayor accepted a glass, and drank to the health of the king and queen, each toast being accompanied by a volley of shot from the musketeers standing by.[23]

When the mayor had finished his beer ('the contry people there present drinking of the remander'), the procession turned about and marched along Fishergate to the Fishergate Barrs, where the same procedure was repeated and there was more ale, 'the people shouting and seizing of the residue left'. Then off to the Friargate Barrs and the same yet again, and back finally to the market place where the master of the grammar school gave a 'learned speech and verses concerning the prossperous Government of his Majestie, and his gracious confirmation of their unparaleled franchises of a Guild Merchant'. At the high cross a hogshead of wine was broached, the health of the king and queen was drunk, musket volleys were fired, the people shouted and acclaimed the event, and then 'in good order' (allegedly, despite the broaching of many hogsheads) the procession returned to the Town Hall. Each company retired to its own rooms or meeting place, with yet more musket volleys and waving of flags, and then to dinner and feasting.

The procession around the streets of the town (which in the mid-seventeenth century consisted only of Fishergate, Churchgate, Friargate and the market place) was, as the evidence of the 1500 Guild orders indicates, a long-standing tradition. It demonstrated to the townspeople the power and might of the Guild and its members. The formal ceremonial procession, its participating dignitaries in their robes, the presence of the gentry, the civic service at the parish church, and the inclusion of the different trade companies, were calculated to make the maximum dramatic impact.

But there was another aspect to the processions. The Guild Merchant was now also a celebration of the town itself, of its importance and civic dignity. In Kuerden's elegant phrase, the Guild ceremonial was 'for the greater Applause and Glory to the Burrough of Preston'.[24] As it was in the medieval period, when the Guild Merchant was young, so it was in the seventeenth century, when it had already acquired a venerable quality; and it is still so in our day, when the Guild is ancient and a remarkable historical survival.

The renewal ceremony

The formal business continued in the afternoon, with the renewal of freedom. The proclamation stated that all those who, by ancestry or by purchase, claimed freedom of the Guild and borough, were to attend the renewal, 'according to the auncient laudable and rightfull customes of this Burrough', there to 'clayme and entitle themselves to all such Libertyes, Preveledges, and Freedomes, as to them or any of them … shall be due or in any wayes belong'.

At the same time they were to be acquainted with 'what Orders, Acts or Statuts, by the Mayor, Stewards, and Aldermen of this present Guild, shall and may be thought fit, either to be added, altered, or abrogated, or confirmed'. This proclamation was reiterated on the next three market days, as laid down in the early sixteenth-century Guild orders, so that full warning could be given to all burgesses. Then, a fortnight before the holding of the Guild, the various minor officials who would attend the mayor, nobility and gentry were appointed by the Guild officers.

During the first day of the Guild, after the church service and the procession around the town, the participants retired to the Guildhall for feasting and entertainment which lasted until the middle of the afternoon. They then reassembled and went to the Town Hall for the opening of the Guild Court, the renewal ceremony and the admittance of new burgesses. The Sergeant made a proclamation by which the 'Grand and Unparalleled Solemnity of the Guild Merchant' was opened. The name of the chief nobleman present—in other words, the man highest in the order of precedence—was then called, and he applied formally for renewal of membership of the Guild. The appropriate oaths were sworn by him, and he paid a fine of sevenpence for his admission. His name was then enrolled at the head of the draft list of names. He was followed by what Kuerden calls 'the residue of Baronets, Kts, Esqrs, and Gentlemen'.[25]

The three guild stewards sat in open court, accompanied by the clerk of the guild, and received the applications for admissions from the burgesses. The first steward had the task of checking the names against the previous Guild Roll, to see whether the applicants appeared there and if they were in-burgesses, out-burgesses, or in any other category. The second steward checked the names of those who did not appear in the previous Guild Roll, either because they had been born during the intervening twenty years or because they had been admitted during the period since the last Guild. The third steward, known as the *bonser*, consulted with the *benchers* (the Guild Mayor and aldermen) to determine the fines and conditions for such admissions, and he received the fines which were paid for renewal. The sum paid was entered in a separate volume, and the official embossed stamp of the Corporation was made on the page at that entry, as a record of payment. The names of those admitted were enrolled by the clerk in a draft book, ready to be written up in a fair hand in the official Guild Roll, after the close of the proceedings.[26]

In the 1680s the fines were sevenpence (3p) for each burgess and for any child being enrolled, 'and some smal reward to the Sarjeant of the Guild, *ad Test. se ipsos esse Burgensses* [to bear witness that they themselves were burgesses]'. After the admissions an oath-taking was held. All burgesses present in court who had paid their fees and were over 21 years of age swore the oath appropriate to their status. There were separate oaths, similar in form, for 'a free burgess, being a nobleman, knight, or gentleman, not inhabiting within the town of Preston', 'a free burgess not inhabiting within the burrough', and 'a free burgess inhabiting within the burrough'. Each man swore loyalty to the king and his successors, to uphold the Guild, to maintain the peace and the king's laws, to warn the mayor of any conspiracy against the town or king, and to uphold the laws and customs of the town and realm. Ordinary burgesses, resident and non-resident, also swore to observe the trading regulations of the town and Guild, and to pay their dues, customs, taxes and charges.[27]

The admission of the nobility and gentry occupied the proceedings for the remainder of the day. Their numbers were not large, but it was considered desirable that the special guests and those of high standing should not have to participate in the same ceremony as the ordinary burgesses. The first afternoon was therefore reserved for this group. Having taken wine with the mayor they retired to their lodgings and recovered from the exertions of the day in readiness for the evening, which was occupied by further feasting.

On the second day of the Guild Merchant a morning service was held, and afterwards the Guild Mayor gave a banquet to those members of the gentry and nobility who had not been in town for the first day's events, or who were staying in Preston. This pattern was repeated on succeeding days, with banquets for the dignitaries (provided that they had given due notice of their arrival) and more modest, but nonetheless substantial, dinners for the ordinary burgesses of 'the greater and better sort'.[28] The junior and inferior burgesses, especially the younger men, were given entertainment and sustenance in other rooms, not in the presence of the mayor. During the Guild fortnight the poor inhabitants of the town were not entirely forgotten: they were given food and drink as a charitable gesture.

When the time came to close the Guild the companies of traders and the burgesses went to the Town Hall to attend the Guild Mayor at the last session of the Guild Court. The orders of the different companies within the Guild were read and sealed, after three proclamations, and the new book of Guild orders was read. It was then held up before the assembled inhabitants and accepted by popular acclamation, ending with a cry of 'God Bless The King'. The clerk of the guild then affixed the seal of the borough of Preston (the 'lamb and flag') and announced, 'Here is your law: God Bless the King'. By proclamation of the sergeant, the clerk declared the adjournment of the court for another twenty years. All was over as far as the formal business was concerned, but the Guild Mayor and the Wardens of the Companies, and some of the gentlemen, retired to the Mayor's lodging and revived themselves after these wearisome duties with drink and biscuits, before a final session in 'his [the mayor's] own lodging, or ... some publiq Tavern, where they give him many thanks and great applause for his *Great Care, Labour Toyle, and Charge exhibited with such Grandure, unparalleled by other Burroughs*'.[29]

Kuerden's description is based upon his detailed observations of the 1682 Guild and is important not only for its recording of the formal procedures of Guild ceremonies but also for its account of the less formal activities, including the processions, feasts, balls and 'wining and dining' of important people. Kuerden was a noted antiquarian who had a keen eye for historical tradition, so that his description of contemporary events also looks back to what he knew of the past. Without Kuerden and his memoir it would be difficult indeed to ascertain the character of much of the ancient Guild.

The cost of the Guild

Apart from very brief references to the sums paid as fines there is no information as to the cost of the Guilds in the sixteenth century and earlier; nor do we know who found the money and how it was disbursed. It is reasonable to suppose that at least some of the expenses were found from the pockets of the chief participants, since it would need to have been a fairly wealthy man who could afford to sustain a fortnight of extravagant expenditure in a manner that would maintain the reputation of the town. To entertain gentry and nobility with wine and dinners was an expensive business, and the prestige and splendour of the occasion may well have been followed by a lean period for many of the leading families in the town.

In the sixteenth and early seventeenth centuries there is a little more documentary evidence, but the costs of the Guild and the way in which the finances were managed are still unclear. It is known that the stewards collected the cash at the Guild ceremonies, but the financial organisation has produced remarkably little documentary evidence. The sources of income were varied: fees and fines; gifts of sums of money by benefactors and perhaps by the wealthier participants; and compulsory or voluntary levies raised from their members by the trade companies and the Corporation. There were also gifts in kind by the traders and craftsmen. The appointment of the providers of victuals reflects an assumption that meat and other supplies would be forthcoming, and it is probable that butchers, bakers, brewers and others would give such food as their contribution to the success of the Guild.

The amounts paid in fines on admission varied greatly, according to the circumstances of the individuals and the conditions which were placed upon membership. Some people were milked of large sums in return for the honour of being admitted. The sevenpences that were exacted as entry fines for hereditary burgesses seem trivial indeed compared with the amounts taken from those who bought their membership. The levies on individual traders are hard to determine, because in most cases a single sum covers not only the burgess admitted but also the admittances of other members of his family. The sums apparently varied according to factors such as ability to pay, the nature of the trade, and the particular circumstances of each applicant. The majority of admissions by purchase appear to have involved payments of between 10s. and £2 10s.

Assuming that the sums given in the Guild Rolls are at least reasonably complete, income from purchases of freedom would appear to have increased substantially during the late sixteenth and early seventeenth centuries. In 1582 the total obtained from such payments was £98 17s. 10d.; in 1602 £213 4s. 8d.; and in 1622 £289 18s. 7d.[30] Increasing numbers of people were indeed admitted at the Guilds as new purchasers, but the figures also suggest that the cost of purchasing Guild membership grew more rapidly. The Guild did not wish to deter traders from joining, by having fixed high sums that would only be affordable to the largest and wealthiest traders, but neither did it wish to reduce the income from this source by setting a low fixed sum. It may have been decided that charges could be increased gradually without dissuading people from joining. There was, in many senses, a captive market, since it was this same period which saw the Guild exercising perhaps its greatest economic and commercial influence. Higher charges could be levied because traders had no real option but to pay.

From the 1662 Guild comes the earliest detailed information as to costs and management, provided by the White Book of the Corporation and the minutes of the Preston Court Leet (the Borough Court). Although the 1622 and 1642 Guilds are not mentioned at all in the minutes, even though the subject must have been discussed, the minutes from the 1660s onwards are more informative. The first discussion within the Corporation, at least in formal terms, was in early July 1662. On 10 July it was ordered by the Corporation that

> All persons whoe shall disburse and lay out any summe or Sommes of money for or concerninge the Management and careinge [carrying] on the now ensueinge Guild Shalbee reimbursed and paid unto them out of the first money which shalbee received by the Stewards of the said Guild.[31]

In theory, therefore, the stewards were supposed to reimburse those who had spent any money on the Guild, and were then to hand over any balance to the Corporation. The next entry in the White Book which relates to the Guild was made after it had taken place, and the finances were being sorted out (not, as it emerged, at all efficiently). On 30 September 1662 it was ordered that 'the Charges of the Guild may bee satisfied out of the profitts of the Guild'. The Corporation had been negotiating recently with the Crown over renewal of the borough charter, and the mayor and bailiffs had spent considerable sums of their own money on this business. The resolution of 30 September went on to agree that this money should be repaid out of any profits which the Guild had made. The profits from the holding of the Guild were thus to be used directly for communal civic purposes:

> after the aforesaid Charges of the Guild bee Satisfied, then Mr Maiors and Baliffes accompte concerneinge Renewinge the Charter ... shall bee satisfied out of the rest of the profits of the Guild, And if they will not amount to pay the same then to bee Satisfied out of the townes Revenues.[32]

The order was ignored by those responsible for its implementation. On 8 December 1662 a further order was made, requiring the finances to be settled. It is of special interest because it states the income from the Guild and the costs incurred:

> Ordered that the Summe of 401^{li} 10^s now remaining in Mr Thomas Sumpners hands (one of the Stewards of the last Guild merchant held for this Borough) over and besides the summe of 230^{li} 13^s 11^d by him disbursed for defraying the charges of the said Guild and other occasions [which] Mr Sumpner this day confessed to remaine in his hands of the profitte of the said Guild [should be handed to the Mayor].[33]

The total proceeds from the 1662 Guild were therefore about £600, perhaps a little less, while the expenditure must have been over £200. The monies disbursed by Sumpner did include some payments on other, unspecified, occasions, but the great bulk of his costs must have been associated with the Guild. The overall profit, even after the other costs were taken into account, was thus about £400. It is apparent that in this period the Guild, if properly managed, could represent a sizeable (though only occasional) source of income for the Corporation.

The tone of the 8 December resolution indicates that it was felt there had been time enough to settle the account as over three months had elapsed since the Guild. That patience was running out is shown by a further order of 12 December, noting that Sumpner had still not handed over the money.[34] The Corporation minutes are silent about the eventual outcome of the differences with Thomas Sumpner, but the court leet records continue the story. The court leet (one of the borough courts) dealt mainly with infringements of byelaws and other matters concerning the administration of the town. On 16 April 1663 it ordered that the Mayor should be fined £5 for not publishing adequately the Guild orders made the previous September, and also that he should give to the next meeting of the Court:

> a particular accompte in writeinge how and in what manner they have disposed of the said 600l., and to what uses, that soe the said Burgesses may be satisfied how they have discharged the trust they have undertaken on the said Burgesses behalfes[35]

Evidently the financial management of the 1662 Guild had been so suspect that the burgesses, with good reason, feared the worst. The court leet which sat on 20 October 1665, more than three years after the Guild, was told that

> divers presentments have beene heretofore brought against Mr. Willm. Bannester for that he hath not accompted togeather with the common councell of this towne for the profitts of this last Guild merchant, therefore wee present [him] and the councell of this towne ... as yet they have not as yet accompted to the ffree Burgesses of this corporacon ... they have 600l. and upwards remaining in theire

hands, And that they shall ... make a particuler accompte in writeing how and in what manner the same hath beene disposed for the satisfaccon of all, which as wee thinke is most reasonable.[36]

Reasonable indeed, since £600 was a huge sum and the Corporation had persistently refused to give an explanation of what had happened to the money. The records of the court leet note that the present mayor was to order the former mayor to make up an account, or be fined £10 himself. It was all to no avail, for on 3 April 1668 the court again dealt with the matter:

We continue all presentments heretofore made by severall other juries of this Leet concerning an accompt to be rendred to the Burgesses of this Incorporacon of the sume of 600[li] and upwards raised by the last Guild.[37]

The mayor was ordered to make an account, in writing, on or before 1 August 1668, or be fined no less than £100. He apparently did so, for a marginal note in the court minute book states that an account of the money was entered into the White Book of the Corporation for 23 October 1668, but in fact there is no such entry and it is very unlikely that there ever was: who was playing a game of deception?

The affair illustrates a special problem of such bodies in this period. In the absence of banks, accountants, auditors and public scrutiny, the accounts of Preston Corporation were purely an internal matter. Without regular, reliable and predictable sources of income it was frequently necessary for individual councillors and officials to defray costs from their own pockets and then seek reimbursement from the Corporation. But the money owned by the Corporation was often in the personal possession of other officials and councillors. Thomas Sumpner, as well as being the man who collected the money at the Guild, also kept it and looked after it. Successive mayors after 1662 seemed to have evaded and avoided properly accounting for the money, and although the business dragged on until 1668, no satisfactory conclusion was reached. A dishonest, feckless or simply incompetent person holding the purse could play havoc with Corporation finances and with those of its individual members, and the burgesses were powerless to do anything to prevent it or to find out what was happening.

The accounts presented for the next Guild are written up in the White Book with more detail and greater efficiency than those of 1662 (probably because of the unseemly and acrimonious events of the 1660s) and they seem to have been settled to the satisfaction of all parties. The financial statement is given below:

An account of the moneys received and disbursed relating to the Guild at
Preston held the 4 day of September 1682

	li	s	d
Recd. by Mr Lawr. Wall one of the Stewards of the same Guild as by a note of the perticulers	267	03	04
Recd by Mr Thomas Hodgkinson another of the Stewards (as by a note of perticulers) the summe of	225	14	02
Re^d by the deputy steward for Entryes of names in the Guild being vii^d a piece for each admittance	75	11	09
Tot	568	09	03
Disburst by Mr Hodgkinson as appears by a note of perticulers	165	05	08
disbursed by Mr Sudell as appears by a note of perticulers	151	15	08
disbt. by Mr Lawr. Hall as by a note of perticulers	14	18	00
To the Steward for his fee	2	00	00
Tot	333	19	04
Remains	234	09	11

The account was not presented to the Corporation until its meeting of 6 August 1683, almost a year after the 1682 Guild.[38] It was neatly arranged and its phrasing shows that each steward kept a separate personal account of monies spent, as well as an account made during the celebration of the Guild to show the money that came into his hands. The accounts of income and expenditure by each steward were then merged to produce the account for the Guild as a whole. The Corporation resolved at its August 1683 meeting that

the accompts abovewritten ... were this day exhibited to the Councill [and] the same be and are hereby allowed and that Mr Lawrence Wall and Mr Lawrence Hodgkinson (two of the Stewards of the said Guild Merchant holden within this Burrough) bee and are hereby fully and absolutely discharged of the moneys in the said accompts.

The profit from the 1682 Guild was £234. The amount spent was not significantly different from that of 1662, and the reduction in the profit appears to have been mainly the result of a fall in income from fees and fines, although it may also be that money from other sources (untraceable now but perhaps including gifts, donations and special payments) was less.

As early as 1682 the Guild was becoming a festival in which social events played an important part, and these aspects—the feasts, balls and entertainments—had become a dominant feature by the middle of the eighteenth century. This trend is reflected in the next set of financial statistics which survive. The Corporation records, including the White Book, make no reference to the 1702 Guild, but the accounts for 1722 are written into the minutes. The figures show a startling change from the profitable and lucrative Guilds of 1662 and 1682. In those years the entertainment and ceremony, although lavish, were kept well within budget, and the Corporation received a hefty profit to be used for other purposes—such as, in 1662, the payment of the costs of renewing the charter. That was not to be the case in later Guilds.

On 9 July 1723 the Council received the final account for the Guild of the previous year. The former Guild Mayor reported that income was £1,347 9s. 9d., and expenditure was £1,318 6s. 5¼d.[39] The profit therefore, was a mere £29 3s. 3¾d. Although income was very much greater than in 1682, having increased by 237 per cent, expenditure had grown by no less than 395 per cent, as a direct result of an ever more ostentatious display of entertaining and socialising.

The account for the following Guild (1742) is the only reference to the holding of that Guild which appears in the Corporation minutes. In July 1743 the Guild Mayor, Henry Farington, presented the final accounts. These revealed that the income had been £1,389 7s. 2d., and the expenditure £1,376 6s. 10½d. giving a profit of only £13 0s. 3½d.[40] There was no longer any expectation that the Guild would produce a sizeable revenue to be used for Corporation purposes. Spending the money on lavish festivities had become the aim and intention of the organisers.

CHAPTER FOUR

The Guild from 1762 to 1835

T HE PERIOD between 1720 and 1760 marked a fundamental change in the character of the Guild. It lost its role in regulating the trade and economic life of the town, and developed instead a prominent social and political function. That political function was derived from the right of the in-burgesses to elect Preston's two members of parliament, and it culminated in the dramatic Preston election of 1768. The disputed election results were sent for adjudication to the House of Commons, which decided to extend the franchise to almost all adult males in the town. Many of the newly enfranchised voters were not members of the Guild and had not been admitted as burgesses. Indeed, because they were employees or had not served as apprentices, and had no hereditary rights, they were ineligible for admission to the Guild.

With the waning of the trading role, and the end of its political power, the Guild lost its significance. After the mid-eighteenth century the intervals between the celebrations saw the Guild existing in name only, its practical work long ended. Its new role, as an upper- and middle-class social club, meant that it had minimal relevance to the daily life of Preston and its people. In retrospect this can be seen as inevitable. It would have been impossible for an institution which was fundamentally medieval in its character and in many of its practices to have survived without change. It was beyond the capabilities of a body such as the Guild to control the economic life of a town experiencing major population growth, urban expansion, industrial development and social change. In any case, by the mid-eighteenth century it was generally considered undesirable even to try to do so. The argument that guilds and corporations restricted trade and hindered economic development was already well rehearsed by the 1720s, and it was widely felt that the success of Manchester and other unincorporated towns was in at least some measure the result of their lack of such restrictive and irksome practices.

The character and circumstances of the Corporation were in many ways similar to those of the Guild, with which it was so inextricably linked in previous generations. The Corporation was a self-appointing closed body, which remained almost unchanging while everything around was in a turmoil of change and flux. Although in the sixteenth and seventeenth centuries it had drawn its strength from the burgesses, by the eighteenth century it had become aloof, detached and out of sympathy with the feelings of the townspeople. The Corporation, fervently Anglican in its religious beliefs and devotedly Tory in its politics, claimed to govern a town which was a religious jumble of Anglicans, Catholics and Nonconformists and was a centre of radical political thought. Catholics and Nonconformists were increasingly influential; the former as penal legislation and other restrictions upon their activities were either removed or ignored, the latter as they grew in numbers and wealth with the increase in population and industry.

In 1700 Preston had been primarily a market and administrative town; in 1800 it was rapidly becoming a major industrial centre. Its population was growing apace. The skyline was changing as the first wave of factory-building swept over the town, and the surrounding fields, crofts and meadows were being submerged beneath a tide of bricks and mortar. Every aspect of its economic, social and political life was in a state of upheaval. But Preston was, more than ever before, a centre for the county gentry. It had been recognised as the county town in all but name long before 1800, and the county's administration was centred there. Areas such as Winckley Square and the adjacent streets, which date from the late eighteenth and early nineteenth centuries, still reflect the grace and elegance of the town at that time, when Preston was widely recognised as the commercial, social and cultural centre for much of Lancashire.[1] Only Manchester and Liverpool, among its rivals in the county, outstripped it.

The Corporation, increasingly out of touch with the townspeople as a whole and unrepresentative of them politically and socially, had no wish to take up the many challenges of those exciting and troublesome times. It was, like many such bodies the length and breadth of England, content to do little and to initiate even less. Civic dignity and ceremonial, regalia and robes, the annual round of dinners, services, formal Council meetings and inactivity, were quite sufficient for its members. The Corporation did not disappear, but the increasing need to give serious attention to the problems of the town was eventually met by a different body—the Improvement Commissioners, established in 1815. They carried out a wide range of tasks, including street paving and lighting, policing and provision of sanitation, and their vigour was in very marked contrast to the inactivity of the gentlemen's club which Preston Corporation had become.

This stagnant period in the life of the Corporation, and the ever-growing contrast between its sloth and the dynamism of the town, was ended by the Municipal Corporations Act of 1835. This was part of the programme of radical reforming legislation introduced by the Whig government in the wake of the Great Reform Act of 1832, and was designed to sweep away the corrupt, inefficient or moribund—and usually very undemocratic—municipal corporations in over 200 boroughs in England and Wales. It was preceded by a detailed and thorough, though far from impartial, investigation by a royal commission, whose reports are a valuable source of information about borough government in its unreformed state.

In Preston the Guild Merchant, because of its formerly intimate role in the administration of the town, received special and unfavourable attention. The commissioners set out on their investigation with the intention of collecting evidence to support the case for municipal reform, and so it was perhaps to be expected that their reports were rarely more than lukewarm in their praise, and often vitriolically hostile to the corporations which they inspected. That they had frequent (although by no means invariable) justification for such views should not obscure the fact that they were not entirely dispassionate in their opinions.

The Act of 1835 abolished almost all of the old corporations and substituted a new and uniform system. Borough councils, which took office on 1 January 1836, were to be elected by a democratic franchise, though it was still very restricted and limited to property owners and tenants of larger properties. Many of the ancient, quaint survivals that characterised unreformed municipal administration disappeared, because the new system was uniform in all boroughs, and so allowed little scope for local variation. In Preston this meant that all the particular and general powers of the Guild Merchant were abolished. It was no longer possible, even in theory, for the new Corporation to exercise any control over the economic life of the town or its trade, or to impose any customs, dues, tolls and charges other than those, such as rents for property and market stalls, levied in the normal course of events.

At a stroke, therefore, the Guild, though not itself specifically abolished, lost all its rights, liberties and powers. In respect to the franchise, these had in practice been abolished in 1768, and in respect of trading had been abandoned more or less voluntarily in the 1780s, but from the end of 1835 all vestiges of them disappeared entirely. As a result it was widely argued in Preston that the Guild itself had effectively ceased to exist.

Planning and preparation, 1782–1822

As noted in the previous chapter, the Guild of 1762 was marked by the building of a Guildhall adjacent to the Town Hall, although the older building was retained. Its survival was of short duration, however, for on 3 June 1780 the roof and some stretches of wall collapsed only a couple of nights after a ball had taken place there. It was therefore necessary to rebuild the Town Hall completely during the following two years, in time for the forthcoming Guild of 1782. The new building, which survived only until 1862, was plain but imposing, and blended in reasonably well with the Guildhall of twenty years earlier.

On 18 June 1782 the Corporation discussed the anticipated costs of the Guild, and passed a resolution concerning 'in what manner with regard to Expence the ensuing Guild should be carried on'. It was decided that 'it ought to be conducted in a genteel and handsome manner with regard at the same time to the State of the Corporation finances' (an uncharacteristically virtuous sentiment, since financial rectitude was not a prominent aspect of the Corporation's budgeting).[2]

There was other building work to be undertaken in readiness for the 1782 Guild. In 1738 an obelisk had been built in the market place, on the site of a disused water conduit, but it cannot have been properly constructed, for in 1782 it was stated that it was 'formerly standing [but] some years ago lately fell or was taken down'. On 30 June 1782 the Corporation signed an agreement with William Roper of Preston, whereby he undertook to 'Build and compleat in a substantial and Workmanlike manner ... a good and sufficient Obelisk upon the Base of the old Obelisk ... of good and sufficient Longridge Stone ... thirty three feet and seven Inches high to be computed from the Surface of the said old Base'. He also agreed to repair and restore the steps, flagstones and stonework around the obelisk. The work, for which he would receive £53 6s. (£53.30), was to be completed no later than 29 August, a mere two days before the start of the Guild.[3] The rebuilt obelisk was pulled down in 1853 and taken to Hollowforth, from which it was recovered a few years ago and then rebuilt in its old position.

The advance preparations for the 1802 Guild are recorded in some detail. The minutes for that year are longer than usual, and for once plenty of time was allowed for the consideration of Guild matters. Usually work was started only a few months before the holding of the Guild, but in this case it was decided on 2 July 1801 that a committee of the Corporation should be formed

> for the purpose of taking into consideration what entertainments must be given by the Corporation at the approaching Guild and as to the general management of such Guild Merchant and what part of the premises about the Guild and Town Hall's [sic] will be necessary for the accommodation of the Company at that time.[4]

The committee considered these questions during the summer of 1801 and reported back on 11 September. Its report was unusually detailed, giving a valuable impression of the organisation of a Guild almost two centuries ago. It begins with the need for rooms:

> the large room in Guild Hall and also the Town Hall will be wanted for the Assemblys Mayors Balls and Masqued Ball and ... the two rooms part of Mr Aspinwalls House will be wanted as Tea Rooms ... the two rooms now used as a Grocers Shop and a parlour by Mr Beeston at the west end of the Guild Hall will be wanted for the Guild Committee who will renew and grant freedoms there and dine each day Sundays excepted according to custom heretofore observed.[5]

The Guildhall of 1762 had been designed for conversion to dwellings and shops after the end of the Guild Merchant. The snag, as far as the residents and shopkeepers were concerned, was that every twenty years it was necessary to vacate the premises for a fortnight to allow the Guild to take place. As the report says, the Guild events required the use of two of Mr Aspinwall's rooms and two of Mr Beeston's. The Corporation ordered that these people should leave their rooms in good time, 'but in such a manner as to render it the least inconvenient to them'. It was also decided that 'the double staircase approaching to the Guild assembly room should be opened and that all the before mentioned rooms ought to be repaired beautified and furnished in good time before the Guild'. The committee report then listed the entertainments that might be required:

> the entertainments at the Guild should be managed with economy and at the same time with a proper liberality becoming the consequence of this Body Corporate, that they should continue a fortnight and consist of two Assemblies in each week on Mondays and Fridays and one Mayors Ball on Wednesdays and also of a public Masqued Ball on some convenient night during the Guild, the price of admittance to the Assemblies and Masqued Ball to be settled hereafter and the two Mayors Balls to be given at the expence of the Corporation with Tea Wines Negus [spiced sweet sherry] and Cake.

The accounts for the 1802 Guild are also very detailed, and are the earliest to survive which are arranged in modern style. Income was £3,438 6s. 11d. and expenditure £3,136 15s. 1d., leaving a profit of £310 11s. 10d. By far the largest category of expenditure was catering, refreshments and entertainment. The list of sums spent begins with 2s. 10d. for the 'Carriage of a Hamper of Wine from Manchester' and includes musicians' fees, hire of glassware, cutlery, chairs and tables, and payment for cakes and ale, wine, water and candles.

There are many miscellaneous entries of interest, such as the payment of a guinea to the boy who wove at the loom in one of the processions, payments for printing, tickets and advertising, and fees of two guineas paid to the ringers at the parish church. The Guild Mayor, Nicholas Grimshaw, went with his wife to Liverpool in person, to 'hire Servants and to engage Confectioner, Musicians, and for various purposes', a journey which cost the extraordinarily large sum of £12 13s. 6d. For twelve shillings a new book was bought for use at the Guild ceremony, to record the names of those who were admitted, while a new book for the Guild Roll cost fourteen shillings and writing it up another six guineas. It is sad to record that expenditure included writing off half a guinea, paid for a freedom at the Guild and found to be a counterfeit coin.[6]

At the 1802 Guild there was another major expense, of a type repeated in future Guilds, and which was a case of the Corporation rewarding its own. On 4 October 1802, at the first meeting after the Guild Merchant, John Horrocks proposed that some piece of plate should be presented by the Corporation to Nicholas Grimshaw Esquire and his lady the Mayor and Mayoress as a token of their approbation of their management and manner of conducting the late Jubilee the Guild.

The Corporation readily assented to this proposal, and voted a sum of fifty guineas for the purchase of an item of silver for the Grimshaws.[7] This was an extremely large sum in 1802 (perhaps £10,000 in modern values would not be an unreasonable estimate). The closed, exclusive circle which constituted Preston Corporation was happy to use public money on a grand scale for private gain. There was a similar instance of the extravagant use of funds at the 1822 Guild. On 29 June 1821 it was agreed by the Corporation that:

a Cup value one hundred Guineas be given by this Corporation to be run for by such horses, carrying such weights as shall be hereafter arranged between the Mayor and the Gentlemen conducting the Races at the Guild in September 1822, And that this Offer be communicated to the Right Honourable the Earl of Derby, by a letter from the Town Clerk.[8]

Partly as a result of such extravagance the 1822 Guild made a loss of £1,885 7s. 7d., even after all the takings from the entertainments and events had been taken into account.

The Corporation discussed rich gifts to its members, but the Improvement Commissioners had more practical matters on their minds. Their minutes for 1822 show concern not for horse-racing and expensive prizes, but for crowd control and maintaining security during the Guild. Huge crowds, then as now, caused the authorities tremendous disquiet. The 1820s were lawless times; civil unrest and popular discontent were widespread, and it was feared that while the gentry raced horses on the Moor the crowds of ordinary people might be causing trouble in the town. The Commissioners met on 15 July 1822:

Mr. Robert Park gave notice that at the next meeting of the Commissioners he would move to take into consideration the propriety of making application to the Magistrates for the appointment of an additional number of Constables to preserve the peace of the Borough during the approaching Guild Merchant.[9]

At the next meeting, on 5 August, a committee was appointed to oversee the question of policing the Guild, and a number of additional special constables were appointed for the duration of the celebrations.[10]

Guild Mayors and burgesses, 1762–1822

The policy of choosing particularly important people to fill Guild offices became general during the eighteenth century. As already noted, it had long been customary for large numbers of the nobility and gentry to attend Guild ceremonies and so the Guild Mayor had to occupy a high social standing within the town and beyond. Henry Farington in 1742 and Robert Parker in 1762 were followed by Robert Atherton in 1782. He was of an old Preston family. One ancestor, John Atherton, had been entered on the 1682 Guild Roll as a woollen draper and served as mayor in 1696 and 1704. Robert Atherton's father, William, had been an alderman from 1731, and was mayor of Preston in 1732 and 1738. The Atherton family is an excellent example of the way in which the Corporation, which was non-elective, filled its vacancies from a small close-knit circle, made up of related families and with the hereditary principle uppermost. Richard Atherton himself had been an alderman from 1771, was mayor in 1773, and after being Guild Mayor in 1782 served a third term as mayor in 1786.[11]

Nicholas Grimshaw, for many years a dominant figure in Preston politics and society, had the distinction of being chosen to serve twice as Guild Mayor, in 1802 and 1822. He was the only man ever to hold that office twice, and it is doubtful if anybody will ever do so again. He was born in 1757, the son of Thomas Grimshaw, a lawyer of Fence near Burnley who had settled in Preston in the early 1730s and founded a powerful dynasty. Thomas was chosen as a common councillor in 1756, alderman in 1768, served as mayor in 1768 and 1775, and was a guild steward in 1782. His elder son, John Grimshaw, was a councillor from 1768 (taking his father's place on the common councillors' bench), a steward in the 1762 Guild, became an alderman in 1782, and was mayor in 1782, 1788, 1799 and 1806. He was also guild steward in 1802 when Nicholas, his brother, was Guild Mayor.

With a family background so interwoven with the Corporation of Preston, Nicholas could not fail to advance in local affairs. He was a guild steward in 1782, became a councillor in 1790, and in 1793 was chosen by the Corporation as town clerk (there being at that time no bar to a member of the Corporation serving such an office). He held this position until he became an alderman in 1801, was almost immediately chosen as Guild Mayor for 1802, and after the Guild served again as mayor in 1808, 1812, and 1817. Even his term as Guild Mayor in 1822 was not the end, for he went on to be mayor in 1825 and 1830 as well. This record, seven times as mayor including twice as Guild Mayor, is unequalled in Preston's post-medieval history. He was a lawyer by profession, and had a lucrative practice as a solicitor in Preston, one of his partners being Richard Palmer, his successor as town clerk. Grimshaw also had great influence within the county, being clerk to the magistrates for 36 years, eleven times under-sheriff of Lancashire, and a leading county magistrate.[12]

The numbers of burgesses and the balance between in- and out-burgesses varied during the eighteenth century, in line with the changes in the Guild itself. The in-burgess category grew as existing out-burgesses were granted an upgrading of status, and as the hereditary principle worked its inevitable result of increasing the numbers of potential burgesses. By the end of the century the overall numbers of burgesses had changed comparatively little, but the proportions of in- and out-burgesses were radically altered. At the 1802 Guild almost 3,000 burgesses renewed or were enrolled for the first time, but only about 300 of these were out-burgesses. Among the in-burgesses were most of the noble and gentry families of Lancashire: even the Earl of Derby and his family were now in that category. Names such as Assheton, Blundell, Clayton, Clifton, Hesketh and Hornby are part of Lancashire's history, and all, with many other illustrious names, appear in the in-burgess list of 1802.

Celebrating the Guild, 1762–1822

From 1762 onwards there are detailed accounts of the celebration of the Guild, with souvenir volumes, eye-witness accounts and newspaper reports. Although the framework remained the same, the Guild was on the one hand becoming more exclusive, but on the other it was increasingly a popular feast. The ceremonies, including the admissions and renewals of burgesses in the mayoral court, and the formal banquets which followed, were now the preserve of the prosperous middle and upper classes, but the fringe activities—entertainments, processions and sideshows—attracted growing numbers of ordinary people. As the town and its industrial population grew, the Guild was seen by working-class Prestonians as a special holiday, and in consequence was eagerly anticipated, while its fame beyond the town and county continued to increase.

The first printed record of a Guild was John Moon's small volume, *The Guild Merchant of Preston*, which included a brief historical account, and a souvenir description of the 1762 Guild. The book is dedicated, most obsequiously, to the Guild Mayor, Robert Parker of Cuerden, 'In grateful acknowledgment of the affability and Candor; the openness and generosity of Heart; the frank Entertainment at his Table; the easy condescension to all subordinate to him, and the Zeal to promote a general Joy, which he had the Happiness of possessing'.[13] As is subsequently acknowledged, these tributes are especially fulsome because the volume was published by express permission of the mayor. It was extensively pirated by rival publishers, who used its information and descriptions without authority from either Moon or the mayor.

The souvenir included a lengthy list, taken from records made at the time, of 'the Nobility and Gentry, who dined with Mr. Mayor and his Lady, at the *Guild Hall*'. At each dinner there were people appointed to record the names of those attending, and the editors of the volume (and its successors at later Guilds) made use of such lists.

They noted that the same could not be done for the mayoral balls, since 'no Tickets were deliver'd, and no Persons appointed to take a List, each night'. The problems encountered in preparing such lists were many, for the editors also point out that 'some few Errors may doubtless, yet remain, in such case they are not to be imputed to the publishers, but to the great difficulty of finding out the Orthography of Stranger's Names, owing to the various ways of Pronunciation of the same Persons Name, in different Counties'.[14]

The Guild of 1762 began on the morning of 30 August, when the mayor, attended by his retinue of stewards and aldermen, went to the Town Hall and opened the proceedings by formally disenfranchising the freemen. The new book for the recording of renewals and admissions was started, and then the party went 'in their proper ornaments, habits &c with their Officers, Regalia, and an excellent Band of Music' to the parish church, for a service, accompanied by 'a most brilliant and numerous appearance of Nobility and Gentry, dressed in the gayest and richest manner'.

After the service the great procession was held. Each of the trading companies had its own band of musicians, its emblems and its banners. The procession wound its way through the principal streets, and it was reported that 'Nothing cou'd be more sumptuous or striking; the whole was splendid and Magnificent, and gave every beholder the greatest Joy and Satisfaction.' Afterwards the mayor and a party of 'Fifty Ladies and Gentlemen of Superior Rank' dined at the Guildhall, with a lavish and impressive feast under the direction of the suitably named Mr Baker of York. The dinners were 'in the utmost Taste and Magnificence ... and no care or pains were omitted to render every thing as commodious and as agreeable as possible'.[15]

On the following days the table was set for fifty at a time, except on the day of the races, when forty men dined with the mayor, while the mayoress entertained forty ladies (and the mayor's chaplain) separately. The second day saw the ladies' procession. The mayoress was attended at the Guildhall by about 300 ladies, 'all splendidly and elegantly dressed', who, two by two, walked to the parish church for divine service. Afterwards they processed around the market place and back to the Town Hall, with the officers of the town in attendance carrying the regalia. The different trades companies were drawn up in lines on either side of the route, 'to prevent the Ladies from being interrupted, or incommoded by the numerous Crowds of Spectators, who were assembled to view this uncommon and memorable sight'.

The authors of the 1762 book, hoping that as many copies as possible would be sold to those who had participated in the Guild and might wish to have a souvenir, ransacked their lexicons for superlatives: the ladies' procession was held 'to surpass any Thing of the Kind, ever seen in the Country, and exceeded the expectation of every one present, as well, in point of Brillancy [sic] and Grandeur, that attended it, as in respect of the Regularity and Decorum, with which it was attended'.[16]

1 The proclamation of the Guild in 1902, from the steps of the Town Hall: in only three Guilds (those of 1882, 1902 and 1922) was this venue available, because the building was partly destroyed by fire in 1947 and subsequently demolished. Since then the balcony of the Harris Museum and Library has been used.

2 Sunlight (which is not always freely available during Guild week) bathes the large party of civic dignitaries and invited guests at the final proclamation of the 1972 Guild.

3 The Guild Court has been the legal and ceremonial focus of the Guild since the earliest records began, and we know that it has followed the same patterns and procedures for at least half a millennium. This view shows the 1902 Court in session.

4 Traditionally the formal start of Guild week was the Guild Mayor's procession through the streets of the town. This event was very carefully managed—the descriptions of the procession as far back as 1682, for example, make clear that elaborate ritual and ceremonial were already enshrined in the order and route. Here the 1922 Guild Mayor's procession is passing the Town Hall, having walked along Fishergate heading for the civic service at the parish church.

5 In this view of the 1952 Guild Mayor's procession in Fishergate, the importance of the borough regalia, ceremonially carried before the Guild Mayor, is apparent. Fishergate itself is scarcely recognisable, as most of the buildings shown had been torn down and redeveloped by the time of the 1992 Guild.

6 Although not the earliest surviving document that refers to the Guild, the Guild Roll of 1397 is the first which gives rich historical detail. Here we see the title, written across the top of the document, which gives the date of the Guild and the name of the Guild Mayor, William de Ergham. Below are two columns of names of those enrolled in the Guild, and (on the right) another column listing those newly admitted and the sums they paid for the privilege.

7 The 1397 Guild Roll was written out in a beautiful script on fine parchment over six centuries ago. Though the document itself was subsequently damaged, most of the names are remarkably legible. This enlarged section shows many places in Lancashire from which the families of Guild members originated: examples include John, son of Robert of *Wygan*, John de *Blakeburne*, and William *Grymbaldeston*.

8 Whereas the 1397 Guild Roll was a simple sheet of parchment, by the sixteenth century its successors were becoming more elaborately decorated. This is the first part of the title of the 1542 Guild Roll, with delightful embellishments to the basic wording. This reads *Gilda Marcatoria Ville de Preston*. Though beautifully drawn, it is in fact badly done: *Marcatoria* should read *Mercatoria*, and the scribe has missed out a key word, *burgensium* ('of the burgesses') and has had to add it in tiny script above the word *marcatoria*.

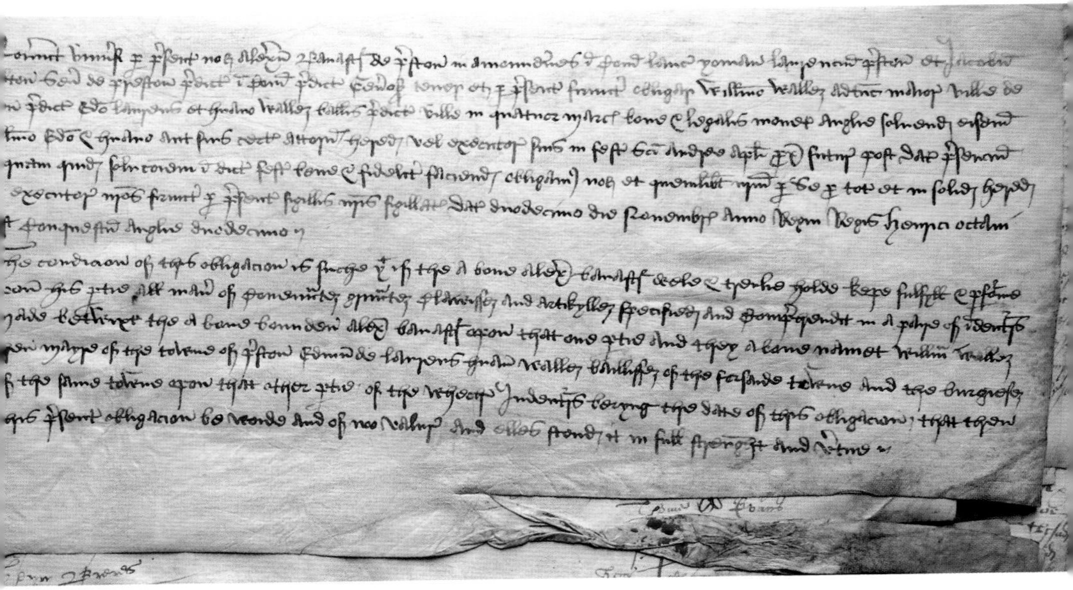

9 This document, the earliest surviving record of the admittance of an individual burgess to the Guild, is dated 12 November in the twelfth year of the reign of King Henry VIII (that is, 1520). The first paragraph is in Latin, the second in English, and the document authorises the admittance of Alexander Banaster of Preston, yeoman. The seal, which was formerly attached to the tag of parchment at the bottom of the page, has long since disappeared. Many hundreds of such documents were issued between then and the mid-eighteenth century, substantial numbers of which survive.

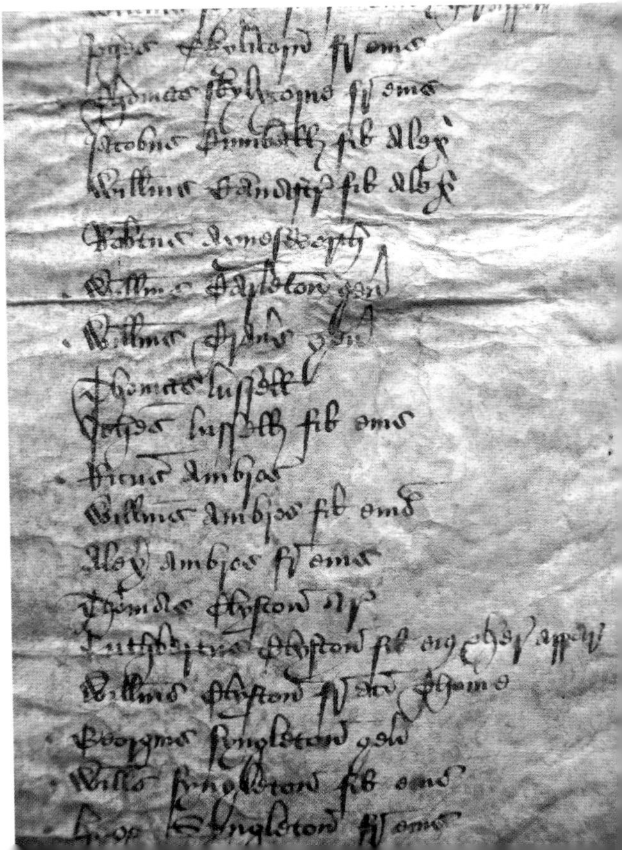

10 This section of the burgess list for 1542 is laid out exactly as all its successors to the present day. The surnames shown here include Ambrose, Clifton (including Cuthbert Clifton, described as 'son and heir apparent' of Thomas Clifton of Westby, the forebears of the Clifton family of Lytham), Skillicorne and Singleton. Many of the entries end with the abbreviation *fil. eius* (his son), emphasising the hereditary aspect of Guild membership.

11 During the seventeenth century the Corporation spent ever greater sums on preparing the Guild Rolls, recognising their great symbolic importance to the town. The Guild of 1662, which closely followed twenty years of warfare and political and social upheaval, was marked by much greater expenditure on the Guild as a whole, reflected in the splendidly decorated title page of the Guild Roll.

Greene Ricus Sadler	Gurnell Johes — jur
Greene Robtus fr ejus	Gurnell Hugo fil ejus — jur
Greskam Andreas fil Antony	Gurnell Johes fil ejus
Graystocke Wittus — jur	Gurnell Robtus fr pd Hugonis
Graystocke Thomas fil ejus	Gurnell Johes fr ejus
Graystocke Evanus fr ejus	Gurnell Wittus fr ejus
Graystocke Jacobus fr ejus	Garlick Johes — jur
Graystocke Henricus fr pd Witti jur	Garlick Thomas fil ejus
Graystocke Thomas fil ejus	Grymbaldeston Johes de Treyles jur
Graystocke Ricus fr pd Henrici jur	Gregory Benjaminus
Graystocke Petrus fil ejus	Garstang Jacobus Miller — jur
Graystocke Philippus fr ejus	Garstang Robtus fil ejus
Graystocke Thomas fr ejus	Grymshaw Jeremia — jur
Graystocke Georgius fr ejus	Greenfeild Chroferus Ar jur
Graystocke Thomas de Reon Hib fr pd Ric	Greenfeild Wittus fil ejus
Graystocke Ricus fil ejus	Greenfeild Chroferus fr ejus
Graystocke Lawrencius fr pd Thom	Goodshaw Thomas Butcher
Gradwell Wittus fil Witti defunct	
Gradwell Matheus fr ejus	
Gradwell Thomas fr ejus	
Gradwell David fr ejus	
Gradwell Thomas Grocer jur	

H.

Hodgkinson Henricus fil Thome vn Scutton Gilde	
Gradwell Wittus fil ejus	Hodgkinson Ricus fr ejus
Gradwell Matheus fr ejus	Hodgkinson Lucas fil Rici defunct jur
Gradwell Jacobus fr ejus	Hodgkinson Wittus fr ejus
Gradwell Josephus fr ejus	Hodgkinson Henricus gen
Gradwell Johes fr ejus	Hodgkinson Lucas fil ejus
Gradwell Edrus Shoomaker jur	Hodgkinson Ricus de Whalley Curne
Gradwell Henricus Butcher jur	Hodgkinson Johes fil Georgii defunct
Gradwell Wittus fil ejus — jur	Hodgkinson Georgius fil Jokis defunct
Gradwell Ricus fr ejus	Hodgkinson Thomas fr ejus
Gerrard Ricus Apothecary jur	Hodgkinson Ricus de London Ribbonweaver
Gerrard Ricus fil ejus	
Gerrard Thomas fr ejus	
Greenfield Thomas fil Luci defunct jur	

12 One page of the list of in-burgesses, from the 1682 Guild Roll. This is the first Guild for which we have a complete eye-witness account, and it is clear that even then the Guild itself was regarded as a remarkable and venerable historical survivor. The importance of tradition and continuity is highlighted by the adherence to the use of Latin for formal Guild documents.

Orders Concerning Brick and diging of Sodds

Whereas wee finde by daily Experience that the Common belonging to this Towne, And being the Antient Inheritance of this Corporation, are now much Strayed, Wasted and impared, by the profuse makeing of Brickes, and the ounertsarie getting and Siging upp of Sodds for the perticular beniffitt of some private persons, and not only to the prejudice of the Herbage and Pasture of thesame, but to the great hindrante of the Antient wayes, and passages about this Towne, and also to the great Losse hindrante of the Common Burgesses, the Inhabitants of this Towne, for remedy whereof for the due prevention of the like Inconvenienties in time to come

13 From the sixteenth century onwards the Guild orders (in effect, the byelaws of the borough of Preston) were read out at the Guild Court and then carefully written up in successive Guild Rolls. These were the formal rules by which the citizens of Preston were supposed to conduct themselves (… though it is hardly necessary to add that they rarely did). Here in the 1662 Guild Roll, Prestonians are ordered not to dig up clay (for brick-making) and turf on the commons at Deepdale.

14 Like the elaboration of the Guild Rolls, decorating the town for the Guild became a matter of high priority for the Corporation. By the middle of the nineteenth century the scale of the event, and the crowds (and income) which it attracted, meant that the Council put the business out to tender. Here, in 1862, Messrs Womersley & Co. of Leeds showed by vividly painted sketches how they proposed to decorate the Public Hall, scene of dances, assembles and banquets throughout Guild week.

15 The construction of ceremonial arches across the main roads leading into the town became a feature of Guilds in the nineteenth and early twentieth centuries. There was considerable competition to create impressive and spectacular designs, as the Moorish Arch which was erected over Church Street in 1902 clearly demonstrates.

16 The arch constructed for the 1902 Guild across Garstang Road close to Moor Park, was less complicated than some but nonetheless impressive both in its scale and the lavish expenditure of time and money which went into decorating the structure. In more recent Guilds the building of triumphal arches has unfortunately gone into terminal decline ... mainly for traffic reasons (the middle of Garstang Road is no longer really suitable for a group photograph)!

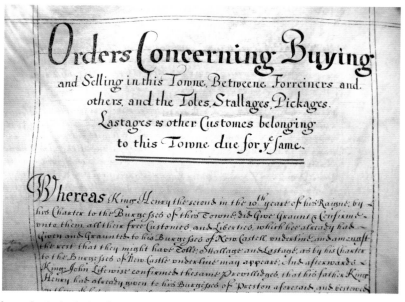

17 The first order (or byelaw) to be written out in successive Guild Rolls was that concerning the powers and privileges of the Guild itself. This extract from the 1662 Guild Roll refers to the fiscal aspects—tolls, stallages (stall rents), pickages (a charge for pitching booths or tents at the market) and lastage (charges for carriage of goods). The main text begins with a recitation of the legal basis of the Guild in the royal charters of the borough. The first line wrongly states that the charter of Henry II was granted in the 10th year of his reign—it was in fact the 25th.

18 The earliest visual portrayals of the Guild date from the middle of the eighteenth century. For the Guild of 1762 a series of somewhat stylised drawings was produced, showing each of the trade companies that walked in the procession. Here the Weavers Company walks carrying (apparently very precariously) a handloom at which a child sits and weaves—a device that was put to much more dramatic effect in the Guild of 1802.

WEAVERS Compy

SKINNERS·&GLOVERS·

19 Also from the 1762 Guild, here we see the Skinners and Glovers, preceded by a couple of musicians playing the whistle and the fiddle, but without any symbols of their trade apart from the flag or banner. This and the previous engraving are taken from Wilcockson's 1822 history of the Guild, but were first published (as part of a larger set) in advance of that of 1762 to act as a form of guide or programme for visitors.

20 This charming hand-coloured print from the 1842 Guild, showing the 'car' of the Gardeners Company, shows something which is recognisably a float in the sense that we understand it—a moving tableau that could be hauled along the streets as part of the trades procession. It is evident that the organisers of the individual trade contributions were going to considerable lengths to prepare a really great visual spectacle, a feature of particular importance as the element of popular participation increased rapidly.

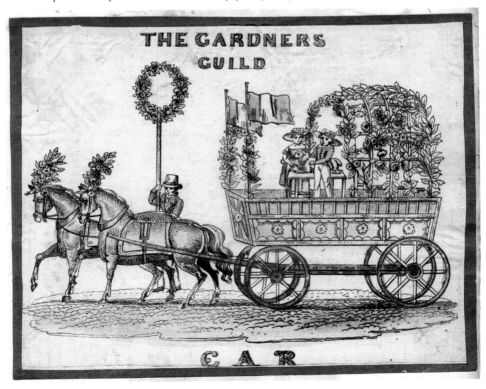

GUILD.

Cotton Spinners
AND
Weavers' Procession.

The COTTON SPINNERS and WEAVERS, resident in PRESTON, who intend to join the Procession on Monday and Tuesday next, are hereby informed, that the said Procession will form between the North End of Chapel Street and Ribblesdale Place; and they are particularly requested to be on the ground, with their Sashes on, at half-past Eight o'Clock in the Morning precisely.

The following is the Order of Procession.

Mr. W. C. CROLE, Marshalman.

BAND OF MUSIC.
COTTON TREE.
FLAGS.
Mr. CATTERALL,
Mr. BAIRSTOW,
Mr. EDWARD CLAYTON,
Mr. JOHN PALEY.
Strangers and other Gentlemen connected with the Cotton Mills, with a Rose of Crimson Ribbon.

Forty Men.
Steam Engines.
Mr. T. AINSWORTH,
Mr. G. HORROCKS.

Forty Men.
Carding Engine.
Mr. CATON,
Mr. W. TAYLOR.

Forty Men.
DRAWING FRAME.
Mr. JOSHUA PALEY,
Mr. OXENDALE.

Forty Men.
FLY FRAME.
Mr. CHEETHAM,
Mr. CRANSHAW.

Forty Men.
MULE.
Mr. ANDREW FERGUSON,
Mr. JAMES SAXTON.

Forty Men.
Band of Music,
COTTON TREE.
FLAGS.
Mr. G. JACSON,
Mr. SEP. GORST,
Mr. JOHN SWAINSON,
Mr. T. PETTY.
Strangers and other Gentlemen connected with the Cotton Manufacture, with a Rose of Crimson Ribbon.

Forty Men.
WINDING MACHINE.
Mr. DILWORTH,
Mr. JOHN HORROCKS.

Forty Men.
WARPING MILL.
Mr. VOSE,
Mr. POLLARD.

Forty Men.
LOOM.
Mr. J. DEWHURST,
Mr. JOHN PARK.

Followed by the remainder of the Workmen employed in the Cotton Trade.
The Gentlemen leading each Division to have White Wands.

BY ORDER OF THE COMMITTEE,

W. Davis, Secretary.

Preston, August 30th, 1822.

W. ADDISON, PRINTER, CHURCH-STREET, PRESTON.

21 The detailed evidence for the appearance and organisation of processions increases rapidly from the 1782 Guild onwards. Here is the proposed arrangement of the 1822 Cotton Spinners and Weavers Procession. The emphasis is on technology, with floats bearing full-sized examples of steam engines, a carding engine, drawing frames, mule spinners and winding frames, as well as the more symbolic cotton trees carried aloft. Some 360 men and 24 masters, together with an unspecified number of 'other gentlemen connected with the cotton mills', walked in the procession, followed by any cotton worker who wished to participate.

22 The 1862 trades procession, which has passed under the triumphal patriotic arch on London Road and is now doubling back to return to the town centre. In the foreground is the float carrying members of the Preston Volunteer Fire Brigade, complete with axes, and on the right are the fishermen, in a flag-bedecked rowing boat on top of a cart, supported by other members of the trade carrying creels and imitation fish stuck on the end of pointed poles.

23 The trades procession in 1952 reflected both the past and the future. The most famous of all floats, perhaps, was the giant pig of Myerscough's the provision merchants. Constructed for the 1902 Guild, it had become a firm favourite with the Guild crowds. The pig, like the firm itself, was a reminder of Preston's ancient role as the main market and retailing centre in mid-Lancashire.

24 Provisions of a quite different sort were represented in 1952 by Frosted Foods, with the catchy new slogan 'Quick Frozen Foods—Save Time And Money'. The lorry carried two large commercial-sized chest freezers, and not a lot else.

25 In 1952 Preston and its people fervently hoped that industries based on the new technologies would be able to compensate for the rapid decline in cotton, the staple industry, that had taken place since 1922. The technological revolution was perhaps best exemplified by the float representing the Ministry of Supply's new atomic energy research and development centre at Springfields, which placed the Preston area in the forefront of progress.

26 During the Second World War the aircraft industry had grown with extraordinary speed in Preston itself, and at nearby Samlesbury and Warton. The pride of Preston was the Canberra bomber, and in the 1952 Guild this was paraded through the streets—albeit in portions, as it was too large for a single vehicle to carry. Here, before the Trades Procession, the gleaming Canberra and a fleet of lorries line up outside the English Electric works in Strand Road, then, amazing to think, still setted.

27 In the 1952 Exhibition an extraordinary range of trades, industries and commercial concerns was represented. A particularly popular exhibit was the Atkinson's Bedding stand, with its king-sized bed, spectacularly extravagant upholstered headboard, and copious use of satin and velvet (or near approximations to the same). After years of austerity such excess was highly appealing—as was the enticingly under-dressed lady who sprawled on the bed. Even better, she (and it) were also prominently displayed on a lorry during the trades procession ... though unfortunately it poured with rain and the bed had no built-in umbrella!

28 As well as the trades procession, Preston's industrial economy has been showcased in the Guilds of 1952, 1972 and 1992 at exhibitions and trade fairs during the Guild. The programme and catalogue for the 1952 Industrial Exhibition encapsulates the nature of the Guild—a medieval-style trumpeter, bearing the Lamb and Flag of Preston, proclaims the exhibition against a silhouetted background of the industrial town. Many councillors at the time would, however, have preferred a more contemporary image.

On the third day was the great procession of the trades, in their companies 'with their respective Colours flying, Kettle Drums, French Horns, Trumpets, &c.'. Two grand balls were held in each week of the Guild, 'to which every Person, who went properly dressed, was admitted'. There was also a ladies' assembly twice a week, on Tuesday and Thursday, and a trades assembly on Wednesday. The various groups associated with the Guild were thus carefully segregated with appropriate events for each: gentlemen, nobility and persons of superior rank, ladies, and persons engaged in trade were each awarded full participation, but rarely did they come together at the same events. The great majority of the townspeople did not participate at all, but enjoyed themselves by watching the proceedings and visiting some of the entertainments, amusements, exhibitions and sideshows which the Guild already attracted in 1762.

The Guild was a spectacle known throughout Lancashire, and beyond. It is clear from the 1762 account that there were sizeable crowds in the town, watching the processions and the other official events, and partaking of the fairground amusements and sights. This was not a new phenomenon: in 1742, for example, Richard Kay, a very sober and serious doctor from Bury, had recorded in his diary:

30 September 1742 This Day in the Morning Sisters and I went with Cousin Pilkington's and some other Friends to Preston Guild, heard a Sermon preach'd at the Church by Mr. Peplo [the vicar of Preston] from Esther 9.18,19 for that Solemnity as he observ'd which happen'd only once in 20 Years, after Sermon we saw the procession of the Handicraft Men and Gentlemen according to their custom.

Kay was accustomed to end his diary entries with a worthy sentiment. Perhaps he found the levity and extravagance of the proceedings rather disturbing, for this entry concludes with the solemn plea: 'Lord, In all Places and Companies ever keep us in sober serious and good Frame; O, thro' Grace ever keep us watchful and careful, humble and dependant.'[17]

The wide public interest which the Guild now attracted is shown by the lengthy reports that appeared in Manchester, Liverpool and London newspapers, giving details of preparations and comprehensive accounts of what took place. The *Manchester Mercury* reported on 27 August 1782 that 'we hear from Preston, that no expense is spared to render their approaching Guild agreeable'. It stated that the Guild would last two weeks, the first being largely devoted to the usual ceremonies and the second to the races and other diversions, both weeks being interspersed with 'Oratorios, Concerts, Plays, Masquerades &c.'. Its correspondent had heard that 'A good deal of the genteel Company is expected from all parts of the Kingdom, as many Lodgings are already engaged for their reception'.

The 1782 Guild programme followed broadly the same pattern as that of 1762, a pattern which is recognisable to this day and parts of which can be identified in Kuerden's description of the 1682 Guild. The diversions which had been secondary to the main Guild celebrations grew more and more numerous and varied from at least 1742. After 1842 they become one of the chief reasons for holding the Guild.

The celebrations were described by journalists in a style so florid and elaborate as to seem almost a parody. In 1782, as in 1762, it was the procession of the ladies which particularly attracted their attention: the *Manchester Mercury* for 24 September 1782 reported that 'The Procession of the Ladies afforded a Sight to the Lovers of the Fair, truly delightful; they were all dressed in the extreme of fashion, the height of the ton, and shone with a brilliancy and splendour that dazzled the eyes of the beholder.' A writer describing the 1802 Guild said that 'Lancashire is certainly the envy of the world for beautiful women ... Such an assemblage of beautiful women has seldom been seen under one roof.' [18]

Smoothness of organisation, orderliness and regularity during processions, and adherence to the traditional procedures were all features noted with approval by the writers of 1762 and 1782. That these were certainly not guaranteed is revealed by events at the Guild of 1802. It began, as usual, with the formal opening of the Guild Court by the mayor, attended by the trade companies with flags, regalia and bands of musicians. The *Manchester Mercury* then describes how, after the arrival of all the companies had been announced to the mayor he attempted to progress to the parish church for the civic service,

> but in vain: and in making the attempt a scene of great confusion took place, for the crowd was so immensely great, that although the street where the Hall is situated is very wide, it was completely blocked up from one side to the other; the shopkeepers were obliged to shut up their shops to prevent the windows being broken. The noise and confusion that prevailed was not in the least inferior to what takes place at a large assemblage of persons in London, on a public exhibition. The time being arrived for the Corporation to go to Church, which they always do agreeably to ancient custom at every Guild, they gave up the idea of forming a regular procession at that time, and got to the Church in the best manner they could. The Church was in a short time so completely filled that there was no possibility of getting near the door.

The raising of extra constables for the 1822 Guild has already been mentioned, and the events of 1802 make it clear that there was a genuine if, with hindsight, remote potential threat to public order. Guild crowds have almost always been good-natured, but there were many grievances which a less friendly and more hostile gathering could have exploited—after all, the Guild of 1822 was only three years after Peterloo. This was one reason for the careful segregation of the more delicate participants from the rough boisterousness of the masses. In 1762, as the contemporary account says, the procession of the ladies was kept safe from the crowd by the trade companies which lined the route. In 1802 the Guild organisers not only made sure that constables were available (special constables had been sworn), but also that the military was brought in. A detachment of the Seventeenth Light Dragoons was on hand and these, it was reported, 'materially assisted in keeping the multitude from pressing in upon the procession'.[19]

Multitudes there certainly were. Readers of the *London Chronicle* of 30 August 1802 (just before the start of the Guild) were told that Preston was 'London in miniature; for the number of pedestrians passing and re-passing through the principal streets was astonishingly great, while carriages of all descriptions poured, in one almost continuous line, from all the roads leading to the town, and particularly from Liverpool and Manchester.' The *Annual Register* for 1802 was of the opinion that the Guild had been celebrated with extraordinary splendour, and that 'it never fails to bring from all parts of the Kingdom crowds of visitors to so unusual a spectacle'. All contemporary accounts comment upon the numbers of people involved, the traffic jams, the crush of humanity during the celebrations. In 1802 the heat and crowds were so great that the Countess of Derby almost fainted, and the populace pressing at the doors of the Guildhall before the procession of the ladies was so numerous that the constables and soldiers, though armed with long staffs, had the greatest difficulty in preventing the people bursting in.

The extraordinary enthusiasm for the Guild, and the widespread popular interest that it generated, are shown by the quantity of souvenirs and memorabilia which were produced from the early eighteenth century onwards, and which became a veritable flood by the middle of the nineteenth century. At the Guild of 1742 there were already sellers of souvenirs. The *Preston Journal* of 24 September 1742, for example, includes a large advertisement inviting subscriptions for 'A Just View of the Procession, of all the Companies with their respective banners; the Corporation in their proper Habits; also the Gentlemen, Ladies, &c. at the GUILD in *Preston*.' The view, 'Drawn on the Spot by Mr. WORSEDALE, Painter from London' was to be 'engrav'd with all Expedition, and printed on a Sheet of Super royal Paper'. The pre-publication price to subscribers was 2*s*., the normal price 2*s*. 6*d*. The list of places where the engravings would be on sale indicates how wide was the interest in the Guild: Lancaster, Liverpool, Ormskirk, Wigan, Warrington and Manchester, as well as Preston itself.[20]

Thereafter the production of Guild souvenirs gathered pace rapidly. Commemorative medals were first struck for the 1762 Guild, and became a standard feature of all subsequent celebrations. From 1842 it was customary for medals in cheap base metals to be given to schoolchildren, originally just to those who had participated but later to all children in the borough. Medals in bronze, silver and gold were struck for presentation to visiting dignitaries and for purchase by burgesses and others who could afford them.

By the mid-nineteenth century, the medals were a useful source of additional Guild income for the Corporation. In the nineteenth century, too, as the age of mass-produced souvenirs dawned, increasing numbers of cheap gifts and ephemera were available at each Guild: mugs; plates and cups; programmes and handbills; paper serviettes; rosettes and ribbons, and many other items.[21]

Souvenir booklets and brochures also appeared at every Guild from 1762 onwards, and publishers and booksellers competed strenuously to produce the most detailed and comprehensive publications, and to have them on the bookstalls and news-stands as early as possible. These publications are, of course, an invaluable source of information about the Guilds, though naturally they tend to flatter the participants. The Corporation published programmes of events for each Guild from 1802, but official retrospective volumes did not appear until 1882. There was a considerable market for an official record, including the opportunity to give presentation copies to visitors and dignitaries, but the Corporation also wanted a lasting account of the organisation and celebration which made the record quite clear (including the record of its own involvement). The idea immediately caught on, and after each subsequent Guild a volume entitled *The Official Record* has been produced. They have usually been written in a deeply grave and ponderous style, perhaps as a corrective to the exuberant and florid prose of the journalists who described the Guild events as they happened.[22]

The Guild processions

In 1682 there was only one procession, which included the official party and the trades companies. Although there were other mayoral visits to church, with attendants and followers forming a train, there was no formal public procession except on the first day. Nor was there any ladies' procession, although, as will be seen, there were already special events for ladies. The 1702 and 1722 Guilds are not described in sufficient detail by eyewitnesses for us to be able to say what processions there were, but in 1742 Richard Kay went to see the procession of the 'handicraftsmen and gentlemen' after church, which implies that this was a similar public procession to that in Kuerden's description.

In 1762, however, the procedure seems to have been altered extensively. The formal public procession that opened the Guild, and which followed the pattern of Kuerden's description, took place on the first day. On the second day was a separate ladies' procession which, like the mayor's procession of the previous day, involved a walk to church and then a short perambulation around the town centre. This is the first record we have of such a procession, and it seems reasonable to suppose that it was an innovation for this Guild in response to growing pressure from the ladies to be allowed to participate.

Equally innovative for that Guild was the first recorded procession of the trades alone. On the third day, Wednesday 1 September, the companies gathered at the Town

Hall and paraded through the town centre streets with musical accompaniments and flags and banners flying. Hitherto the trades had had no separate part in the Guild. Thereafter their procession became a very important event, which attracted special attention and which was increasingly elaborate in its organisation. Whether the change was intended to give greater publicity to the trades or (perhaps more likely) that the gentlemen no longer wished to walk with the craftsmen and artisans is not clear, but it was a development which profoundly affected the future character of the Guild. A 1762 Guild record published by Thomas Anderton may have been sold as a programme for those who came to witness the pageant, to tell them which company was passing by.[23] It lists the trades which marched and briefly describes their dress and emblems. The list includes:

1. The Tanners' Company; musicians; the flag of the company; the wardens of the company, bearing wands; members of the company in the dress of their trade

2. The Weavers' Company; musicians; a weaver working at a handloom, on a frame carried by four bearers; members of the company

3. The Woolcombers' Company; musicians; banner; man on horseback, with gown and wig, carrying a comb; wardens with wands and streamers; members of the company

4. The Masons' Company; musicians; banner; wardens bearing staves; members of the company in trade dress

5. The Cordwainers' Company; musicians; banners; two men in 'antique' costume with long cloaks and plumed hats; wardens bearing wands; members of the company

6. The Carpenters' Company: musicians; banner; marshall of the company; boys bearing wands topped by bunches of oak leaves; wardens bearing wands; members of the company in trade dress

7. The Butchers' Company; musicians; banner; wardens bearing wands; members of the company in trade dress

8. The Vintners' Company; musicians; banner; wardens bearing wands; members of the company

9. The Tailors' Company; musicians; banner; 'two figures, nearly nude, representing Adam and Eve'; wardens; members of the company

10. The Skinners' and Glovers' Company; musicians; banner; wardens; members of the company

11. The Smiths' Company; musicians; banner; a figure on horseback carrying an axe, representing Vulcan; wardens; members of the company

12. The Mercers' Company; musicians; banners; wardens; members of the company.

The list suggests that the procession had already acquired the basis of its modern form. Previously there had simply been groups of men marching with flags and emblems as part of the general procession. Now, since they formed the focus of attention, some ambitious companies decided to include more elaborate and impressive props. Thus the weavers had a form of float: a large frame carried by four men, on which sat a man weaving at a loom. The tailors, in token of their role in clothing mankind, had nearly nude figures of Adam and Eve. As the procession had become more popular it was being designed deliberately to appeal to the crowds who would be lining the streets. No longer were the companies concerned with the trading privileges which went with Guild membership, for these had almost vanished: instead, they were part of a spectacle, and were rising to the occasion with showmanship on an unprecedented scale. Thomas Wilson, author of a verse on the 1762 Guild, found the sight of Adam and Eve worthy of special mention:

> I'd the pleasure to see our old Grandmother Eve
> but how Adam was tempted I cannot conceive
> For her face & her Eyes seemed no fitted for slaughter
> & I'm sure she scarce has so ugly a daughter
> I cannot observe on peruseing her face
> the Remains of one dimple or trait of one grace
> & if truth may be spoken our Grandfather Adam
> is stupid & awkward & clumsy as madam.[24]

The division into separate processions was evidently successful, for the same procedure was followed in 1782 and again in 1802, when the order of the companies remained basically the same as in 1762. For the 1802 Guild there are detailed descriptions of the costumes and insignia worn by participants and, as befitted a town in the throes of industrialisation, there were many signs of modern factory industries.[25] Although the Guild was an ancient celebration the new trades were very anxious to participate fully, and they made a deep impression on observers.

The Tanners' Company wore blue coats. Their hats were trimmed with green ribbons and oak leaves, while the wardens of the Company had sashes of office over their coats reading, in gold lettering, 'Success to the Tanners'. Some of the Company carried a banner with the motto, 'We trust in God alone'. The joiners, cabinetmakers, carpenters, coopers, chairmakers and millwrights formed one large group. Two tall masked men carried large hatchets and leather cases, as though they were going to cleave timber; on the cases were a brass saw and a hatchet, symbols of their trade. Six boys followed them, clad in green jackets with velvet collars and gilt buttons, and green caps trimmed with green feathers and bunches of oak leaves: they symbolised foresters and forestry. All the men in the Carpenters and related companies wore blue ribbons in their hats.

The hats of the tailors were decked with ribbons of blue and pink, and ten apprentices wearing green pantaloons and white hats with oak leaves brought up the rear of their procession. The splendid symbolic theme of their 1762 procession, Adam and Eve, was used again in 1802. Near-nudity may have been too shocking, or perhaps the weather was too cold, for on this occasion the two wore white cotton gowns with large fig leaves sewn on in the appropriate places. Eve carried a large branch laden with apples, and as they passed through the streets she tempted Adam to eat. It is easy to imagine the pleasure and delight which this tableau must have given to the watching crowds.

The spinners and weavers came next. John Horrocks had opened his first mill only a few years before, but Preston was fast becoming a major textile centre. This trade company was thus especially symbolic of the changes that were transforming the town, and the manufacturers went to a great deal of trouble to depict the modern age of industry. The spinners and weavers headed their band with a large board edged with a white cotton fringe and painted dark blue, on which had been written 'Prosperity to the Cotton Manufactory'. Then came a spinning mule of the latest type, belonging to one of Horrocks's factories, drawn on a stage. It was worked by a little boy, his hair powdered, dressed in a white cotton turban with blue silk trimmings, and his clothes all of white cotton which he himself had made. His attendant was a small girl, about ten years old, who mended the thread when it broke. She too wore white cotton, and had her hair powdered, and on her head was a wreath of white cotton flowers.

This tableau was received with rapture by the crowds. There were repeated rounds of applause, and the *Manchester Mercury* reported that 'the little creatures worked the machine, and performed their work with as much composure as if they were not seen by a single person, although they were viewed by several thousands, and with no small degree of satisfaction'. How difficult it is, with hindsight, to regard such a spectacle with the same degree of enthusiasm. That particular evil of the Industrial Revolution, child labour, is here sentimentalised, even glorified. The use of little children to work the machines is repugnant to us, but it was accepted by contemporaries. The conscience of society as a whole was not stirred until the 1830s, even though individuals were already campaigning for reform.

After the children came 24 young women, 'selected from different manufactories for their attractive charms', and dressed in cloth made in Preston—white cambric with blue ribbons and cotton fringes. Each carried an artificial cotton 'tree' in her hands, the blooms and leaves being made entirely of cotton: 'the ingenuity with which the leaves were formed, and the whole of the execution, do the highest credit to the taste of Mrs. Horrocks and the female part of her family, who made them.' The women were led by two men, superintendents in the factories, who wore 'white cotton jackets and trowsers, with white cotton epaulets on their shoulders, and tassels of the manufacture of the town, and with white cotton turbans ornamented with purple silk'. They, too, carried artificial cotton trees. The comments of their friends in the crowd might well be imagined.

Behind them came the factory owners. John Horrocks and John Watson, the great rivals within the Preston cotton industry, marched arm in arm and carried white wands, to symbolise the peace that reigned between them (but only for the duration of the Guild).[26] Then came more than a hundred workmen, two by two, and another board, topped by a silver urn and inscribed in gold letters 'May the ingenuity and industry of the Cotton Manufacturers ever find protection and support in this United Kingdom'. It was carried by a man with powdered hair, an 'uncommonly white' shirt with purple ribbons on the sleeves, and, daringly perhaps, no coat or waistcoat.

Another power loom was drawn on a stage or carriage by twenty men: on the stage were two boys, all in white except for gold fringes on their turbans. One, aged thirteen, was weaving, the other, aged eleven, was winding on bobbins. And finally, fifty master weavers and their sons and between two and three hundred ordinary workmen completed this lengthy and spectacular part of the procession.

Eliza Parker, a spectator at the 1802 Guild, wrote (without punctuation!) to her father that

> in my opinion the Cotton Trade was best worth seeing five and Twenty of the Handsomest Girls out of factories was pick'd out and was dressed in Cambrick Muslins with head dresses of Purple silk these went first with vasis of Cotton put on little green sticks ornamented with green leaves and then a Boy winding Bobbins and a nother weaving it is said that the machinery cost Mr. Horrocks eight hundred pounds.[27]

When the 1782 Guild was held the cotton industry in Preston was in its infancy. By the time of the next Guild, in 1802, the town had been altered dramatically by the boom in textile manufacturing. This was the first Guild in which the cotton manufacturers were represented. Though new to Preston this trade was able to participate fully in the Guild partly because it had taken over the existing Weavers' Company. The new and immensely rich cotton manufacturers were clearly determined to make the maximum possible impact at the 1802 Guild. With their huge resources and large workforce Horrocks and his colleagues could put on a magnificent display, and no expense was spared. The results were a great success with the crowds, and gave them a thrilling spectacle of colour and novelty, but it might perhaps be wondered what the old-established merchants and townsmen thought of it all: 'only been in the town ten years and now look at him'.

After the cotton trades procession the other companies must have seemed an anti-climax. The butchers came next, about forty of them, with new white aprons and steels, and with twelve of their sons dressed in a similar way. All the butchers had white and red ribbons in their hats. The farriers, or shoers of horses, followed, with an impressive display led by a man representing Vulcan, dressed in steel armour and with a plumed helmet. He rode a horse covered with a scarlet saddle cloth, ornamented with gold lace, and was followed by eight boys in shirts with blue ribbons, carrying gilt-headed white staffs. The members of the Company wore blue trousers and blue jackets with red collars. Their caps were red with tassels on top and fur at the front; they had new leather aprons, and carried new pincers and hammers.

Then came the smiths, plumbers, painters, glaziers and watchmakers, each a small company in its own right. Their wardens led them, carrying black staffs of office headed with gilt, and about thirty men of each company marched in blue coats with dark cockades edged with gold fringes. The 'Peace and Unity' Lodge of Freemasons processed in full regalia, carrying before them an open Bible on a red velvet cushion. There were about fifty of them, finishing with 'an officer called the Tyler. He was dressed in scarlet with a hairy cap, and carried a drawn sword.' The Ancient Company of Cordwainers or Shoemakers was led by two of its Wardens, carrying staffs and sashes emblazoned with the motto, 'Preston Guild, and Success to the Cordwainers'. Their apprentices carried long poles on which were placed ladies' and gentlemen's shoes of different fashions. All wore new red morocco aprons bound with light blue ribbons. And finally came the vintners and innkeepers and the grocers and mercers, all of whom were apparently too unremarkable to be described in detail.

The novelty of the 1802 procession was considerable, and the weavers, in particular, attracted a great deal of attention. The organisers had a remarkable flair for publicity and, for example, arranged that when the ladies' procession paraded around the market place there should be a beautifully made working model of a steam engine 'exhibited for [their] instruction and amusement ... This very curious and singular piece of mechanism attracted great attention.' The descriptions of the 1802 procession, full of colourful details of costumes, tableaux and regalia, show how exciting and dramatic the spectacle must have been. The different companies vied with each other to produce ever more impressive sights, with special effects, floats and tableaux depicting their trades.

The 1802 Guild marked something of a turning-point, for the large-scale and very ambitious procession put on by the weavers was in a different league to anything that had gone before, and set an example by which other companies might in future measure their success. This is very clear from the descriptions of the 1822 Guild.[28] The idea of a moving scene or a tableau, introduced by the tailors in 1762 with their highly effective Adam and Eve, stood them in good stead, for in 1822 Eve again tempted Adam with forbidden fruit. This time, however, the temptation took place on a large carriage, which was decorated with 'an immense Alcove of Fruit Trees', and the tailors embellished the scene with a serpent in a fruit tree, tempting Eve, while she tempted Adam. One reporter noted that 'He resisted her wiles as long as we observed him'.

For this Guild the majority of the companies had upgraded their displays. No longer were mere banners and sashes sufficient. Instead, elaborate and doubtless costly displays, preferably involving moving scenes, were *de rigueur* for any self-respecting trade. Wilcockson's very detailed and informative account of this Guild shows how magnificent some of them had become in response to the show put on by the weavers in 1802. The Tanners, Skinners and Curriers' Company had two flags, beautifully embroidered with the arms of their company, the arms of Preston, the roses of Lancaster and York, a thistle, a shamrock and a leek. They wore blue and white rosettes, and purple morocco aprons. It is, indeed, difficult to imagine how the tanners and skinners could have done anything more than this: moving scenes or tableaux depicting their disagreeable trade would not have been at all seemly.

The cordwainers had a float, drawn by two horses, on which three youths were making shoes and a young woman was doing binding work with leather. As an excellent publicity stunt, two pairs of the shoes made on this occasion were presented to the mayoress, Mrs Nicholas Grimshaw, and the Countess of Derby. A third pair, much more controversially (and, it may be added, in opposition to the political views of both the mayor and the Earl of Derby) was sent as a special gift to the celebrated Orator Hunt. Henry Hunt, later to be Radical MP for Preston, was at the time of the 1822 Guild languishing in Ilchester Gaol for his part in the Peterloo meeting of 1819. This was a daringly radical gesture on the part of the cordwainers, which no doubt earned them a great deal of approval from the people even if the gentlemen and nobility shook their heads in dismay. The cordwainers also bore a banner which asked that their products should be trampled underfoot by all the world!

The carpenters carried the symbols of their trade, while two of their number were dressed as woodmen, 'with hatchets, brown hats, and their faces painted brown, to give them the appearance of men belonging to the hardy ages of yore'. The butchers and vintners were in costume (the butchers bearing 'rosettes of flesh colour and white'). The smiths, represented at the previous Guild by the magnificent figure of Vulcan, this time had two Vulcans, one wearing steel armour and the other brass, 'each attended by two Cyclops in coarse blue trowsers and jackets, with sugar-loaf shaped red caps, and white leather aprons'. Two mounted trumpeters accompanied the smiths, 'playing flourishes occasionally as they passed along'.

There was one new company in 1822, the Letterpress Printers and Bookbinders, who had a float with a working printing press and a man cutting paper at a binder's press. With ostentatious patriotism, they had adorned the printing press with a large bust of King George IV, and the whole assemblage was wreathed with laurel. The printers, although new to Guild processions, clearly knew a thing or two about obtaining good publicity and produced about 3,000 copies of a special commemorative handbill during the procession. Two, one for the mayoress and one for the Countess of Derby, were printed on satin, and the remainder were distributed as souvenirs. There was also a display by the Gardeners' Company or Paradise Lodge, a friendly society, in which a float decorated with a huge crown made of flowers and evergreen foliage was accompanied by three men carrying pineapples, grapes and other fruit. Other members carried between them, on their shoulders, a miniature garden with two little children sitting in it, and there was also, somewhat bizarrely, 'a hollow cone formed of leaves and flowers, with a man in the middle of it bearing it along'. An open Bible was carried by another member of the society, and finally a man, 'dressed in the skins of animals', bearing a naked sword. The gardeners also indulged in mild publicity-seeking when, on the second day, they went to the mayoress and while their band played *God Save the King*, presented her with a tray of fruit grown by themselves.

And what of the weavers and spinners? Having revolutionised the Guild processions in 1802 by the splendour and elaborate nature of their display they could not fail to do even better in 1822, and to overshadow the efforts of their fellow companies. No amateur trumpeters and fiddlers for them: their procession was headed by no less than the band of the 3rd Regiment of the Royal Lancashire Militia. Then came a whole series of tableaux and working machines, each separated by a group of mill owners and managers and by groups of forty millworkers. A working steam engine led this part of the display; then came a carding engine, worked by a man and two boys; a drawing frame, also worked by a man and boys; two men working a fly frame; a spinning mule; a cotton tree; a winding machine worked by (in Wilcockson's odd, perhaps even slightly lascivious, phrase) 'four interesting young females in white cotton dresses' and two boys; a man working a warping mill; and, to conclude the procession, a handloom worked by a weaver, with a reedmaker on the same stage.

'The different machines,' Wilcockson says, 'were fixed upon stages or platforms, and each stage was drawn by a pair of fine grey horses, and conducted by men in clean white waggoners' frocks, made of thick calico.' With so much weaving in progress the mayoress and Countess of Derby would naturally have been expecting some souvenirs, and they were not disappointed. During the processions fourteen yards of calico were woven, and half was given to each lady. The weavers' and spinners' procession included almost 800 workmen and 24 gentlemen mill owners and managers, as well as eight floats and many flags, banners and emblems—all in all, an unprecedentedly large and impressive display. By 1822 cotton was the greatest industry in Preston, and so such a magnificent and dramatic show was in keeping with the importance of the trade. The weavers were no longer just one of several companies: they were now, by far, the most important company in the Guild.

Wilcockson reports that after the processions were over the cotton machines were left working in the market place for the public view. He pays tribute to the skill and ingenuity of the organisers of this procession, and says that 'to a stranger to mechanics, or the process of weaving and spinning of cotton, the exhibition of the numerous machines connected with that process ... was particularly interesting and instructive'. He goes on to link the procession and the Guild display by the weavers' and spinners' with national greatness: since the 'perfection to which the art [of mechanics] has arrived in this country', the technical accomplishment of making machinery, and the wealth produced by the use of machines were, he thought, 'all circumstances which demand the warmest approbation for those who have contributed, not less to our prosperity as a nation, than to our domestic comforts; and in this instance, our public amusements'.

In 1822 the idea of floats and tableaux, pioneered by the tailors and brought to perfection by the weavers, was taken up by most of the major companies, and thereafter the Guild processions became a theatrical spectacle. There had always been colour and entertainment, but now the Guild had become a grand show, aimed at publicising industry and trade. Once upon a time the traders and craftsmen had walked to demonstrate their exclusive hold over the business and commerce of the town; now they walked to show off their trades and to attract publicity, in the manner of an industrial exhibition.

While the processions of the companies undoubtedly provided the most remarkable sights at the Guilds of 1802 and 1822, the other parts of the procession were just as colourful, and the descriptions of them just as lyrical. In 1802 the civic procession which opened the proceedings was specifically called, for the first time, the 'gentlemen's procession'. The companies, with their emblems, were present to honour the Guild Mayor, but the main participants were the civic dignitaries, accompanied by the gentlemen and nobility, who went as usual to a church service and then paraded around the town. The ladies' procession was on the second day, and gentlemen and company members lined the parade route, carrying white rods as a badge of status. The ladies walked in pairs, in order of rank: the Guild Mayoress first, accompanied by the rector; the Countess of Derby and her eldest daughter, Lady Charlotte Hornby; other ladies of the Stanley family; other wives and daughters of the nobility; and members of gentry families from Preston and beyond.

There were, in total, almost four hundred ladies in the 1802 procession, 'all superbly dressed, and adorned with a profusion of the richest jewels. Each of them wore an elegant fashionable plume of feathers, branching from the *coeffure*'. This procession, as before, allowed the reporters to scale unprecedented heights of prose: 'such a brilliant display of beauty, elegance, and fashion, deservedly attracted universal attention and admiration, and produced one of the grandest, most uncommon, and charming sights ever beheld ... So splendid an exhibition of female attractions has seldom been witnessed in this part of the country.'[29]

The 1822 processions took place in fine weather after a week of heavy rain, which was generally thought to be a good omen.[30] The bells of the parish church were rung early on the Monday morning, with a 'select band' from all over Lancashire ringing a complete peal of grandsire triples of 5,040 changes. The trades companies began to assemble at

7 o'clock, and at 9.30 the Guild Mayor, in a carriage drawn by four bay horses, left his house in Winckley Square and drove to the Town Hall, where the nobility, clergy and gentry paid him their respects before going to the parish church for the civic service. The trades companies had assembled in Fishergate and adjacent streets, for by this date there were too many people for a single starting point to be possible, and after the proclamation of the Guild at 10.30 their part in the procession began. They moved down Church Street to Stanley Street, and then came back to the parish church where they waited in ranks to form a guard of honour for the mayor and gentlemen who emerged from the service.

The procession re-formed and went up Church Street, along Cheapside and the west side of the market place, down Friargate to Canal Street, up Lune Street and into Fishergate. It went west as far as Pitt Street before turning back along Fishergate to Chapel Street, through Winckley Square and Winckley Street to the Town Hall.

The description of the procession shows that, because the town had grown, the route of the parade was lengthened so that it passed through the newly developed areas. This policy was to present major headaches for the organisers later in the nineteenth century, when Preston had far outgrown its pre-1800 core. By the 1880s not only did the timetable of the processions have to be worked out with immense care, to accommodate a very much longer route and many more displays, companies and organisations, but the organising committee was bombarded with requests and petitions from residents of areas beyond the centre, asking that the route should pass through their districts.

After the first day's procession in 1822 all the companies 'proceeded to their respective houses of entertainment, and passed the remainder of the day in convivial enjoyments'. The event was said to be a beautiful sight, although Wilcockson had reservations about the enthusiasm with which it was received: 'nothing seemed wanting but a few exhilirating [sic] shouts to make up the character of a gay and most spirited spectacle ... if the crowds below were not rapturous in their plaudits, they appeared, by their eagerness to gain front situations, to enjoy, with satisfaction, the passing shew.'[31]

The second day started with poor weather, and it rained early in the morning or, as Wilcockson contrives to phrase it, 'the clouds about seven o'clock, commenced a discharge of their contents'. The sun came out by the time the ladies' procession began, and 'joy and hilarity again swelled every heart'.[32] The Guild Mayoress, Mrs Grimshaw, felt unable to participate in the 1822 Guild because of the tragic death by drowning of two of her sons in a boating accident on the Ribble, only a few weeks before. Her daughter, Mrs Atkinson, therefore took her place, and favourable comment was made upon 'the peculiar dignity with which she led the magnificent train up the centre isle [sic] of our venerable Church'. Wilcockson, as always, pens an exhaustingly lyrical description of the scene in the parish church during the ladies' service. He claims to be unable to compose a satisfactory description, but has a good try all the same:

to give an adequate idea of the whole, even the combined powers of the most skilful pen, and the animated application of the purest tints of the pencil, must confess their inability to do justice. The bright gems which shone in the head-dresses, surmounted by plumes of nodding feathers; the spangled beauty of the rich flowing dresses; and, above all, the graceful movements of the fair promenaders, must be seen before an adequate feeling can be impressed upon the mind.

Carried away by his own eloquence (he was a journalist) Wilcockson describes the scene when the mayoress left the church: 'the sun shone resplendently; the air, cooled by the rain which had fallen in the morning, felt most refreshing; and we will venture to say, that such a galaxy of beautiful females, was never before assembled in the full glare of the day, canopied only by the azure vault of heaven, since the last festival of Preston Guild.'[33] Of the assembly of ladies in the Town Hall just before their departure for the parish church, another writer, trained in a similar school of journalistic prose, recorded that:

We have not room to expatiate upon the scene, of which, by special favour, we were the only witness; but let our readers imagine everything that is beautiful in female attire, enriched by all the combined efforts of skill and fancy; that attire displayed by persons in whom all the advantages of wealth, rank, education, beauty and fashion were concentrated ... one hundred and sixty ladies ... promenading an elegant room; happiness glowing on every countenance; music playing in the adjoining apartments and among the crowds in the streets; the bright sun shining upon crimson and gold curtains, dazzling chandeliers, pictures, beaming eyes, snow-white feathers, and costly gems; then they will have *some idea* of what we beheld.[34]

The processions of 1822 were described in jaunty verse by the anonymous author of *A New Song on Preston Guild*:

> To see this grand sight, we soon got a good place,
> It surpass'd all the world for beauty and grace,
> There were feathers and flounces and bosoms like snow,
> In beautiful ringlets their hair it did flow,
> The ladies procession was walking,
> The noblemen laughing and talking,
> While each jolly farmer was gawping,
> To catch all the fun at the Guild.[35]

The costumes of the ladies in the 1822 Guild are described with a good deal of accuracy and an eye for detail. The mayoress, Mrs Atkinson, wore 'an elegant silver gauze robe, with head-dress of diamonds and feathers'. The Countess of Derby had 'an elegant gold lama [*sic*] dress; head-dress; plume of feathers and diamonds'. There was lavish use of feathers, diamonds and artificial flowers (this was the end of the Regency period, and these were the height of fashion) and all the ladies wore white or silver except the Countess. Mrs Townley Parker, for example, had 'a petticoat magnificently embroidered in silver lama, with apron and fichu to correspond; head-dress, feathers and diamonds', while Mrs Whitehead wore 'a figured lace dress, over white satin, festooned with flounces of lace and beads, &c, turban with plume of white feathers and pearl ornaments'.[36] Recording the details of dress and costume was crucial, to give the readers a better image of the scene and to explain what those at the height of fashion were wearing. Before television and photography, mass communication and instant access to pictures, descriptions such as these were the only way in which a scene could be conveyed … perhaps the journalists may be forgiven their enthusiastic and extravagant prose!

CHAPTER FIVE

The Guild
as a social event

N OBODY knows what manner of events accompanied the formal enactment of the Guilds in the medieval period and the sixteenth century. The first hints of other activities at the Guild celebrations do not occur until the late sixteenth century, when we know a little of feasts and music. The seventeenth century is better documented, because of Kuerden's invaluable description of the 1682 Guild, while from the eighteenth century we have many other eye-witness accounts. By this time, too, there is an abundance of more or less accurate newspaper reporting, which gives details of the sideshows and banquets, races and galas accompanying the official Guild.

Undoubtedly entertainment and feasting were part of the medieval Guilds, and Kuerden makes it plain that there was already a great deal of tradition and ancient custom about the way the feasts were held. By 1682 some of the social events, such as the mayoral dinners, were already incorporated within an official programme. Others, including the dances and balls, originated outside the formal proceedings but, because they were held for the leading participants (the gentry, nobility and civic dignitaries) must quickly have been accepted as part of the regular programme. Still others, such as the races, began as extras, held during Guild celebrations to attract the crowds and entertain the gentry, but were soon recognised as a special feature of Guild week even though they were not included in the official programme until the early nineteenth century. And then there was a motley and miscellaneous assortment of entertainments which provided the popular holiday fun for the masses—peepshows and puppetshows, fairground stalls, exhibits of curios and many more.

Feasting and banquets

Holding feasts and banquets on special occasions, such as saints' days and mayor-makings, was a widespread medieval custom, and there can be no doubt that such events took place at the Guild even though nothing is known of them. Not until 1582 is there any specific reference: in the Guild orders of that year a cook was admitted as a burgess provided that he agreed to serve the mayor of Preston by providing meat and drink at any feast to which the mayor should call him, upon reasonable warning.[1]

In 1612 the Corporation ordered the abolition of the civic banquet at Easter, on the grounds that the cost had become too great. The bailiffs had traditionally paid for the 'Wine, Beare, Breade, Cheese, Ayle and other Banckettinge Stuffe and provision', not only for the mayor and Corporation but also for any burgesses and others who chose to turn up. This free-for-all feasting produced scenes of chaos, described by the Corporation:

> the concourse and assemblie of people att the same tymes did growe greate, verie turbilente, and unrulie, tendinge (not onely) to the breache of his Majesties peace (but also) divers others Inconvenience thereof.[2]

It was to prevent such scenes of disorder, rather than to relieve the burden on the civic purse, that Guild banquets and feasts were held in private. The cost was a less material consideration, for groaning tables of expensive and luxury food and drink were a feature of the mayoral feastings. Kuerden, who gives the impression that he was a man who enjoyed his food, has a detailed account of the feasts at the 1682 Guild and their complex organisation. The officials who managed the dinners are listed, and the quality and variety of the fare are described with obvious relish. Although Preston was a sophisticated town by Lancashire standards it could not supply many of the luxury goods needed for such an event, and so much of the preparation for the Guild involved menu planning and ordering food and drink, to allow time for delivery from further afield.

Some of the foodstuffs were provided by the burgesses themselves. The butchers, bakers, grocers and other merchants would set aside choice items for the mayor's table, and other burgesses were appointed to make up any shortfall in 'fatt Beef, Veal, Mutton, Pullen, Venison'. The Town Hall cellars and nearby storage areas were made ready for beer, ale and wine. Wine and sack were ordered, 'the best that may be procured from home merchants or from London'. The local brewers were asked to supply 'the best Malt that can be had', and 'the most expert Brewer to be appointed to brew the same'. Before being sent to the cellars it was sampled to see if it reached the 'excellent good' standard required.[3]

The mayor's banquets were supervised by the 'Controller of the Household', who was chosen for this task from among the twelve aldermen.[4] Carrying a white rod of office and wearing his formal robes and gown, he gave directions to the servants, discussed each menu and the preparations for the dinners with the master cook and the clerk of the kitchen, and each morning received the accounts of the expenses incurred in the previous day's feasting. The 'Clerk of the Kitchen' (the title has a fine medieval sound) was in charge of the provisions. Kuerden's description of his duties indicates the great range and variety of food that would be prepared:

> to give order to the Master Cook and Butchers, what beef, muttons, and veals to kill; what venison to prepare, what rabets or variety of fouls, as phesants, green geese, ducks, capons, pulletts; and the Caterars to provide and to be delivered to the Larderer and Cook, to bee in readinesse with other necessarys of the like nature, and with the Baker what bread and flower for the pastrey.[5]

He also supervised the wines and other drink, kept accounts to submit to the comptroller of the household, and was responsible for the other kitchen staff. He was usually a professional, since his was a specialist task involving a wide knowledge of the quality and condition of food and drink, as well as accounting procedures and finance. In many senses the clerk of the kitchen was the lynchpin of the whole operation, and officials with similar duties, brought in from outside, were employed at most subsequent Guilds.

The chief cook saw to the food itself. He gave orders to the under-cooks 'for prepairing such victualls, boyld, roast or baked as he, with the Clerke of the Kitchen and Controller, have considered to be needful ... and to see each dish furnished and sent up with what art, or ornament can possibly be perform'd'.[6] There were under-cooks (who had 'to obey their *Maisters* with all diligence'), servants in the scullery, turnspits, and servants attending to the slaughter. The animals to be eaten were brought alive to the kitchens of the Town Hall and were killed on the spot unless, as in the case of venison and some game, the meat had to be hung beforehand.

Serving the meal involved another group of staff. The chief butler made sure that the plates and serving equipment moved smoothly in and out of the buttery, and entertained strangers 'with all kindness and curtesse [courtesy]'. The strangers were people who, although not entitled to attend the main dinner, were of superior social status and might expect a free snack. The under-butler, perhaps appropriately, looked after the cellars, supervising the drawing of ale and beer for strangers and making sure that the supplies of drink for the great banquets also flowed freely. He was assisted by the 'Yeoman of the Wine Cellar', who was above stairs and ensured that glasses were kept filled, that there were plenty of bottles and casks in reserve, and that the service in the dining hall was efficient. Ordinary servants did the menial and routine work—the officers of the wine cellar, who kept an eye on the operation of the cellar, and the drawers of wine (the men who actually tapped the casks and pulled the corks).

Dining hall staff included the 'Bread Baker and Pantryer', who kept the stocks of bread, cheese and butter, and served them from a pantry which opened onto the dining hall. He was accompanied by the 'Guardian of the Spicery and Sweetmeats', or *spicer*. In medieval England the spicer was the supplier of exotic and rare herbs, medicines and drugs. The spicer at the Guild feasts was in charge of the sweetmeats at the end of the meal. These dishes included sugar and fragrant spices but he also supplied tobacco and pipes. This was less than a century after the introduction of tobacco to England but its use had become ubiquitous, and at an event such as this smoking would be regarded as essential. One writer has commented that 'by Charles I's reign [1625–49] tobacco-smoking was regarded as one of the rites of good fellowship [and was] one of the fashionable habits of the upper classes'.[7]

The table waiters were part of a veritable chain of servants who kept the diners supplied. They were 'young men appointed [dressed and uniformed] decently to carry up meat [from the kitchens], and to attend at dinner or supper, to furnish each guest with plates, beer, or wine, or other viends'. Many of those dining would have brought their own menservants to attend them on their Guild visit, and it was customary for these gentlemen's servants to join with the table waiters, helping their own masters and (if they were not too proud, as the servants of gentlemen were often held to be) lending a hand with other jobs as needed.

The dishes of food were not handed by the table waiters directly, but were brought to the table by two gentlemen servers, who took the dishes as they were brought from the kitchens and then placed them 'decently and in order upon the Tables, the one upon the one side, the other upon the other or opposite side': thus, each man had one side of a long table to supervise.[8]

Before the feast the tables were laid by the butlers, who put out plates, napkins, bread and salt. Supplies of these and of drink would be kept at hand in side cupboards or on serving tables, from which the dining tables could be easily reached. 'Gentlemen of the Napery' looked after these cupboards, issuing instructions to the table waiters about 'where to be furnished with botles of sack, white or claret, and Renish or Frontiniak, or ale strong, or small beer'. They also had to ensure that every gentleman had clean plates and glasses, ample cutlery and table linen, bowls and tankards.[9] Finally, among the army of staff who scurried around at such events was the 'Dapifer', the gentleman-carver who stood at the Mayor's table and ceremonially carved slices of each of the meats as the menu dictated, this being a signal to carvers at other tables that they might begin their work.

But the list of staff does not end there. The 'Marshall of the Procession' or, as Kuerden also calls him, the master of the ceremonies, had a somewhat different task from his modern counterpart. He had to see that dinner was conducted in a dignified way, with all appropriate ceremony, and his duties included supervising the processions and the order of the different companies who walked. He had to conduct the gentry and nobility to their places, in due order of precedence to avoid inflamed tempers or hurt sensitivities, and 'to comit the method thereof to writing for future Guilds remembrance'. All that happened in a Guild was guided by what had gone before, and the recording of procedures and events was of special importance.

The 'Usher of the Hall', in conjunction with the butlers, dealt with unexpected gentlemen visitors. He wore his gown and carried a black staff of office, and if those who came were of sufficient rank and importance he would personally usher them up the stairs to the dining room. Some specially honoured guests might be conducted into the presence of the mayor by the marshal of the procession himself. The groom porters, dressed in black gowns, were the bouncers of the 1660s: one stood at the front door and one at the back, 'to keep of Crouds and lett in Gentry and Strangers'.[10]

The account given by Kuerden also includes a description of the dinner itself.[11] On the first day of the Guild the Royal Standard and the Holy Lamb of Preston were hung out from the Town Hall, to signal the arrival of the mayor and his party at the end of the procession. The groom porter made a way for them, and they passed between the crowds into the dining room, conducted by the comptroller of the household and the usher of the hall. There the party was welcomed, and refreshed 'with good Sack and Biskett' until dinner was brought up. The feast on the first day was the most formal, at which the first course was brought into the hall by the twelve aldermen, as a mark of their deference to the Guild Mayor and his party of gentlemen. The first dish was handed to the waiting gentlemen servers, who placed it 'decently and reverently' upon the table, at which point the mayor and his guests took their seats.

Grace was said by the mayor's chaplain, the meat was blessed, the dapifer carved the first slices, and the dinner began. Music played, the plates were constantly replenished and the glasses refilled: 'nothing is wanted that might give a plenary contentment to the Guests or credit and honor to Mr. Mayor.' Toasts were drunk to the health of the royal family, the nobility and other worthies, and for this purpose 'good liquor, passeth round and round all the Tables'. The last courses were 'great variety of Fruites and Sweet Meates' and then what Kuerden calls the 'concluding dish … all store of Pipes and Spanish Tobacco, drenched well with healths in Spanish Wine'. The chaplain said a closing grace, and then 'the memory of Absent Frends is … revived in the best Wine or Sack, as the Cellar will afford'.

This impressive and lavish meal took place at midday, immediately after the morning procession around the town. The mayor hosted the dinner for the gentry and nobility, and the members of the different companies of tradesmen held their own separate dinners at the same time. These were nominally held in the company halls, and Kuerden suggests that this was the case, but few of the Preston companies had their own premises, so most of the dinners were in fact held at inns and taverns in the town. The companies provided their own 'splendid provisions', but in addition each received a gift from the Guildhall ('a Venison pasty, piping hott, and a great store of Wine and Sack presented from Mr. Mayor').[12] Despite the scale of the feasting and the large amount of drinking in the middle of the day, the participants had to be ready to continue the ceremonies immediately after dinner. The banquet ended between 2 and 3 o'clock, and then the Guild Court was held, with the enrolling of the gentry and nobility who renewed their freedoms. Afterwards the mayor returned with them to the Guildhall, where he 'treat[ed] the Nobles and Gentry very splendidly, with choice of wines', before conducting them to their lodgings.[13]

That was by no means the end of the day's feasting. The departure of the mayor and his guests in mid-afternoon was followed by the frantic clearing of tables and preparation for the evening, when there was a banquet for the ladies who were 'pleas'd to honour Mr. Mayor with their presence'. Kuerden, a witness to these events, gives a personal testimony: 'I have known 200 or more Ladyes & Gentlewomen entertain'd at supper, at 3 or 4 sittings down.' He does not describe the food and drink, but we may be sure that it was less in quantity and richness than at the midday banquet. Ladies would not be expected to indulge hearty appetites for food and drink, but instead to eat in a delicate and genteel way, of more refined and dainty foods, washed down with much less strong liquor—and, of course, there was no smoking.[14]

Further banquets were held on succeeding days, although the costliness and abundance of the food were reduced. The nobility would not have been present later in the week, and there was less need to present a display of extreme quantity and luxury. On the middle Sunday of the Guild the mayor held a dinner, after morning service, for the wardens and other officials of the different trade companies. This was a markedly more basic meal, for these were not men of rank or fortune. While the mayor entertained the leaders of trade upstairs in the Guildhall, 'the young men of an inferior rank' were treated in the buttery below and provided with wholesome fare and plenty of ale. Every day the different companies held their own dinners, for members and guests.

In the seventeenth century the Guild celebrations were very much longer than they would be between the late eighteenth and mid-twentieth centuries. Kuerden thought that six weeks was the usual length of time, and that meant a very great deal of eating and drinking. The importance of the feasting in the Guild celebrations did not diminish as time went on: rather the opposite. As the Guild became increasingly a social event, and the nobility and gentry were more dominant in its proceedings, grand entertainments and lavish dinners were even more essential. In the eighteenth century the mayoral dinners became more exclusive and expensive, and the element of public participation (such as the inclusion of younger men, who were accommodated in the other rooms for food while the great feast was held) was reduced. The Corporation firmly believed that only the best was good enough, and no expense or pains were spared to provide the highest quality ingredients, the most fashionable dishes and table settings, and the finest wines. It was inevitably very costly indeed, which was a main reason why profits from the Guilds became ever smaller even though income rose rapidly. Much of the surplus was literally eaten up during the course of Guild festivities.

In 1702 Ralph Thoresby, a noted Leeds antiquarian and a gentleman of good family and connections, visited Preston during the Guild and recorded his experiences in a journal.[15] It appears that Thoresby was alarmed by the effect that feasting and drinking might have on his constitution, for he attempted to avoid some of the more excessive consumption. One evening, for example, he went to a play with some ladies of his acquaintance in order to escape a session of heavy drinking:

> Dined at Lawyer Starkey's with Justice Parker and much good company. Afterwards at tavern involved in more; to avoid inconveniences, Mr. Kirk and I went with the ladies to a play, which I thought a dull, insipid thing ... but I was the better pleased to meet with no temptation there.

It is clear from his journal that as well as attending the lavish public feasts, the gentlemen and their families who were in town for the Guild had substantial private dinners, either at their own houses or at inns and taverns. The visiting party of which Thoresby was one was 'treated at a banquet' at the 'Guild House' and given choice wines, on the same day as the dinner referred to in the above quotation. The digestive systems of many must have suffered during the Preston Guild.

The published accounts of the 1762 Guild emphasise the quality of the feasts, though it must be borne in mind that the publishers were anxious to sell copies to those who had participated, so they may have over-indulged in flattery. The description notes that on the first day:

> Fifty Ladies and Gentlemen of Superior Rank dined this Day with Mr. Mayor and his Lady, at the Guild-Hall. The entertainment (which was provided under the direction of Mr. Baker of York,) afforded much pleasure. The Table was cover'd with the utmost Taste and Magnificence, and supplied with all the Delicacies, that the most Luxurious fancy cou'd invent, that the Season could furnish, or Expence procure; and no care or pains were omitted to render every thing as commodious and as agreeable as possible.[16]

The feasts were meant to impress the visiting dignitaries, and to show how prosperous and fashionable Preston was. The account points to this feature: 'Mr. Mayor's Table was, during the Guild, adorned with a great Variety of emblematical Ornaments, and no Expence was spared, that might serve to improve its Splendor, Eligance and Accommodations.'[17] Kuerden had shown how the comptroller of the household, a professional caterer, had been the key figure in the arranging and running of feasts a century earlier. By 1762 the elaborate administration had been almost entirely turned over to professionals. From this Guild onwards the caterers, usually brought from far afield, are regularly referred to in the records—often in connection with handsome gifts of money or plate given as rewards for the success of their endeavours.

In 1762 there is also information about the refreshments provided at other events. The grand balls, the social highpoints for many visitors, were a chance to demonstrate the sophistication of the town. Thus visitors were regaled with 'an elegant cold Collation (with a rich Desart of Sweetmeats, and the choicest Wines of all Sorts)' in one room adjacent to the main hall of the Guildhall,[18] while in another room chocolate and tea were provided. Forty years later, dancers at the balls of 1802 were provided with 'Tea Wines Negus and Cake' at the expense of the Corporation.[19]

Wilcockson's account of the 1822 Guild gives less detail about what was actually eaten, but is extravagant in its use of adjectives to praise the quality of the banquets and suppers. He reports that, at the mayor's banquet on the first Tuesday of the Guild, over fifty members of the nobility and gentry sat down to a meal that was 'spread out in all the inviting forms that the skill and ingenuity of the first epicurean talent could suggest'. Special attention was paid to the selection of wines (naturally, of 'very superior quality') and 'there was a profusion of every thing essential to render the banquet at once inviting, hospitable, and inspiring'. As this was a banquet mainly for gentlemen, 'the glass circulated freely, and several toasts were given'.[20] Some idea of the food on offer at these banquets, and the immense variety of drink available, is given by a poem written in advance of the 1842 Guild, but reflecting the experiences of 1822:

> Come up too ye *topers*, of merry good ale,
> Here are plenty of barrels that never will fail;
> Ye drinkers of brandy and swiggers of rum,
> And ye tipplers of punch, too, come up my lads, come.
>
> Ye *drinkers of gin*, which ye'd fain pass for tea,
> And ye, too, ye ladies, that love ratifia,
> Noyeau, cherry brandy, and prime Curacoa, [*sic*]
> Will drive away vapours, and cure the 'heigho!'
>
> Ye *drinkers of water*, the Ribble runs by us,
> Adam's ale is in plenty, so come up and try us;
> *Eau de vie*, ginger beer, soda water, and pop
> Spruce beer ye may drink, till you'r ready to drop.
>
> Ye *gourmands*, your watering mouths ye may wipe,
> We've venison, turtle, grouse, partridge, and snipe;
> Welsh mutton, Scotch salmon, Duch hams we'll bring in,
> Then tuck up your napkins close under the chin.[21]

In 1822 a particularly popular attraction was the 'Mayoress's Public Breakfast'. More than seven hundred people applied for tickets, and the seating arrangements meant that 320 people could sit down to eat at one time. As always, the meal was described as being of the highest quality:

> of the delicacy and profusion of the viands, it would be impossible to speak in too high terms of commendation. Mr. Lynn, of the Waterloo Hotel, Liverpool, who superintended the whole of these arrangements was eminently successful ... The festive board was supplied with all that could invite the eye and please the palate; to enumerate the various dishes and choice viands that decked the banquet, would be to reprint 'Jarrien's new Confectioner'. There was every delicacy of the season, with a most liberal supply of fruit, confectionary, lemonade, ices, tea and coffee.[22]

Mr Lynn was subsequently paid 63 guineas for his invaluable services to the Corporation in providing refreshments, and his assistants, Mrs Bird and Mrs Booth, 25 guineas and 15 guineas respectively.[23] Lynn had been employed as a professional caterer by the Corporation on previous occasions, and his services were held in such esteem that twenty years later he was appointed as the caterer to the 1842 Guild.

Great banquets and magnificent spreads of delicacies were the fare for the gentry, the nobility and the more prosperous townspeople. The ordinary townspeople enjoyed a holiday, too, and the 1762 account records that 'Large Quantities of ale and Beer, and cold Provisions of all Sorts were ordered to be distributed among the Populace each Day'. Generally, though, the populace found its own food: the poem, *A New Song on Preston Guild*, written in 1822, records the less dainty fare of the ordinary folk as well as suggesting the noise and confusion of the time:

> There is mutton and beef, bak'd, roasted and boil'd,
> With cordial for women, and cakes for the child,
> Sausages, puddings, and gingerbread hot,
> Potatoes and dumplings just out of the pot,
> > There were hungry children a crying
> > And some with thirst were a dying
> > While others fat bacon was frying
> The day that we din'd at the Guild.[24]

At the races on Preston Moor during the 1822 Guild the gentry rubbed shoulders with the ordinary people, the 'honest countryman and the industrious mechanic', for whom there was 'no want of temporary places of refreshment [they] quaffed the nut brown ale, for which Preston has always been famous'.[25]

Musical and theatrical entertainment

Music must have been part of the Guild from the earliest times. Then, as now, no procession would have been complete without its bands and marching tunes, and such evidence as survives from the period before 1662 suggests that the town made use of musicians in the celebrations. Thus, in 1562 James Taylor, 'mynstrell', was admitted as a burgess, and it is reasonable to suppose that he would have participated in the musical events of the Guild itself.[26] In the earlier Guilds there would have been pipers and fiddlers, but as the banquets, dinners and processions became more sophisticated the musical entertainments must have become correspondingly more ambitious.

Kuerden conveys well the impression of noise and colour that was characteristic of all Guilds. The church bells rang frequently, with special peals to mark the major events, and bands paraded through the town. At the opening of the Guild, on the first Monday, from 8 o'clock in the morning the trades companies awaiting the arrival of the mayor passed the time by marching 'regularly up and down the streets ... and variety of musick attending each Company'. The young men who were not yet in a company marched in the same fashion, 'with their drums and musiq', and the mayoral procession went through the town 'drums beating, musick of al sorts playing'.[27] The noise, to which was later added the firing of volleys of muskets, must have been tremendous.

The elaborate ritual of the serving and eating of the food took place against an appropriate musical background. When the gentlemen had arrived at the Guildhall and were being refreshed with 'good Sack and Bisket' before dinner, their chatting was dramatically interrupted by a great fanfare, played by '6 or 8 able Musitians, with their wind Instruments', to announce the arrival of the food.

More gentle and restful was the musical accompaniment provided during the banquet. The guests were ushered into the dining chamber, and there ate to the seventeenth-century version of background music, created by placing musicians 'playing upon their stringed Instruments, at a due distance in or near unto the Dyning Roome, as may be most pleasant and audible, to the contentment of the Nobility and Gentry attending at this great Solemnity'. The musicians gave suitable fanfares of farewell and greeting as the dishes were changed. As soon as each course had started, they would 'betake them again to their stringed Instruments as before, their playing melodiously all Diner time, where is all verietye of mirth and good victualls'.[28] The trumpeters had a busy time, for each of the major events included fanfares and when, at the close of the Guild, the Clerk announced its adjournment for a period of twenty years, his announcement was greeted with 'great acclamations by all, "God save the King," and ecchoed [sic] with Drums, Trumpets and a Volley of Shott'.[29]

That was the formal music, for the grand entertainments. Less is known of the other musical events and the informal entertainment provided for those who did not participate

111

in the Guild itself but who took advantage of the celebrations to have a holiday and let their hair down. Ralph Thoresby gives some idea of the din that must have filled the streets of the town throughout the 1702 Guild when, on 3 September, he recorded that he had been 'Disturbed with the music, &c., that I got little rest till three o'clock in the morning'. After his visit to the theatre to avoid excessive drinking he may have hoped for some decent sleep, but if so he hoped in vain. The entry for 5 September notes sourly that he 'rose by five, having got little rest; the music and Lancashire bag-pipes, having continued the whole night at it, were now enquiring for beds'.[30] The pipers and musicians had disturbed the night for everybody, and now wanted to sleep themselves.

A brief report of the 1722 Guild stating that there were 'Concerts of vocal and instrumental music' is the first reference we have to the formal musical events, attached to the official celebrations, which were soon to become an outstanding feature of the Guild.[31] Public concerts and musical events were a development of the late seventeenth century, for until then concerts had been essentially private affairs.

After the Restoration in 1660 it became increasingly common for people to pay for tickets to public musical events, and by the early eighteenth century concerts and public performances by famous singers and musicians had been added to the Guild programme. The music of composers such as Handel and Purcell, whose large-scale religious works were ideally suited to public performance, attracted large numbers of people to such events. Handel's oratorios, in particular, were ever popular at the Preston Guild, and are noted by many writers and diarists.

At the 1762 Guild some of the musical features were little changed from those noted by Kuerden a century before. Each company in the processions was preceded by a 'good Band of Music', and the mayoral party by an 'excellent Band', while during their own procession the trades companies 'paraded the Capital [i.e. main] Streets of the Town, with their respective Colours flying, Kettle drums, Horns, Trumpets, &c.'.[32]

The same account records that during the various breakfasts, banquets and 'concertos' there were many vocal and instrumental soloists, including (as was almost obligatory in eighteenth-century England) a number with Italian and French names (even if they were not always genuinely Italian or French): 'Miss Brent, Signior Tenducci, Dr. Arne, Mr. Arne, jun. Mr. Desaubrys, Signiors Dasti, Blanck, Richter, Mr. Richardson.' There was also Mr. Bromley '(on the Harp)' and Mr. Lambourne, who performed on the 'Musical Glasses'.[33] 'Dr. Arne' was Thomas Arne, most famous as the composer of *Rule, Britannia!*, but also a prolific writer of oratorios, masques and music for theatres and pleasure grounds.

It may well be that during medieval and sixteenth-century Guilds plays and dramas were performed—perhaps mystery plays and mummers in the medieval period, and popular drama in later Guilds—but there is no specific evidence for these. Kuerden's account of the 1682 Guild makes no reference to theatrical entertainment, but as it is concerned with the formal celebrations this does not mean that there was none. As with concerts and public musical events, public theatre flourished after the Restoration and enjoyed immense popularity, and the late seventeenth century saw its introduction to the Guild as part of the ever-widening range of additional attractions.

Although Thoresby went to the theatre to escape from the taverns during the 1702 Guild, the scheme was not a success. In his somewhat jaundiced view, the evening provided a very inadequate form of entertainment: 'a dull, insipid thing, though the actors from London pretended to something extraordinary.'[34]

What is of special interest in this short record, the first account of a play in the history of the Guild, is that it was felt worthwhile to import actors and dramatic companies from London. Likewise, in Thomas Arne the Preston Guild could attract the man who was arguably the most celebrated—as well as one of the finest—English composers of his era. It is apparent that by the beginning of the eighteenth century the Guild was sufficiently important and prestigious for performers to be brought from all over the country, and half a century later it could boast national celebrities. Local talent was not considered to be adequate for the entertainment of the more sophisticated visitors to the Guild, and famous names were therefore an essential component of the programme.

No doubt the actors and musicians received handsome financial inducements to make the long and difficult journey to Preston, but perhaps there were other incentives. It was reported that at the 1722 Guild there were 'two Companies of Comedians' (actors of light, humorous or happy plays and pieces), and there survives an *Epilogue*, written by James Heywood of Manchester, which was apparently recited by one of these actors. It refers, as was the flattering custom, to the remarkable beauty of Lancashire women:

> Ye Batchellors, that lead unsettled Lives,
> In this fair County make your choice of Wives:
> Not only Fair, but Virtuous you'll find,
> Not prone to Vice, nor Vanity inclin'd

And then, in one version, the actor added more lines to hint at one of the other handsome rewards for appearing at the Guild:

> From such our Author prizes one more kiss,
> Than thousands from a Covent Garden Miss.[35]

According to the souvenir volume the 1762 Guild was well provided with theatrical entertainment, because a 'commodious temporary Theatre was built (for the Purpose) in Church street'. The old theatre in Fishergate, built at the beginning of the eighteenth century, was used for popular entertainments, but the new temporary building was the choice for theatregoers of quality. Plays were performed 'by his Majesty's Comedians, from the Theatres Royal in London: viz, Mr. Yates (Manager) Mess. Holland, King, Lee, &c. Mrs. Yates, Mrs. Ward, &c.', with a troupe of dancers as well. Mr Yates was from the Drury Lane Theatre, and was a man of varied talents; he was also responsible for putting on the popular circus-style events at the old theatre.[36]

At the 1782 Guild the programme of concerts, plays and other events was published in advance by the *Manchester Mercury*, among other newspapers. The cultural and social attractions were by this time at least as important as the ceremonies in bringing visitors of social or financial distinction to the town, and there was also plentiful and varied entertainment for the masses throughout the Guild. The *Mercury* told its readers that 'the first week will be taken up with the usual ceremonies attendant on that occasion, interspersed with Oratorios, Concerts, Plays, Masquerades, &c.'. The list included concerts on Tuesday evening and Thursday morning, and morning oratorios on Wednesday, Friday and Saturday. These were accompanied by many balls, masquerades and assemblies, and 'Messrs. Austin and Whitlock's Company of Comedians will perform every Evening during the Guild'.[37]

The descriptions of the 1782 Guild in local and national newspapers include detailed accounts of the musical and theatrical events. The *Manchester Mercury* included a flattering description, apparently to refute a hostile piece written by someone from Liverpool which had appeared in another newspaper. Austin and Whitlock and their company 'had selected the best Performers they could get out of London', but the writer notes that there was a second company of actors in the town during the Guild, an 'Itinerant one' which must have given performances to the populace at much lower and more affordable prices. The oratorios and concerts were 'conducted with a propriety that reflects honour on the Director, and supported by the most celebrated Performers both vocal and instrumental'.[38] A Liverpool newspaper, the *General Advertiser*, recorded that the audiences at the theatre were:

> not less crowded than they were judicious and respectable. The boxes, in particular (which were filled every evening) exhibited scenes of beauty and elegance such as are rarely to be met with even in the theatres of the Metropolis; nor were the performances in any respect unworthy of such distinguished patronage, none but the newest and most celebrated pieces being represented during the fortnight.[39]

A contemporary observer whose record was not published until 1822 also emphasised the variety and glamour of the entertainments and social occasions of the 1782 Guild: 'some of the first rate performers of the day exhibited their vocal and instrumental powers to crowded audiences of nobility and others. The races were excellent and afforded great sport to the lovers of our old English custom of horse-racing. The assemblies were numerously attended by the young and gay, of both sexes, some of which were exuberantly ornamented in the prevailing fashions of the day a *capite ad calcem* [from head to toe].' [40]

The 1802 Guild records include details of the payments made to musicians who were hired for the event. The method of hiring seems more than a little arbitrary—witness the comment appended to the first name on the list—and evidently much depended on the personal taste and the musical discernment of the mayor.

The Mayor offers the following terms to all or so many of the Military band undermentioned as choose to accept the same:

Mr. Snell (if a good performer, but not else)

George Bramwell	James Thompson
Henry Moss	Joseph Farmer
James Parker	James Hegg

Wm. Parker (the Mayor having first heard him play and approving of his playing – not else)

Wm. Parker (Serpent)

Those playing in the mayoral procession were to receive a guinea each and half a guinea for the mayoress's procession (the latter 'being a very short one'). Players at the mayoress's public breakfast were to be paid half a guinea, and those at the assemblies, balls and masquerades would receive twelve shillings per night. They were to include three violinists and a cellist, in addition to which the mayor himself undertook to engage a fourth violin. [41]

Theatrical attractions in 1802 included the famous actor-comedian, Joseph Munden, who played Sir Anthony Absolute in *The Rivals*: 'on his entrance he was greeted with reiterated plaudits by the whole house, which was extremely well filled.' On the Tuesday evening, at the new theatre in Fishergate, *The Poor Gentleman* was performed, with Munden playing Sir Robert Bramble. [42] In the same play were names which are much better known to us: the celebrated Mr and Mrs Siddons, the latter playing the heroine, Amelia. The oratorios were performed at the parish church, with celebrated soloists making special appearances. The first to be performed was *Messiah*, 'composed by Mr. Handel', while the second oratorio concert comprised a selection of pieces of sacred music including *Judas Maccabeus*, *Israel in Egypt* and *Samson*, all works that could be guaranteed to fill the church. [43]

The performers were not paid in advance, and so their expenses were not covered. After the 1802 Guild the mayor, Nicholas Grimshaw, received a letter from Sophia Dussek, one of the soloists. She and her companion, Giovanni Cimador, had gone to

Liverpool after their Guild engagements were completed, and had run out of money.[44] They were due to leave for Birmingham, to fulfil other engagements, and had used up the £60 for expenses which they had allowed themselves. She begged Grimshaw to forward £25 extra, to cover pay for an additional, fourth, Guild performance which they had given, because 'the expenses at Preston were enormous'. Grimshaw had already paid her postage bills and the costs of carriage of her harp from London, and she asked him to deduct these sums from the money, in total £150, which was due to her for her Guild performances.[45]

These sums illustrate well just how expensive and ambitious the Guild had become: £150 in 1802 would be the equivalent of perhaps £40,000 today. The Guild was attracting the leading actors and musical performers of the age, and they were expecting, and receiving, large sums for their attendance. The full accounts for the 1802 Guild show the very great expenditure on musical events:

	li	s	d
Ringers at the Guild [i.e. bell-ringers]	2	02	00
The Band of Music for the processions and public breakfasts	17	11	00
Paid Blennerhasset, an additional clarionet from Liverpool	3	17	00
Three musicians from Halifax, for playing at the Mayor's Ball and Mayoress' Breakfast	6	6	00
Paid the Preston Musicians, for playing at the Public Ball and Breakfast	11	18	00
Payments to 29 musicians and soloists	470	01	00
Conductor and his music	23	14	06
Blennerhasset, for concerts	4	18	00
The Chorus Singers	115	00	00
Removal of pianoforte to and from Penwortham Lodge	1	00	00
Carriage of M. Dussec's Harp and letters	1	06	00
Supply of sheet music	4	10	00
Preston musicians, for assemblies, promenade and masqued ball	42	00	00
Mr. Blennerhasset, for same	8	01	00
Musicians from Halifax, for same	15	15	00
Total spent on musical events in 1802 Guild	724	01	06

The importance of the musical events is clear: as a proportion of the total expenditure on the Guild of 1802, musical events and the provision of musicians accounted for no less than 23 per cent, a remarkably high figure. The Corporation was taking great pains to ensure that its special guests, and the many important and influential people who crowded into the town during the fortnight of the Guild, would be entertained by people with a national or even an international reputation. That this was already accepted is seen by the quality of the acting companies obtained for the 1782 Guild; that it was regarded as money well spent is indicated by the continuation of this policy to the present day.

The last of the old Guilds was in 1822. By that date every detail of the celebration, and all the attractions that were available, were thoroughly recorded. This Guild was the first which had a proper official souvenir programme, published in advance so that the various entertainments and special events had maximum publicity. It included two theatrical evenings in the first week, as well as races, firework displays, balls and assemblies. In the second week, however, the musical events were brought together under the umbrella title of *A Grand Musical Festival*, 'for the Benefit of the PUBLIC CHARITIES of the Town'. The programme noted proudly that 'The First Vocal and Instrumental Performers in the Country will be engaged, whose Names will shortly be published'. It would have been unwise, in view of possible last-minute cancellations, to be too definite. The festival week included three oratorio mornings and two concerts in the evening, together with the traditional balls and assemblies.[46]

The *Liverpool Mercury*, reporting on the success of the 1822 Guild, noted that preparations had been in progress for a year beforehand. Although the main object of the article was to show how the town had succumbed entirely to 'Guild Fever', the description gives a valuable impression of the activity and colour of this, the last Guild held under the auspices of the unreformed Corporation. It states that handbills and posters had been put up all over the town, some of them as long as the side of a house, advertising such attractions as 'De Camp's Theatre, during the *Guild*, with new performers, new decorations, new plays, new scenery, and new dresses'.[47] Everything was novelty and excitement, everything referred to THE GUILD!

Over a century earlier, the theatre was already sufficiently respectable to be attended by ladies and gentlemen. By 1822 it was *de rigueur*, and all those who had the slightest claim to social status and significance clamoured for tickets to attend performances at which the nobility and dignitaries were to be present. The programmes offered seem a little curious to modern taste, but were evidently immensely enjoyable and created a magnificent spectacle. The first night of the Guild included a musical play, *Rob Roy*, at the Theatre Royal in Fishergate. It was claimed that 'the lower boxes presented an assemblage of Nobility, beauty and fashion rarely to be witnessed in a provincial Theatre'. The theatre was 'crowded to excess by the nobility and gentry' and 'a very large part of ladies, friends of the Earl and Countess of Derby, nearly filled the box from the commencement of the performance'.[48] The theatre itself had been completely redecorated and refurbished for the Guild and was, for the first time, lighted by gas.

On the following night the management offered 'the favourite Comedy of *Exchange no Robbery, or Who to Father Me*', a musical farce called *The Agreeable Surprise*, and a re-enactment of the coronation of King George IV that had taken place a few months earlier. This entertainment had already played to packed houses in Liverpool, Manchester, York and Birmingham. The Thursday evening programme was especially popular, and the theatre was attended, in the words of the *Preston Chronicle*, by 'all the fashionable in town'. The fare included a stage version of Sir Walter Scott's *Ivanhoe*, and Sheridan's satire, *The Critic*. The mayoress was present, and the local newspaper noted that the 'stage boxes right and left were fitted up in very tasteful style; the former was occupied by the Earl of Wilton and his lovely Countess, with the Stanley family; and on the other side the party of the Mayoress appeared to great advantage.'[49] The plays, it said, were 'well got-up, well acted, and well received', but the report leaves the impression that the main attractions might well have been celebrities in the audience.

The great music festival, in aid of local charities, was something of a risk on the part of the organisers. Giving to the poor and needy usually involved the distribution of beer, meat and bread dinners, but the 1822 Musical Entertainments Committee attempted to extend the scope of charity. They had to persuade visitors that the musical performances were as socially necessary as the theatrical evenings and the great balls and dinners. On the first morning a 'grand selection' of sacred music at the parish church was attended by 'all the persons of rank and consequence in the town'. It was followed on subsequent days by a 'miscellaneous concert' (one with a variety of short items, rather than a long set piece); a programme of pieces of sacred music in the parish church between 11 in the morning and 3 in the afternoon on the Friday; the inevitable and, as always, very popular performance of *Messiah*; a second miscellaneous concert; and a full performance of Haydn's *Creation*.[50]

Wilcockson was full of praise for the music itself. At a morning concert the audience was

> delighted by the strength, justice and correctness, displayed by Mr. Mori the leader. Braham was in fine voice, and his singing of Handel's Jephthah was an astonishing effort ... 'Behold rude winter flies' from the Seasons, by Haydn, displayed the full deep tones of Kellner's voice to great effect. His fine taste and science was a treat of the first order ... Master Smith is a most astonishing boy; the hymn of eve was sung by him with great taste and science. Mozart's Requiem was never better performed, and was encored.[51]

An evening concert at the Theatre Royal included a flute concerto by Charles Nicholson (1795–1837), an almost forgotten composer who enjoyed much esteem in his lifetime. Liverpool-born and a virtuoso flautist, he performed his concerto in person, 'one of those astonishing efforts of science which no one but himself can execute. The audience were electrified with delight, and testified their approbation by continued plaudits.'[52]

Despite their high quality, Wilcockson thought that these events were less well patronised than the glittering social occasions. He implies that the visitors were not convinced of the social importance of the musical performances: going to the theatre might count as a social occasion, but a concert required a good deal more devotion to culture. Those who had been dancing until the early hours presumably preferred a morning in bed to serious music at the parish church. He says of the evening concert that 'the boxes were quite full, but every other part of the house was very indifferently attended', while his overall verdict is that 'it was evident that the numbers assembled were not equal to the great expence which had been incurred in concentrating so much talent'.

His verdict is supported by the financial statistics. Partly because attendance was lower than expected, and partly because so much expense had been incurred, the great musical festival was a financial disaster. The charities received no benefit from the event. The detailed sets of accounts include such items of expenditure as 'Green Baize for Church Gallery, £13 19 7' and 'Hire and Carriage of Piano Forte £5 14 0' as well as candles and wine for the refreshment of the performers. The fees for vocal performers and instrumentalists cost £1,513 18s. 0d., not far short of the total takings from attendances. Despite £84 in donations from Lord Derby, the bishop of Chester and other patrons, the festival made an overall loss of £265 5s. 2d. In August 1823 a circular letter was sent to the Indemnifying Committee which, wisely, had been established before the Guild. The Musical Entertainments Committee stated that it had applied to the Corporation 'for the liquidation of the deficiency' but its request had been turned down: 'the Committee find themselves very reluctantly obliged to call upon you for your Contribution.'[53] Only a glittering social occasion could guarantee financial success: the highest artistic merit was in itself insufficient.

Attendances at the theatrical performances during the 1822 Guild were also disappointing, perhaps because prices were too high. This, too, was considered by Wilcockson to be a great pity, for the performances were excellent. The performers had been very well paid for their attendance in Preston, but as a further reward in 1822 the leading performers, the great names of London stage and musical life, were entertained at dinner with the mayoral party and 84 gentlemen and noblemen. Some had to sing for their supper: the company was regaled with 'the brilliant singing of Mr. Braham, Mr. Kellner, and Mr. Nicholson'. The 'best vocalists and instrumentalists who could be secured were engaged for these occasions, and the performances are stated to have been admirable'.[54] There is no reason to doubt that verdict: the best was always sought, and usually found, for Guild musical performances.

Balls, masques, dances and assemblies

The participants in the Guild had music wherever they went. Where there was music there was also dance, revelry and merry-making, and this had probably been part of the Guild tradition from its earliest beginnings. In the seventeenth century the dances were the only aspect of the Guild festivities in which the gentlewomen took much part. Many of the other proceedings, including most of the formal business, were either exclusively male, or included women only as incidental onlookers and bystanders. The evening balls and assemblies, on the other hand, gave them a role which always charmed the reporters and record-takers, and inspired the heights and sometimes depths of prose style.

Kuerden devotes a long paragraph to the 'Entertainment of the Ladies', describing how the Mayor was honoured by the presence of 200 or more at supper, at three or four sittings. The evening was passed 'most nobly with a splendid supper, rich banquet, pleasant musick, Balls and revellings, where their excellent skill in dancing is expressed to the full'. No gates, he said, were shut upon any persons of gentry and credit who wished to be spectators, if not participants themselves. The hall was lit by torches held by gentlemen, and the dancing area was cordoned off to keep away, as he phrases it, 'the more intruding spectators'. Around the hall were 'ascents', or raised platforms or stands for viewing the dances:

> Corantes, Galliards, Serabands, with their Castinetts, French and Country Dances, with great delight to the spectators, and glorious reputation to the deserving actors, coming hither from all parts of the County and neighbouring parts upon this occasion ... Morning and Wearines having concluded these revelings; after a new treatment all depart to their severall apartments with their attendance.[55]

This ball, held by the mayor on the first evening of the Guild fortnight, was part of the official programme. In contrast with, for example, the theatrical performances and many of the other entertainments, the balls and assemblies were always integral to the celebration of the Guild itself. Although it is impossible to give a date for the first inclusion of this event in the proceedings, it is likely to have been long before Kuerden wrote. The 1682 Guild was itself based closely on that of 1662 and perhaps the origins of the assemblies may be traced, like those of the banquets and feasts, to the medieval beginnings of the Guild.

In 1682 there was just one ball but, as the numbers of nobility and gentry swelled, the demand for such entertainment grew. Of all the events held during the Guild the balls and assemblies offered the best chance by far for public display. To see and be seen, to wear the latest finery and the most costly jewels, to dance the latest steps—

new to Preston but quite the rage in London—and to show off the skill, grace and elegance of one's dancing technique: what could be more desirable for anybody with a claim to quality? Once in twenty years, to be invited to the dances and balls by the Guild Mayor, to rub shoulders with the nobility, to study very carefully what Lady Stanley and the Countess of Wilton were wearing ... it is not surprising that so much attention was given to this aspect of the Guild, both by those involved and by those who reported on the proceedings.

In 1722, it was noted, there were 'Balls and Assemblies almost every night' attended by a 'great concourse of Nobility. Gentry, &c.'.[56] The Corporation spent an increasingly large proportion of the Guild budget on decorating rooms for the balls and assemblies. The Guildhall itself, built for the Guild of 1762, had a great state room which, like the adjacent chamber of the Town Hall, was (according to the 1762 Guild souvenir booklet) illuminated every night for the assemblies and balls by 'some hundreds of Wax Tapers, in several grand Chandeliers, Girandoles and Sconces': it was reputed that the cost of the candles alone amounted to £200.[57]

The construction of the Guildhall, with its large chamber, made it possible to hold splendid grand dances and assemblies. One feature of the design was that the two halls could be made into a single linked chamber, a huge room 'capable of containing near one thousand People; which Number, it was conjectured by many, appeared therein each Ball Night'. From the 1780s onwards there are detailed newspaper accounts of the assemblies and balls, in which journalistic writing reaches ever more remarkable heights. Special attention is devoted to the masked and fancy dress balls, with long lists of those who attended, giving descriptions of their costumes and, frequently, amusing and sometimes hilarious comments upon the disguises. The Liverpool *General Advertiser* of 19 September 1782 reported that there were more than 300 people at the masquerade held in the previous week, 'a number of whom assumed characters'. The implication is that a full fancy dress ball had not yet been contemplated, but that some of the braver souls hired costume or character masks instead of the customary black facemasks.

If that was so, the notion evidently captured the imaginations of those present, for in 1802 a great ball, still called a 'masqued' ball but with fancy dress obligatory, was held on the last evening of the proceedings as one of the social highlights of Guild fortnight. The ball was attended by over 700 of the gentry and nobility, and the newspapers gave the closest attention to the behaviour, as well as the costumes, of those present:

A Squadron of Lancashire Witches, with Hecate at their head, affected their superiority over hers with great success ... The character of Robinson Crusoe, his man Friday, and a Cherokee Chief, were well supported ... Counsellor Whitehead was very lively in the dress of a clown; though he did not always stick close to his character, his attention being more directed to the Lancashire Witches

... Major Brooke, of Liverpool, drew upon him the eyes of all in the character and dress of an Infant, of 6 feet 4 inches high.[58]

The costumes at the 1822 Guild masked ball were a great deal more elaborate and adventurous.[59] Some of the very important people chose not to conceal their identity too much, and some were downright cowards: the Earl of Stamford, who was lord lieutenant of Cheshire, came dressed as the lord lieutenant of Cheshire. The Countess of Wilton, a well-known figure at court, wore her court dress, and Edward Bootle Wilbraham MP, Baron of the Cinque Ports, came in the uniform of a Baron of the Cinque Ports. It was an unwritten diplomatic rule that the most expensive costumes should be those worn by the highest nobility present. Thus, although the Countess of Derby is described as wearing fancy dress, she wore 'a profusion of diamonds, a train and cloak formed of striped cotton, ornamented with gold. This part of the dress was woven in the procession during the *Guild*.'

But other people really entered into the spirit of the occasion. Lord Stanley was in 'the very characteristic dress of a Neapolitan Woodman. The disguise was so great that very few of his Lordship's friends could, for some time, recognize him.' Thomas Trafford of Trafford was dressed as his own heraldic crest, Robert Townley Parker as an Albanian chieftain; several men came as Highland chieftains, and the Earl of Wilton, more daring than his wife, was in a 'most splendid dress of Turkish costume, richly embroidered with gold and heightened by a profusion of diamonds'. *His* jewels alone were said to have been worth £10,000.

The ladies were much given to the wearing of European peasant costumes, perhaps with the same motives as Marie Antoinette when she dressed as a milkmaid. The Misses Johnson of Knutsford came as Bernese peasants, and the correctness of the costume was 'noted by many who had been in Switzerland'. Miss Greene was a Norwegian peasant, with a 'curious stomacher of fancy buttons', Miss Miller a German peasant, and the three Misses Lyon wore Russian costume. Mr John Haigh, clearly worried that a single costume would fail to make the desired impression, arrived wearing 'superb Turkish dress' and at some point in the evening slipped away to reappear, somewhat improbably, as 'Robin Hood in full costume, with black velvet cap, diamond loop, and white feathers'.

The most adventurous disguise was that of Mr Waterton of Walton Hall in Yorkshire, who came entirely in feathers, as Montezuma: he was an eccentric who had a large private museum, and this was a genuine Aztec cape from his collection. But perhaps the greatest sensation was Mr Gregson of Lancaster:

a Rajah, attended by a native Hindoo servant, with his Hookah ... The impenetrable gravity which he maintained throughout the evening, rendered the illusion complete; his features were finely adapted for such a representation

... The Rajah conversed with several gentlemen present, who had been in India, and excited general interest and attention. The fragrant perfumes of the Hookah which he smoked in the saloon, was very grateful to a crowd of admirers.

The setting for these glittering occasions was new. In time for the 1822 Guild the Corporation had opened the first part of the new Corn Exchange building at the bottom end of Lune Street. This offered greatly improved facilities for holding great assemblies, since the Guildhall chamber of 1762 was by this time already regarded as too cramped and outdated. In his exceptionally thorough account of the Guild of 1822 Isaac Wilcockson notes that the Town Hall and Guildhall were spacious, but that in 1802 'some inconvenience was felt ... from their too crowded state, on a few of the most attractive occasions'.

It was anticipated, correctly, that in 1822 'a much more numerous assemblage of rank and fashion' would attend, and so more capacious accommodation was needed. Most of what was provided was temporary, since the Corn Exchange was intended as a commercial building. Within its shell a suite of rooms was constructed, and richly decorated to disguise the basic and mundane function of the Exchange. Wilcockson, in characteristic vein, felt that the building would be 'consecrated to the memory of all the gay and happy visitors who resorted to [it] in pursuit of innocent amusement, long after [it] has been turned to other uses than those of mirthful jollity'.[60]

He describes the interior decoration, giving a good impression of the setting for these early nineteenth-century occasions. The curtains and couch covers were of 'rich blue moreen, handsomely trimmed with gold coloured fringe, except the saloon, which was hung with scarlet moreen. The principal room was illuminated each night from a massive gilt chandelier ornamented with beautiful glass drops, and containing ten argand lamps [gas lights in which the burner produced a cylindrical flame of great brightness] in globes of ground glass; and from four other superb cut glass lustres for wax-lights.' The Town Hall and Guildhall, setting for the Guild Court and various mayoral events, were also redecorated in a 'handsome Gothic patterned paper', with scarlet curtains and regilded picture frames, and a newly painted wooden plaque which listed the names of past Guild Mayors.[61]

The dances and assemblies, as usual, produced the most lyrical descriptions. Wilcockson thought that the Mayor's Ball was 'a most unprecedented display of fashion', and noted how the company poured into the hall from 9.15 p.m. until 10.30 p.m. from a line of carriages that stretched from Lune Street along Fishergate into Cheapside. 'A more enchanting spectacle it is not possible to conceive, a more agreeable and delightful society never, perhaps, met together; all was harmony, good humour and condescension; a smile of pleasure dimpled every cheek, and the careworn countenance of age refreshed and brightened in the anticipation of the joyous scene.' They danced until dawn: 'the grey hint of streaky morn had spread her cheering light in the horizon, before the sons and daughters of Terpsichore had ceased to trip around the magic circle of her sphere.'[62]

Popular entertainment

All these attractions—the theatre and the concerts, the dances and the assemblies, the feasts and the banquets—were for the benefit of the few. Although over a thousand people attended some of the banquets and balls held in the Guilds of 1802 and 1822, that represented only a tiny proportion of the people living in the town or visiting for the Guild fortnight. The Guild, as contemporaries make clear in their descriptions and records, attracted large crowds of ordinary people, and by the beginning of the nineteenth century the numbers were such that there were serious traffic problems and a desperate shortage of accommodation. How did the ordinary visitors and residents—those who were neither of the noble or gentry classes, nor prosperous professional or business people, and who did not have the money (nor perhaps the inclination) to go to the grand events—amuse themselves during Guild celebrations?

Many, of course, had to be content with the spectacle of the processions, which, as already noted, increased in size and splendour as the eighteenth century progressed. They gave an opportunity for a free show, the like of which was rarely seen: ladies in their lavish and fashionable costumes; gentlemen in uniforms and fine clothes; the mayor, officers and Corporation in their full robes of office; the magnificent horses and carriages; the bands and the shining regalia. All these could be watched free of charge in the streets of the town centre.

The trades processions, too, were an object of immense interest and excitement, with the colourful costumes specially made for the occasion, the chance of seeing a friend or relative marching, and, after 1762, the open-air theatre provided by still or moving tableaux carried on floats and carts. And then, as now, the idea of the Guild had enormous power in its own right. This was not just another celebration, but something quite exceptional. As one ballad about the Guild put it, this was 'our greatest Carnival', and there was a great deal of excitement and pleasure to be gained simply from being present at the Guild.

But the presence of large numbers of people meant that there were many commercial opportunities for those who provided popular entertainments. Sideshows and stalls, curiosities and competitions, circuses and music-hall shows, appeared at the Guild for the benefit and pleasure of the masses. Kuerden, as befits a gentleman antiquarian, makes no mention at all of any of these somewhat vulgar additional events or activities. He lists in great detail the official and formal celebrations, but is silent upon the pursuits of the majority of the visitors to the town. Yet we know that many ordinary folk came even in his day, for he refers, in his account of the procession, to 'the contry people there present'.[63] The Guild was an attraction for those living well beyond the town, but that is his only reference to these people. All these attractions were outside the official proceedings of the Guild, and until well into the nineteenth century did not appear in the programmes of events. Some, indeed, were 'unofficial' until the late twentieth century.

Thoresby gives a very important piece of information. He arrived in Preston on 3 September 1702, the first day of the Guild, and found the town 'extremely crowded'. He was too late to see the formal opening of the Guild Court and the procession, but what he did see was a part of the celebration nowhere else recorded. He and his party

> were in time enough for the appendices, the Pageant, &c., at the bringing in the harvest, ushered in by two gladiators in armour, on horseback, &c. The Queen discharged her part well, but the King was too effeminate. I was best pleased with a good providence that attended a fellow clad with bears' skins, &c., who, running among the mob in the Low-street, by the Churchyard, happily chased them away just before the wall fell, whereby several lives were saved.[64]

It seems, from this evidence, that after the formal procession had finished, and the mayoral party, the gentry and nobility and the trades companies had departed to feasts and banquets, the people of the town had their own carnival. The references to the bringing-in of the harvest and to the figures of a king and queen suggest very strongly that this was an otherwise unrecorded survival of an annual celebration based on folk traditions, rather than specifically a Guild event. It is known from other towns that urban festivals were often derived from very ancient rural traditions, perhaps pre-dating the growth of the town itself. The harvest theme points to this conclusion, since it is clearly rural in its associations. There is another reason why that theme indicates that this was not just a Guild event: a harvest feast must surely have been celebrated every autumn, not just every two decades—but no doubt the carnival in Guild year would have been particularly special, with large crowds and much excitement.

Thoresby refers several times to the music and noise in the night. The people of the town continued their revelry and merry-making while their betters were enjoying themselves at assemblies and dinners. He also went with 'several Lancashire and Yorkshire Justices' to see a remarkable sight: a 'posture-master, who not only performed several uncommon feats of activity, but put his body instantly into so strange and misshapen postures, as are scarce creditable'. A visit to watch a contortionist was clearly not something which attracted only ordinary people—the superior classes were equally eager to see the sideshow. This is the first reference we have to an attraction of this sort, but again it seems certain that such sights must have been part of Guilds long before 1702.

The brief programme of the 1722 Guild refers to 'generous hospitable Entertainment', and also to the Preston horse-races, an event that was soon to become a particularly renowned feature of the Guild and would be included in the official proceedings by the middle of the eighteenth century—largely because the participants, spectators and speculators were almost exclusively drawn from the gentry and nobility.[65]

Moon's souvenir of the 1762 Guild lists many more entertainments, including some which were undoubtedly aimed at the mass of the people. Indeed, he explicitly states that some shows and attractions were put on so that 'no Rank of Persons might be deprived of Amusements, agreeable to them'. While the persons of superior rank were enjoying the London theatrical companies, those lower down the social ladder—but still able to afford tickets—thrilled to exhibitions of daring and feats of acrobatics at the old theatre in Fishergate:

> various Performances on the Slack Wire, by a celebrated Equilibrist; Ballancing, Dancing, Musical Glasses, Singing, Pantomime Entertainments, humorous Farces, &c. as at Sadler's-Wells. There was likewise a Company (in St. John's Weend) of eminent Performers, from London (viz. Francisco, Rayner, &c.) in Lofty Tumbling, Vaulting, Dancing on the Stiff Rope.

Such circus entertainments were not intended to attract upper-class visitors (though some of that class might well visit), and the souvenir points out that 'these and many other Entertainments [were] adapted to the peculiar Taste of People of every Rank'. All around the town—on street corners, in yards, and on open spaces behind the houses and shops (for Preston was still a small town, with no more than three main streets)— were fairground amusements and sideshows. The 1762 souvenir gives a brief but vivid impression of these, and it is clear that they were of the sort that had existed for centuries and were to remain popular until our own age. In several parts of the town, it says, 'were to be seen Puppet Shews, Wild Beasts, Horses of Knowledge, &c. &c. &c.'—and no doubt fat ladies, cows with two heads, strong men and all the other traditional fairground exhibits.[66]

The races on Preston Moor may possibly have started as popular entertainment, although the horses themselves were always owned by the more moneyed classes, but from an early date this event became the special favourite of the gentry and nobility, and was adopted by them. The horse-racing was an annual event, but the prizes and the numbers attending were much greater in Guild years, and the races received a great deal of attention from the journalists. By the mid-eighteenth century they had become a semi-official feature of the Guild, and attendance was almost obligatory for those of quality.

The 1762 account reported that the mayor did not entertain at the Guildhall on race days, because all those who might otherwise be invited to his dinners and assemblies were out at the Moor. Accounts given in the *Manchester Mercury* show that at this Guild there were four days of racing (for four-year-olds, five-year-olds, six-year-olds and allcomers, each for £50). The list of winners includes horses owned by notables such as Lord Strange, Lord Grosvenor, Charles Towneley and the Hon. John Smith Barry. In 1782 the whole of the second week of festivities centred, at least for the gentry, on the races during the day and plays and concerts during the evenings. The four-year-olds' race was won by Lord Surrey's bay colt, with the charming name of Sir Thomas Jellybag.[67]

In 1822 the weather was very poor and heavy rain fell during the first two days of the Guild, which 'considerably spoilt the pleasure of the sport', but according to Wilcockson the crowd of spectators, who were 'of all classes' was still large: 'By two o'clock, the time when the horses started, there was a grand display of splendid equipages, all arrayed in new liveries, glittering in the sun like a birth-day meeting at St. James's.'[68] There were several more races by this time, among them a 'Twenty Pounds for Horses &c., of all ages, that never won Plate, Match or Sweepstakes' on the first day, with a 100-guineas Old Gold Cup, a 10-guinea sweepstake over three miles, a £70 over the same distance, another 10-guinea sweepstake, and a gold cup for three- and four-year-olds, over two miles.[69]

Cockfights were also held, and were well patronised by visitors of the superior ranks. In 1782 advertisements appeared for cockfights, including one between the 'mains', or teams, of Sir Frank Standish and Mr Banister Parker. Cockfights remained popular into the nineteenth century but they were increasingly regarded as unacceptable, and the Guild of 1822 was the last time they were included in the programme.[70]

The author of a letter to the Liverpool *Kaleidoscope*, written on 31 August 1822, just before the start of the Guild, reported that there were scenes of remarkable exuberance and merry-making in the streets. He claimed that 'Preston has become the focus of an immense number of itinerant exhibitions, and altogether presents an appearance of so much gaiety and bustle, as to defy description'.[71] The presence of travelling folk and 'itinerant exhibitions' was widely commented upon, and descriptions make it clear that many of the open spaces on the edge of the town had been used for fairgrounds and amusement parks. Another reporter, this time for the *Liverpool Mercury*, also wrote in 1822 of the bustle and vigour of Preston in Guild week, noting that

There were ... bills announcing a grand circus, with forty performers, and twenty horses, during the *Guild*; there were Races during the *Guild* ... Mr. Ryley's Rooms, with Adam's performances on the musical glasses, during the *Guild*; a Steam-Chariot exhibited during the *Guild*; a mass of Vauxhall entertainments at the Bowling-Green, with Fire-Works, by Madame Hengler, during the *Guild*; Wombwell's Menagerie, during the *Guild*; Livingston's Balloon, exhibition and ascent, during the *Guild* ... Marshall's Panorama of the bombardment of Algiers, during the *Guild*.[72]

These exciting diversions were located in and around the town centre. Adam's and Powell's circus was pitched in Woodcock's Yard in Fishergate, while Wombwell's nationally celebrated menagerie, a travelling zoo, was first in North Road and later in the market place itself. The firework displays were held in North Road, on the edge of the town.

Undoubtedly the greatest sensation of the 1822 Guild was the balloon ascent, which provided a level of popular excitement unparalleled in previous Guilds. Everyone could observe the ascent of the balloon from the streets, and the whole town came to a standstill as the moment of lift-off approached. Livingston, the 'aeronaut', had been asked by a number of Preston gentlemen to provide a balloon ascent as an extra attraction for the Guild. The proprietors of the Preston Gas Company, formed in 1816, saw a wonderful opportunity for free publicity, and offered a supply of gas to inflate the balloon. A plot of vacant land between Fishergate and Friargate, near the present St George's Centre, was hired, and inflation began at eight in the morning. The doors opened at 10 a.m., the admission charge being no less than five shillings. Almost seven hundred people paid to enter, though 'the great majority ... were satisfied with such a view of the phenomenon as they could obtain outside the ground, and, of course, added nothing to the emoluments of the voyager'.

The balloon, 38 feet high and 30 feet in diameter, was inflated inside a temporary wooden building so that any glimpse would be impossible until the critical moment. At 2.30 p.m., when 'the roofs of adjoining buildings and every conspicuous situation in the town were covered with spectators', the doors opened and the balloon was brought out into the open, 'and had a most majestic appearance'. A basket was attached, and the 'intrepid' Mr Livingston (who had done this frequently before, even though this was a first for Preston) was presented with tokens and colours by the Countess of Wilton and the mayoress. A cannon was fired, and at 2.40 p.m. 'the balloon rose majestically into the air to a considerable height, nearly perpendicular, clearing the roofs of the buildings and presenting a most sublime appearance, accompanied by the cheering shouts of ten thousand voices'. The journey was short but extremely rapid, for the 'aerial voyager' at least: observers reported that at about 3.05 p.m. the balloon was seen to descend, somewhere near Clitheroe. News reached the town, later in the afternoon, that it had come towards ground at Billington Moor, but in the course of landing Livingston had fallen out and was badly hurt. The balloon had then risen again and, unmanned, crossed the Pennines to come to rest, much damaged, just outside Selby.[73]

Preston during the Guild: impressions and opinions

By this time the Preston Guild had become a great spectacle. For many people the formal celebrations were almost incidental, since there was so much else to see and do. Trading rights, voting rights and the privileges of the burgesses were forgotten. Instead there was, every twenty years, a gigantic fortnight-long carnival that was without rival in England.

The first account of the town during a Guild celebration is found in Thoresby's journal of 1702. Kuerden describes the procedures for the holding of a Guild but with only minor exceptions he keeps to a purely factual and detached style, and does not give impressions. He conveys the noise and excitement of the first day, with its procession, firing of musket volleys, drinking of toasts, and general celebration, but does not give opinions. But Thoresby was recording, for private purposes, his own impressions and activities, so in his record we have the earliest view of the Guild by an interested outsider. Those describing official celebrations tend to ignore the informal and incidental, but Thoresby's account gives, for example, an idea of the noise and music that went on all night, and of the popular carnival which followed the mayoral business. As already seen, he noted the way in which the town was 'extremely crowded with the Gentry as well as Commonalty', and the enormous numbers of people. The congestion and the crowds are one of the abiding impressions of every Guild for which descriptions survive.[74] It really was something remarkable, and by the late eighteenth century the amateur statisticians were busily producing figures of the numbers who came, the numbers of carriages they used, and the size of the crowds at all of the events.

The Guild was an occasion for versifiers and would-be poets to try their hand at capturing the spirit of the moment, usually with results that are less than outstanding. The Guilds from 1722 onwards all had their ballads and broadsheets; verses, both printed and (usually deservedly) unpublished, have come down to us. They convey, often better than the more ponderous descriptions in newspapers and souvenir volumes, the extraordinary excitement that the Guild generated. The *Epilogue* spoken by an actor at the 1722 Guild concludes:

> May this gay Season add to your delight,
> Pleasures each Day, and Happiness each Night,
> Let no contentious Broils your Thoughts divide,
> Debates of *Whig* and *Tory* lay aside;
> Be chearful, merry, innocently gay
> This joyful Time, this *Preston Jubilee*.[75]

That was the joyful spirit which many versifiers attempted to capture, and which was undoubtedly felt by almost everybody who attended the Guild. With every succeeding Guild the fame and attraction of the festival grew, and with every Guild the crowds coming from far and wide grew likewise. As transport became easier, with the building of canals, turnpikes and, by the 1842 Guild, railways, so thousands more were able to travel to Preston, and the throng became ever larger. As early as 1762 it was reported that the procession on the first day was watched by 'a crowd of many thousand spectators, more than ever known before'. The town was filled with 'an amazing Concourse of People, from many Parts of the Kingdom, and from all parts of the County', who had come to see a 'Spectacle [which] was allowed to surpass any Thing of the Kind, ever seen in the Country'.[76]

The newspapers, as might be expected, were especially interested in the 'genteel Company' and so their accounts are heavily biased to the formal and grand events, but it is clear that very large numbers of ordinary people also came. Such crowds inevitably offered rich pickings for thieves, swindlers and especially pickpockets. The 3 September 1762 issue of the *Manchester Mercury* included an advertisement, placed by the mayor and Corporation, warning visitors to be on their guard. They had had information from the Bow Street Runners that there were 'in divers parts of the kingdom several large Gangs of Housebreakers, Pickpockets, and Sharpers who usually attend Horse Races and other public Meetings, and who are grown so audacious as to commit the most daring Burglaries and Robberies'. These gangs, it was said, were expected to be in Preston during the Guild, and in order to protect the people and property in the town a 'Nightly Watch, consisting of a Great Number of stout, able-bodied Men, properly armed' had been established by subscription among the gentlemen and tradesmen of Preston.

Worries about similar dangers were expressed at later Guilds. In 1802 it was thought that the crush and confusion at the entrance to the Town Hall was partly caused by the presence of pickpockets, who used the opportunity to ply their trade. The police presence at later Guilds was increased and, as already seen, the Improvement Commissioners were very concerned that there should be adequate policing in 1822. 'Prestoniensis', a correspondent of the *Preston Chronicle* writing in its issue of 3 August 1822, expressed these worries (Scotland is mentioned because George IV had just completed a royal visit to Edinburgh):

> It is not improbable that the influx of strangers at Preston may be increased by many of those who have been in Scotland returning this way, at the time of the Guild, and it will be incumbent upon us 'Natives', to keep a sharp look out against bad characters of various descriptions. There will also be a number of 'acquitted felons', fresh from Lancaster Castle, but some of our own constables will probably attend the Assizes, and obtain a knowledge of their persons, so as to keep an eye upon such as may quarter themselves in Preston for the Guild.

The danger of crime did not, of course, deter visitors to the Guild, and only the most timid and inexperienced criminal was likely to have been deterred by the threat of action on the part of the Preston constables. The police were few in number, untrained, and without any experience of the wider criminal world, and catching a thief would have been largely a matter of luck. *A New Song on Preston Guild* (1822) made light of the danger, and hinted, delicately, at there being prostitution as well:

> There was constables doing their duty,
> Young ladies exposing their beauty,
> And pickpockets making their booty,
> The time that we stayed at the Guild.[77]

The Reverend Thomas Wilson, master of Clitheroe Grammar School, was present at the 1782 Guild, and wrote a long verse description of the event, dedicated to Mrs Maria Aspinall, wife of the Recorder of Preston. There is great deal about the beauties of the women, and in particular of the 'Lancashire Witches', the young women who 'with the magic of eyes, and profusion of charms ... bind us with spells and display all their art, to wind with soft fetters in wreaths round the heart'. But the following lines give an excellent impression of the crowded colourful streets of the town:

> All the world is at Preston, the Multitude spreads,
> So thick through the streets, 'tis a pavement of heads;
> Whilst feasting and dancing and music and noise,
> Are the soul of a Guild and the chief of its joys.[78]

Within the town there was an astonishing number of pedestrians, and at all the great events of the Guild the spectators occupied every possible vantage point. During the ladies' procession, in 1802, the mob was so great that bystanders and participants were in serious danger of being crushed, and extra security had to be provided. The windows and rooftops were crammed and, according to one reporter, the roof of the parish church, the steeple itself, and the trees in the churchyard, were all 'thronged with people'. He thought that he had never seen such a crowd when he was in Preston for the opening of the Guild on the Monday, but on the Tuesday the numbers were far greater: 'every street was filled with people, and there was hardly any possibility of passing.'[79]

The anonymous writer of the *New Song on Preston Guild* gave a colourful picture of the crowds and the confusion in 1822:

> Such shoving, such squaling such squeezing between,
> Such tearing of clothes sure there never was seen,
> Such rattling of coaches, upsetting of gigs,
> With their loss of their aprons, their garters and wigs,
> > There was some with their petticoats trailing,
> > And some their new bonnets bewailing

> While the boys tumbled over the railing,
> To get a full view of the Guild.

At the Guild of 1802 an old complaint was revived. It is one which is found in accounts of the Guild (and especially in the private grumbles of diarists) for many years, and was not entirely absent during the 1992 Guild. Preston people, it was claimed, exploited the Guild by charging exorbitant prices, especially for accommodation and transport. The correspondent of the *London Chronicle* reported that 'as much interest is made to procure a lodging as if it were a permanent situation in life … enormous sums are demanded; fifteen guineas a week having been asked for three rooms; houses have been built upon speculation to let during the novel festival.'

Another correspondent of the same newspaper described the 'distress for beds' as being very great, and, far outdoing the other correspondent in horror stories, had been told that fifty guineas had been asked for three beds in a house near the town centre.[80] The rapacity of landlords (and later of cabdrivers) was a familiar theme for the more sour or cynical commentators. A poem written in advance of the 1842 Guild sums up the view of this group:

> All you that come this *Guild* to see,
> With money well provided be;
> For wanting this, your case is bad,
> You'll want both Victuals and a bed!
> A bed of Straw or Chaff, is very high,
> And in the streets all night come lie:
> For Barn or Stable, charge they will,
> One-shilling a night, at *Preston Guild*.[81]

In 1822 everything was gaily decorated. The townspeople had spent twelve months in preparing for the Guild; repairing and decorating housefronts, mending and repaving the streets, refitting shops, repainting public buildings. 'So brushed up, painted, and beautified is the good town of "Proud Preston", that, on entering it, we had pleasure in recognising "an old friend with a new face",' wrote the correspondent of the *Liverpool Mercury*.

On the Saturday before the Guild the visitors began to arrive in their hundreds, and then in their thousands, 'in every description of vehicle, from the carriage-and-four of the Peer down to the humble cart of the Peasant'. Many people came during the Sunday night or the early hours of the following morning, in readiness for the formal opening of the Guild at 10 a.m. on Monday. The *Liverpool Mercury* described the scene and pointed, incidentally, to another very important aspect of the Guild, that of the reunion and reacquaintance of Prestonians from home and from foreign or distant lands and places:

The bells rang merrily; flags waved in the breeze, and all was life in Preston. During the preceding night and early in morning, hundreds of persons had flocked in from all parts. At one private house, on Sunday evening, persons arrived from east, west, north, and south, namely, from Blackburn, Dublin, Carlisle, and Liverpool. It was well remarked by a gentleman who has generally been absent from Preston, but who has attended three Guilds, that such festivals, if they had no other object, were extremely useful in bringing together old acquaintances, and reviving 'auld lang syne' among those old friends, who might otherwise have lost sight of each other for ever.[82]

Preston people often invited old friends and scattered members of their families to visit them for the Guild. William Cross of Preston (the grandfather of Richard Assheton, 1st Viscount Cross), sent this letter to his old, and very close, friend Robert Greaves of Liverpool. William wrote on 24 April 1802, in plenty of time for the September Guild:

Our Guild you know approaches fast & I expect among my Guests our friend Sam & his excellent wife & Mr. Robert Greaves—perhaps you may not know him—but I do, & I hope very shortly to receive his promise by which he now has it in his Power to add another real obligation to the Debts of his very faithful Friend Will Cross.[83]

Invitations were sent out by the Corporation to their special guests, the distinguished patrons and benefactors of the borough. At the top of the guest list was the Stanley family, headed by the Earl of Derby himself. In August 1822 the formal invitations were sent out, though all those who would attend were well aware of the forthcoming Guild long before that date. The replies were expressed in the most respectful terms and, although many of those present were far higher in social status than the mayor and Corporation, the protocol of the Guild meant that on this occasion even the nobility were suitably deferential to their hosts.

Lord Derby wrote in person to the mayor from Knowsley on 24 August 1822: 'It will give me great pleasure to accept your obliging Invitation to dine with you on Tuesday the 3d September at the Guild Hall in Preston.' Lord Derby and his party, when in Preston, stayed in the town house, Patten House in Church Street, which had been in the family since the late seventeenth century. He continued that 'in compliance with your wish expressed in your Letter of this Morning, I have the honor to inform you that I expect ... on this occasion Lord Wilton Lord Stanley & his two elder sons & the two Misses Hornby, & I am sorry that the size of my House will not permit me to have more Company.'[84] Even the greatest nobleman in the county had to limit the size of his party when visiting the Guild, so limited was the accommodation.

Amid all the pleasure and merriment and among all those who eagerly flocked to Preston for the greatest carnival in England there were of course some who were less than enthusiastic. We do not hear very much about them, because their still, small voices tended to be quite overwhelmed by the mighty noise. But occasionally a dissenting note is heard: Richard Kay, the very serious doctor from Bury, whose visit in 1742 has already been quoted, asked the Lord afterwards to keep him ever sober and serious, as though he had doubts about the revelry which he had seen. Another sober observer was Benjamin Shaw, a mechanic, industrious and self-educated, who in 1802 had just been converted to Methodism. Twenty-five years later, in his autobiography, he recalled that:

> Preston guild was Held in august, but such was my deadness to pastimes & austontation, that I never went up the Street, or saw any thing belonging to the guild all the time, for such was my contemp for these things, that I wuld not pertake in the folly as I considered them to be.

By the time of the 1822 Guild Benjamin was more relaxed, and allowed himself to record some of the events of the Guild, noting that the 'Baloon went of Mr Livingston went in it', and that there were 'Races cockings & fair' with 'Horitory [oratorios] in Church'.[85] The 1822 Guild, though, had its gloomy aspect. The *Kaleidoscope* of Liverpool published a poem by 'Adolescens' in its 17 September issue entitled *Meditations at the Guild Fancy Ball Friday, September 6, 1822*: not a very memorable title, and not a very memorable poem. 'Adolescens', it has to be said, was evidently not the life and soul of the party, and must have sat glumly in a corner to pen these doleful lines:

> Few, who so happy now around are seen,
> Shall live to look upon another Guild;
> Full many a spirit, buoyant now, I ween,
> Ere then, Death's icy finger will have chill'd.

> Ere Preston hold this merriment again,
> How many, happy now, shall sleep beneath the urn ...

But perhaps the clearest indication that some, at least, were very unimpressed by the Guild and all its glories comes in a letter written to William Blundell of Ince Blundell by his friend William Statham. The letter is dated 20 September 1822, just after the festivities of the Guild had drawn to a close. Statham states, sourly, that 'The Preston guild interfered a little with our Shooting excursions'.[86] It was all a question of priorities ...

CHAPTER SIX

The 1842 and 1862 Guilds

T H E 1842 and 1862 Guilds have a crucial place in the history of the festival. In 1842 it was decided that the celebration of the Guild should continue, despite the loss of its ancient privileges and the reform of the Corporation in 1835. The decision came at a time of great social and economic change. By the beginning of the 1840s Preston had become a major industrial centre and the railways had arrived. No longer was it a pleasant country town, the residence of gentry and professional men. Instead, it was sprawling, grimy and industrial (the unfortunate inspiration for 'Coketown' in Charles Dickens's *Hard Times*), and the gentry and professionals, although they still had their offices in town, lived elsewhere if they could—in Penwortham, Fulwood and Ashton, or even further afield.

As these changes continued, profoundly and irreversibly altering the town, the Guild also changed. There was more participation by 'ordinary' people, and more pressure for the Guild to involve all groups within the town, rather than just its social and commercial elites. The management of the Guild became a middle-class preserve during the later nineteenth century, under the guidance of a Corporation which was predominantly composed of professional and business men. They used the Guild as an opportunity to make money and to publicise the town and its industries, while introducing (albeit, after considerable public pressure) such elements as the churches and the schools. Their attitude is eloquently displayed by the experience of 1862, when the Guild was held in the midst of the appalling suffering which resulted from the Cotton Famine.

From 1842 Preston was ever more easily accessible. The Guild, as the most famous carnival in the north of England, one whose name had entered the language, was visited by hundreds of thousands of people making good use of extraordinarily cheap railway trips to flock to the town. These invasions were partly attracted by, and partly responsible for, the ever-growing number of fringe activities—the funfairs, the pageants, the concerts, the circuses, the processions of schoolchildren, the military bands, the sports, the spectacular firework displays. In 1842 the Guild was already surrounded by popular entertainments, but the carnival character became even more apparent as additional attractions were added to the official programme. Although the medieval forms survived at the core, they were dwarfed by the showmanship and commercialism of the nineteenth century. These two Guilds set the pattern which has been followed ever since and is in many ways the model for the 2012 Guild.

'To hold or not to hold'

The Municipal Corporations Act of 1835 abolished the old unreformed Corporation, and replaced it with a directly elected body which took office on 1 January 1836. At the same time the customs and traditional privileges of the old Corporation, including those relating to burgesses, burgess rights and trade restrictions and powers, were swept away. These had already become irrelevant in practical terms and, as noted in chapter 4, the role of the Guild in controlling trade and business in the town had been an illusion for many years. The last attempts to enforce the ancient powers had been over half a century previously. But by the 1835 Act these privileges, for so long redundant, were legally and definitively rescinded and, although the Preston Guild was not itself formally abolished, it survived only in name.

This analysis has the benefit of hindsight. To contemporaries the legal position was a good deal more ambiguous. The privileges of the Guild had been abolished—that was certain—but there was much doubt as to whether the Guild itself had ceased to exist. Had it retained a shadowy and vestigial existence even though formally stripped of all power and purpose? The major unanswered question was whether or not there could be any further celebration of the Guild Merchant. If the Guild had been abolished, who could possibly hold a Guild celebration? And if the Guild remained, was there any point in holding such an event? The next Guild was due in 1842, and as the time approached there was much speculation in Preston about what would happen. Would the Guild go ahead as before, would it take place in another form, or would the event simply be abandoned and centuries of tradition ended?

Feelings in the town were divided. Those disposed to legal argument debated the precise implications of the 1835 Act, a piece of national legislation which made no specific provision for purely local institutions such as the Preston Guild. Members of the business community pondered on the obvious commercial advantages offered by the Guild, seeing it as a unique chance for the town to capitalise on visitors coming from far afield—the shrewd among them no doubt noting that the new railway would enable very many more to visit the town than in earlier Guilds. Antiquarian sentiment and concern for historical tradition gave others cause to regret the possible end of the Guild.

Some traditionalists were so angered by the loss of rights and powers that in their view the holding of a Guild would be a hollow mockery and a farce. Others, equally traditionalist, suggested that mere Acts of Parliament should not be allowed to interfere with and interrupt a great and illustrious tradition in a proud and independent town. Many, unconcerned for such high-flown sentiments, simply saw the Guild as an entertaining and enjoyable spectacle, a chance to celebrate and be regaled with exciting amusements and shows. Preston now had a large new working-class population, for whom the Guild provided a rare chance to witness such treats—and, for some at least, to participate in them.

The Corporation itself was very little interested in this contentious topic, and did not think the matter worthy of any serious discussion until almost the last minute. At the end of February 1842 the question of whether or not to hold a Guild Merchant in September of that year was put to the Corporation by the town clerk as an incidental point between discussion of the reform of the grammar school and consideration of a lengthy petition from traders and merchants concerning a proposed new market hall:

> The Town Clerk stated, that he had introduced this matter because it had been the custom in ancient times; but having consulted the Recorder, who was not able to be present this day, and who said that he did not think it desirable to advise that the holding of a Guild Merchant should be adopted at present; the better way would be perhaps to pass over it.[1]

Evidently the town clerk had no personal enthusiasm for the idea. But the opinion of councillors was divided. Councillor Armstrong suggested that since several of his colleagues were known to be in favour of holding a Guild it would be better not to dismiss the idea completely, while Alderman Taylor pointed out that it would not be necessary to make a decision at that stage (the last week in February) because 'not advertising it now, would not prevent a Guild being held'. Since the Guild had to be held in the first week of September, the limited amount of time available might seem to us alarming and the Council's complacency even more so. The time normally allowed for preparations was admittedly much less than today, but even so Taylor was being remarkably nonchalant. It was agreed that discussion should be adjourned until a later (unspecified) meeting.

There matters rested, but within the town the issue was hotly debated and discussed at length: a correspondent to the *Preston Chronicle* on 28 May described it as 'the much talked of question of whether a Guild is to be held or not'. He referred to a meeting of the Council which had been held two days before (26 May) at which they 'did not even condescend to allude' to the holding of a Guild. The correspondent proposed that a public meeting should be held 'at an early day, to devise means for having a festive week in celebration of the Guild, according to royal charters and ancient customs'.[2]

The question of the Guild's future was in danger of passing out of the hands of the Council altogether. On 1 June a meeting was held at the *White Horse*, Friargate, by the pro-Guild campaigners. It was attended by 'several of the most influential members of the Council', indicating that the Corporation was becoming seriously divided over an issue which, only three months before, had appeared to have little relevance. The influential townspeople wanted a Guild even though circumstances had so greatly altered since 1822. At the meeting 'the warmest feeling in favour of a Guild was manifested, and ... it was resolved that a requisition be forthwith prepared and presented to the Mayor, requesting him to call a public meeting of the Inhabitants of the Borough, to make the necessary arrangements for celebrating the Guild Merchant in a manner heretofore accustomed'.[3]

The reference to the customary manner of celebrating is important. Those agitating for a Guild were concerned not just for the continuation of the celebration itself, but also that the traditional forms should be observed. This meant, in particular, that the enrolling of burgesses and the ceremony of renewal should continue, even though it was quite clear to all concerned that it no longer had any practical significance or benefit.

Sentiment apart, the signatories of the address to the mayor knew quite well what the main function of a future Guild would be: they were 'of the opinion ... that the festivities and amusements hitherto attending the celebration of our ancient Guild' should be continued, since this would 'greatly conduce to the interests of trade, and be otherwise beneficial to the town, and a gratification to the inhabitants generally'. Trading benefits and an entertaining spectacle were, henceforth, to be the role of the Guild. Such thoughts were in the mind of a correspondent to the *Preston Chronicle*, who wrote that his friend from Liverpool was asking about the Guild and had said, 'really you should not suffer the thing to fall to the ground'. The friend had proposed processions and other features as usual and, to give the ordinary folk a share in the celebration, 'a good old English dinner for the poor'.[4]

The anticipated commercial advantages of holding a Guild were well expressed by a contemporary (though very unpolished) verse:

> When trade was good in Preston streets, you would not then be met
> With papers stuck o'er many a door, saying, This House To Let;
> But let us hope trade will revive, and they may all be fill'd,
> Then people will more pleasure take at famous Preston Guild ...
> Then in the hope of getting gain some people will attend
> Just to pick up the odd brass which other people spend.[5]

On 8 June what was described by the *Preston Chronicle* as a 'highly respectable and numerous meeting' of the pro-Guild campaign was held in the Town Hall. It was chaired by Alderman Jacson, who was supported by other members of the Council and 'influential gentlemen of the town'. Reports of the meeting show that the enthusiasm for the proposed Guild was in considerable measure engendered by local patriotism and pride, and by a good deal of nostalgia for the supposed Golden Age before the 1835 Act. There was also a lot of interest in the considerable part which a Guild might play in promoting the welfare and prosperity of Preston. One speaker believed that, whatever his personal feelings, the mayor could not fail to be persuaded by the strength of support for a Guild among the townspeople. He felt 'quite sure that there was no reason why [the mayor] should not surrender every sympathy of his nature to promote the honour and glory of Preston'.

The same speaker noted the great distress in the town and the acute problems faced by many Preston citizens, 'especially of the operative class', as a result of a slump in the cotton trade. He hoped that the Guild would encourage business and so help to alleviate these problems. By holding the Guild it might be possible 'to relieve that suffering, and withdraw from the trade of the town that which was so deplorably affecting it … He hoped sincerely that the poor, even the most wretchedly poor in the town, might become active and almost equal participators in every enjoyment, in every pleasure, in every comfort, and in every happiness, aye, even in every gala which … might crowd into the week of enjoyment.'

Waxing still more lyrical, and carried away by the emotion of his own eloquence, the speaker boldly stated that unless the poor were happy as well, there could not be 'that prevailing happiness, that universal accord of benevolent sentiments which ought to characterise the rational enjoyments of intelligent man'. Ending with a noble oratorical flourish, he proclaimed his confidence that 'all would unite in prayer, that, by holding of this guild, the ancient days of glory of Preston would return; and that there should be no strife but as to who could contribute most to each other's happiness; the only rivalry being, that he should most enjoy himself who could best promote the welfare of his whole community, by wiping away the tears from the eyes of the sorrowful, by ameliorating the suffering of the distressed, and thus perform his duty as a guild burgess of the town, in accordance with the highest duties of morality and the high behests of religion.'

Not a dry eye in the house? Certainly, the newspaper report notes, there were prolonged cheers! Faced with such flights of dramatic fancy, and with such persuasive arguments—that the holding of a Guild was no less than a Christian duty and was morally essential—the outcome of the meeting was of course in no doubt. While it may be questioned whether the gentlemen present would really have welcomed the attendance of the most wretched of the poor at all the galas, balls and dinners, and whether all would really subscribe to the notion that their duty was to promote the equal happiness of all, it was very difficult for them to resist the nobility of the thought that lay behind such speeches. No doubt all those who attended, and voted to address the mayor formally, went home bathed in a rosy glow of virtue and contentment.[6]

The Corporation had little choice but to bow to the wishes of the meeting. On 23 June a special meeting was held to discuss the matter. Alderman Monk opened the discussion by stating that at the meeting of the inhabitants a resolution that a Guild should be held had been carried unanimously, and that the Council would 'not be doing justice to those people not having a vote in the council, if they did not endeavour to carry out the wishes of the inhabitants of the town'. With startling disregard for the events of the previous four months, he suggested that 'the corporation were the persons who ought to take the lead in bringing forward the celebration of the guild'.

The Corporation at this period was composed largely of traders, merchants and industrialists—the mayor was no less a person than Samuel Horrocks, cotton magnate, and nephew of the more famous John—and Alderman Monk went straight to the heart of their special concern. The Guild, he said, 'would be the means of bringing together a great concourse of people, who would, no doubt, bring to the town a considerable sum of money'. He reported that the gentlemen who had promoted the public meeting did not wish to say how the Guild might be celebrated, or to imply that the procedures followed in past Guilds should necessarily be used in that of 1842. But they were of the opinion 'that a week's amusement might be got up, both to the pleasure and the benefit of the town at large'.

Monk referred in some detail to the depression in trade that was affecting the town: 'if there was ever a time when it was necessary to induce persons to come to the town to spend money, that time was now.' There followed a lengthy discussion among the members as to the holding of a Guild and, more particularly, about what form that Guild might take. Their worries centred on the legal and constitutional position of the Guild and the burgesses following the reforms of 1835. Alderman Haydock pointed out that the 1835 Act effectively removed all real purpose from the Guild and that, it might be argued, it even made the holding of a Guild by the Corporation impossible. He suggested that the Guild could not be held for trading regulation, or for enrolling burgesses (who were now enfranchised independently of the Guild) or for the promulgation of byelaws, or for any other form of regulation of the government of the town, and thus it had no function. It would, therefore, be simply for the purposes stated by Alderman Monk: entertainment and making money. In that case, Alderman Haydock argued (with ample logic but little sentiment), it should simply be called a festival, and the title 'guild' should be dropped completely.

As chief spokesman in favour of a Guild, Councillor Armstrong replied by claiming that the holding of a Guild was legal under the 1835 Act. That had removed the elements of voting right, freedom from tolls, and the ability of the Guild Merchant to restrict trade to its members or to pass byelaws for the town, but it had not abolished the Guild Merchant, and Guild burgesses therefore still existed. He supported strongly the argument that the Guild would bring trade and income to the town: 'He had had letters from Liverpool, from which he learned that several thousands of people would visit Preston from that place, if there was a jubilee, who would not come if that was not the case ... these persons would of course bring considerable sums of money with them.' Armstrong, an elected councillor, also made another telling point: 'by countenancing the guild, which was all that they asked of them, the council would be fulfilling the wishes of their constituents: and that when the guild of 1842 had passed away, as their memories dwelt upon the occasion, their constituents would say to them, "Well done, good and faithful servants; enter ye into the joy of your Lord".'

Such was the persuasive argument: the economic well-being of the town, the happiness and welfare of the poor and the unemployed, the civic pride and honour of Preston, and even the councillors' chances of being re-elected at the next poll, all apparently depended on the holding of a Guild. The outcome was inevitable, and gone was the uninterested, casual attitude of late February. The motion to hold a Guild was carried by fifteen votes to one, only Alderman Haydock dissenting from the majority. It should be noted, however, that there were actually three aldermen and twenty councillors present, as well as the Mayor and the Recorder, so at least seven must have abstained. Clearly the holding of a Guild was by no means unanimously favoured, and a number of members were still not prepared to commit themselves.[7]

Having passed the motion the Council voted to advertise the Guild Merchant in the *London Gazette* and other appropriate publications; to form a committee to supervise the necessary arrangements; to ask the Mayor to preside at the Guild in accordance with ancient tradition; and to appoint the aldermen, recorder, clerk and other officials of the Guild. The *Preston Chronicle* concludes its report of this important debate: 'No sooner had the intelligence of the result of the deliberations of the council been publicly announced, than the bells of the Parish church commenced ringing their lively and ancient peals.'[8]

So, despite the doubts and the debates, the 1842 Guild went ahead after all. Outwardly it was little changed. The formal proceedings remained as before, and it seemed as though the continuity of the celebration was being maintained. But there were crucial underlying differences. Most notably, the holding of the Guild had become a public matter, involving the town as a whole—or, to be exact, the more articulate and influential members of town society. It was no longer the sole preserve of the Guild members and the unreformed Corporation. Immediate differences were small, but after 1842 it was increasingly accepted that the formal business was a small part of the Guild, and that most of the week would involve the participation of the rest of the town. Other elements in Preston society—the churches, employers' and (eventually) workers' organisations, schools, cultural and civic groups—were anxious to become actively involved.

Some have thought that the Guild was captured by the middle-class business and commercial interests of Preston for purposes more sinister than making money and having a good time. One writer a quarter of a century ago suggested that the Guild was perpetuated not only for commercial gain but to 'undermine class conflict', keeping the workers quiet at a time of Chartist agitation by making them think that they had a place in society.[9] In this view the inclusion of spinning operatives in the processions as early as 1802 had been 'an inducement to them to accept the prevailing community values without disturbing social unity',[10] while the 1842 Guild was intended to project 'a new, more bourgeois value system asserting order, hierarchy, prosperity, and rational pursuits ... this new harmony would be contrived and manipulated from above, and not naturally dispelled from all levels of the community as in the past.'[11]

This seems a curiously idealised—indeed, naïve—image of a pre-industrial Preston where peace and harmony and popular democracy reigned. It also implies that the middle classes of 1842 were outstandingly Machiavellian in their plans for the Guild; motivated by vested interests and the prospect of financial returns they may have been, but the notion of the Guild as an anti-working-class conspiracy does not really seem to be supported by adequate evidence. To hold a carnival once every twenty years would have been, to say the least, an odd way to pacify anyone: the employers and the middle classes had far more powerful weapons at their disposal. This view also does less than justice to the intelligence of the workers, who were certainly not the credulous dupes which it implies.

Many local people must have been very cynical about the continuation of the Guild, and about the motives which lay behind the agitation, and some at least did see a clear difference between the 1842 Guild and those that had gone before. The anonymous author of *A New song on Preston guild 1842* (not to be confused with *A New Song on Preston Guild*, published in the same year), although generally approving of the Guild and looking forward to its excitement, did note the unfortunate circumstances of the workers and a contrast with 1822:

> The times are hard, the wages low,
> Some thousands to the Guild cant go,
> From Blackburn, Burnley, & Chorley still,
> They will roll on to Preston Guild ...
> So young and old, I'll tell you true,
> It's different now since twenty-two.
> The men did labour with good will,
> Its not so now this Preston Guild,
> But let us hope the times will mend,
> When the poor man can the poor befriend,
> We want our rights and then we will
> Have plenty of sport next Preston Guild.[12]

Nevertheless, there is a clear difference between the nostalgic view of how things were 'in the old days' and the idea that there was a deliberate plot to manipulate the workers. Making money seems to have been a far stronger—indeed, the overriding—objective of the organisers of the continued Guild.

The same writer also argued that the holding of the Guild was intended to 'provide for the working class, in its dearth of leisure pursuits, wholesome activities that would be uplifting and enriching'.[13] He claims that many of the events 'reveal a distinctive middle-class aura of respectability and self-help' (he cites cricket matches, boat races and wrestling matches) and says that 'The bourgeois councillors, the Guild officers, and their social entourage wanted the best of both worlds; exclusive status and prestige for themselves, and conciliatory, stage-managed rational pursuits for everyone else.'[14]

In his view these attempts failed because the working classes organised their own informal events, and the 'stage-managed' events were, he claimed, poorly attended. This overlooks the evidence which shows that similar popular and informal events, enthusiastically patronised by the working classes, had been part of the Guild for generations. Working-class entertainment at the Guild never appeared on the programmes and received only the scantiest of mentions in the press, but there is no doubt that it had been flourishing for a very long time. To suggest that this was something new, a working-class rejection of the offerings of the organisers of 1842, was totally to misunderstand the character and evolution of the Guild. It also seems to underestimate the desire of the middle classes to enjoy themselves. It is more probable that the organisers held wholesome and rational pursuits—cricket and wrestling matches and boat races—for their own entertainment, rather than to enrich and uplift their inferiors.

Without question, in 1842 the Guild became even more of a commercial, money-making event. In that it bore a close resemblance to the five previous Guilds, while the trend towards commercialism had been apparent for well over a century before that. Decisions about the Guild were, in the nineteenth century as in the seventeenth and as in the early twenty-first, taken by those who occupied positions of social, economic and political power. That has always been the case. The Guild was organised by the Corporation, which was made up of the leading professional and commercial men in the town, so (regardless of the merits of their actions) it was inevitable that they represented their own interests. But there was a genuine growth in a truly popular element, and participation by the townspeople did widen and increase. Schoolchildren walked, churches carried their banners, and workers in large numbers were involved.

The view of the Guild as something more than a grand carnival overestimates its real importance. In the long years between its celebration few gave it serious thought, and any grievances or working-class discontent which it might temporarily have concealed would have surfaced again within days of its conclusion. After 1842 the Guild was an occasion to promote and publicise Preston, to celebrate the town, and to let collective and individual hair down. It had a very high degree of symbolic significance, as it does today. In the year or two before a Guild was due, and in the Guild year itself, the town would have been very conscious of the institution, and have experienced growing excitement— again, a phenomenon which has manifestly grown since the mid-nineteenth century.

Nevertheless, very few people imagined it had practical significance between those times, even though most would have approved of it in principle.

The 1842 Guild is important because, as a result of the deliberations which took place in the spring and early summer of that year, the final say on whether or not the Guild should be held and the manner in which it should be celebrated was left to the Corporation. The impetus for its celebration came from the town, rather than the Corporation, and the management of the Guild could very easily have passed to a self-appointed committee which directly represented leading business and professional interests. Instead, because time was short and the Corporation had always managed the previous Guilds, the pressure groups left the matter in their hands. In consequence future Guilds were, without any significant opposition, run by the council and not by outside committees, although at all Guilds after 1842 the commercial and community representatives were vital to the decision-making process.

Thus continuity of procedure was maintained. Had the management passed out of the hands of the borough council the formal Guild Court and the place of the enrolment of burgesses in the procedures of the Guild would certainly have vanished, since no lay committee had, or could have had, any power to confirm or renew burgesses in the Guild, or to admit them for the first time. Since the Guild Court and renewal of membership had for centuries been central to the whole event, the character of the Guild would have been drastically altered if they no longer took place. Furthermore, it is easy to imagine how, once the formal renewal of admissions had ceased, there would have been nothing to prevent the organisers from holding the Guild more often than every twenty years, and thereby removing its special uniqueness.

The acceptance by the Corporation in late June 1842 that a Guild should be held left at most only two months for its preparation and organisation, and a committee made up of the mayor, four aldermen and five councillors was requested to tackle the matter. They met for the first time on 18 July, when they formed themselves into a series of sub-committees to deal with each major aspect of the Guild. There were then only six weeks left. One sub-committee had the task of obtaining plans and estimates for the temporary conversion and decoration of the Corn Exchange as a ballroom; another was to 'conduct the Musical Department'; and another to organise the processions, except for the school processions. Finally a large group, including several people co-opted from outside, dealt with the public breakfasts and balls.[15]

This method of organising such a great event at short notice was efficient and effective, even though the 1842 Guild saw a major increase in the number and length of the processions and a very much wider range of official activities as well as the strictly formal business. The conclusion of the *Illustrated London News*, that the 'proceedings of the present Guild have not been inferior to those of any on modern record', is a tribute to the success of the organisers who triumphed despite a daunting challenge.

They were helped in this task by another, crucial decision. It was agreed in mid-July that the 1842 Guild would be much shorter than those that had gone before. Up to the Guild of 1822 the proceedings had lasted a full fortnight, with most of the ceremonial in the first week; entertainments, including the races, in the second; and banquets, dinners and assemblies throughout. The reduction in length to one week, primarily because of shortage of time for organisation, made the celebration far more manageable, and so became the pattern for future Guilds.

To emphasise the continuity between this Guild and those of the past the Corporation decided, on 27 July, that its members would be obliged to wear their full robes during the Guild: 'it appears that at the opening of all previous Guild Courts, the Corporation have assisted at the ceremony in Gowns [and so] it appears desirable that at the opening of the Guild Court of 1842, the Stewards of the Guild, and the Members of the Council generally, should assist at the same in Gowns.'[16]

Continuity was also to be emphasised by the preparation, after the Guild, of a splendidly illuminated Guild Book containing the names of those admitted as burgesses. As the power of the Guild had waned, the cost and elaborateness of the Guild record had grown, but after 1842 the lavishness and brilliance of the decoration were unprecedented. The estimate for the costs of the 1882 Guild Book (not written up until 1894) states that vellum would be used, as it was 'much superior to parchment for this purpose', and 'the Binding will be Red Levant Morocco full Bound polished or Plain & elegantly finished with the Borough Arms stamped on if desired', at a cost of £25 10s. 0d.[17]

With the respect for tradition firmly established, all should have been well with the 1842 Guild, but its prelude was far from being the happy celebration anticipated by the organisers. A fortnight before the start of the Guild there were huge demonstrations in Preston and neighbouring industrial centres against the low wages in the cotton industry. The authorities claimed that the demonstrators were inflamed by Chartist agitation, which was then at its height. On 13 August there was a major confrontation in the centre of the town between the marchers and the 72nd Highlanders, who had been called in by the magistrates to try to prevent trouble. Serious rioting began. The soldiers fired upon the crowd at the bottom end of Lune Street, and five men were killed. Since the authorities were particularly nervous about the dangers that might result from the presence of vast crowds in the town, they called in further troop reinforcements. The auspices for the Guild were not good, but there were no incidents during the celebrations: the large numbers of armed soldiers standing guard undoubtedly had a deterrent effect.[18]

The Guild began in the customary fashion, with the mayor presiding at the opening of the Guild Court. The clerk of the guild, Richard Palmer, announced that all rights and privileges must be renewed or be forever lost, and then the Corporation members and Guild officials renewed their freedoms, marking the opening of the new Guild Roll. It was announced that, following the usual pattern, the Guild Book would remain open throughout the week. The ladies' procession, on the third day, was accompanied by representatives and members of the Preston Friendly Societies. This procession saw a departure from tradition, when the ordinary service and sermon was replaced by a performance of Handel's *Messiah*.

On the Thursday there were more changes, of great importance to the future character of the Guild. In the morning a concert of sacred music was held in St Wilfrid's Roman Catholic Chapel. This was the first time that there had been any official involvement of the Roman Catholic Church in Guild festivities. Before 1835 the Corporation, exclusively Anglican, had studiously avoided any recognition of the existence of a very large and growing Roman Catholic population in the town.[19]

On the same day the 'Guild Mayoress's Breakfast' (which was in fact a luncheon) was followed by the first ever procession of schoolchildren. This was particularly symbolic of the way in which the Guild had been altered since its previous celebration in 1822. Although the customary forms were retained for the official business, on the Thursday the Roman Catholics and the children of the town were both publicly admitted as participants, features that would have been unthinkable only twenty years before. On the Friday there was another procession by schoolchildren, many of whom were later treated to parties and visits to the circus. The weavers, to emphasise their special status in the town, had refused to participate in the general trades procession, and instead held their own procession on the Friday. Under the original plans for the procession they had been given a place which they regarded as inferior and unworthy of their importance.[20]

The speeches made in June had emphasised that the poor might benefit from the holding of a Guild, and a verse published before the Guild anticipated that this would be funded by subscriptions from the more prosperous townspeople:

> Because the times are hard, some generous gentlemen we hear,
> Will strive their best, that week at least, to banish grief and care.
> And if they should succeed in gathering a bounteous store,
> Then in the good old English style they'll entertain the poor.
> From low diet and scanty fare 'twill be a kind relief,
> If they for once should chance to dine on plum-pudding and beef
> And many a heart will happy be and all complaints be still'd
> While all rejoice together at famous Preston Guild.[21]

The organisers, and the would-be subscribers, quietly forgot this laudable aim in the few weeks which followed, and it was left to the Preston Poor Law Union to make a token gesture in that direction:

Through the exertions of Mr. W. Melville Lomas, one of the Guardians of this

Union, and lately Chairman of the Board, the inmates of the several workhouses were regaled, on Saturday last, with plum pudding, in addition to their ordinary dinner fare, so that even the most humble individuals in the town were, in some measure, enabled to participate in the general festivities.

A portion of plum pudding scarcely seems equal to the 'active participation in every enjoyment' spoken of three months before, but no doubt the application of a slab of pudding salved many a conscience in the town.[22]

The 1842 Guild was a triumph of organisation and a great commercial success and, without doubt, was well received in the town. That was despite the very real threat not just to the holding of the Guild but also to public order following the fatal shootings of 13 August. But in 1862 the Guild was again threatened, for the first time in its history, by outside factors. No Guild had ever been seriously affected by what was going on beyond Preston—the Guilds of 1642 and 1662 fell, very conveniently, just before and just after the Civil War and the Commonwealth period—but in 1862 another war was wreaking havoc in the town. The Cotton Famine, the product (at least in the popular opinion) of the American Civil War, had created the most acute economic and social distress which Preston had suffered in four centuries.[23]

That the Guild should have fallen during this period was a most unhappy chance, and many in the town felt very strongly indeed that to hold an ostentatious celebration in such circumstances was entirely unacceptable. The Guild would inevitably produce many public and prominent examples of conspicuous wealth and excessive consumption. That would, in the view of these people, have been an inappropriate exhibition of the prosperity enjoyed by a few in the face of the near-starvation which was being experienced by thousands in the town. There were numerous letters of objections, and public meetings expressed the gravest misgivings.

Nonetheless, undeterred by the serious reservations or outright opposition of many in Preston, the Corporation went ahead with the Guild. Against the background of distress a guild committee was appointed on 27 February to organise the celebrations. It did not begin serious planning until 11 April when, reflecting the customary importance of the musical aspects of the Guild, its first action was to appoint a special sub-committee to arrange musical events and a music festival. It was also decided that the Corporation should 'transmit a Memorial to the Queens Most Excellent Majesty requesting Her Majestys permission to invite the Prince of Wales to lay the Foundation Stone of the Town Hall'.[24]

Deliberations about music—and particularly about an invitation to Charles Hallé—occupied much of the time of the committee. In early May, realising that the cost of the Guild would be very high and that the trade crisis might result in a lower than expected income, it agreed to establish a 'Guarantee Fund' to cover expenses. It was felt that the

Corporation should not agree to guarantee the losses of private firms and individuals who were involved in Guild events, but that it should instead give a lump sum (£500) to a general fund. This was duly done, with the proviso that, should the guarantee fund not be required in full, any surplus should be handed over to the Relief Committee which was organising the collection and distribution of financial and material help to victims of the Cotton Famine.[25] In that way consciences could be clear: if the Guild was a success, the destitute might in some small way benefit.

This vexatious matter having been sorted out, the committee could return to the more complex and pressing question of deciding what events and entertainments should be on offer. Discussion during June and July covered a diversity of topics: inviting Lord Zetland, the Masonic Grand Master, to be present at the laying of the Town Hall foundation stone (he could not come, but offered the services of the Deputy Grand Master, Lord de Grey of Ruthin, instead); advertising for tenders to provide facilities for the orchestra in the Corn Exchange; making arrangements for processions; arguing with tenderers over the cost of converting the Corn Exchange; and approving designs for commemorative medals.[26]

During July and August the committee was involved in continuous negotiations with a very wide variety of individuals and firms: the railway companies, the different religious organisations and churches within the town, the caterers, builders and decorators, suppliers of food and drink, the police chief, the ratepayers' groups and representatives of particular streets which wanted to see the processions.

The minutes of the Guild Committee for 1862 are especially detailed, and give an excellent impression of the complexity of—and the disturbingly short time allowed for—arranging the Guild. Following the example of 1842 the scope of the official celebrations had been greatly widened. No longer was there a relatively modest and straightforward programme. Instead a whole host of groups within the town had demands to make and wanted to become directly involved in the Guild. The planning was thus more complicated and intricate than ever before. Rather less than five months, all the time the committee had allowed itself, was probably insufficient.

Guild processions, 1842 and 1862

The processions, with their musicians and bands, the various companies and their regalia, the formal robes of the Corporation, the civic service with plenty of bell-ringing, and the walk through the streets with toasts and the firing of salutes, combined to produce a splendid centrepiece for the celebration. Processions impressed visitors, they impressed the spectators and, no doubt, they impressed the participants as well. Initially there was a specific motive for all this: the processions were a very visible assertion of the dominance of the Guild in the life, and particularly the economic life, of Preston. As the character of the town and the Guild altered another motive came to the fore—that of emphasising to all concerned the importance of Preston (and, by happy chance, of the Corporation and its members). Thus, the processions and the panoply of ceremonial turned into a celebration of the greatness of the town.

Descriptions of all the Guilds from 1762 onwards emphasise this role. The scale of the events, their sophistication, the good taste and wealth of the town (a match for any other city, it was thought) and, increasingly, the range and modernity of its industries, were all pointed out. Preston, the Guild proclaimed, was prosperous, a great industrial centre, a cultivated and up-to-date place. It was not a small provincial backwater but a thriving town capable of entertaining the greatest in the land. All these qualities, contemporary writers felt, were reflected in the Guild, and increasingly the appearance of the Guild reflected those qualities—witness the rapid elevation in importance of the weaving industry in the trades processions, and the inclusion of the modern textile machinery as exhibits. Although medieval in origin, the Guild adapted with surprising speed to the changes within the town and its life, and indeed to its own new role. By the end of the eighteenth century the Guild had already acquired some of the characteristics of a twentieth-century trade fair.

In 1842 the Guild Procession was held on the second day, not on the opening day as had been customary. The Guild Mayor and Corporation, their guests and other dignitaries, walked from the Town Hall to the parish church. While they were inside for the civic service the rest of the procession, instead of waiting to accompany the mayor afterwards, marched around the town on its own.

It covered new ground. Processions up to 1822 had been confined to the old centre, but from 1842 onwards more streets were included to take account of the rapid growth of Preston and the development of new industrial suburbs. The route from the church followed North Road to the Walker Street corner and then went along Park Road (the line of the modern Ringway) to the junction with Stanley Street and Ribbleton Lane, before turning back along Church Street to the parish church. The marchers therefore passed through New Preston, the large area of working-class housing which had developed east of the old town in the previous forty years.[27]

Among the trades marching in 1842 were many which were traditionally associated with the Guild: the joiners; plasterers; plumbers, glaziers and painters; smiths; coachmakers; letterpress printers and engravers; glass-cutters; and butchers. As was customary, each trade had symbols or floats with displays of its work. The joiners, for example, pulled a stage on wheels, on which men and boys were working at carpentry, while those on foot carried set-squares, compasses and wooden models of buildings. The *Preston Chronicle* considered that at least some of the ancient trades failed to make a good impression. The blacksmiths 'seemed shorn of the almost pre-eminent distinction which they have never failed to secure at former Guilds'. It regretted that the smiths did not include the figure of Vulcan wearing armour, a display for which they were celebrated: 'any breach in the observance of customs ... is much to be grieved.'

But some of the trades were new, while others used their symbols to portray new aspects of the town's industries. The coachmakers, 'whose craft is not perhaps of equal antiquity to that which may be claimed for some of the other ... trades', had models of different vehicles which were 'indeed well deserving of the expressions of admiring applause with which they were everywhere greeted'. The models included, from 'Mr. Kerr's factory', a 'beautiful Victoria Cab Phaeton ... The use of this elegant Lilliputian equipage was satisfactorily shown to the applauding crowds, a sweet little girl occupying it with all the perfect nonchalance which could have been manifested by royalty or nobility.' To represent the most modern transport in Preston, the coachbuilders of the North Union Railway Co. had produced a superb model of a first-class railway carriage.

The ladies' procession on the third day was better attended than the main procession, partly because the weather had improved but also because, as always, it was a great attraction with its abundance of expensive fashion, and was extravagantly praised in advance by the newspapers. The ladies met the mayoress to drink a celebratory toast beforehand, using 'besides the loving cup and the punch bowl, several pieces of the Corporation plate ... including the Queen Anne's Cup'. Although there were 'about 113 ladies of position' in the procession, there was not a single noble title among them. Most of the county gentry families were represented, but there had been only very short notice of the Guild, and that meant that attendance by the nobility and gentry was inevitably reduced. More important, though, was the widespread alarm after the riots and bloodshed of a fortnight before, and the risk of further civil disorder. Fearing for their personal safety, the most important people stayed away: if revolution was to break out at the Preston Guild, they did not want to be there.

The first of the processions newly introduced in 1842 was held by 'the Scholars of the Established Schools'. A service was held for 2,500 children in the parish church and then, after an uplifting and morally improving address by the vicar, they (and 2,000 others who could not fit into the church) walked through the town centre. The processions by churches and schools in the nineteenth and early twentieth centuries were characterised not only by rigid segregation of the denominations, but also by bitter and acrimonious rivalry between the organisers over precedence, choice of routes and suggestions that guild committees were displaying favouritism towards a particular denomination. This inter-Church hostility was a major headache for the administrators of successive Guilds, but the Church of England scholars inevitably had the first place in the processions. Not until 1842 was there any recognition at all of the other Churches, and there was never any doubt that the Established Church would have precedence.

On Friday the fortunate Church of England scholars were again involved. The Sunday Schools and Church of England National Schools, the youthful armies of God,

29 The first Guild medals were struck for the 1762 Guild, but from 1842 they became the standard popular memento, mass produced in cheap alloy and distributed to all the schoolchildren of the town. Special medals, of gold, silver or high-quality bronze, were also produced as gifts for visiting dignitaries or collectors' items for burgesses and townspeople who could afford to buy them. This example, from the 1922 Guild, shows on the reverse Mr and Mrs Astley-Bell, the Guild Mayor and Mayoress, in regal pose. The obverse is a representation of the goddess of the Ribble (the river is pouring from the pot by her side) with, of course, the Lamb and Flag of Proud Preston.

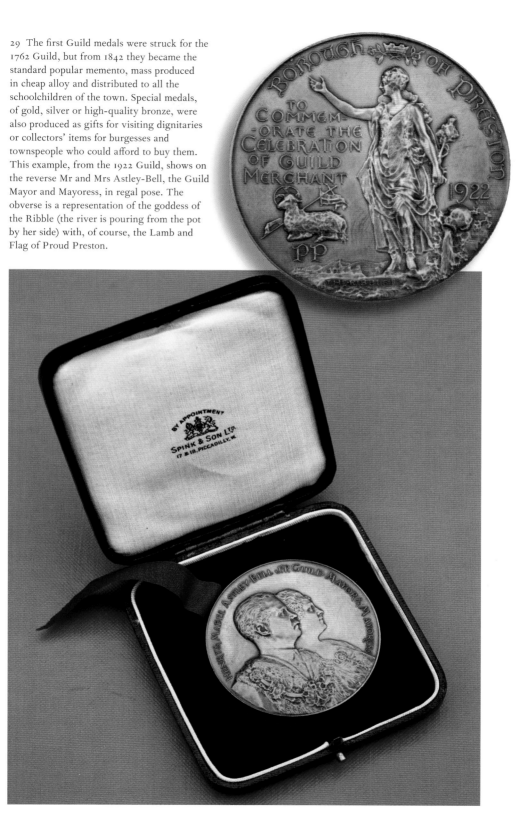

30 A religious element in Guild processions can be traced back to the medieval period, but it became much more important from 1842 onwards when the Churches, which were considered to represent the townspeople as a whole, had their own processions. This is a small section of the huge Anglican procession of 1922. The tradition of children walking in white and carrying posies and garlands of flowers is very familiar from Whit Walks throughout north-west England.

31 A later nineteenth-century innovation was the Friendly Societies procession, reflecting the powerful Victorian feeling that self-help and financial prudence were essential for the working classes. Towns such as Preston had a multitude of societies, some of which (such as the Masons, the Oddfellows and the Buffaloes) were national or even international, while others were purely local. Here the 1902 Friendly Societies procession walks along Fishergate past the Miller Arcade.

32 The 1952 Catholic Churches procession, passing the Cenotaph having walked up Friargate. The three main denominations—Anglican, Catholic and Nonconformist—each had its own procession from 1842 until 1952, because bitter sectarian rivalry was characteristic right through the period up to the Second World War. The Roman Catholic processions always placed great emphasis on statues, images and banners of the saints and, especially, of the Virgin Mary, something that would also have been typical of the medieval processions up to 1522, the last Guild before the Reformation.

PRESTON GUILD,

1802.

THIS JUBILEE
WILL OPEN
ON MONDAY THE THIRTIETH OF AUGUST NEXT,

IN THE MORNING,
AND CONTINUE A FORTNIGHT.

THE BOOKS
FOR THE RENEWAL OF, AND ADMISSION TO THE
FREEDOM OF THE BOROUGH
WILL REMAIN OPEN
At the Guild Hall for twenty eight Days.

AMUSEMENTS.
FIRST WEEK.

MONDAY.—In the Morning a Procession of the Mayor and Corporation, and such others as may honor them with their Attendance, and the different incorporated Companies of the Borough, with their Flags and Bands of Music, will proceed from the Town-hall to the Parish Church, and after Divine Service and Sermon, parade through the principal Streets of the Borough, according to ancient Usage—In the Evening an Assembly at the Guild Hall.

TUESDAY.—In the Morning a Procession of the Mayoress, and such Ladies as may honor her with their Attendance, and the incorporated Companies, from the Town-hall to the Church: After Divine Service, the Procession will return by the Market-place to the Town-hall——In the Evening a Play at the New Theatre.

WEDNESDAY.—In the Morning a Procession of the incorporated Companies; afterwards a Purse of 50 Pounds, given by the Right Honourable the Earl of Derby, and also a Sweepstakes of 20 Guineas each, will be run for on Fulwood Moor: In the Evening the Mayor's Ball.

THURSDAY.—A Maiden Plate of 50 Pounds, and afterwards a Hunter's Sweepstakes of 10 Guineas each will be run for—In the the Evening a Play.

FRIDAY.—The Members' Purse of 50 Pounds will be run for—In the Evening an Assembly.

SATURDAY.—A Sweepstakes of 10 Guineas each for all Ages, will be run for, to which will be added 50 Guineas by the Corporation of *Preston*; and 10 Guineas, to the Owner of the second Horse—In the Evening a Play.

SECOND WEEK.

MONDAY.—In the Morning a Grand Miscellaneous Concert in the New Theatre, under the Direction of Mr. YANIEWICZ :—The Vocal Parts by Madam DUSSEY, Mr. CIMADOR, and Mr. MEREDITH.—In the Evening an Assembly.

TUESDAY.—In the Evening a Grand Miscellaneous Concert at the New Theatre.

WEDNESDAY.—In the Morning a Grand Miscellaneous Concert at the New Theatre—In the Evening a Play.

THURSDAY.—The Mayoress's Public Breakfast at the Guildhall.——In the Evening a Promenade.

FRIDAY.—In the Evening a Masqued Ball, and Supper.—In the Evening a Play.

SATURDAY.—In the Evening a Play.

ORDINARIES will be provided each Day at the principal Inns; and an ORDINARY for Ladies and Gentlemen at the BULL INN.

Preston, 23d July, 1802.

PRESTON: PRINTED BY W. ADDISON.

33 Entertainment has been part of the Guild for centuries, but in 1762 and 1782, as the original trading role dwindled and died, it became the dominant theme. Special efforts were made by the organisers to provide a large and varied programme of concerts, assemblies, plays, dances and banquets, and during the day horse-racing was a particularly well-patronised activity. This programme from the 1802 Guild reveals the wealth of amusement on offer for the elite of the town and their visitors from further afield.

To be Let,

DURING THE GUILD.

A COMFORTABLE SITTING-ROOM and BED-ROOM, situated in Fishergate.—Apply to Matthew Shaw, House Agent, 2, Jordan-street, Fishergate.

August 5th, 1842.

PRESTON GUILD.

FASHIONABLE DANCING FOR THE APPROACHING FESTIVAL.

Mr. Balderston

PURPOSES opening an ACADEMY for those Ladies and Gentlemen who may wish to perfect themselves in WALTZING, GALOPS, QUADRILLES, &c.

For particulars, apply at his Academy, or at 27, Avenham Lane.

Preston Guild Races.

NOTICE.

THE Committee appointed to conduct the Preston Guild Races, respectfully inform the Subscribers to the Race Fund, that the Gentlemen whose names are added below have been appointed to collect and receive the amount of their respective Subscriptions, and that the same will be called for without delay:—

J. Bickerstaff, Esq.	Mr. J. L. Cotton,
T. D. Clayton, Esq.	,, Mitchell,
H. Corbett, Esq.	,, Coupe,
Mr. L. Billington.	,, Whiteside,
Mr. Heaps.	and
Mr. Rainford.	,, Whittam.

34 Preston's first newspaper, the *Chronicle*, appeared in 1811. For the Guilds of 1822 onwards we can therefore use the small ads and other advertisements as a source of historical information. Here, from the *Preston Guardian* of 5 August 1842, are some typical examples: renting out upper-floor rooms or window space in Fishergate (and to a lesser extent Friargate and Church Street) was a lucrative opportunity for property-owners, while the socially insecure could take a quick course in accomplishments, such as dancing, so as not to disgrace themselves at grand events.

35 The uniquely concentrated series of social events, and especially the dances, assemblies and banquets, required a commensurately large and varied wardrobe in the most fashionable styles. For many weeks before each Guild, milliners, tailors, dressmakers and costumiers advertised their wares, usually (as in these instances from 1842) making much of the fact that these were the latest London fashions.

36 The Guild of 1862 was without doubt the most controversial of all, since it took place during the darkest days of the great Cotton Famine, and there was widespread condemnation of the lavish and conspicuous consumption by a minority, while the majority were unemployed, destitute or starving. Nonetheless, for those who were able to spend money the attractions were plenty. It was even possible to purchase a specially prepared Guild perfume, prepared 'from the choicest flowers of many climes'. Sadly, no specimens of this choice fragrance are known to survive and the recipe was, of course, secret. A lady wearing such a 'bouquet' would also require sweet breath and good teeth: Ondontine dentifrice was strongly recommended.

THE GUILD FESTIVAL.

J. W. PIPE,

HAIR DRESSER & PERFUMER, FISHERGATE,

Is prepared to execute all orders with which he may be favoured by those ladies and gentlemen who purpose patronising the Dress and Fancy Balls during the forthcoming Guild. Having secured the services of first-class Assistants from London, and Bold-street, Liverpool, he confidently solicits the early commands of his friends, feeling assured that he will be able to give the greatest satisfaction to all who may patronise him.

J. WHITEHEAD,

37 Although (perhaps fortunately) the concept of the unisex salon had not entered the imagination of the Victorian hair entrepreneur, J.W. Pipe of Fishergate was advertising special Guild hair-dos for ladies *and* gentlemen in 1862. Note how, when the citizens of the town had to be impressed, it was almost obligatory to refer to London fashions. In this case—and there are many other examples—the other centre of contemporary style was Liverpool ... never Manchester.

PRESTON GUILD,

1862.

BANQUET

GIVEN BY

R. TOWNLEY PARKER, ESQ. MAYOR.

1st SEPTEMBER, 1862.

Potage Tortue à l'Anglaise.	Potage à la Julienne.

Saumon de Gloucester, Sauce Homard.	Turbots à la Cardinal.
Soles farcie à la Normande.	Anguilles, à la Spatchcock.
Filet de Turbot à la Holandaise.	Pouding de Merlan, à la Suprême.
Saumon à la Norwégienne.	Truite à la Tartare.

Cotelettes de Mouton aux Concombres.	Timbal de Maccaroni à l'Italienne.
Chartreuse de Legumes à la Financière.	Compote de Pigeon aux Champignons.
Cotelettes de Veau aux Tomates.	Paté aux Huitres.
Kari de Poulet, au Riz.	Vol au Vent à la Financière.
Paté de foie Gras.	Rognon de Mouton au Vin de Champagne.

Hanches de Venaison.	Bœuf à l'Anglaise.
Selles de Mouton.	Filets de Bœuf à la Jardinière.
Filets de Veau à la Rutland.	Jambons de Bayonne.
Langues de Bœuf.	Epaule d'Agneau farcie.
Poulardes à la Montmorency.	Poulets à l'ivoire, Sauce Suprême.

Grouse.	Perdreaux Roti.

Salade d' Homard en Mayonnaise.

Gateaus à la Victoria.	Charlottes Plombiere.
Crêmes à la Brunswick.	Crêmes Imperial.
Charlottes Russe.	Gateaus Neapolitan.
Gelée au Marasquin.	Gelée à l'Ananas.
Pouding à l'Exposition.	Pouding St. Clair.
Tourtes à l'Anglaise.	Patisserie à la Francaise.
Soufflé à la Preston.	Pouding à la St. Petersburg.

DESSERT.	GLACES.

WINES.

CHAMPAGNE, SHERRY, MADEIRA, HOCK, MOSELLE, SAUTERNE, CLARET, PORT, BURGUNDY.

LIQUEURS.

F. E. Morrish,   Parсуσ Liverpool

38 Guild banquets in the eighteenth and nineteenth centuries were extravagant and luxurious, as this menu from 1862 reveals. There were eight courses (soup, fish, entrée, meat, game, lobster mayonnaise, a choice of fourteen different puddings, and dessert—that is fruit and nuts—and ices), five wines together with champagne, sherry, madeira and port, and liqueurs to finish. All this was paid for from the rates. A century later that sort of opulence was quite impossible and politically unacceptable—at one of the 1972 civic events the fare on offer was 'chicken in the basket'.

39 While most publicity was directed at events and entertainments for the elite, the ordinary townspeople were not ignored. By 1842 participation in the Guild had grown to such an extent that impresarios put on events and attractions for the masses. In 1862, despite the desperate crisis in the town, and the shocking weather, crowds flocked to see a legendary international celebrity, the tightrope walker Blondin, cross the River Ribble at Preston Marsh—hardly Niagara, it must be conceded, but exciting nonetheless.

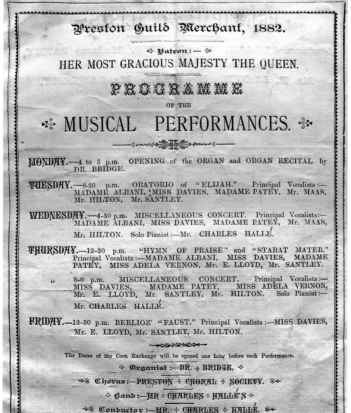

40 Musical entertainments were part of the Guild programme from at least the early eighteenth century. For the 1882 Guild the attractions included Dr Joseph Bridge of Chester Cathedral, perhaps the most famous organist of his day, and the Hallé Orchestra, founded 24 years earlier and still described as a 'band'. Charles Hallé himself was the piano soloist in the Wednesday afternoon concert, and many of the singers, whose names are now forgotten, were renowned celebrities at the time.

41 The decorating of the main streets of Preston, and particularly the processional routes, became important in the early nineteenth century, and was very lavish by 1862. Flags, banners, bunting, illuminations and ornate signage were typical. In contrast, the decoration of small streets in residential areas was not general until after the First World War. From 1922 onwards, encouraged by 'best dressed street' competitions run by the *Lancashire Evening Post*, local communities made strenuous efforts and also began to hold street parties. Here we see Fleetwood Street, behind Fylde Road, in 1952.

42 The balls and dances were eagerly awaited, and local newspaper reporters produced lengthy accounts of the guest list and the costumes. Throughout the eighteenth and nineteenth centuries costume, or fancy dress, balls were especially popular. In 1882 a ticket for the costume ball cost £1 11s. 6d., which is equivalent to about £95 today.

43 The 'Calico Ball' was held for the children of the great and good of the town and their visitors. A much more low-key affair, costing only five shillings in 1882, it was in the early evening and of course included no alcoholic refreshment.

44, 45 Of all the many and diverse aspects of the Guild in the twentieth century, that which is remembered most vividly and most fondly is the children's events—the pageants and grand performances in Avenham and Miller parks. Now a Guild tradition, these began in 1922 with what was then, and may well still be, the largest ever Guild event—the Great Historical Pageant. Every schoolchild in the borough participated in a hugely ambitious and triumphantly successful *tour de force*, recreating Preston's long history in a great series of dramatic scenes. The costumes were outstandingly good, and the children had a wonderful time, as every one of the numerous photographs reveals. Here we see, above, Saxon peasants tilling the soil when Preston was a mere agricultural village and, below, an Elizabethan miscreant pilloried by the officers of the borough.

46 The 1952 Guild Schools Pageant combined historical re-enactment with dancing, singing and other styles of performance.

47, 48 The Torchlight Procession was introduced at the 1882 Guild and was an immediate success. Described by one contemporary as 'a most sensational; eccentric revel', it allowed the people of the town and the numerous community groups, clubs and societies free rein to devise fantastical costumes. Here, in 1922, we see (above) a group of fearsome grotesques, one of whom (third from the right) appears to anticipate Margaret Thatcher, and (below) a charming group of masculine Lancashire witches.

49 The 1972 schools' event was the Prospect of Preston which, although it did have a substantial historical element, also included plenty of music, poetry and drama about the present-day town and its future prospects. The 3,000 participants performed before a total of almost 11,000 spectators.

The **ONLY** Chocolate Casket Souvenir carrying sanctioned portraits of Preston's Guild Mayor and Mayoress.

Price at all Sweet Shops, etc. **3/-**

Get this handsome Souvenir.
Filled with Beech's famous chocolates.

Every Preston Citizen and visitor to the Guild Festivities from outside will wish to possess an inexpensive souvenir of the famous celebration in which they may have taken part, or, at all events, witnessed. Beech's have prepared this attractive and handy little Souvenir Casket filled with a generous assortment of their finest fancy chocolates—the most delicious tasting in the world. **Buy a Box to-day at any Confectioners, Sweet Dealers, Etc.**

Beech's Chocolates Ltd

50 Souvenirs of the Guild have been produced since the mid-eighteenth century. Some are purely ephemeral—the printed paper napkins, ribbons and bars of soap which only survive by chance, and often in fragile condition. In the case of this souvenir edition of Beech's Preston Guild Chocolates 1922, quite a few of the tins are still in private and public collections, but—not unexpectedly—the chocolates themselves have been gone for ninety years.

51 In contrast, Guild china, like the medals and glassware, has a special collectable quality which ensures that many examples remain. This cup and sugar basin, floridly decorated in red on white, were produced for the Guild of 1882.

52, 53 A Guild tradition was invented in 1952, made possible by the development of intercontinental air travel. The Guild scrolls, taken around Australia, New Zealand, Canada, the United States and South Africa to be signed by exiled and expatriate Prestonians, captured the public imagination. In the upper picture we see one of the scrolls, which had been housed in a model of the tower of the fire-damaged town hall, being handed over by the Guild Mayor, John James Ward, at Manchester Airport for its onward journey. In the lower, Harry Harwood of Preston Harriers arrives from Liverpool delivering the second Guild scroll at the moment of the final proclamation of the 1952 Guild.

54 The 1952 Guild was the first in which some of the proceedings were recorded and broadcast on the wireless. Here, in April 1953, the Guild Mayor receives two records from Robert Stead, head of the BBC Northern Region, containing the BBC's recorded commentary on the Guild of the previous year.

55 In 1952 a party of Blackburn teetotallers came to the Guild to pay homage to Preston-born Joseph Livesey, the founder of the movement. In contrast to the social excess and freely flowing drink which had characterised many Guilds in the past, this sober delegation held a religious service beside Livesey's grave, enjoyed a modest meal and free time, and then returned to Blackburn.

56 The 1972 Guild was the first in which the ethnic communities of the town played a significant part, although the Polish and Ukrainian communities were represented in the Catholic procession of 1952. In this picture children from the African and Caribbean communities participate in the ecumenical Walk of Witness at the beginning of Guild week 1972.

PRESTON · GUILD · MERCHANT ·
PP
SEPTEMBER · 1st. – 6th
1952

The First Teetotal Pledge—that of the " Seven Men of Preston "—was drawn up by Joseph Livesey, and signed on 1st September, 1832

Mrs. Lewis' Teetotal Mission

LEES HALL, BLACKBURN

(Founded . . 1st September, 1883)

Seven of the Preston Teetotallers came to Blackburn in a 'Teetotal Car' to spend Easter Week here in 1835

A Party of Blackburn Teetotallers will go to Preston on the first day of Guild Week—1st September—to do homage, and offer thanks to the Giver of every good and perfect gift, beside the tomb of Joseph Livesey in Preston Cemetery . Service papers will be provided

Coach leaves Lees Hall punctually at 10-30 a.m. Mid-day meal will be taken in Lancaster Road Congregational School, Preston, about 12-45

Afternoon Free . The coach will be at the Lancaster Road School at 4-15 to bring us home again . This ticket covers coach and meal

Seat No.   (Eccles Trust Fund, Lees Hall)

57 Preston's twin towns, now four in number (Almelo, Recklinghausen, Nimes and Kalisz) have been involved in the Guild since 1952. In 1972 a particular attraction were Les Majorettes Nimoises, who performed at many Guild events and 'added warmth and colour to the festivities'.

58 Eighteenth- and nineteenth-century Guilds were usually marked in permanent form by new buildings, or by the laying of commemorative foundation stones. In 1992, however, there was no such scheme. Instead, the Borough Council courageously commissioned the artist Maggi Hambling to paint a portrait of the Guild Mayor, Harold Parker. The result was highly controversial but gave the town a fine picture by one of the greatest British portraitists of the second half of the twentieth century.

'mustered in the Market Place', where 'with their numerous flags and banners, and neat dresses, [they] constituted a pretty sight'. The band of the Rifle Corps played music, and the children, again 4,500 in number, gave cheers for Queen Victoria and for the Guild Mayor and Mayoress, before going for a celebration dinner at their respective schools. The children of the Nonconformist schools had a different, and perhaps much greater, pleasure: many of them were sent on a monster day trip to the seaside at Fleetwood, travelling (in most cases for the first time) by train, along the Preston and Wyre Railway, which had opened in 1840. The Catholic children met at the school in Fox Street, were 'refreshed', and then visited Pablo Fanque's circus, 'where 1,500 of them witnessed the performances in riding and walking'. The Wesleyan Sunday School children had a separate procession of their own, to Preston Moor (now Moor Park) for games and sports. Most schools of all denominations presented Guild medals to their scholars.[28]

In 1862 there was a pressing need to ensure that the various processions were properly organised, in order to satisfy all the competing organisations which might feel aggrieved or badly treated and to ensure that order was maintained. Processions had to be very carefully routed; meticulous timetable planning was required to avoid clashes of events; and the organisers had to be as tactful as possible with touchy and sensitive delegations. All the work had to be done in only two months, for it was not until 30 June that a sub-committee was appointed to consider arrangements, to negotiate and to instruct.

The first problem, one not hitherto of much significance but now a major consideration, was the question of marshalling. In the past the numbers in the processions had been relatively small. The experience of 1842 showed that when the schoolchildren were involved space had to be found for assembling several thousand people at a time, in an orderly way and at a point suitable for starting a procession route. Many of the areas of vacant land around the old town, formerly used for assembly points, had now been built over, but after some deliberation the sub-committee decided that Avenham Park, then being laid out as a public works scheme for the relief of unemployment, was the most suitable site. Its size and proximity to the town centre allowed even the largest processions to begin there without difficulty, and its availability was therefore very timely.

The administration seemed to be going smoothly when, on 5 August, the Guild Committee received a memorial presented by ratepayers and others living or having businesses in Cheapside, the Market Place and Friargate 'as far as Lune Street',[29] asking that all Guild processions should go along those streets. It might have been thought that these important central streets would have been included anyway, but the anxieties of the inhabitants were probably based on a realisation that, with a new starting point and with many new streets having been laid out around the old centre, alternative routes might be chosen.

This memorial was followed, four days later, by a petition from the inhabitants of Lancaster Road, also asking for all processions to be routed in their direction.[30] How the organisers must have reflected, with nostalgia, on the simple times when there were only four major roads in the whole town and all the inhabitants automatically had a procession past their doors. And how, too, they must have wished for those simple times when there was a mayoral procession, a ladies' procession and a trades procession, and no more. In 1862 they had friendly societies, schools and churches, trades and—for Joseph Livesey affected the Guild as well—the Temperance Society to consider.

On 11 August they chose routes for the Friendly and Benefit Societies and the Temperance (or Teetotallers) processions. The routes chosen were different, partly in response to requests from the organisers, who wanted to pass through the areas of their greatest support, and partly to spread the attractions as widely as possible.[31] There was also very detailed consideration of the order and route of the main trades procession. This was estimated to be 2,235 yards (1¼ miles) in length, and consequently was very difficult to arrange. It had to be routed in such a way that the head could not accidentally catch up with the tail. All such planning was, however, in vain: on the day the procession was twice the estimated length because of last-minute and unscheduled additions, and at several places en route confusion reigned as it came into collision with itself. A good deal of 'unruliness' was reported, as different trades struggled to pass each other.

The church and schools route was also selected by the committee, and it was agreed that children from Ashton and Fulwood, which were not yet within the boundaries of the Borough of Preston, should be allowed to join in.[32] It had already been decided that, for the sake of simplicity and to give the most impressive appearance, there would be one very long procession. It was to be carefully sub-divided into different denominations and into schools and churches within each denomination, but all would walk together. The arrangements were, it was thought, finalised. But on 12 August came a resolution of the Wesleyan Methodist Schools Committee, protesting strongly against the position which had been assigned to them in the procession, because

> by the arrangement now adopted by the Guild Committee the great Protestant family are divided by placing the Roman Catholics between the Church of England Schools and the remainder of the Protestants and because also the deputation appointed by this Committee has not been treated with proper courtesy, not having due notice of the meeting of the sub-Committee.[33]

The Wesleyan Methodists requested that they might hold their own separate procession or, failing that, should be relocated within the planned procession, but they were told that arrangements which had been made could not be altered. On 18 August, only two weeks before the opening of the Guild, the committee received a letter from the Sunday School Union, urging that 'the whole of the Protestant Schools shall walk together in the Guild Procession otherwise the said Schools shall take no part in the same'. A deputation from the SSU met the committee, which then hastily sought the advice of the Church of England clergy to see what they felt on this vexed issue. The clergy announced that they were 'perfectly satisfied with the arrangements already made by the Guild Committee; that they will be guided by precedent; and that they will leave the matter in the hands of the Mayor'. The Wesleyans, all too conscious that the Church of England had precedence in the procession anyway, thought that this answer was entirely predictable.[34]

The Guild Committee, its resolve strengthened by Anglican approval, told the Wesleyans that they had 'anxiously considered the differences which have arisen as to the Order of the Procession of the Schools' but 'regret that they find no means of reconciling such differences'. No change could therefore be made. That answer was quite unsatisfactory as far as the Wesleyans were concerned. They replied two days later, pointing out that they represented about 8,000 children and teachers and noting the decision of the committee and the views of the Church of England. The Anglicans had evidently annoyed the Wesleyans considerably: it was pointedly remarked that the Church of England clergy had themselves resolved that they would only walk 'at the head of the general Schools Procession' and had implied that this was their prerogative. Since, the letter continued, 'the Protestants of this Borough are not to be allowed to have one united procession', the Wesleyans once more requested a separate procession, and asked whether, if that did happen, their schools would also be the recipients of Guild medals and 'bounty'. The Guild Committee, weary and impatient, once more rejected these applications.[35]

But still they tried, and Wesleyan tenacity bore fruit. On 27 August, only a week before the beginning of the Guild, the Wesleyans presented completely new proposals. They protested, yet again, about the decision of the committee to place the Roman Catholics (numerically the second largest group in the town) in second place behind the Anglicans. This, they made quite clear, was unacceptable, and they asked for a third time if they might have a separate procession. It would be arranged to start from Deepdale Road and pass through the town to Avenham Park, there to meet the Church of England and Roman Catholic children: the Wesleyans would sing 'certain devotional hymns' and then all the children would join in patriotic songs. Exhausted by their persistence the Guild Committee finally gave way, and agreed that the Wesleyans should have their wish.[36]

Perhaps it was impatience with the issue of schools processions which hardened the hearts of the committee when it met on 9 September, the Tuesday of Guild week itself. It had received a request from the Guild Schools Procession Committee asking for a grant by the Corporation towards the cost of refreshments for the children in the schools procession. In the 1842 Guild the children had been given treats, and the Procession Committee had asked for help this time because of the dire effects of the great cotton famine in the town. Without a grant, it was said,

a great number of the children will be deprived of the usual Treat for there are no funds applicable for the purpose and as the children form a great portion of the population of the town who are suffering from the pressure of the times they are consequently unable to contribute towards the expenses.[37]

The application was peremptorily rejected, and the Guild Committee refused to allow this contribution which might have made the Guild more enjoyable for those young Prestonians who were suffering the hardship brought about by the Cotton Famine. It is perhaps worthy of note that £516 0s. 6d. was spent on refreshments for the various balls during the Guild week.

The processions of 1862 were, despite all the bad omens and the inauspicious circumstances, regarded as a great success. The old Town Hall, built for the 1782 Guild, had recently been pulled down, so on the first day the Corporation and gentry processed instead from the grammar school in Cross Street. At the parish church they attended a full Anglican service, while at the same time the Bishop of Liverpool celebrated a Roman Catholic high mass at St Augustine's (the first time a bishop had appeared in an official capacity at the Preston Guild).

On the following day there was an extra procession, to mark the laying of the foundation stone of the new Town Hall. The ceremony was performed by the Guild Mayor, Robert Townley Parker of Cuerden, who was a freemason. The freemasons from all over the county accompanied the mayor and Corporation. Masonic choirs, bands and choruses provided a musical background: 'an ode composed for the event was sung by the Brethren while the block was lowered.'

> The Procession again formed, but ere it could start, a thunderstorm burst upon the town; the crowd melted away; the Mayor's tail gradually diminished; and that good-humoured and hard-worked gentleman, after bowing to the constant few who attended him, dismissed them at last, and retired, dripping, to his apartments. After some hours, however, he shone out with renewed effulgence at the Masonic Ball.[38]

On the third day was the procession of the Friendly Societies, who splashed and squelched in a line stretching 1½ miles through torrential rain. Abram quotes an anonymous description: 'The Free Gardeners walked behind a lurry [sic] bearing a section of the Garden of Paradise, with the antediluvian Gardens, in flesh-coloured tights, seated therein. Seen between the intervals of the fall, they produced a wild sensation amongst the Prestonians, who received their gracious bows with infinite delight.' The same writer suggested that during the subsequent Temperance Procession, the 'water drinkers [had] beautiful water' *ad nauseam* in the afternoon. The rain, he says, was incessant, and the procession was more or less invisible, like most of that in the morning, because there were so many umbrellas. It was 'possible, now and then, to catch a sight of the flags, bearing a variety of most trenchant and defiant mottoes, such as 'The Pump and the Teapot', 'The Bar, the Barrel and the Grave'.³⁹

The centrepiece of the 1862 Guild was the trades procession. The number of spectators was also thought to be greater than at any previous Guild, and the procession the longest ever. It included representatives of twenty trades, was 2½ miles long, and comprised 2,500 men, 120 horses and 35 wagons.

Participating in this vast gathering was a sad little group. Edwin Waugh recounted how the unemployed men, laid off because of the Cotton Famine, were working on a landscaping project at Moor Park. A foreman told Waugh that 'One o' the men coom to me an' axed if i'd allow 'em hauve-an-hour to howd a meeting' about havin' a procession i'th' guild week'. The outcome was a 'parish labourers' procession, strictly regulated so that the spectacle should not be too distressing to sensitive observers: 'all persons joining the procession should be required to appear on the ground washed and shaved and their clogs, shoes and clothes cleaned.'⁴⁰

Those still at work made more of a show. The cotton managers and overlookers had 400 men and six 'lurries' carrying machines used in the various stages of manufacturing cotton cloth: lap machines, a carding engine, drawing, slubbing and roving frames, throstle and spinning frames, a spinning mule and a warping mill.

As before, the different trades tried to outdo each other in the scale and daring of their displays. The smiths had a working forge on a cart (a hair-raisingly dangerous idea), and were shoeing a horse which stood on a lorry. The printers turned out souvenir handbills and programmes to shower upon the crowd. The tailors used their century-old device of Adam and Eve, the first people to need tailors. The fishmongers had a large expanse of canvas sea, on which were three fishermen in a boat (one rowing, one drawing in a large salmon in a net, and one mending nets). The masons had two men carving a moulding for an arch, and a group of men erecting a tall Gothic window. There were many new trades, reflecting the still-changing character of Preston's economy. Although cotton was the largest employer, the role of engineering was becoming more significant, especially as the riverside industrial area developed. The procession therefore included the steam-engine makers and the amalgamated engineers.

On the Friday the much-troubled Church Schools Procession finally took place. All went well, and even the Wesleyans seem to have had a good time. The appalling weather of the first half of the week had given way to brilliant sunshine, so the schoolchildren did not have to suffer the misery of a sodden march through rain-lashed streets. The various denominations congregated in the great natural amphitheatre of Avenham Park, and were marshalled according to schools. Each child was given a Guild medal on a blue ribbon, and the different groups were arranged to form segments of a giant circle.

Thousands of spectators sat on the slopes of the hollow, but many hundreds of others were sitting, in a good deal less comfort and security, on goods wagons which were stabled along the railway viaduct crossing the park: passing trains (the line was in use throughout the day) signalled salutes with their whistles, and showered the spectators with soot and cinders. At 5 o'clock the marshalling was complete—it had taken three hours—and the children sang *Hurrah for England's Queen!* and the national anthem. There was a 21-gun salute from a battery on the riverbank, and then the children, 25,000 in number, marched through the town and back to their schools, where they were 'liberally feasted'. This was perhaps the largest public gathering which Preston had ever seen: there were said to be 100,000 spectators and 25,000 children.[41]

Balls, feasts and entertainments, 1842 and 1862

As already noted, the holding of a Guild in 1842 was far from universally popular. Some people condemned the way in which, they believed, the ancient festival was being ruined by commercialism. A reader who had written to the *Preston Chronicle* must have made his views known in no uncertain terms, and the editor rebuked him in magisterial fashion: 'The letter of this correspondent would be out of place in the columns of a newspaper. Besides which, we have no desire to prevent innocent amusements, or to decry those who partake in the festivities of a celebration so ancient and honoured as that of our Guild Merchant.'[42] Such views were soon eclipsed by enthusiasm for the Guild and its fringe activities, an enthusiasm encouraged by the commercial interests which had been crucial in its continuation and which rushed into action as soon as the decision to hold a Guild had been taken.

Sporting events were more prominent than they had been in previous Guilds. The Ribble Yacht Club held a regatta on the river, with the first day including a special race for the Guild Plate. As with horse-racing in the years after 1782, the prizes for the socially superior sporting events of the nineteenth century were expensive and elaborate. On the other days of the 1842 Guild there were such attractions as Cumberland wrestling (for the Guild Belt) and cricket matches. Rowing competitions were held as part of the Ribble regatta (with the Guild Cup, Borough Cup and Ribble Cup as prizes):

> Boat races too they did attract
> For prizes pull'd so gaily
> Upon the Ribble's silvery stream,
> The boatmen they tugg'd rarely,
> The prizes won did back return,
> Again to Preston Guild sir,
> And drunk the health of carpenters,
> who the winning boat did build sir.[43]

There was horse-racing, which in this year was held on Penwortham Holme since the Preston Moor racecourse had been abandoned some years before.[44] As usual, the racing was for large prizes, although the absence of the nobility at this Guild meant that attendance was smaller than usual and the event had less social style. Nonetheless, the reporter from the *Preston Chronicle* found the lesser races enjoyable: 'On Monday some more homely heats were run, the prize being a cart, saddle, and breachings. This afforded capital fun; for what with some horses "bolting", some throwing their riders, and some turning tail, roars of laughter resounded on the course.'[45]

There was a grand firework display in the Market Place on the opening night of the Guild with, as its highlight, a wheel, 'in green, scarlet, and purple flames, changing to four lofty revolving spiral columns, in purple and crimson, supporting a kind of frieze or entablature, on which were inscribed in many coloured lights the words "PRESTON GUILD", surmounted with a bouquet of Roman candles, which on being discharged formed a canopy over the whole device, of crimson, blue, green, silver, lilac and orange-coloured stars, and concluded with a royal salute of imitative cannon'.[46]

In the market place on Monday night
There was a glorious sight, sirs,
With fire works, the sky rockets
Flew nearly out of sight, sir
The wheels did whiz and rattle round,
Each breast was with joy fill'd, sir
The flames burst forth, red, green & blue,
And blazed out Preston Guild, sir.[47]

Cultural attractions included the usual series of concerts and theatrical entertainments (some of superior quality, some not) and there were, of course, the balls, assemblies and mayoral banquets during the week. In keeping with firmly established tradition, the Guild ended with a grand costume ball on the last evening. Among the guests on this occasion was Mr P.E. Townley, attending in fancy dress his fourth costume ball at a Preston Guild. Such achievements always caught the imagination of the press and public. An even more impressive feat was that of Lawrence Crookall of Poulton-le-Fylde, who 'arrived at the patriarchal age of ninety years' in May of that year and who had walked from Poulton to Preston to attend each of the previous four Guilds: 'He anticipates paying us another visit, but ... he will not, of course, be able to walk here. The railway affords him, however, a good opportunity of a quick journey, and when he comes we hope he will enjoy his fifth visit to Preston Guild.'[48]

At the 1842 Guild newspapers were used for extensive commercial advertising for the first time. Advertising can be traced back to the earliest papers, in 1742, but in 1842 large sections of each issue of the *Preston Chronicle* were filled with tempting descriptions of the goods on offer for the balls and masques:

> Messrs. Nathan, GREAT COSTUMERS, OF LONDON, AND DRESSERS TO HER MAJESTY'S FANCY BALLS, Having made arrangements with MR. SINFIELD, their Agent, respectfully inform the Nobility, Gentry and the Public, that, in consequence of the number of Applications, they intend to visit Preston with a Motley and Costly WARDROBE of FANCY BALL and CHARACTER DRESSES, of all Nations, which, for variety, elegance and taste, *cannot be equalled.*
>
> Mrs R. Baldwin Begs respectfully to inform the Ladies of Preston ... that she has just returned from London, with a magnificent and appropriate stock of goods for the approaching GUILD, consisting of Ancient and Modern Brocade Dresses, Embroidered Tarlatan Muslins in White and coloured, old Point Lace Capes, Cloaks, Berthes, Ruffles, &c, Also, a splendid assortment of Ancient and Modern Head Dresses, Point Lace Bonnets for Full and Demi Toilette; with a large collection of coloured Prints of National Costume, to assist Ladies in selecting their Fancy Dresses; all of which will be open for inspection on WEDNESDAY, the 10th of AUGUST, 10 Fishergate.[49]

The poem *Summons to the Preston Guild,* written in advance of the 1842 Guild, pokes fun at the pretensions of those who felt themselves in the fashion, and who were susceptible to the blandishments of the purveyors of costumes and make-up:

> *Old maid's* [sic] leave your cats and your monkeys behind
> And look in your glasses new beauties to find;
> Buy fresh curls and washes to get a new skin,
> Like ruins well white-washed come simpering in.
> Ye *dandies,* starch'd, padded and puff'd into man,
> Tho' you bear no fatigues except holding a fan,
> Bring your whiskers of mouse-skin, your heads made like mops
> Come show in perfection the new breed of fops.

The same versifier mocked the musical entertainments on offer, inviting 'Ye *lovers of music* and catgut' to listen to 'our scraping, and squalling, and squealing'.[50] But music was in fact taken ever more seriously by Guild organisers, undeterred by the financial failure of the 1822 charity concerts. In 1862 the first and most important business considered by the organisers was the arranging of a music festival for Guild week. It was agreed that the Corn Exchange should be used for some of the concerts, and that *Elijah* and

Messiah, both much-loved and familiar Guild fare, should be the oratorios. The meeting of 14 April 1862 instructed the Town Clerk to 'communicate with Mr. Charles Halle as to his conducting the Musical Performances at the Guild'. The resolve to secure the services of the best performers and artists may have been behind the rejection of Robert Clarke's offer that 'the Volunteer Amateurs would arrange to have an amateur Dramatic Performance either in the Theatre or in the area of the Exchange'.[51]

Negotiations with Charles Hallé went well: on 9 May the committee was able to recommend to the Council that he should be appointed as 'conductor of the Musical Arrangements' at a fee of £150 for conducting the four concerts, playing at two of them with his orchestra, and making any preliminary arrangements. It was also decided that several leading soloists and opera singers should be engaged to appear at the Guild, at fees of no less than 200 guineas in the case of Mr Sims Reeves and 250 guineas for the celebrated Mademoiselle Tiethjins. The Hallé Orchestra had been founded only five years earlier, in 1857, but it had already established an international reputation, and Charles Hallé's acceptance of an invitation to the Guild was a coup for the organisers. The total cost of the concerts, when finally added up later in the year, was £2,063 17s. 0d.[52]

The conversion of the Guild into a popular festival was well advanced in 1842, and became more or less complete in 1862, when there was a host of special events which were purely for entertainment or publicity purposes and had no connection with the old-style Guild. Perhaps the earliest instance of such an event had been the laying of the foundation stone of St Peter's Church in Fylde Road, which took place during the 1822 Guild.[53] On the first day of the 1862 Guild, in the afternoon, the local militia volunteers held a review and a sham fight on Preston Moor: this, unfortunately, was a washout, because of continuous heavy rain, but even so there were estimated to be 30,000 spectators. The event could have been a disaster in another way, since one of the temporary stands collapsed and several people were injured.

The same afternoon saw an athletics event on the marsh (doubtless even wetter than usual), close to where Preston Dock was to be built a quarter of a century later. For many thousands the evening was made memorable by a breathtaking display from the legendary Blondin. Those with elevated tastes of a different kind enjoyed another Guild 'first' on the same night, a performance of Verdi's opera *Il Trovatore* at the theatre in Fishergate. The rain was ceaseless throughout Tuesday night, and the Ribble rose in flood, carrying away a temporary wooden bridge that had been built from Broadgate to give access to Penwortham Holme. Here, during the dripping, grey Wednesday, was held the annual show of the North Lancashire Agricultural Society. Visitors were few, the show was a disastrous failure, and although 1,700 people (including Lord Derby) braved the elements to attend a vast dinner, held in a huge marquee during the afternoon, the roof leaked so badly that much of the food was ruined.

The improvement in the weather during the Thursday night of Guild week was fortunate: not only did it allow the magnificent display by the schoolchildren to go ahead, but it also made possible a second firework extravaganza, also in Avenham Park. The Guild closed with the usual costume ball, but there were also what Abram patronisingly calls 'two or three supplementary entertainments on a minor scale', including a Juvenile Ball, for what would now be termed teenagers, on the Saturday and for the rather less affluent, a 'popular Ball' on the Tuesday evening and a 'cheap Concert' on Friday.[54]

All affluence is of course relative. Those who could afford tickets to the popular and 'cheap' balls and concerts were still among the fortunate few in a town which was going through agonies of misery and distress. Many had condemned outright the holding of the Guild, and yet there was a good deal of genuine popular demand for such a celebration, because of the pleasure it would offer as well as because of factors such as historical tradition and sentiment. Opinion was sharply divided in 1862, and it is easy to be wise after the event, but it is very hard to escape the impression that the 1862 Guild involved a good deal of fiddling while Rome burned. The profit from the Guild was £704 19s., and most of this was handed over to the Preston Charitable Relief Committee. It was a not inconsiderable amount, but it represented only 7½d. per head for each person being relieved by the committee. The average weekly relief per head was about 1s. 6d., so the contribution to the welfare of the town's poor—about 22,000 people were then being helped by the emergency authorities—was enough for only three days' relief.[55]

That, perhaps, was better than nothing, but the expenditure on costly trivia and ephemeral decoration was prodigious. The contrast between the stark reality in the streets outside and the comfortable unworldliness of the Guild is well illustrated by the discussions within the committee concerning the purchase of food and drink and the decoration of the halls. The 1842 Guild had confirmed that banquets and assemblies would continue to be prominent in the celebrations. Even though, in that Guild, the noble visitors had been fewer than hitherto, the Corporation had provided lavish hospitality, and nobody had any doubt that in 1862 the same would be the case. Dinner for many was provided by the Relief Committee, which during Guild week distributed 55,000 pounds of bread, 12,000 quarts of soup, and almost 5,000 quarts of coffee to the starving unemployed.[56] The distress in the town and the deeply depressed state of Preston and its industries seems to have made no difference to the thoughts of the Guild organisers. There were to be no grand gestures, no sacrifice of a dinner so that the poor might have the money or food instead.

In July the caterer, Mr Morrish of the Merchants Dining Rooms in Tithebarn Street, Liverpool, visited the Corn Exchange. He was unhappy about the 'very scanty [kitchen] accommodation' available. The committee therefore authorised the construction of a temporary kitchen, with gas stoves and ovens, to be brought from Liverpool at a cost, including installation and removal, of £40 10s. There was lengthy consideration of the question of drink, demonstrating that the life of a Guild Committee member was not all hardship: 'The Sub Committee have further to report that on Monday last they tasted very many Samples of Wines, consisting of Sherry, Champagne, Claret and Port from Mr. Morrish's Cellars.'

It was recommended that sherry at 6s. a bottle, champagne at 10s. a quart, the best 1846 claret at 10s. a bottle, and moselle and hock at 8s. a bottle, should be purchased. The wines purchased seem to have been of especially good quality. Not so the port, for none could be recommended, as it was not 'quiet [sic] satisfactory on Monday, owing probably to the shaking it had received on the Railway'. Overall, though, it was felt that 'the quality of the various samples of wines tasted ... was excellent'. The samplers also recommended that contracts should be agreed for the supply of 'Ices lemonade Negus attendance of every description and no extras whatever' at the dances, at 5s. per head for up to 350 guests and 3s. 6d. per head over that figure. At the Juvenile Ball (where, all being well, the guests would eat less and where they would certainly drink only lemonade) the cost was to be 2s. per head. Morrish also undertook to provide refreshments for performers at concerts and oratorios, at 1s. 6d. per head. They, being perhaps of a lower class than the guests or perhaps in greater need of sustenance, were to be given less delicate, heartier fare: 'Tea and Coffee, Bread and Butter, Hams, Sandwiches, Fowls, Tongues &c.'.[57]

When the Guild Committee was approached in late July by a deputation asking that a special treat should be given to the poor of the borough during Guild week, it rejected the idea, saying that the Charitable Relief Committee had already announced its intention of providing 'additional relief and assistance' out of the donations it received—that is, out of the hard-pressed general relief fund. But at the same meeting the Guild Committee did approve expenditure of £550 on decorations at the Guildhall, including 'Modelled Lambs and Flags with rays, 108 flags, Gothic canopies, Gothic figures with Shields, Gothic Fret-work', canvas canopies across the roof painted in imitation of Gothic ornament, banks of flowers, imitation flowers for the balconies, and leaves with which to entwine the columns. The eventual total cost merely for decorating the Guildhall and the Corn Exchange was no less than £746. The amount given to the Relief Fund was £704. As ever, it was all a question of priorities.[58]

Preston and the Guild, 1842 and 1862

In its coverage of the 1842 Guild the *Illustrated London News* gave prominence to the rioting in the town two weeks earlier, when five people had been killed. It reported that 'some persons of rank' had been deterred by these events, fearing that there were plans for massive demonstrations by the Chartists and other forces. It clearly regarded all such activity as revolutionary and outrageous, and it welcomed the presence of large detachments of regular soldiers and militia in the town and at Fulwood. They, it considered, were an effective deterrent to further Chartist activity, and 'By the excellent arrangements of the Mayor and Magistrates' these plans (which were in fact a figment of the imagination of the authorities and the *Illustrated London News)* were said to have been frustrated.[59]

It was, however, officially admitted that there had been a wave of serious crime during the Guild: troops might apparently deter the revolutionary, but they did not deter the petty thief. As usual, the London gangs were held primarily responsible—it was said that they had been able to travel even more easily to Preston because of the new railway. One woman from Blackburn, with more money than sense, had sold some property for £4,000 and was in Preston to bank the proceeds. She lost £1,900 in cash which she was carrying through the crowd.[60] Such crimes were scarcely a surprise in view of the prevalence of pickpockets, petty thieves and swindlers, and many others taking advantage of huge numbers of people, plenty of money in circulation, and a police force which was almost powerless to deal with the situation and which could only try to prevent the worst manifestations of crime.

There were said to be 80,000 spectators in the town on the Wednesday morning to watch the ladies' procession, and the *Blackburn Standard* reported that on that morning the toll bridge over the Ribble at Brockholes (near the present *Tickled Trout*), collected £37 10s. in halfpenny tolls from pedestrians alone.[61] That meant that about 18,000 people had walked into Preston from the east on that single morning, a figure which of course excluded those who travelled in the endless stream of carriages and carts and other conveyances, or who came in on horseback.

This was the first Guild after the railway had reached Preston. By 1842 the lines to Wigan and the south (including Manchester and Liverpool), Fleetwood, Lancaster and Longridge were all open, and it was possible for excursionists to come in unprecedentedly huge numbers. One special train in 1842 is said to have carried over 1,000 people. The *Preston Chronicle* noted that the middle-class visitors came not by special train but in private hired railway carriages:

the influx of visitors of the middle classes to the Guild was very large on Saturday and Sunday, and on the evening of the latter day, no less than nine extra carriages arrived at the North Union Station, filled with such persons, and the stream was largely swelled on Monday on that line, and also on the Lancaster and Preston Railway.[62]

It was recorded in a contemporary verse that

From Blackburn, Burnley, & Chorley still,
They will roll on to Preston Guild,
From Wigan – Bolton – Lancaster,

From Liverpool and Manchester,
The Railroad brings them on it still,
To see the fun at Preston Guild.[63]

Twenty years later the railway was firmly established, and the organising committee made every effort to negotiate agreements with the railway companies for advertising, cheap trains and special fares, and to try to manage the huge numbers of people emerging from the stations into Fishergate. It was decided that notices advertising the Guild and its attractions should be put in all the leading newspapers of northern England, as well as in *The Times*. Advertising posters were displayed at major railway stations throughout the North and Midlands, including places as far afield as Carlisle, Scarborough, Worcester, Gloucester and Leamington. The Guild, it was realised, was destined to be not just a local, or even a regional, attraction but could now draw its visitors from all over the country and even from abroad.[64]

In 1862 over half a million people used the station during Guild week, and it was widely reported that the inadequacies of the old, cramped and unsavoury building produced a great deal of difficulty. This was despite the planning carried out by the Corporation and the various railway companies: perhaps they had left it too late, for the discussions did not begin until 12 August, only three weeks before the opening of the Guild. Meetings with the East Lancashire Railway Company produced an agreement for a special train to leave for Accrington via Blackburn at 3 a.m. on the three evenings when balls were being held. A similar service was to operate at 11.30 p.m. on the two concert evenings, and at 11 p.m. on the Saturday after the Juvenile Ball. The return fares were to be less than the third-class single fare: clearly the committee struck a hard bargain. The ELR also undertook to provide trains in the early hours on the Liverpool line, while the Lancashire & Yorkshire Railway was to do the same for the Chorley, Bolton and Manchester line and the Blackpool, Fleetwood and Lytham lines.[65]

Within the town the control of crowds and of traffic was a serious difficulty. In 1862 the committee liaised with the police chief to try to work out access and departure routes for evening events (when the gentry and nobility, and those who wished to emulate them, would come in their carriages). Even forty years earlier the congestion had given rise to comment, but in 1862 it was so acute that Preston's first temporary one-way system was introduced. Particular congestion was experienced on the evenings when balls were held at the Public Hall, as carriages deposited and collected the guests at the foot of Lune Street. It was decided that 'all Carriages going to the Concerts Oratorios and Balls [were] to go down Lune street from Fishergate and returning up Fox Street ... all Carriages returning from the Concerts Oratorios and Balls to go down Fox Street and return by Lune Street'.[66]

The safety of the public—not previously a matter of particular concern—was also given consideration, as were the many requests for the construction of viewing stands and seats. To prevent the blocking of the streets and the restricting of views, it was ordered that temporary balconies were to be permitted on the shopfronts of Fishergate and other main streets, but that these were not to project beyond the shopfront (which sounds like a contradiction in terms).

The construction of triumphal arches across main roads (a feature of most later Guilds) was also agreed: in 1862 there was one over Fishergate at the tram tunnel (where the Fishergate Centre is today), another over Church Street where the Ringway traffic lights are now, and a third in Friargate. The chief superintendent of the Preston Borough Police urged successfully that there should be a check upon the safety of all the carts, floats and machinery to be used in the processions, and that there should be safety barriers at appropriate points where the crush of the crowd might be dangerous.[67]

Diarists give us more personal impressions of the town and the Guild. Nicholas Blundell of Ince Blundell came from a diary-writing family, and his own account of a visit to the 1862 Guild is full of interest. The arrangements were largely left to his wife Agnes, who on 30 August 'was very busy arranging a fancy dress for the Preston Guild, We having arranged to form a quadrille all wearing Hungarian Peasant dress.' The Guild opened on 1 September, 'a dull day with heavy showers'. Nicholas and his family went to see the opening of the Guild and then on to the review of the troops on Moor Park: 'very heavy rain after my arrival which retarded the arrival of the troops.'

They were staying at Crook Hall near Chorley, and on the following day did not bother to go into town but stayed with their hosts, the Weld Blundells, and with various other relations and friends, playing croquet. But in the evening they 'drove in for a grand Miscellanious [sic] Concert in the Corn Market which was very handsomely decorated for the Occasion'. On Wednesday he and his brothers went to the agricultural show on Penwortham Holme: 'Pouring rain most of the day [the dinner] being in a tent the rain came through to such a degree, that the people were obliged to keep up their umbrellas.'

Friday saw the enormous procession and display by the schoolchildren in Avenham Park. Reliable contemporary sources suggest that there were about 25,000 children present, but Blundell, perhaps unused to humanity *en masse*, estimated that there were 'above 1,000 children', a startling discrepancy and an instance of how the size of a crowd is almost invariably the subject of wildly differing estimates. 'After dinner,' he goes on, 'drove in for the Fancy Ball which was a very beautiful sight and many of the dresses very handsome.' Blundell and his party thus gave up the whole of their week to the Guild, driving in every day, and sometimes twice a day, from Crook Hall to attend particular events which attracted them.[68]

Local residents, of course, did not need to worry about travelling in. James Foster, a Preston man, went for a walk to Hoghton on the morning of the first day of the 1862 Guild, and then returned to watch the proceedings. On the Wednesday he was much disgruntled, perhaps because of the foul weather, for this Guild was particularly miserable for many of the participants and spectators: 'Saw the Benifit Societys walk morning Did not care much for them saw Lor Derbys procession and then the balloon ascend on afternoon. Very wet day.' In contrast, on the Thursday, although it was also 'a very wet day', he had more appreciation of what was on offer: 'Saw the trade's [*sic*] procession was very good enjoyed it very much.' [69]

But to many outside observers in 1862 the Cotton Famine, and the contrast between plenty and want, were particularly noticeable. Some were encouraged by the Guild, seeing it as a way in which those in desperate circumstances had their burdens lightened, albeit temporarily. Arnold, in his *History of the Cotton Famine* (1864), notes how Preston 'presented the strange contrast of a carnival and a famine'. He felt that 'the gaunt grim spectre of famine which had stalked about the streets was laid by the appearance of gay processions, of famous singers, and of the prince of tight-rope performers'. In his view the wealthy classes in the town were to be blamed not for holding the Guild, but for their miserly and grossly inadequate contribution to the relief effort over the whole period of the Famine.[70] But others, angered and shocked by the blatant extravagance of the event, saw the Guild as a frivolous and expensive diversion for a few, and emphasised its ephemeral, transitory, wasteful nature. *The Critic* reflected upon 'the evil effect which all this useless display of medieval mummery and luxury must have upon the suffering brooding minds around' and asked whether 'the whole affair has not now become an utterly vain and useless piece of folly'.[71]

Perhaps the last words on the 1862 Guild should be those of a compassionate and concerned, but anonymous, writer who compiled *The Distress in Lancashire: A Visit to the Cotton Districts*:

> The Guild Festival was over, and nothing but a few gaudy archways, with dead flowers hanging about them, as mementoes of the occasion, were remaining ...
> It seemed strange in a town where so much suffering is being experienced to see on every hand relics of gaiety and rejoicing, play-bills and programmes, banners and triumphal arches, and to look round at starving crowds idling about the streets gazing listlessly at them. Joy and sorrow, real life and counterfeit, seemed to have met face to face.[72]

CHAPTER SEVEN

Preston Guild, 1882–1922

T HE 1862 GUILD was held at a time of bitterness, division and unparalleled suffering within the town. The Guild itself may have diverted the minds of some, but it angered and sickened others. Twenty years later, though, basking in the glow of late-Victorian prosperity (in reality, perhaps, veiled in the smoke and grime of late-Victorian industry), Preston seemed to have no doubts about holding another Guild. The stark contrasts of 1862 had troubled the consciences of many, but the organisers of that Guild were themselves in no doubt that it had been a triumph. Regardless of the 'spectre of poverty which haunted the streets', many hundreds of thousands had flocked to the celebrations, and financially it was a considerable success. The Guild now included the schoolchildren and the churches, the employers and their employees, the gentry and—if only in the form of a plum pudding dinner—the paupers in the workhouse. To the local newspapers, and in the opinion of those who planned the Guild, it was a true celebration of Preston. The 1882 Guild was thus seen as developing this ideal of harmony, unity and civic pride to an even greater extent.

Schools, churches and the Guild

The greatest success of the 1862 Guild was the procession of the schoolchildren of Preston, followed by their gathering in Avenham Park to sing patriotic songs. This event, very carefully organised and executed, was widely praised: the participation of the children was especially popular with the townspeople ... so many adoring parents, grandparents, aunts and uncles! In 1882, therefore, the children were given even greater prominence, and a vast procession was held on the opening day of the Guild. This comprised all the Church of England Sunday School scholars and most of those from Nonconformist Sunday Schools, a total of 19,581 children. The procession was accompanied by school bands, and each school had produced its own flags and banners: 'altogether the display they made was of a grand and delightful character.' [1]

The Church of England took advantage of the Guild to hold its annual procession, which in normal years was held on Whit Monday. The parish magazine for St Paul's,

Home Words, devoted a great deal of attention to the Guild in its 1882 editions, claiming that it would 'long be memorable on account of the wonderful Processions, the elaborate Decorations in streets and on houses, and for the fine weather which with one exception, viz. on the Tuesday, prevailed throughout the week'. *Home Words* was, naturally, especially proud of the contribution of its own parish. The Church of England and Nonconformist procession, so long that 'the head of it caught up with the tail, and the different schools walking four abreast took three hours to pass a given point', was meticulously organised, and looked enchanting:

> The young women and girls all wore very neat white muslin aprons, and many of them white hats, and the boys wore white straw hats trimmed with blue ribbon and white ties, so that altogether the effect was most pleasing, and we believe that it was generally remarked that no school in the whole procession marched better or looked nicer than St. Paul's ... After the procession the usual refreshment of coffee and buns was provided in the school for the scholars, and the Workhouse children were similarly entertained, by the liberality of a friend, in the Mission Room.[2]

The scholars in some schools derived a very tangible benefit from the Guild: extra holidays. Thus in 1882 the children of All Saints' Church of England School had a longer holiday than usual, 'on account of the Guild coming so near the Midsummer holidays',[3] while at St Augustine's Roman Catholic Girls School the teachers tried, in vain, to maintain attendance in the week before the Guild. The logbook for the week ending 2 September 1882 records: 'Attendance for the week very poor—Holiday on Friday afternoon. School closed during the Guild week.'[4]

The 1882 Guild saw another important change, one which would be a pattern for every subsequent celebration. This was the elevation of the Roman Catholic contribution so that it formed an entirely separate and important element in the programme of processions. Hitherto the Catholics marched in the school and church procession with the Anglicans—which had been the cause of such fury on the part of the Wesleyan Methodists in 1862.

The Catholics had the particular advantage of a guild system of their own. In 1838–39 the Roman Catholic community in Preston had established the St Wilfrid's Guild, a friendly society which provided sickness benefits, death grants and medical care, as well as organising communal events and social gatherings, all for the welfare of its members. In 1839 a women's guild, attached to St Ignatius Church, was founded, and this was soon followed by others, including some for boys and girls. Each of these guilds was well organised, with its own regalia and banners. The St Wilfrid's Guild had marched with the friendly societies in the 1842 Guild, but in 1882 it was decided that all the Catholics would join in their own special procession, to rank with those of the other churches and with the trades and friendly societies among the highlights of Guild week. The Catholic Guilds marched on the Thursday, and Hewitson, in his *History of Preston*, gives an eye-witness account. The procession was, he thought,

> a gigantic and magnificent demonstration. Never before was there such a muster, such a march of Roman Catholics in Preston. For this Guild they exercised all their spectacular skill, and aggregated all their available processional forces. Splendid flags—banners innumerable, of all forms hues—crosses, crucifixes, images, &c., adorned their ranks; a world of artistic beauty and emblematic elaboration was manifested; and, well attired as the members of the various guilds were—many of the females being in white, while all or the greater part of the processionists wore sashes—they made a most admirable and long-to-be-remembered display.[5]

The number of Guild members marching totalled 5,147, while behind them came many members of the United Catholic Brethren. After the procession ended many of the marchers were addressed at the Larkhill Convent (now Cardinal Newman College) by a remarkable group of worthies, led by Cardinal Manning and including the bishops of Liverpool, Salford and Leeds. All expressed their admiration for the procession, and the way it reflected upon the strength and fervour of Catholicism in Preston, Cardinal Manning saying that he had 'never looked upon anything that touched him more and moved him more than the procession'.[6]

On the first morning of the Guild the attendance of prelates had been even more remarkable, for high mass was celebrated simultaneously in all the Roman Catholic churches of the town: at St Wilfrid's by the bishop of Clifton, at St Augustine's by the bishops of Liverpool, Salford and Leeds, at St Walburge's by the bishop of Shrewsbury, and at English Martyrs by the bishop of Middlesbrough. In 1882 the Roman Catholics mustered no fewer than six bishops and a cardinal. At this Guild the official Church of England representation also included bishops for the first time. The bishop of Manchester (whose diocese included Preston) preached the sermon at the civic service, and he and the bishop of Carlisle (who since 1856 had had Furness within his diocese) walked in the mayoral procession on the opening day.

The separate processions for the Protestant churches and Roman Catholics worked very satisfactorily and suited all parties. In 1902 it was agreed that the Nonconformist churches should also separate and form a procession of their own, a logical step which produced a neat and workable approach to the problem of the different denominations. The Guild organisers from 1882 thus overcame the vexing and acrimonious public disputes between the church officials which had been so serious a matter in 1862. But at a local level there was still extensive antagonism and friction, and often bitter and sometimes violent rivalry. In 1882 the Roman Catholic Guilds procession was attacked by the Preston branch of the Orange Order, and there was serious street brawling. The anti-Catholic fever of the Orange Men was at its height in the early 1880s, and religious antagonism was strong in Preston, with its very large Catholic and Irish population. While the violence of 1882 was not repeated at later Guilds, the strong religious tensions within the town remained, and the segregation of the processions was undoubtedly necessary not only to ensure administrative harmony, but also to make possible a public face of contentment.

One of the features of the Guild since the early eighteenth century had been that each succeeding celebration has been more elaborate and more complex, and required more organisation. As technology has advanced, and as the commercial, publicity and artistic aspirations of the organisers grew ever more ambitious, so the time, resources and energy devoted to planning the Guild expanded inexorably. It became big business in the nineteenth century, and continued to grow bigger. In the case of the schools and churches this is reflected in the sophistication of their displays and in the elaborate spectacles which by 1922 were expected of them. The 1862 gathering in Avenham Park set a high standard and thenceforth no Guild organiser could possibly afford to receive or read the comment, 'Not as good as twenty years ago'. In 1922, therefore, the organisers excelled themselves with events which were remembered as remarkable by those who took part or watched, and were still being talked about at the beginning of the twenty-first century. As *The Times* reported on 7 September 1922, 'the Guild Merchant gets more amazing as the week progresses'. Its Preston correspondent was awestruck by the scale and ambitiousness of the Guild.

The theme of the 1922 Guild was 'history'. The Catholic procession, for example, included tableaux of Catholic history, not only relating to Preston but also to Britain and overseas, and there were many figures in costume representing, for example, St Joan of Arc. But the masterpiece of this Guild was the grand historical pageant, conceived and organised by A.J. Berry, Director of Education for Preston. Berry was by training an historian, and he had a great enthusiasm for imparting the history of the town in a digestible form: his book *The Story of Preston*, written for children, was extremely popular for many years. In his pageant at the 1922 Guild he attempted, in memorable and spectacular fashion, to portray Preston's history by a series of dramatic scenes and setpieces, spread over three full days of the Guild. Almost all of the actors in these were children, with a few adults taking particularly demanding roles.

Preparation for the pageant was a lengthy task, and most of the schools in the borough had to devote a good deal of time to detailed instruction in the songs, recitations and actions that would be needed. This was more than just a play or a concert: it was a massive and highly complicated *tour de force*. The logbook of All Saints' Church of

England Girls School shows how this affected the routine of school life,[7] and how at times the headmistress was somewhat exasperated by the time taken up in rehearsals:

10 July 1922	Mr. Ellison [headmaster of the Boys' School] brought his top standard boys across to sing the Guild songs
12 July 1922	Mr. Ellison brought across Stds. IV to VII to sing Guild songs from 11 AM to 12
13 July 1922	All the children except Domestic Sci: children are going from 2.30 to 4.30 to the Palace to practise the songs for the Guild
19 July 1922	Sent for Gild Pageant Bks to Office—60 sent down. Third Term examinations this week Teachers each taking their own as work has been & is dis-arranged through the Guild
20 July 1922	Sent for 2 dozen more Guild Bks
21 July 1922	Sent for another 2 dozen Guild Bks
27 July 1922	Received some Guild sewing from Miss Houseman
21 August 1922	Time Table will not be kept to at all this week on account of Gild work
23 August 1922	[School Photograph day] The children dressed in their White Guild frocks
25 August 1922	Went at 9 o'clock to the North End Football Ground for a rehearsal of the 'Lamb' Went on Avenham Park this afternoon for a rehearsal of the 3rd Day Pageant
28 August 1922	Received word this morning to take the children on Avenham Park at 9 o'clock for an extra Rehearsal of the 'Lamb'. Sent children home at 11.30. Registers not marked this afternoon, but children met at School to go to see Rehearsal of 1st Days Pageant
29 August 1922	Work as usual this morning. School closed @ 11.30. Registers not marked this afternoon but children go on Park for a Rehearsal of third days Pageant
30 August 1922	School as usual this morning Registers not marked this afternoon
31 August 1922	School as usual this morning Closed @ 11.30 to enable school to be opened and registers marked at 1.15. Children go on Park to see Rehearsal of 2nd days programme. Children receive the ticket for their parent to see rehearsal tomorrow

1 Sept. 1922   School as usual this morning. Closed at 11.30 to enable children to meet at school @ 1 o'clock for a rehearsal on Park School closed for Gild Week & week following—reopens on Monday Sept 18th.

Other logbooks tell a similar story of two whole months of Guild Pageant preparation, with all the disruption to classes and problems of timetabling that went with it. The headmistress of St Augustine's Catholic Girls School recorded on 3 July that she had had to rearrange the timetable for the whole school to allow time for singing practice for the Guild Pageant. It was not enough: on 24 July she had to do it all over again because 'These classes have still one hours singing every afternoon, Stds V, VI & VII still require two hours daily for Singing & Rhythmics'. On 11 August 270 of her girls went to Avenham Park to rehearse their part of the first day of the Pageant, leaving at 2.05 p.m., but they 'did not return as the Rehearsal continued until 5.45 p.m.'. On 4 August, worried by the deficiencies shown up during rehearsals, she had allotted even 'more time ... to be devoted by each class to memorizing the words of the choruses, during this week'.[8]

It is hard to avoid the impression that Preston's teachers must have breathed a loud collective sigh of relief at the end of the third day of the pageant. It was an extraordinary project, probably the most spectacular and ambitious ever undertaken at a Preston Guild. About ten thousand children, all in costume, took part, and it is estimated that the audiences numbered at least 30,000 on each of the three days. The Preston correspondent of the *Daily Mail* indulged in that peculiarly winsome style of reporting that was popular between the wars. As befits somebody who had (apparently) travelled from the Deep South to see this curious Northern spectacle, the musical hall view of Northerners is clear. Under the heading *Merrie England at the Children's Ball* he or she reported that:

Today's part of the historical pageant took us off to the 14th and 15th centuries, with sonorous Latin set to Mozart. 'Have in the pageant,' cried the 14th century mayor, and down the hillside came streaming maids with tall conical hats, flying veils, and dresses richer than a painting. Next a mystery play, with a company of sweet angels whose wings the sun caught and turned to gleaming fire and silver ... Preston folk were blunt then (as now), robust, spirited fellows, 'The king's a rare good customer when they're givin' things away for nowt,' cries a townsman, and the parish priest delivers himself of 'We thought bluff King Hal was bad enough, this Protector Somerset is worse'. With merry swing and bang of bladders, jesters in motley sing 'There's a good time coming, boys'.[9]

The trades and their processions, 1882–1922

Thus, Guild events steadily became more elaborate, and required increasing amounts of long-term planning (no longer would a few weeks in the summer of Guild year suffice). The trades and industries of the town increased the scale of their contribution, and Guilds after 1882 saw growing involvement by the workers and their organisations, working alongside or parallel with the employers. It was not a contribution which was universally welcomed. As soon as they were sufficiently organised and representative, the trades unions were anxious to participate on the same terms as the friendly societies and other local organisations, and to have their members marching not only as employees of particular trades or industries, but also as trade unionists. At first this was difficult, as the employers were reluctant to cede any of their role in the organisation of the trades procession, and to appear to acknowledge the union movement. The unions themselves had limited time and modest financial resources, and their contributions were not easy to achieve.

In the heyday of the old Guild, before the 1740s, the trade element had been especially important. After all, the Guild was in large measure an organisation designed and empowered to control and restrict trade. In theory it had not functioned as an employers' organisation as such, although inevitably it had included many employers. Instead, it was based on the 'craftsman or trader-plus-apprentice' principle, whereby a reliable and trusted apprentice would graduate to craft or trader status and so become a full Guild member. The factory system and the development of the employer/employee relationship effectively ended this (admittedly simplistically explained) pattern. It was obviously impossible for all the employees of, for example, Horrockses, to graduate to Guild membership just because John Horrocks himself was a leading member of the Guild. The Guilds after 1762 had therefore increasingly been dominated by the employers and the factory managers, who selected some of their employees to march in the processions and who produced and financed the elaborate displays.

In the processions the decorations, floats, tableaux and regalia were provided by the employers, and the workers marched as employees, not as equals. A paternalistic attitude was usually displayed by the employers at the time of the Guild. In 1842 it was reported that 'On the occasion of the trades walking procession last week, a handsome dinner was given to their men by the master butchers. A dinner was likewise given by the master coachmakers to their operatives. These friendly demonstrations on the part of the masters towards their men are highly pleasing, and must tend to promote and cherish kindly feelings between the employers and the employed.' [10]

The remaining craft and trade industries—for example, the glaziers and painters—were gradually eclipsed in prestige and prominence, as suggested by the comments on the blacksmiths in 1842. Even in these trades, which were once the preserve of small independent craftsmen, the factory system became dominant. Marching with such trade companies as the smiths and the carpenters were men who, by 1842, were employed in the factories and mills, not in their own workshops.

But unionisation, and the growth in feelings of common identity and interest among the workforce, led to changes later in the century, and the somewhat idealised view of harmony expressed in 1842 no longer satisfied. The representation of the workers separately from their employers became more apparent at succeeding Guilds, though naturally many workers still marched with employers, and the union marchers generally participated in the trades procession. For example, almost all the very numerous crafts and processes within the textile industry had its own union, each with a Preston and District branch, and each of these formed a guild committee to organise its particular contribution to the textile trades procession.

The Preston & District Power Loom Weavers' Union participated in the 1882 Guild, as might be expected of the body which represented the largest group of workers in the largest trade of the town. The minutes of the union are concerned, in large part, with the preparations for the march in the trades procession, and raising money to pay for decorations and garlands. Union funds were not only limited, but also had to be reserved for the serious and urgent requirements of the welfare of the members, so none could be set aside for the Guild procession. On 16 May, therefore, the union committee resolved that at each mill the management should be asked 'for permission to make collections to defray our Guild Expenses'.[11] This was successful, and sufficient money was collected for the plan to go ahead.

The power loom weavers appointed banner carriers, stewards and other officials in late May 1882: they adopted the patterns and customs of the Guild, rather than trying to break with convention and tradition. This is in large measure why there has been a continuation of the forms and institutions of the Guild: each new body or group included in the processions or other ceremonies has taken what went before as a model. In June came another gesture towards the custom of the Guild: it was decided that the officers should wear special sashes, such as had been used in trades processions for at least 140 years. Those who marched were to wear artificial flowers, and 600 were ordered (300 for men and boys, 300 for women) at a cost of £1 18s. 6d. The union motto was to be embroidered or painted on its banner: 'He that permitteth oppression shareth the crime.'[12]

But strict economy was essential. In contrast to the unlimited resources of the employers, the workers of 1882 had to make do with the minimum. On 27 July, in response to a request from a member, it was agreed that 'we do not entertain the question of having medals', and at the meeting of 8 August the committee chose a 'Ten shilling Banner', which was far cheaper than others on offer. The centrepiece of their procession was, curiously, to be a model of a handloom: it may have been intended to show the origins of the trade, but more probably it was there because the employers who had used it in a previous Guild procession no longer wanted it. In mid-July the committee had agreed to have the 'model-loom restored', which suggests that it had indeed been brought out of a retirement that had lasted, at the very least, twenty years. The model was to be mounted on a cart, the two drivers of which were paid 5s. each for their services. Money was desperately short: on 14 August it was resolved to *sell* the artificial flowers to the marchers, because even £1 18s. 6d. was too great a burden upon the Guild account.[13]

The union also entered into another ancient Guild tradition, again on a modest and restrained scale. It has been noted how, as long ago as the mid-seventeenth century, it was customary for the members of the different trades companies to march with the mayor to the Town Hall or Guildhall on the opening day, and then to disperse to their own halls for feasts and banquets. This custom had been carried on ever since, and as well as the civic banquets there were numerous private or semi-private dinners in the town each day. Inevitably the power loom weavers could not afford a grand feast, but they adhered to the spirit of the custom by providing instead a good old Lancashire tea—but here, too, they could not afford to give a free tea to allcomers. On 22 August the committee agreed that 'the tickets for the Tea at the Guild be 1/6 for men and 1/3 for females'. The latter were presumably expected to eat less![14]

The trades processions in 1882 were described by one observer as 'the most interesting, the greatest, and by far the most attractive of all the outdoor displays during the Guild festival'.[15] The textile procession began at 9.00 a.m. in Garstang Road, and between 2,000 and 3,000 people walked through the town, headed by the managers and overlookers, with all the different crafts and sections of the trade following, each with its guild committee: carders, spinners, ring frame throstlers, slashers, winders and warpers. Every group carried its own banners and emblems, and most had prepared displays or tableaux of the sort which the power loom weavers had considered: bales of cotton, models of machinery and mills, 'scutching, slashing and carding engines; drawing, winding, doubling and ring and fly (throstle) frames; mule and head stocks; handpower, dobby, and jacquard looms'. The most remarkable exhibit was the machine which had changed Preston's, and Lancashire's, history—Samuel Crompton's original spinning mule, now 92 years old, which had been lent by Dobson & Barlow of Bolton and which was operated by Robert Ainsworth, aged 78.

The 1882 Amalgamated Trades Procession began in Winckley Square at ten in the morning: 'the total length of the route was extravagantly long—about seven miles; and though now and then, towards the latter part of the journey, an elderly person, naturally enough, dropped out of the ranks, the great majority, so far as we had a chance of forming an estimate, went right through the processional ordeal, from beginning to end.' The order of the procession was decided by ballot, because of the competing claims of so many different trades. Such diversity was a reflection of the complexity of the economy of Preston, but it also indicates the way in which all the new and existing trades were starting to organise themselves to join in the Guild procession. Those present in 1882 were:

Tinplate workers	Gasfitters
Stonemasons	Saddlers and harness makers
Boilermakers	Shipbuilders
Black and white smiths	Butchers
Soapmakers	Ironfounders
Marble masons	Plumbers
Housepainters	Carpenters and joiners
Cabinet makers	Upholsterers
Bricklayers	Coachmakers
Mungo [shoddy] makers	Lamplighters
Engineers	Brickmakers
Paviors and flaggers	Letterpress printers
Lithographers	Bookbinders
Tailors	Lace and underclothing makers
Plasterers	Wireworkers

Fire brigades (from Preston and nineteen other towns)

The historian Anthony Hewitson wrote that 'The display they made was gigantic; their operations and productions were pre-eminently interesting; and, of its kind, this demonstration surpassed, in both extent and variety, any made at any former Guild in Preston.'[16] They have said that about every Guild, and it has usually been true.

In 1902 the general trades and the textile workers marched on the same morning, but their routes varied and they were in two distinct sections. The range of the general procession was very much greater than before: additional trades represented included farriers, grocers, french polishers, hay binders, railway servants, tobacco manufacturers, bakers, braziers, excavators and drainers. Some of these, such as the bakers, were of course ancient trades, but they had not hitherto been separately represented. Others, such as the railway workers, were new trades which were of growing importance in the economy of the town.

In 1922, the last Guild before the cotton industry's swift decline, the textile trades gave very detailed attention to their performance. The minutes of the Preston & District Textile Trades Federation record extensive negotiations and discussions, and much work was done during a series of joint meetings between the Federation and the Cotton Employers Association, beginning a year in advance of the Guild in September 1921. The first question—a crucial one for the workers—was that of holidays. It was pointed out that in 1882, when the workers had first played a significant independent part, there had been no summer holidays, and Guild week had been given by the employers as a special holiday. By 1902 the unions had secured a four-day annual summer holiday, and the employers refused to concede this as well as the Guild week. Therefore the workers 'gave the whole of these four days up and got Seven days in September'.

Since then there had been further change, and the meeting was told that 'now our people had got used to having a weeks holiday we should try to maintain that during 1922'. The agreement of the employers was sought for an arrangement whereby the workers would give up their August summer holiday in return for having the whole of Guild week. The modesty of the proposal is startling: the workforce was prepared simply to move its holiday from August to September, and did not ask for any extra time—no more, therefore, than confirming the pattern of the 1902 Guild. The employers, who perhaps had anticipated a request for an extra day or two, agreed with alacrity.[17]

Most of the discussions in the spring of 1922 related to detailed planning of the trades procession, and to balancing all the competing claims to space, money and publicity. The mayor asked that the procession should be 'curtailed somewhat', because the planned length was far too great, and he had to insist that fewer machines should be exhibited. The Federation eventually decided that only one machine from each process could be included. However, so complex was the textile trade, with so many processes, that there were still too many machines. The Federation wanted maximum publicity for its industry, and was anxious to avoid being mixed up with the other trades of Preston: 'this meeting favours a Textile Procession at a time when there are no other processions in the streets—say Textiles half a day & other Trades half a day.'[18] Such a division had been made in 1882, so there was a precedent for the separation into textile trades and other trades. However, in 1882 the two processions had walked at the same time but in different parts of the town: now the textile trades wanted nothing to detract from their own special status. The request was rejected by the Guild Committee, and instead, on the lines of the 1902 Guild, the textile trades procession was followed immediately by that of the amalgamated trades, a parade totalling four miles in length.

Money was less troublesome for the workers of 1922 than it had been forty years before. There was a joint effort by the employers and the employees, and so the resources for floats and tableaux were found, in most cases, by the firms which participated. The meetings considered the thorny question of advertising and came up with a fine solution: advertisements on tableaux were to be forbidden, but any firm which provided the money for one or more tableaux would have 'the right to one or more exhibitions of their own where advertisements could be used'. That meant, in effect, that there would be additional advertising tableaux and floats.[19]

The number of firms which asked to participate in the textiles section grew rapidly, and by March 1922 twelve tableaux had been agreed, three of them being allotted to

Horrockses. In May it was calculated that there would be 1,180 people marching trade by trade, but that there would also be a similar number marching for the firms. Eventually it was decided that there would be a limit of 500 employees per firm, each being dressed in cloth manufactured by his or her employer—a particularly colourful form of advertising and, as the descriptions of the 1802 Guild show, one with a long history.[20] To produce final plans proved almost impossible: every decision was followed by further requests for a place in the procession, or for a change of route, or for extra machines and displays to be included. In July, for example, a deputation from Plungington and Adelphi Street came to a meeting to urge that the route should be altered to pass through that district, which had a population of over 21,000 and was the most densely populated part of the town. Their representative 'spoke in this strain for 16 minutes, when the chairman drew his attention to the time he was taking up': eloquence which failed, since the request was rejected (though the same streets tried again a week later, still to no avail).[21]

The Times described the textile section of the trades procession of 1922, the end product of all this deliberation:

> The textile parade gave the story of the cotton industry from the growing of cotton to the wearing of the finished product in home and foreign lands. First came a cotton-picking scene, with workers picking cotton from growing plants specially imported from Texas. Then came the various processes of manufacture, with machinery in motion producing goods in miniature factories on lorries … Finally appeared hundreds of girls and men dressed in the multitudinous cotton costumes of the world, the gay colours of the East contrasting with more homelike materials down to overalls. Many fine tableaux followed, one showing symbolically the cooperation of capital and labour in industry, and another … showing how cotton is the keystone of Lancashire industry.[22]

The 'miscellaneous' trades could not easily manage such an ambitious and integrated theme, but each made use of the modern technology available: for example, large motor lorries could now be used instead of the horse-drawn floats of the past. The boilermakers had demonstrations of steel-cutting and welding (perilous activities on a moving lorry), the electrical workers—another instance of an industry which had sprung up since the previous Guild but which immediately became part of the Guild tradition—showed a 'pageant of light', from flint and tinder to electric filament lamps (samples of which were made by girls during the procession). A rubber trades pageant showed 'coolies' at work in a rubber plantation. There was also a procession of historic transport, promoted by the various firms and workers in the transport industries: a stagecoach 150 years old was followed by a Rolls Royce; a replica of Stephenson's *Rocket* was the prelude to the newest royal train coach, and old and new fire engines and lorries were driven past.

177

Entertainments, feasts and banquets, 1882–1922

All Guilds since 1842 have combined the traditional and customary with the novelties and special events of the time. Thus in 1882 a particular attraction was the opening of the magnificent organ in the Corn Exchange, which had been given to the town by John Dewhurst, coal merchant, at the immense cost of £3,000. There were the usual balls and banquets and (almost a tradition in itself) a balloon ascent from Avenham Park. An increasingly common feature of Guild year was that county organisations held their annual shows or meetings in the town: in 1882, for example, the Manchester, Liverpool & North Lancashire Agricultural Society held its annual exhibition and show at Moor Park, its annual luncheon being graced by the presence of Lord Winmarleigh (the president of the society), the duke of Cambridge, Lord Derby and Lord Lathom. The floral, horticultural and bee show was held on the same site, and at the presentation of prizes on the Wednesday there was 'a fashionable assemblage of ladies and gentlemen'. Events such as these not only added variety to the Guild programme, and increased the importance of the event: they were also a reflection of the trend whereby the Guild drew its patronage from further afield. It had become not only a county event, but one known and eagerly awaited throughout the North West.[23]

By now the ceremonial laying of the foundation stone of a major public building had become a Guild tradition, traceable to the laying of the foundation stone of St Peter's church during Guild week in 1822. The attendance of royalty or a leading county dignitary was a special attraction and gave these events a particular appeal. The 1882 Guild, like that of 1862, saw such a formal ceremony—on this occasion at the Harris Library and Museum. It had been hoped that Prince Leopold, Duke of Albany (a son of Queen Victoria) would perform the ceremony. That would have been the first time that the Guild had had a royal visit, but at the last minute illness prevented him from coming. All the special souvenirs and medals had been produced, and a lot of money and effort were wasted. The queen asked the duke of Cambridge (her cousin, the uncle of Queen Mary) to go as substitute, and he graced the 1882 Guild with his intermittent presence (he commuted from Knowsley, where he was staying with Lord Derby). The ceremony itself was performed by Lord Lathom and, like the laying of the foundation stone of the Town Hall in 1862, it was dominated by the freemasons—some 1,500 of them. Later the duke planted an oak tree in Avenham Park using 'an elaborate, bejewelled, silver spade', a feminine fancy which had been made on the expectation that it would be the duchess of Albany who performed the tree-planting.[24] At the 1902 Guild the Guild Mayoress, the Countess of Derby, opened the new Diamond Jubilee Wing and the Robert Charles Brown Operating Theatre at the Royal Infirmary, and laid the foundation stone of the out-patients' department.

The musical performances in 1882 were on tried and tested lines: nothing too radical or revolutionary would have been acceptable. The new Public Hall behind the Corn

Exchange was the setting for the obligatory performance of *Elijah*, before an audience of 1,900 people. Members of the Preston Choral Society took part, and the organ was played by Dr Bridges, the organist of Westminster Abbey, who had played at the grand opening of the organ two days before. The Hallé Orchestra played at the miscellaneous concert on the following day,[25] while on the Thursday the Public Hall was the setting for Mendelssohn's *Hymn of Praise* and Rossini's *Stabat Mater*, with an illustrious array of soloists from London. The musical events of 1882 concluded with Berlioz's *The Damnation of Faust*, before another huge audience. This performance was described by Hewitson, a less than outstanding music critic: 'the choruses were rendered by the Preston Choral Society; and the instrumental portions were given by Mr. Halle's band. The style in which "Faust" was gone through amounted to a great musical treat.'[26]

In 1902 the well-loved, traditional pieces were performed, with *Elijah* of course on the programme, but there was also Dvořák's *The Spectre's Bride* (which had been written specially for English performances) and that Edwardian favourite, Coleridge Taylor's *Hiawatha's Wedding Feast*. Planning the musical entertainments had, as always, occupied a lot of time. The 1902 Guild Committee was appointed as early as November 1900, and was interviewing impresarios and performers by February 1901, ready to make firm bookings at the earliest possible date. The man chosen to arrange, conduct and organise the music was Luigi Risegari of Rusholme in Manchester, and throughout 1901 he bombarded the Guild Committee with letters asking for information and approval for his decisions: 'I would beg you to kindly help me by telling me of anything which I might possibly notice as being expected of me; I am so sure of your great kindness that I confidently ask you to guide me so that I may not unintentionally commit any errors.' The committee must, at times, have wished for a man rather more confident in his own judgement.[27]

There were many other events, and all the fun of the fair. In 1882 attractions included the inaugural ball, the Guild Mayor's banquet, two athletics events, a 'pyrotechnic display, of a varied and brilliant character', and a military tournament and brass band contest ('open to all England') at West Cliff. As always the reports of the events concentrated on the glittering social occasions, with their abundance of titled guests and elaborate and expensive costumes. The costume ball held on the Wednesday was claimed, predictably, to be the best ever: 'like a beautifully fantastic, moving mosaic it looked … the gay and the saturnine, the regal and the rustic, the calmly quaint and the flashingly sensational, potent Knighthood with its lamellated exterior, and gentle, lattice-breasted Love with its flowers, Fashion with its patches and fans, homely Girlhood with its beauty and blushes.'[28]

The hearty English banquets of earlier centuries had long ago made way for more sophisticated and fashionable fare. The introduction of expensive wines, champagnes and liqueurs was an accompaniment to the increasingly French, or pseudo-French, food.

Mayoral banquets were still the scenes of lavish feasting, with even greater expense and even more noble and gentry guests to impress: the queen's cousin was among the guests at the Guild Mayor's Luncheon of 1882, for example. On that occasion there was a long menu written entirely in caterer's French, with a choice of two soups (one of them 'Clear Turtle'), two fish dishes, two entrées, twelve varieties of roast, five other main dishes, four game dishes, seven sweets, ten sorts of pastry and ice cream, and a wide range of fresh and crystallised fruit, all washed down with copious quantities of sherry, champagne, punch, claret and hock.[29] The champagne was Heidseick Dry Monopole 1895, at 105 shillings per dozen bottles.[30] The ordinary folk ate substantially but a great deal less extravagantly at their Guild dinners and teas. In 1922, for example, the textile workers, after their procession, sat down to a lunch of sandwiches, meat pies, cakes, tea and coffee.[31]

The last day of the 1882 Guild saw excitements galore. Perhaps the most sensational event of the whole Guild, to those who thirsted after novelty, was the 'meet and procession of "cyclists"', when 359 bicyclists (including half a dozen tricyclists) met at West Cliff at 4.30 p.m., some wearing badges and pink sashes, and with all the riders 'attractively attired'. They came from as far afield as Kendal, Chester, Llandudno and Bradford, as well as from local clubs, and held their own equivalent of a procession: preceded by four mounted policeman and a trumpeter of the 5th Dragoon Guards they rode along Fishergate and Church Street to Moor Park and on to Fulwood Barracks, where they were photographed and had what was described as 'luncheon' but which was eaten at about 6 p.m. Cycling was in its infancy, and such a gathering was an extraordinary sight. The spectacle caused amazement: 'the sight was a very beautiful one, and so evenly and quietly did the riders proceed, that they appeared to be sailing, rather than moving on wheels, through the streets.'[32]

And to conclude a Guild full of novelty, there was the first example of what immediately became a Guild tradition: a torchlight procession on the Saturday evening. About a thousand people congregated at the end of New Hall Lane and marched through the town to Fulwood Barracks, dressed in grotesque and bizarre costumes: 'the comic and the grotesque, the grim and the laughable, the ludicrous and the fantastic—soldiers, demons, musicians, brigands, aesthetes, witches, clowns, dragons and elephant figures, monkeys.' The procession was illuminated by torches, flares and lanterns, and was 'a most sensational, eccentric revel—a wild, laughable, flammivorous display'. Adjectives were, as ever, in short supply, and the dictionaries were certainly raided by the reporters of 1882.[33]

The Guild of 1902 followed the pattern of 1882, with a multitude of additional entertainments and a whole series of processions for different groups and denominations. An entry in the minutes of the 1902 Guild Committee highlights a developing problem. It had been usual for the Corporation to authorise a programme of events, which could then be used in official publicity and its own published programmes. The information could also be included in the souvenirs, guides and publicity handouts of private firms. In 1902 there were several requests from the organisers of fringe events that these should be included in the Guild programme. They would thus gain invaluable publicity, and have an official seal of approval which might bring them extra custom or visitors.

The Guild Committee accepted one of these proposals, but very late in the day, at the end of July 1902, the full council rejected its decision: 'the North End Football Club Events which the Club was holding in the Guild Week' should not, it decided, be included 'because it also opened the door to the inclusion of every other unofficial entertainment organised for the week'. There had to be some degree of restraint in the official programme, even though the Corporation wholeheartedly welcomed any event which might add to the attractions of Guild week.[34]

Subsequently, the Nonconformist Sunday Schools complained (echoes of 1862!) that the Military Tournament, part of the official programme, would take place at the same time as their procession. The Guild Mayor was to attend the tournament, and so it had been included as an official event, but as a result of these protests it was agreed that 'the tournament should be expunged from the Programme'.[35] These decisions had the desired effect in 1902, but the defences were crumbling: it would not be long before the Guild programme included every conceivable (and some almost inconceivable) 'unofficial entertainment'.

Guild Mayors and their guests, 1862–1922

The nobility and gentry remained faithful to the Preston Guild despite the setback of 1842. Although uncertainty over whether the 1842 Guild would be held, as well as fears of Chartist demonstrations and civil unrest, had kept the upper classes away in that year, they returned in force in 1862. In 1882 the presence of royalty—albeit minor royalty (the duke of Cambridge was a grandson of King George III)—lent a particularly elevated social tone. However, distinctions between the old gentry and the newly rich merchants and manufacturers were already very blurred, and the Horrocks family in particular had climbed with extreme rapidity to the highest social circles.

The 1842 Guild Mayor was Samuel Horrocks, who enjoyed the fortune and prestige of his uncle, the legendary John Horrocks, and of his father Samuel the elder, for many years MP for the borough. In 1862 the Guild Mayor was Robert Townley Parker of Cuerden, grandson of Robert Parker, Guild Mayor in 1762: his family had been closely connected with the Preston Guild since the fifteenth century, and had many times filled other Guild offices. He himself had been high sheriff of Lancashire as long ago as 1817, MP for Preston 1837–41 and 1852–57, and was elected as a councillor in 1861 solely to allow him to be made Guild Mayor in the following year. After officiating in that role, he retired from the Corporation—a very efficient massaging of the democratic process.[36]

The 14th Earl of Derby, the leader of county society, was also from a family which had been intimately associated with the town for centuries. He had been prime minister briefly in 1852 and again in 1858–59 (and would serve as such again in 1866–68). Lord Derby played a prominent part in the 1862 Guild, and personally presided at a number of 'county' events, notably the agricultural show on Penwortham Holme which was a watery disaster. As usual he brought an illustrious entourage of titled family and friends—Lord Stanley, the Earl of Sefton, Lord Skelmersdale, Lord de Tabley, Sir James Yorke Scarlett and Colonel Patten were among those singled out for mention in contemporary descriptions. The earl and his family and companions were special guests at the Masonic Ball on the Wednesday evening and they, with many other county gentry, were distinguished but disguised at the Costume Ball on the last evening—though the newspaper reports make it clear that the disguises were thin, since the nobility present always wore plenty of *real* jewels.

In 1882 the office of Guild Mayor was again filled by a rich manufacturer, Edmund Birley. His guest list was particularly grand, being graced by the presence of the duke of Cambridge, but in 1882 all of the great families of Lancashire turned out in force. The ceremony of laying the foundation stone of the Harris building was attended by 'the Duke of Cambridge, the Countess of Lathom, the Earl and Countess of Derby, noblemen from different parts, [and] many county gentlemen',[37] while at the magnificent banquet which the Mayor gave afterwards there was 'a large and brilliant attendance, including the duke of Cambridge, bishops, earls, countesses, members of Parliament, provincial mayors, county squires, military officers, members of the local Town Council, and many ladies and gentlemen belonging to the town and neighbourhood'.[38] From 1862 onwards invitations were sent to the lord mayors and mayors of all the Lancashire boroughs, a list which grew fast as many towns were incorporated in the three decades before the First World War, and which produced a fine display of civic robes and regalia in the mayoral procession.

The Derby family was greatly admired in Preston (though it had been treated with much less reverence earlier in the nineteenth century when its politics failed to meet with the approval of the town's large and volatile electorate). In 1902 Frederick, Earl of Derby, was honoured by being chosen as Guild Mayor. He had succeeded to the earldom on the death of his brother in 1893, since 1897 had been lord lieutenant of Lancashire, and in 1895 he had been chosen as the first lord mayor of Liverpool (another instance of a city council honouring an outsider in this way). The Countess of Derby, in her role of Guild Mayoress, took a particular interest in the Guild. Learning of discussions within the Corporation regarding the flags and banners belonging to the town, and of the Council's wish to have a new standard made, the Countess made a romantic gesture, the reference to which in the minutes of the Corporation strikes a curious note among expenditure on new sewerage schemes and other mundane business:

the Mayor reminded the Committee that in the days that had been it was not unusual for Banners to be presented by Ladies when sending forth their Knights, and with the Committee's permission he desired on behalf of the Countess of Derby to express her wish to make the presentation to the Town, of the Standard.

The Countess's 'graceful and generous offer was most cordially and gratefully accepted'.[39] It was indeed a fine banner, and the workmanship was of the highest quality. Which solid middle-class gentleman, sitting on Preston Corporation in 1902, could have resisted the chivalrous and elegantly phrased offer of Countess Constance of Derby? In November 1902 the Corporation voted unanimously that the earl be granted the honorary freedom of the borough of Preston,

> in recognition of his long and distinguished connection with this Town, and to worthily mark the high appreciation of the Inhabitants of the Town of the eminent services rendered by him during the Mayoralty for the year 1901–2, especially in connection with the celebration of the Guild Merchant of 1902.[40]

It was a fitting tribute to the earl, but thereafter the family, although it did not entirely sever its connection with Preston (George Frederick Stanley was MP for Preston 1910–23), became less significant in Guild affairs. The Guild Mayor in 1922 was Henry Astley-Bell, a leading cotton manufacturer and director of the firm of A. and J. Leigh of Preston: he lived at Garstang, but had close links with the town. In 1952 a significant number of councillors and others 'favoured a return to titled patronage' as a means of overcoming party political issues, which had vexed the discussions on the choice of Guild Mayor.[41] Eventually, as a compromise between the political parties, John James Ward, a former mayor and a political independent, was chosen. The Guild Mayors of 1952, 1972 and 1992 were Preston people, and the practice of bringing in notable outsiders to give a special cachet to the office of Guild Mayor has ended, though not without debate.[42]

Preston and the Guild, 1882–1902

The journal of Edward Harrison, a Southport solicitor who visited the 1882 Guild with his family, gives interesting insights into this great event.[43] Harrison, it must be said, was a rather sour and jaundiced observer: he came for the Guild, but was far from delighted with what he found. Accommodation was extremely scarce, and he had to pay through the nose for a house which was less than conveniently placed and had too few beds:

> Saturday, left home at Southport with my wife & 6 children, for the house of the Revn. S. N. Smith 1, Athol Terrace, Ashton on Ribble about 2 miles

from Preston which I had taken for £10 for the Guild Week ... arrived in the evening—we brough [*sic*] 2 officers bed steads—attended Ashton Church with family. The Rev. Mr. Ramsbottom read & preached well sermon 10 mins long, not condemning the looked for pleasures of the coming week. The prices of cabs were doubled for this week.

Harrison and his family watched the processions, having, in common with thousands of others, paid large sums to take window space in the shops along Fishergate and Church Street: 'Tuesday we witnessed sundry processions from Mr. Hayhursts Shop window Fishergate.' The word 'sundry' suggests a definite lack of enthusiasm for the magnificent sights of the day. On Wednesday he and his wife and the two eldest daughters went to the fancy dress ball at the Corn Exchange. He wore 'half court dress', his wife was a sixteenth-century German lady, the elder daughter, Agnes, was an oyster girl, and Gertrude went as Nancy Redfern, a character in Harrison Ainsworth's *Lancashire Witches*. The costumes were selected from pictures well beforehand, a practice commended in advertisements as early as 1842: in a slightly ambiguous comment he noted that Gertrude, the witch, 'looked just the part [and] her dress according to the plate was perfect'. Thursday saw a cultural event, a visit with the elder daughters to see 'Halley & his band [and] Madam Patey' (the celebrated Dame Adelina Patti). But he ends this part of his journal with a short and irritable outburst:

It may be mentioned that had it not been for my son Richards getting a cab after half past eleven on the night of the first fancy dress ball, we might probably not have got there at all owing to the Cab from Hardings not coming as appointed at 10 P.M. when all our preparations would have been thrown away.

It is scarcely surprising that accommodation and cabs were in very short supply, and were very expensive. The statistics of visitors to the Guild became more extraordinary with every twenty years. In 1882 arrivals by train were estimated at 10,000 (Monday), 25,000 (Tuesday), 175,000 (Wednesday), 85,000 (Thursday), 25,000 (Friday) and 100,000 (Saturday), a total of 420,000 visitors by rail alone.[44] The differences from day to day are illuminating: the opening ceremonies were clearly of limited interest to people from beyond Preston, for whom the real draw was the magnificent spectacle of the Wednesday trades processions. There was comparatively little to attract outsiders to the various church and society processions, but on Saturday the closing ceremonies and the torchlight procession drew well over 100,000 people into the town. The railway companies had to cope with staggering numbers of day trippers, while the roads were saturated with streams of carriages, coaches and huge crowds of pedestrians walking into the town from its outer suburbs and the surrounding countryside. If these are included the numbers at the 1882 Guild must have been approaching three-quarters of a million over the six days of the celebration.

In 1922 the correspondent of *The Times* found the numbers almost incredible. He noted how the visitors were enterprising in sustaining themselves during the day. By the time of the 1922 Guild the visiting hordes were swelled by the fleets of motor coaches which disgorged their passengers at the edge of the town. The correspondent noted that soon after daybreak these fleets began to arrive: most of the people had come well prepared with food, 'and depended on good-natured householders only to make them tea and lend them pots. Thus the problem of feeding multitudes day by day, which had troubled many people, does not seriously exist.' He reported that by seven in the morning the streets were lined with people, and that so great were the crowds that vehicular traffic had ground to a halt well before nine o'clock.[45]

Negotiating with the public utilities and the railway companies was time-consuming for the Corporation. Fortunately, most firms saw the Guild as a marvellous opportunity to make money or indulge in extensive advertising and publicity (and ideally both). The Preston Gas Company, for example, usually offered a 20 per cent discount to the Corporation for supplying gas at Guild events (a service it had provided since 1822). In 1902, however, there was competition from the new Electricity Company. The Gas Company had already found that balloons (which certainly could not be electric) were an excellent means of getting some publicity, so it offered a reduction of no less than 60 per cent on its gas tariff for use in the balloon ascents and in special illuminations during the Guild, with pipes supplied free, and charges made only for time, labour and the carting of materials. The National Electricity Supply Co., not to be outdone, offered an even better bargain. It would supply *free* current to all outside illuminations at the Town Hall, the Harris and other public buildings, during the Guild week *and* the Coronation celebrations that were to take place shortly afterwards. The Corporation would only have to pay for wiring, fitting and removal.[46] Electric lighting on this scale was still a novelty, and its brilliance, regularity and reliability still provoked gasps of wonder and admiration.

With its own publicity requirements in mind (for electricity was the symbol of an up-to-date and modern town) the Corporation accepted the offer of the Electricity Company, and chose electric lighting for the buildings and for special areas of the town where evening events were to be held. The new illumination was only part of an extensive facelift. Redecorating the Public Hall, Assembly Room and other facilities at the Corn Exchange and lighting them by electricity cost £2,900 alone. The Town Hall was upgraded, with new kitchens, a lift, and improvements in the strong room where there was to be a display of charters and regalia. In the Public Hall the walls were newly covered in painted lincrusta, there was abundant fresh plaster ornamentation and many potted plants, and most of the floor was repaired for dancing.[47] The streets were decorated by house and shop owners, with some help from the Corporation. Each application for temporary structures had to be vetted on safety and amenity grounds: arches, a favourite device in several preceding Guilds, had to be 21 feet above the street, and had to allow a 16-foot carriageway with pathways at least 6 feet wide on the pavement edges.[48]

Organising the processions in 1902 was exceedingly troublesome. They were a major headache for Guild Committees long before then, and matters had not improved with time. The town was still spreading outwards, with new housing estates and new roads sprawling north to Fulwood, westwards to Ashton, and eastwards to Ribbleton. Clearly it was not possible to include these areas in procession routes, but there was strong pressure for the inclusion of new streets and districts in the inner town. In January 1902, for example, the Guild Committee decided, after petitions and counter-petitions, that the route of the textile trades procession should be the same as that of 1882 but with the addition of New Hall Lane, Skeffington Road and Ribbleton Lane.[49] At the same time, many newly formed local organisations were requesting either that they should be awarded a place in a procession, or that they should have processions of their own, or were objecting to the earlier decisions of the committee. In 1902 the Royal National Lifeboat Institution asked for a procession place but was turned down because, as it was not unreasonably pointed out, 'it is deemed desirable to adhere to the local characteristics that have always prevailed in the Guild Processions'.[50]

Once the procession routes had been decided, the whole plan had to be sent to the chief constable of the borough police. He then assessed the practicality of the routes, their timing and their lengths, to try to avoid collisions between processions and to prevent any threat to public order or safety. In March 1902, for example, he wrote to the Guild Committee to point out that his detailed calculations had shown a major potential hazard—the clashing of the textile procession and the trades procession:

> supposing the route suggested for the 'Trades Procession' be adopted, it will be absolutely necessary, In order to avoid collision, that the 'Textile Procession' should start from one to one and a half hours later than the former ... should the 'trades Procession' start as suggested at 9-a.m. and proceed about the rate of 2 miles per hour and covers as at the last Guild, a distance of 3 miles (though of this I cannot have any assurance), it will not clear the Town Hall end of Cheapside, much before 11 o'clock, while should the 'Textile' Procession leave Garstang Road at 9-a.m. and travel over the route already suggested, at the same rate, that is 2 miles per hour and be of the same length, that is 3 miles, its head will reach Cheapside, by the Town Hall, about 10-o'clock nor will it clear Fishergate before 12.[51]

A talent for mental arithmetic was certainly an asset in such circumstances ... and a talent for diplomacy was essential for Guild Committee members. In May 1902 they had lengthy discussions with a deputation of trades employers and employees after the chief constable, assiduous in his checking of the plans, had requested this group to assemble its procession east of the town centre in London Road, rather than at the top of Fishergate Hill as they intended. In 1882 there had been serious trouble at the station entrance when crowds coming from the trains collided with processions marshalling in the street, and the police were anxious to avoid its recurrence. The trades representatives objected strongly to the proposed revision, because most of the iron foundries and engineering works were at the western side of the town, and marshalling in London Road would thus be very inconvenient. It was also pointed out that the station had recently been rebuilt with a more spacious exit. These arguments were eventually accepted, and the chief constable was overruled (as were the two railway companies, which had expressed similar fears).[52]

The 1902 Guild week had perfect weather, perhaps the best of any Guild between 1842 and 1992. Many thousands of people came into the town by rail, and to cope with the crush an extra series of temporary platforms was erected at the bottom of Charnley Street, in the sidings east of the main line. The crowds were so great, however, that one young man, at least, was scared stiff. James Spencer, writing in 1952, recalled that on the final Saturday of the 1902 Guild he had watched the torchlight procession ('which I did not find impressive') and then 'the great mass of people, as if by common consent, surged like a tidal wave towards the railway station. I was lifted off my feet and carried willy-nilly with the surging crowd—and, breathless, gasping for air, I was frightened. The fear of suffocation was my last memory of the 1902 Guild.'[53]

Improvements in transport and communications in the later nineteenth century increased the opportunities for foreign and expatriate visitors to come to the Guild. From 1862 Guilds were seen, at first unofficially but after 1902 with official support, as a means of keeping Prestonians who had gone overseas in contact with their home town or the town of their forebears. As early as 1822 there were visitors from overseas: a very bad poem written for the Guild of 1842 says that:

At the last Preston Guild so many thousands came they say
From France, Holland, and Germany, likewise America,
From east and west, from north and south, such thronging crowds did meet,
They scarcely could find room to meet each other in the street.[54]

The *Preston Herald* reported that at the 1882 Guild there were 'Visitors by tens of thousands from all parts of the United Kingdom, and even from the British Colonies, the United States, and the Continent of Europe'.[55] Former Preston residents in the Empire or former colonies—especially Australia, New Zealand and the United States—made special efforts to keep in touch with each other and to celebrate or commemorate the Guild. Thus in 1902 the Guild Mayor, Lord Derby, and the Corporation received an illuminated address from New Zealand, beautifully bound in leather with inlaid marquetry using native woods:

> an Address of Congratulations from former Residents in your Town, now Citizens of this far distant land, wishing you, and all your fellow townsmen, health, wealth, and prosperity. The Preston Lads now resident in Dunedin, New Zealand, have not forgotten, though we have traversed 16,000 miles of our naval field, that you are about to celebrate in our Ancient Town of Preston, the first Guild of the New Century, and we offer you our united congratulations.

Lord Derby replied in a similar vein, but with a sting in the tail, saying that the borough and its people 'will feel with yourselves that many thousands of miles of distance, so far from weakening old ties, serve only to strengthen the memory of our connections'. Going on, he wished the 'Preston Lads' well, and in a noble but not necessarily honourable comment upon the industrial smog of early twentieth-century Preston, referred to the 'brighter skies under which you live, [which] present features which compare favourably with your former surroundings'. *Very* disloyal, but of course he did not live in Preston.[56]

In 1922 it was noted that there were over 300 overseas visitors at the Guild, including people from Ohio, Calcutta, Cairo and Melbourne. Henry Pye of New York was interviewed by the *Daily Mail*: 'a typical young American, of 73, with a deep banded straw hat and no waistcoat … and looking not a day more than 50.' He was at his fourth Guild and intended, he said, to come for his fifth: he entertained the reporters by speaking 'Lanky'. Edward Woolley of Woonsocket, Rhode Island, had come to renew acquaintance with Preston, accompanied by his wife and four sons. He talked 'real American' and was, according to the *Daily Mail*, very smitten by the mayor's 'sweet wife'. Mrs Woolley roguishly said that she was quite taken by the mayor. The Woolleys had themselves filmed, 'so that [they] may exhibit it in Rhode Island': the Guild had entered the modern age.[57]

CHAPTER EIGHT

The Guilds of 1952 and 1972

O N   T H E   S U N D A Y at the end of Guild week 1922 the correspondent of the *Daily Mail*, who had been in Preston all week, described the closing hours of the celebrations: 'The comedy is ended; Preston's Guild is over for another 20 years.' It was, he said, a wonderful scene, with people waltzing to a melodeon at two in the morning, thirsty dancers offering a shilling just to have a cup of tea at one in the morning, torchlight processions and speeches from the Town Hall balcony. The crowds in the Market Place were shouting 'We want the Mayor; We want the Mayor' and the mayor, who had already made one formal speech, had to go out again and kiss his hand to the assembled crowds. The reporter thought that there were 30,000 people waving streamers, holding balloons on strings, and showering confetti. Many were in carnival dress: 'the heads of prehistoric beasts (direct from the torchlight procession) poked in tall inquisitiveness. Pierrette stood in Harlequin's arms ... and a well-directed lassoing string of paper, pink or blue, was good as any Cupid's shaft for starting a flirtation followed by linked arms, ices *alfresco* and kisses from the captured.'[1] Well, it was the *Daily Mail*: *The Times* had given rather more attention to the industrial exhibits and the details of the Royal Lancashire Agricultural Show.[2]

The close of the official proceedings had been marked by an emotional speech from the Guild Mayor, Henry Astley-Bell. At 11.50 p.m. he stood on the balcony of the Guildhall and addressed the crowd below: 'Preston has been a proud town; we are prouder than ever tonight. God bless you all; may you be spared to see the Guild of 1942.' Hindsight gives those words an especially poignant quality. There was no Guild in 1942, and many of those who stood below the Guildhall balcony were not spared. For the first time in its history, war intervened to prevent the holding of a Guild.

The Second World War began in September 1939, shortly before detailed planning for the 1942 Guild was due to begin. By this time preparations for a Guild were taking at least two years, and such crucial business as booking leading musicians and performers, and arranging for the redecoration and alteration of the buildings to be used for Guild events, should have been under way by the spring of 1940. It was very quickly apparent that there were insuperable obstacles to holding a Guild in wartime. With strict rationing of most commodities there was little chance of a celebration, and with full conscription there were few people available to celebrate or to carry out such non-essential work. More importantly, few people felt like celebrating: there was an incontrovertible moral argument that even to try to hold a Guild was contrary to the spirit of national self-denial and the devotion of all resources, mental and physical, to the war effort.

Nothing serious was done, and on 3 July 1941 the Corporation passed a long-predicted formal resolution that 'the celebration of the Guild Merchant of 1942 be postponed until the first full municipal year following peace'.[3] The initial intention was simply to postpone it, so that the nominal Guild of 1942 would be held as soon as possible after the war, but when peace came in August 1945 it was clear that this was quite unrealistic. The desperate plight of the economy, the acute shortages of foodstuffs, fuel and industrial raw materials, and the consequent rigid rationing, meant that to hold a Guild was impossible. Immediately after the end of the war, on 27 September 1945, the Corporation resolved that the decision of 1941 should be rescinded, and 'that further consideration be given to the question in September 1946'.[4] But when September 1946 came, it was obvious that severe economic problems and very strict rationing would continue for some time.

To plan a Guild would take at least two years even in the most auspicious circumstances. Recognising, therefore, that it would be at least 1949 before a Guild could be held, the council agreed that the most satisfactory solution was simply to defer it until ten years after the abortive 1942 Guild. In this way, although the twenty-year interval had been disrupted by circumstances beyond the control of the Corporation, the Guild would be held at the earliest realistic date, and the neatness of having the years ending in '2' (a not inconsiderable factor) would be maintained. The Corporation had been faced with several options: to abandon the Guild altogether; to abandon the formal business of the Guild so that it was simply a festival (shades of the thinking of 1842); to hold the Guild in 1962 and thereby resume the old pattern, but with a forty-year gap; to hold the Guild as soon as possible in, say, 1949 or 1950 (which would have ended the 'neatness' of the dates); or the solution which was eventually adopted. On 26 September 1946 the Corporation resolved 'that the celebration of the Guild Merchant be held in 1952'.[5]

Planning for the 1952 Guild began in January 1950, when the Guild Sub-Committee of the Corporation was established. This body consulted, as was usual, with the different churches, schools, trade and industry organisations and commercial concerns, as to the best way of conducting the Guild. Despite the official decision to carry on the pre-war traditions, there was a great deal of debate about the form which the 1952 Guild should take. Many were conscious of the changed circumstances and, as always, there were those who argued that it was time the Guild became more 'progressive' or 'up-to-date'. The so-called New Elizabethan Age had dawned by the time of the Guild, but even before then there had been voices urging departures from what were seen as old, outdated ways.

In November 1950, for example, the Corporation gave serious consideration to the question of whether the trades procession should be scrapped. It was felt by some that an old-fashioned procession, or walk, by representatives of the trades was not a suitably up-to-date advertisement for Preston's industrial might, and that instead there should be an exciting modern alternative. The town clerk was instructed to ascertain the views of trade and employee associations 'as to whether it would be practical and desirable to organise Trade Processions as in former Guild Celebrations, or to arrange instead a modern form of Trade and Industrial Exhibition'.[6] The answer was resoundingly old-fashioned: there was overwhelming enthusiasm for retaining the trades procession. The obvious answer to the alleged conflict of opinion was the one eventually adopted. The trades procession went ahead as usual, and a large industrial exhibition was held at Moor Park during the previous week and the Guild week itself. Preston thereby managed to satisfy both views: it was progressive and yet its ancient traditions were maintained.

The 1952 Guild thus retained all the major features of its predecessors as far back as 1842, despite the pressure for a break with tradition. For over a century, and probably much longer, there had been those who felt that the Guild was simply a festival, a form of carnival, and that its historic associations were of no importance. Each time, some members of the Corporation had suggested that the Guild should not be held: in the words of Frank Billinge in the 1972 *Guild Handbook,* they 'questioned whether the whole business was not outmoded and irrelevant to the times'.[7] And it is certainly true that, in terms of its *original* (that is, medieval) conception, the Guild had been irrelevant since 1835, and indeed had had only theoretical relevance for at least sixty years before that.

But to consider it only in those terms was narrow and limited. The Guild remained relevant for three reasons. The first was that it was good for Preston, encouraging commercial activity, bringing income and publicity to the town, and reinforcing civic pride and prestige. The second was that although it had had no more than a symbolic role since 1842, it represented a tangible link with the past and was a venerable tradition which should be valued for its own sake. The importance of that factor cannot be overestimated for, although these feelings are hard to define and may appear irrational, the antiquity of the celebration undoubtedly gave it a special status and produced a special pride in, and affection for, the Guild. On various and usually dubious grounds, the Victorians swept away many of the customs and traditions which they inherited from the past, and the Guild was almost lost too. As long ago as 1682, Richard Kuerden had recognised the particular historic quality of the Guild, and already he venerated it as a rare survival. Three centuries later, its rarity and importance had increased many-fold.

The third reason for the relevance of the Guild was perhaps less elevated, but even more important. It was simply that people enjoyed it. All the evidence, as far back as there are eye-witness accounts, suggests that every Guild has been an occasion for mass public enthusiasm and enormous popular enjoyment. As a spectacle, as an excuse for a good time, as a holiday or carnival, as a time when the sense and thrill of being present at a remarkable event was strong, the Guild had always been a triumph. There has often been a tendency to take the Guild too seriously, and to forget that since the 1760s it has been completely irrelevant in day-to-day terms. That does not matter. It is a symbol, it is immensely popular, it has a history that can be traced back for well over eight centuries, and people have a deep and strong identification with it. Those seem to me to be good enough reasons for its continuation.

In 1952 there was a great deal of doubt about this. The uncertainties over the holding of a Guild, the lack of enthusiasm from some quarters, the criticism of its 'old-fashioned' character, and the continued effects of rationing, led to fears that the event would be a failure. According to Frank Billinge, not until the May of Guild year did any public enthusiasm begin to show, and even then 'the torpor of those not directly involved seemed to continue, indicated by the initially poor response to the side street decoration competition'. It had been thirty years since the previous Guild, and some feared that the longer break had damaged the continuity of the celebration. And then, spontaneously and suddenly, 'the whole thing caught light, the town came alive. Enthusiasm blossomed with the June roses and the Guild celebration was an assured success, come rain, wind or a fresh visitation of austerity.'[8]

The Guild had the customary separate processions for the Church of England, the Catholic Guilds, the Nonconformist Sunday Schools Scholars, and the Friendly Societies. The trades procession went ahead as it had done since the late eighteenth century, still separated into a large textile section and a general trades' section. As was subsequently noted, this was the last Guild in which the textile trades played a major part, for in the following two decades the collapse in the town's cotton industry wrought havoc. In 1922 the textile section had more than fifty vehicles, and eight bands (out of thirteen in the trades procession); in 1952 there were just nineteen vehicles, with four bands. In 1972 this, once by far the largest and most impressive of the participants in the Guild processions, was reduced to a rump: there were only nine vehicles, and the list of these reveals how dramatic had been the decline in the industry. All that was left of the trade which had dominated the industrial structure of the town were rayon, surgical dressings, velvet, Evvaprest, woollen knitwear, under garments, school wear, stretch covers, and dusters, mops and tea towels ... how the mighty were fallen.[9]

The 1952 Guild themes reflected the divergent views of the event itself. There was a prominent historical element, under the umbrella title of *Merrie England*, with pageants and exhibitions on nostalgic or retrospective themes. There were also strong overtones of the New Age, and the industrial exhibition was only one of several events and attractions which looked to the future of the town and lauded its prospects. Preston was in transition: it was experiencing industrial upheavals, the loss of its major industry, and the first of the physical changes—the clearance of large areas of older housing and planning of new roads and redevelopment schemes—which by 1980 would radically and irrevocably alter the appearance of the town.

The Historical Pageant of 1922 had been a remarkable success, and was still clear in the memories of many in the town. James Spencer (who wrote the historical material in the 1952 Guild programme) recalled that he had never 'witnessed anything so beautiful as the miming of those children in their colourful historical costumes. It was the outstanding event of the 1922 Guild and it will be remembered whilst life lasts by the people who saw it.' [10] In 1952 the concept was repeated, again with great success. On the Wednesday and the Thursday a schoolchildren's pageant was held. The first day was entitled *Children of Yesterday*. It was in full costume and covered the period from the 'first recorded Guild' in 1328 to the first Guild of the twentieth century, that of 1902: 'appropriate sports and pastimes' were depicted. On the second day, *Children of Today*, the games and activities of the children of 1952 were shown, including a folk dancing festival. Each performance attracted audiences of over 15,000 people, and almost 6,000 schoolchildren took part. Frank Billinge records a story told by Tom Haines, a sergeant in the Preston Borough Police. Haines saw, watching the pageant, two rows of old ladies who had come on a coach trip accompanied by one old man:

There wasn't a single dry eye amongst them. As for the old boy, he was trying to light his pipe. Each time, something new caught his eye, and, as the burned-down match caught his finger, he would with a muttered imprecation throw it away—to repeat the same process over again. At the sixth attempt he succeeded. [11]

The children's pageant was 'vast in conception, superb in organisation and faultless in production ... there was not a single aspect of it that did not merit a superlative.' As in 1922, there was a huge 'behind the scenes' enterprise, with long rehearsals for months in advance, and highly complex planning and organisation: the event, according to a local newspaper, would have 'done credit to an Army operational staff'. [12]

History was also the theme of the 1972 children's event, when the pageant entitled *Prospect of Preston* was given by about 3,000 children in front of 10,659 spectators (the figures are exact: the account-keeping for this Guild was more rigorous than ever before). The children depicted Preston, past, present and future, with displays of Preston Past showing, for example, 'Market and Fair' and 'The Coming of the Factory'. Preston Present was represented by 'Pathways to Preston – North, West, East and South', and by the arrival of people from all over the world, making Preston a cosmopolitan town. Preston Future looked at the trades procession of the Guild of 2012, and the future of Preston as part of the Central Lancashire New Town. Forty years later, many of the ideas conveyed by the pageant seem absurdly over-optimistic and unrealistic, but they represented the enthusiastic spirit of the age, when it was hoped that the Preston of tomorrow would be 'a new city of bright modern buildings, set in green spaces, fresh with the promise of an inspiring future'. There is still no sign of the Preston citizen of tomorrow, who was represented in 1972 by 'a small boy in fluorescent space outfit'.[13]

In keeping with the forward-and-backward nature of the 1952 Guild, another pageant was a production of Sir Edward German's light opera, *Merrie England*, performed in Avenham Park before huge audiences by Preston's various amateur operatic and dramatic societies. *Merrie England* is set in the reign of Elizabeth I and, inevitably in 1952, there was a good deal of talk of the new Elizabeth: 'for the first Guild of the reign of the second Queen Elizabeth ... Preston's leading amateur societies aptly chose a theme of the times of the first Queen Bess.'[14] This romanticised view of history was echoed in one of the major attractions of the 1972 Guild, the 'pageant version' of the hit musical *Camelot*. The inclusion of a musical—as popular in the late 1960s and early 1970s as light opera had been earlier in the century—was another instance of the Guild changing with fashion. The production of *Camelot* (according to the *Lancashire Evening Post*, 'the show with everything—romance, delightful music, simple story, fantasy, comedy and tragedy') was on a grand scale, as befitted both the Guild and the setting, the natural amphitheatre in Avenham Park.[15]

The 1952 Guild was noteworthy as the first to be broadcast by the BBC, that of 1922 being just too early to be so captured. In 1952, as well as giving extensive radio coverage to the Guild, the BBC broadcast Community Hymn Singing from the Lune Street Methodist Chapel at 8.30 p.m. on Guild Sunday, the day before the opening of the proceedings: the hymns were announced by the radio celebrity Wilfred Pickles.[16] Twenty years later television was well established, and the Guild organisers realised the value of that medium for publicity. They also, very shrewdly, appreciated the compulsion of the soap opera. By cultivating executives of Granada TV they managed to get a visit to the Preston Guild written into the script of *Coronation Street* (for many living outside the North West, probably the first time they had ever heard of the Guild). Granada also made two special programmes on the Guild, and the BBC included coverage on *Look North*. Inconsiderately, the organisers of the 1972 Munich Olympics had failed to appreciate that the Guild was to be held in the first week in September, and arranged their own event to coincide. This meant that the BBC gave the Guild a lot less airspace than might otherwise have been the case.[17]

The use of the new media and the types of 'historical' show demonstrate the Guild successfully adapting to changing circumstances and changing fashions. At each successive Guild the style of the times is much in evidence: pictures of the 1972 Guild, with many miniskirts and wedge-heeled shoes in evidence, and the men with flowing locks and flowery ties, now look as historic as nineteenth-century engravings. Among the entertainments the same vagaries of fashion are apparent: the community singing and *Merrie England* of 1952 gave way to the television-influenced Old Tyme Music Hall (with

David Jacobs, Clive Dunn, Ann Shelton, and Mike and Bernie Winters, among others) and the All Star Pop Concert of 1972.

The latter was troubled by the waywardness of the performers: as the *Official Record* of the Guild notes, in its very grave and ponderous style, 'the Entertainments Officer had been able to secure the services of Mungo Jerry, and the Garry [*sic*] Glitter Rock and Roll Spectacular, two acts having a high rating in the popularity charts'. This was after 'much discussion and sometimes heated argument over a prolonged period concerning an appropriate form of entertainment to provide for young people': it was agreed that 'the general consensus of opinion of young people was that the concert would be popular and would attract a large audience'. Unfortunately, Gary Glitter failed to turn up, and 'by way of compensation' (or, after their lucky escape, given the subsequent notoriety of Mr Glitter) the audience was promised free admission to a future concert which he would give at the Guildhall.[18] How troublesome the young people were, wanting special entertainment and expensive groups and acts, with strange names and even stranger behaviour. How the organisers of past Guilds must have turned in their graves ...

The pop concert took place on 13 September 1972, after the official close of the Guild, because of serious problems with the completion of the new Guild Hall. In the mid-1950s it had been decided that the town needed an inner ring road. The plans that were drawn up envisaged the demolition of the Public Hall, which lay in its proposed path. The aim was to pull down the building by 1973–74: the front, the Corn Exchange of 1822, survives, but the demolition of the remainder was finally carried out, sixteen years later than scheduled, in the autumn of 1990. In 1966, partly as a replacement, the Corporation agreed to build a new civic and public hall, to be called the Guild Hall. Work began in June 1970, the contract stipulating that it should be completed by June 1972 to allow it to be used for the Guild in the September of that year.

The work fell behind schedule, and the Corporation therefore had to draw up contingency plans for the events which were to have been held in the Guild Hall. On 9 August 1972, only three weeks before the opening of the Guild, the decision was taken to move events to the Public Hall and the Top Rank Ballroom, or in some instances to defer them until the building had been completed (thus, the Guild Concert by the Royal Liverpool Philharmonic Orchestra was not staged until December). The delay had been exacerbated by strikes in the building and construction trades during the summer of 1972, which also meant that the stands and exhibition buildings at Moor Park and elsewhere were not properly finished: in some cases, as the 1972 *Official Record* noted in its elliptical style, 'there was insufficient time left to cover them to protect spectators from inclement weather'.[19]

Because of problems with the Guild Hall the other great musical event of the 1972 Guild was also staged in the Public Hall at short notice: this was a concert by 'one who had been Britain's most popular singing star over a period of more than thirty years',

Vera Lynn, the Forces' sweetheart. The concert was considered by some as the climax to the whole week of celebrations and, 'singing songs which had made her world famous for three decades, including many of those which had enthralled men in uniform during the long years of the Second World War, Vera Lynn captivated her audience. Patrons needed little encouragement to join in the songs when invited, and when the time came for the show to end they applauded for so long and so vigorously that Miss Lynn was only able to bring the show to a conclusion by singing two encores.'[20]

And of course there was an abundance of other events, official and unofficial, associated with the Guilds of 1952 and especially 1972. By the beginning of the twentieth century the Guild organisers faced increasing pressure to include many fringe events in the official programme, or at least to give them recognition. Just as a series of extra processions and pageants had, because of requests from their organisers, been added to the formal proceedings of the Guild after 1842, so the promoters of sporting fixtures, cultural attractions and exhibitions began asking for the inclusion of their particular events, as evidenced by the request from Preston North End in 1902. The 1922 Guild was the last in which there was any real attempt to exclude the fringe from the official proceedings. From 1952 the views of those who, in 1842, had foreseen the Guild as a gigantic carnival were truly realised. The organisers, recognising that it was no longer possible to pretend that the fringe events did not exist, or to adopt a superior attitude to them, opened the way for their inclusion as part of the Guild proper by allowing them to be mentioned in the official Guild programme.

Most of the events were already far removed from the spirit of the old Guilds: children's pageants, schools processions, firework displays and stone-laying ceremonies were all innovations introduced since 1822. The notion that, suddenly after the Second World War, the Guild lost its medieval feel is incorrect: it had lost that long ago. The incorporation of the fringe events made the Guild into a genuinely popular festival, and removed any residual air of 'elitism': no longer was it tea, buns and gawping at the gentry for the people of Preston, and champagne, ices and the opera for the chosen few. Within the limits imposed by ticket costs and the distribution of invitations the Guild, from 1922 and particularly from 1952, was an event in which all could participate and which all could enjoy. Sentimental idealism, perhaps, but the difference between the 1902 and 1922 Guilds is striking, and between those of 1922 and 1952 even more so.

In 1952, too, commerce officially reared its twentieth-century head, with the holding of the great exhibition of Preston industries at Moor Park. The exhibition was modelled on the industrial fairs which were increasingly popular after the war. The Guild had long ago become a celebration of Preston industries, but this was the first time that the public relations value of a special exhibition of the best of the town and its trade had been realised. But the list of other events reveals the way in which the Guild had become a far more popular and wide-ranging festival than ever before: a veteran car rally; art exhibitions in the Harris; displays by the Preston Scientific Society; a grand swimming gala in the Saul Street Baths; dancing every night in a marquee at Miller Park; laying the foundation stone of an extension to the Royal Infirmary; athletics meetings at the greyhound track in Acregate Lane; cricket matches at Moor Park (Preston & District *v.* Lancaster & District: deadly serious local rivalry), Penwortham and West Cliff; life-saving exhibitions in the river at Avenham Park; football matches (PNE *v.* Servette, a Swiss club, and *v.* West Bromwich Albion); and a parade of the Loyal Regiment, its adoption by the borough, and the laying-up of its colours in the parish church.[21]

Once the floodgates were opened there was no going back. The Guild of 1952 was the culmination of two centuries of evolution, which had seen the Guild change from the great ceremonial event intended to preserve the privileges of the comparatively few, to the great carnival for the very many. Long ago it lasted several weeks, and the ceremonies had been only the core of a long period of feasting and celebration. In the eighteenth century the Guild had been reduced officially to two weeks, and from 1842 was curtailed even further, lasting only from Monday to Saturday in the first week in September. In 1952 the rule was relaxed: a few official events were held on the Saturday and Sunday immediately before the opening of the Guild, and some quasi-Guild events took place in the weeks before and after.

The planners in 1972 placed no particular limits on the Guild, either in its content or its length: there were 'Guild' events before the opening, and several major 'Guild' events long after the formal close of the Guild. A new tradition, and a new direction for the Guild, thus began. The Guild of 1992 included events months before and after the formal Guild week in early September. The wheel turned full circle: the Guild was spread across a much longer time, and in 1992 it was possible to speak of Guild year not just as 'the year of the Guild' but as 'a year of Guild events'. Whether such an enormous expansion of the Guild was necessarily wise or desirable is another matter, considered in the next chapter.

In 1972 pre-Guild events included a 'donkey derby', that symbol of the 1960s and 1970s fete or 'fayre'; the annual conference of the Referees Association, with delegates from all over the world; the grand final of the North of England Crown Green Bowling Championship; and a Guild cruise from Preston Dock to the Isle of Man, with some 2,000 passengers including the Guild Mayor and Mayoress. After the Guild were the Guild Junior Disco (another novelty which would have horrified those who had gone before); the Guild Trophies Philatelic Exhibition; the campfire meeting of the Preston Girl Guides. The Guild itself was almost swamped by the 'extra' events which were now part of the official programme: an orienteering race, the Northern Counties' Archery Society's 1972 championship; 'It's A Knockout'; table tennis tournaments; swimming galas; a coin fair; the Broughton Parish Church Flower and Horticultural Show, which had somehow slipped into the programme; a golf tournament; a Round Preston walk; a film festival; ladies' football at the greyhound stadium; radio and electricity exhibitions, including tours of the Penwortham power station; a friendly football match between PNE and Kilmarnock; barn dances and judo displays.[22]

The dances, balls and banquets which had been so important in the Guilds before 1922 of course continued, and, as with other aspects of the Guild, were extended and increased to cater for all the new groups who wanted to participate. After the final proclamation of the 1972 Guild the mayor and mayoress entertained 483 guests to cocktails and luncheon in the Public Hall: 'the Corporation silver plate adorned the top table, whilst the remaining 19 tables were decorated with red roses.' The menu included salmon with mayonnaise and duck à l'orange, while sherry, chablis, barsac and port were served.[23] The Guild Inaugural Ball on the Monday evening was attended by 898 people 'fully representative of both local and county interests and who included many of the Guild Patrons and some Burgesses'. Cyril Stapleton and his Orchestra provided the music, assisted by the dance band of the King's Regiment, and the Preston Drama Club gave a medieval interlude with dancers and minstrels in medieval costume. The un-medieval supper included cold meats and pies, four sorts of salad (American, Potato, Russian and French), trifle, flans and fruit salad. A champagne bar and three other bars provided the necessary accompaniments.[24]

Many of the old people of the borough were provided with a special Guild luncheon on the Tuesday of the 1972 Guild week. The meal was provided by the catering staff of the Preston Education Department and served by pupils of the various schools in which the luncheons were served: 'The over-seventies enjoyed the memorable occasion, the meal, service and setting earning many expressions of appreciation. Those who were unable by reason of age or infirmity to be present had packed lunches delivered to their homes on various days throughout the week by members of the Social Services Department's staff.' That was another, and very welcome, sign of the times.[25] Whether progress was in evidence in the catering at the Carnival Ball on the Thursday is more doubtful: after dancing to Kenny Ball and his Jazzmen, the guests were entertained by the majorettes from Nîmes, one of Preston's several twin towns, and then served with a buffet supper 'consisting of chicken legs, tomato, bread rolls, Danish pastry and fruit ... in take-away containers'! The caterers of old would have been appalled.[26]

At the final luncheon, after the formal adjournment of the Guild, another menu listed prawn cocktail, garden vegetable soup, trout, blanquette de veau with mushrooms, coupe Jacques, and cheese and biscuits. The fare provided in Guild week 1972 could not match the extraordinary and lavish spread offered in 1882, when there was royalty to be entertained, but it was a great deal more interesting and varied than that on offer in 1952, when rationing was still in force and food was of necessity plain and simple. In that year a typical Guild luncheon, in this case provided by E.H. Booth & Sons (who had access to the best that was available) comprised a choice of fruit juice or soup; cold turkey and ham with stuffing; potato salad and green salad; trifle and 'fruit Melba'; washed down with 'Cyder Cup', champagne, port and coffee.[27]

The reaffirmation of links between Preston and its former citizens overseas, and with other towns and villages of the same name, had been a feature of the 1902 and 1922 Guilds. Before then transport was difficult and there seems to have been relatively little official interest in such ties, but the 300 or so overseas visitors who had made the long journey back to Preston in 1922 captured imaginations. The organisers of the 1952 Guild made special efforts to promote links with former Prestonians and their descendants, and the *Preston Guardian* was prescient in reporting that there was 'an idea which probably founded a new Guild tradition in the despatch on worldwide travels of two guild emblems, carved models of the old clock tower of the Town Hall'.[28] These emblems were sent to the dominions and came back to Preston for the Guild 'escorted' by returning exiles. That from North America travelled on the liner *Empress of Canada* and was handed over to the Deputy Guild Mayor at a ceremony in Liverpool on 29 August 1952. The emblems were accompanied by scrolls signed by hundreds of overseas Prestonians. The idea was guaranteed to appeal to the warmth of sentiment at such a time, and it made excellent publicity—especially since, in the fashion of Olympic torch relays, the emblems were taken from Liverpool to Preston by runners to be handed to the Guild Mayor in another ceremony.

Planning for the 1972 Guild was on very different lines from those in the past. In August 1971 Frank Billinge (former editor of the *Preston Herald*) was appointed Guild Public Relations Office, and it was part of his directive to widen the appeal of the Guild and to publicise it more extensively outside the town. International advertising, especially in Australasia and North America, was thought to be of particular importance, but attention was also paid to the Caribbean and Africa: Preston was becoming a multi-ethnic community. As the *Preston Guardian* had suspected in 1952, sending emblems overseas had become an instant tradition. Thomas Stanley, the maker of the 1952 emblems, was asked to make a new set, and the Guild Committee sent them with scrolls to Australia, New Zealand, Canada and the United States. Scrolls, for signing by expatriate Prestonians, were sent without emblems to 26 countries, one even being 'circulated in the African bush'. Special letters with details of the Guild were sent to 37 towns in North America and Australasia where, after an appeal in the local press for addresses, groups of Preston people had been identified.[29]

All this had the desired effect. Over five hundred people from overseas had attended the 1952 Guild, and a reception had been held for them at the Town Hall. It was decided in 1972 that, as the numbers were likely to be considerably greater, a more formal and extended reception should be held for overseas visitors as part of the official Guild programme. Each of the 1,400 people who attended was presented with a pennant as a souvenir, and the emblems and scrolls were on display. Broadcasts of messages to and from old friends were made during the morning of the reception: 'this facility was much appreciated and many acquaintances were re-renewed.' [30]

In 1948 Preston had become the twin town of Almelo in the Netherlands. The Burgomaster of Almelo gladly accepted an invitation to become a patron of the 1952 Guild, and visited the town during Guild week. The French city of Nîmes, and Recklinghausen in what was then West Germany, were made twin towns of Preston in 1954 and 1956, and their mayors came to the 1972 Guild, as did the mayors of Preston, Ontario, and Preston, Victoria. One cultural benefit of the twinning arrangement with Nîmes which was regarded with particular enthusiasm was the visit of *Les Majorettes Nimoises* to the 1972 Guild. The troupe of majorettes 'endeared themselves to the crowds who watched their performances throughout the week. Such was their youthful enthusiasm, that at the slightest encouragement from the spectators they would prolong, improvise or repeat their performance, much to the confusion of the organisers who found it extremely difficult to bring displays to an end.' [31]

The 1952 Guild was the first in which the town's ethnic communities were represented. This was just before the influx from the Caribbean and Asia, but there were already groups from Eastern Europe, including Poles and Ukrainians. Some previous Guilds had had 'friendship with other lands' among their themes. In 1922 there had been displays by children dressed in the traditional costumes—or what were thought to be the traditional costumes—of other countries, and there was also a group marching under the League of Nations banner, 51 girls dressed as the 51 member states of the League.

Times changed. By 1952 people of other lands had come to live in Preston itself. During the Church of England procession members of the Ukrainian community, 'exiles from their native land, gained a warm cheer from Prestonians as they marched proudly in their native costumes as part of the section from the Parish Church, where they worship regularly'. In the Roman Catholic procession, too, Ukrainians marched in national dress with the section from St Augustine's Church. As part of the torchlight procession which ended the Guild, the Polish Ex-Servicemen's Association produced a grand and impressive float, entitled 'A Polish Wedding'. But such sights were still a great novelty, and the *Lancashire Evening Post* paid special attention to a group of Nigerians, students of local government, who paid a visit to the Royal Lancashire Show during the Guild. They were described, in terms which might now raise eyebrows, as 'picturesque visitors'. [32]

The processions of the 1972 Guild began with the traditional civic procession to the parish church, which as was customary included the Corporation and its officers, the masters and wardens of trades, a host of clergy ('Archbishops, Bishops, Clergy & Ministers of All Denominations'), the senior burgesses, MPs, chairmen and mayors of other local authorities, representatives of the town's professions, guests from twin towns and other overseas communities, and other invited dignitaries. After the service the procession went to the Public Hall to hear the Latin orations which were traditionally spoken by a pupil of the grammar school (by 1972 the Sixth Form College).

On the Sunday before the official start of the Guild there was, for the first time in 130 years of Church participation in the Guild, an ecumenical event. A Walk of Witness, with all major denominations, went through the town centre to Avenham Park for an open-air service. Anglicans, Catholics and Nonconformists also joined in the civic service at the parish church on the opening day. Nevertheless, the main processions were still separate: they included, between them, no fewer than 35 bishops, an archbishop and a cardinal. The 89 floats in the Free Churches procession included 'two groups of girls in saris [who] added a colourful touch to the walkers'. They were reported to have 'brought a delightful display of Eastern charm to the processional route'. In the same procession the Preston Gujrat Hindu Society had a float which was decorated with shrubs, and which broadcast prayers in Gujurati. Forty years on, looking back on the 1972 Guild, we see in these small beginnings the start of another of the great changes in the character of the celebration, one which reflects, as changes in the Guild always have, the history of the town itself.[33]

The scale of the 1972 Guild presented the organisers with major problems. The Lancashire police were particularly anxious to regulate the marshalling of the participants in the various processions, and issued an order that they should all begin in New Hall Lane, a departure from the procedure in every previous Guild. The decision was met with some hostility, and the organisers of processions found that it caused them problems. In the programme of the Church of England procession, for example, it was noted that previously 'each Church joined the procession at the nearest point to their own Church. The new arrangement presents many difficulties e.g. the transport by special buses of all personnel across town to the starting points, besides the carryers of all banners and floats. Both the Police and Church Marshalls have a formidable task ahead of them ... the route will be much longer than in previous Guild processions, but if the Police must keep all other through traffic converging on the town on an even flow then in their opinion starting from this new area is the only way to do it.'[34]

The highlight of the 1972 Guild, as of every other Guild, was the great trades procession. The range of trades and businesses represented had greatly increased since 1952, and especially since 1922. Reflecting the decline in the traditional industries of the town, the growth of a wide variety of services and light industries since the war, and the introduction of new technologies and processes, the trades procession was more diverse than ever before. It covered three miles from head to tail, but only 900 people actually walked. Gone were the days of massive contingents of millgirls, walking four or five abreast, dressed in their own cloth. Now the participants rode on lorries, or joined in one of the 190 tableaux and eighteen bands which were in the procession.

Preston really had changed. Warpers and slashers and winders and reelers were almost history now. The late twentieth century was represented by accountants and aircraft builders, plastics machinery and telecommunications services, mail order firms and nuclear fuels employees, fish and chicken fryers and greetings cards makers, security services and Calor gas distributors. Some of the past was there—painters and decorators, carpenters and joiners, metalworkers and butchers had been at every Guild since Guilds began—but much that was not even thought of only twenty years earlier was now prominent in the Guild procession.[35] This was only the latest stage in a process which had been going on for many Guilds past, and which will go on for many Guilds to come. The change in Preston by 1972 might be illustrated by the words from two songs performed by the Primary Schools Choir at the *Prospect of Preston* event:

> My dad works at B.A.C.
> Making things for you and me,
> His aircraft fly across the sea,
> He's not weaving cotton.[36]
> Where once stood mills against the sky
> Blocks of flats rear heads on high
> Cobbled streets no more resound
> To clattering clogs, all millward bound
> In Preston, proud Preston.[37]

It may be observed that in 2012 BAC is no more, and some of the blocks of flats, new and gleaming in 1972, were blown skywards in great clouds of dust some years ago.

The Guilds of 1952 and 1972 were as remarkable in the degree of popular enthusiasm with which they were received as any that had gone before, despite the doubts expressed, during the planning of both, about the likely degree of public support. In both years the organisers attempted to encourage interest among the townspeople by competitions designed to publicise the Guild. The 1940s and 1950s were the era of the street party, as exemplified by the spontaneous parties that celebrated VE day and the Coronation in 1953. There was virtually no television, so no compulsion to stay indoors to watch what was going on. The end of austerity was approaching, and it was felt that the Guild would offer an excellent opportunity for communal efforts to bring colour and brightness. The organisers were therefore puzzled and disappointed by the apparent lack of interest in the Guild and their competitions.

The solution was a 'best decorated side street' competition, which eventually produced an extraordinary burst of energy, transforming just about every street in the borough with festoons of bunting, forests of flags and banners, and innumerable garlands, flowers, lights, ribbons, streamers and decorative arches. Osborne Street, off Christ Church Street, built a thatched cottage complete with wishing well. In Floyer Street (behind Queens Road), the winner of the competition, every house had temporary trellised porches wound with flowers, hanging baskets and, on the pavement outside, a flower tub. Every lamp-post was decked with floral garlands and ribbons, and from every house bunting was hung across the street. Seven thousand artificial flowers were used in this short street alone.[38]

The town, of course, was brightly decorated. The main buildings were floodlit (itself a relief from years of electricity shortages and rationing), producing some dramatic sights—the 'classic spire of St. Walburge's was poised like a silver sword in the dark sky'. The passion for illumination even spread to one of Preston's ugliest and least appealing buildings, the Penwortham power station, which was floodlit, while the great gaunt coal conveyor bridge spanning the Ribble to the dock was lit by strings of lights until it, too, 'took on a peculiar beauty'. Along the main streets grandstands had been erected, and flags and bunting were strung between all the lamp-posts. Fairylights 'spangled the trees of the Market Place, where in the evenings happy crowds danced on the flagstones to music relayed through amplifiers'.[39]

Similar competitions were held for the 1972 Guild. The Corporation sponsored a 'best kept allotment site' contest, but unfortunately 'none of the sites ... made sufficient effort to win the prize' and accordingly it was not awarded. Far more successful was the competition for the best-decorated side street which, despite a very poor initial response, eventually received no fewer than 86 entries. The winning street in 1972 was Mersey Street in Ashton, which was lavishly bedecked with bunting, streamers, flowers and banners.[40] In the town as a whole the floodlighting and illumination of buildings was much more extensive than in 1952. All the major buildings in the centre were lit, the new bus station, that Brutalist symbol of the brave new world, being decorated with illuminated coloured murals and multi-coloured fluorescent lights. A particularly valuable part of the 1972 preparations was the effort, sponsored by the Civic Trust and other public bodies, towards refurbishing and improving town centre buildings. The decrepit and dilapidated Miller Arcade was completely restored, and most of the public buildings in the town centre, as well as St Walburge's Church and some others in outer Preston, were cleaned of a century or more of grime—work of lasting benefit to the appearance of Preston.[41]

Despite the early fears, the post-war Guilds drew larger crowds than ever before. New records had been set at every Guild since statistics were first collected. In 1882, when the railway network was almost at its peak, 440,000 people arrived by train during Guild week. In 1922 the crowds who came by rail were quite extraordinary: 555,434 return tickets were issued to Preston during the week of the Guild, the vast hordes being carried by no fewer than 504 special trains to Preston and 457 from the town. Almost a quarter of a million visitors came on one day alone, the Saturday of the Guild week: even Blackpool, at the height of its cheap trip popularity, could not match that record. And it has to be remembered that these figures exclude all the many thousands who came into town by motor coach, by omnibus, by tram from the suburbs and on foot from all around: the police estimated that during the week the number coming by road was at least equal to that by rail, so that in total about one million people came.[42]

In 1952 the railway network was less burdened, as motor traffic played a far greater role. The railway still carried many thousands of visitors, but the Corporation had to plan for large numbers of cars and, more importantly in the days before private motoring was ubiquitous, huge numbers of coaches and buses coming to the town. It was very conservatively estimated that three-quarters of a million visitors came to the town in 1952: the true figure was certainly a great deal higher.

In 1972, learning from that experience, the Corporation and the County Council cooperated in planning for the first Guild of the age of mass motoring, while attempting to persuade as many people as possible to come by public transport. The central bus station was closed during procession periods, so temporary bus stations were provided in Corporation Street, Ribbleton Lane, St Peter's Square (Fylde Road) and Queen Street, and many extra car parks were also laid out, although four 'park and ride' car parks at Penwortham, Ingol, Cuerdale and Lostock Hall proved to be a complete failure: 'so little use was made of them that there was virtually no demand for this free transport.' British Rail laid on seventy special trains from Lancashire towns: some of these, as had been the case since the ancestors of British Rail put on special services in 1862, were late-night services to take the merrymakers home from balls and dances. But the numbers who travelled by rail were tiny compared with those of fifty years before: it was calculated that there were but 12,500 people additional to the normal traffic in the whole of Guild week.[43] Estimates of the numbers who came in 1972 vary, but about one million seems to be the generally accepted figure.

CHAPTER NINE

The Guild of 1992
and a new millennium

I N 1946, when it debated the future of the Guild, the Corporation was presented with choices: to end the tradition entirely, to transform the Guild into an occasional trade fair with a bit of a party tacked on, or to maintain the Guild with all its tradition while seeking to adapt it to a troubled and uncertain world. Underlying currents of emotion contributed greatly to the prevailing sense of indecision, for Preston, in common with most Lancashire towns, had lost its confidence. That was a consequence not so much of the war which had just ended, although that had produced a profound mental, physical and financial exhaustion, but rather of the twenty years which preceded the Second World War. After a century and a half of industrial expansion, the emergence of a dominating industry of global importance, and a sense of progress and onward advance, the 1920s and 1930s had produced a devastating period of industrial decline, accompanied by an ever more apparent physical and environmental decay. What was there to celebrate? Of course, there were hopeful signs—the eager optimism of the emergent Welfare State, the 1944 Education Act with its promise (largely realised) of widening educational opportunities, the imminent creation of a coherent planning system, the government's espousal of a great programme of social housing ... these, and other political and social changes, implied that the post-war world would be one where people might well benefit materially and socially.

The Corporation took the decision to carry on with the Guild, retaining all its time-honoured traditional features but adapting elements of the celebrations to suit changing circumstances. The ever-wider sense of community involvement and the inclusion of representatives from all the key groups within Preston ensured that the 'participatory' Guilds of the second half of the twentieth century would be radically different from those of one hundred years before. The decisions taken in the late 1940s can therefore be seen in retrospect as no less important than those of 1842, another year when the survival of the Guild was hanging in the balance.

Those decisions of 1946, and the ideas and ambitions which, though only articulated in a series of vague aspirations, shaped the Guilds of 1952 and 1972 were thus instrumental in the history of the celebration. There is no doubt that those two Guilds were triumphantly successful: there had never been a Guild which could not be described as such in the 250 years since opinion and comment in the press became available to tell us about contemporary reactions. In the records of every Guild in that time observers expressed the view that the Guild which had just gone would linger for ever in the minds of those who had witnessed or experienced it. In 1952, indeed, the *Preston Guardian* somewhat extravagantly claimed that the Guild of that year would 'live as long as human memory and, beyond that, the printed record endure'. The same editorial went on to try to analyse just why the Guild was so significant, so successful and so perennially popular. Its conclusion is undoubtedly correct: 'It was largely a matter of atmosphere. Every Prestonian said to himself, "This is the Guild—and I am part of it ".'[1]

But the Guild of 1992 was different. It took place in a world which had changed quite remarkably since its predecessor had been held in 1972, not only in the sense that Preston itself had changed, but also because some key aspects of the management of the Guild were taken out of the direct and immediate control of the council and its officials. A considerable part of the design and publicity was handed over to outside consultants, while at the same time a new 'philosophy' of the Guild was widely publicised, its sentiments being in accordance with the prevailing attitudes of the early 1990s. The forthcoming Guild was to be more multi-cultural, more egalitarian, and more commercially orientated. Although there had been marketing agencies and outside publicists for the 1972 Guild, the scale of their involvement in 1992 was very much greater, and it changed the character of the Guild celebrations. So the 1992 Guild was markedly different from those which had gone before, in the way it was marketed, the character of the events, and—it hardly needs saying—the sums of money involved.

Organising and preparing for the Guild of 1992

In July 1987 a report by the chief executive was presented to Preston Borough Council, and as a result of this (and a second report prepared in February 1988) a Guild Committee of the Borough Council was appointed. This was in accordance with tradition, for a separate committee to manage the planning of the Guild had been set up for each celebration since 1862. However, three sub-committees were established, to deal with events; civic matters; and 'public relations, marketing and sponsorship', despite the clear evidence of the 1972 Guild that this strategy would not work—it had been tried, and abandoned, then. The problem was that it was unclear where responsibilities lay—were key decisions to be taken only by the full Guild Committee, or could the sub-committees do this? Confusion rapidly developed, and in April 1991 the sub-committees were dissolved. The Guild Committee and the various officers of the Council who would be involved in the planning and organisation also formed a Guild Working Party, and during the three years from the autumn of 1989 this body was instrumental in managing the proceedings.[2]

A period of three years for detailed planning may be contrasted with the six weeks that it took to organise the Guild of 1842![3] But it is clear that the scale of the modern Guild, and the need to coordinate operations, bring in outside attractions, and ensure efficient management mean that a much longer period is essential. Early Victorian officials did not have to worry about health and safety, traffic management, sponsorship or a host of other requirements central to the thinking of their modern-day successors.

The employment of consultants was closely related to a new approach to the Guild itself. There was considerable pressure for the Guild to be dramatically expanded in scale and to be far more than the traditional events of Guild week itself. Hitherto, as we know, the focus of the Guild had been that one week at the end of August and beginning of September. While historically there had been some Guilds which had, quite informally, lasted longer than this—with concerts, entertainments and other informal activities both before and after the last week in August—the heart of the Guild was always then. Now, though, councillors, officials and consultants started to contemplate a whole year of events: rather than being 'the year of the Guild', 1992 would be 'a year-long Guild'. This required planning on an entirely different scale, and it was early on recognised that if events were to continue for almost twelve months the organisation would be beyond the scope and capacity of the Council and its officers. A brief for consultants was therefore prepared, which set out the new thinking. The Guild of 1992, it said, would potentially:

have events and promotions throughout the year, from January to December;

publicise Preston's role as a strategic centre for the North-West region;

keep the town in the public eye for a whole year;

be reshaped, changed from the format of previous Guilds while retaining all the ancient customs and traditions;

be publicised worldwide;

benefit from extensive private funding and investment, including large-scale sponsorship of events and activities, and widespread commercial advertising.

A consortium of two local firms, Heckford Advertising and Glasgow Associates, together with Marketing Consultants Ltd of Edinburgh, was awarded the contract in Spring 1989, with the brief to produce a business plan for the Guild. All the usual features of late twentieth-century marketing were employed to promote the Guild, from publicity packs and press releases, via souvenirs and special postmarks, to the seemingly unavoidable logo and slogans. Whatever the verdict on the Guild, and on the publicity, itself full marks had to be given for imaginative thinking—for instance, Preston Guild commemorative lingerie had no historical precedent (though whether it was sufficiently visible, to enough people, actually to publicise the Guild is not recorded).[4]

Local commercial involvement and financial sponsorship were a particular target under the new strategy. The cost of the ambitious programme of events for a full year was clearly going to be very high, way beyond the funding ability of the Borough Council, so cash support and sponsorship deals seemed the answer. A problem immediately encountered was that many local firms were already contemplating involvement in privately promoted Guild year events and did not want (or could not afford) to give sponsorship to Council-run activities as well, while the Council was bombarded with requests to include such private events in the official Guild programme. Despite these problems, though, the sponsorship policy worked well: it was estimated that over £800,000 was raised for official events in this way, and the official Guild record lists 74 firms and organisations that contributed to events large and small. Some, such as English Nature and Lancashire County Council, were public bodies; others, including the Rotarians and the Friends of the Harris Museum and Art Gallery, were voluntary organisations; and many, including MacDonald's, Sainsburys, GEC Alstom and Yates's Wine Lodge, were commercial companies.[5]

As far as the public were concerned, much of this planning was behind the scenes and invisible. But controversy arose over some aspects—notably the Guild logo, an abstract design with a series of pale blue wave shapes divided by a green wave. There was much speculation about the deep inner meaning and significance of this (was the blue intended to remind us of the River Ribble ... and would brown therefore have been a better colour? did the green represent the environment and ecological harmony?). In fact, there was no hidden message at all: it was simply thought to look attractive, though some complained that it was 'wishy washy' and many expressed the view that using the Lamb and Flag of Preston would have been more suitable. However, although the logo met with derision in some quarters, it soon became familiar. It was accompanied by the 'Guild message', the remarkably unremarkable phrase 'A Celebration of Preston Past, Present and Future'. So that's where the consultancy fees went?

One of the most important decisions to be taken, as far as the people of Preston were concerned, was made at a meeting of the Council on 18 July 1991, when the Guild Mayor was chosen. The unanimous vote was in favour of Harold Parker, the leader of the Council and one of its longest-serving members—he had been a councillor for 27 years and had already served as mayor of the borough in 1976–77. The Guild Mayor formally took office on 21 May 1992, and in his acceptance speech described the office as 'the pivot around which the Guild revolves', noting that the Guild should be 'a time of enjoyment, the pleasures of meeting old friends and making new ones, the re-uniting of family and friends from home and abroad. The Guild has been described as England's greatest carnival. We should enjoy it with enthusiasm and style.'[6]

Traditionally, the new Guild Mayor invited patrons of the Guild to come forward—in past centuries they provided financial assistance from their own pockets and, because they were influential people of high social status, gave a real cachet to the Guild events described in previous chapters. The numbers grew in the twentieth century and in 1972 the Guild had no fewer than 144 patrons. For the 1992 Guild, however, the Borough Council opted in favour of seeking commercial sponsorship, and it was decided to limit the personal patronage to a list of just twelve names: foremost among these was Her Majesty the Queen, who had also been a patron of the 1972 Guild. No other monarch had ever been a patron except Queen Victoria, who consented only once, in 1882. The other patrons were the prime minister (John Major), the leaders of the Labour and Liberal Democrat parties, the lord chancellor, the lord lieutenant and high sheriff of Lancashire, the Duke of Hamilton and the Earl of Derby (whose families had links with Preston going back over five centuries), the Bishop of Blackburn, the Roman Catholic Bishop of Lancaster, and the moderator of the Free Church Council (Preston District).

But there were other, weightier, matters to be debated and changes of major historical importance to be made. As has been shown in previous chapters, the Preston Guild Merchant was, with only the most limited exceptions, an all-male organisation. Apart from a few examples in the late-medieval period and early sixteenth century, women had never been members of the Guild. For the entire period until the twentieth century their role had therefore been as decorative adjuncts to the proceedings, their costumes admired by the newspaper reporters, their enchanting appearance the subject of fulsome description by amateur versifiers. In the later eighteenth century women began to walk in processions, mainly because so many of the employees in the new cotton mills were female, and in the nineteenth century this important role grew rapidly. But, crucially in terms of the ancient antecedents of the Guild that went back to the twelfth century, women could not be burgesses and therefore could not be participants in the formal business of the Guild Court.

In 1918 women over 30 years old had been given the vote in parliamentary elections, and in 1928 they were at last granted equal voting rights with men. For local government purposes women householders had the vote before the First World War, and it was possible for women to stand and be elected as borough and district councillors. In 1921 Mrs Avice Pimblett was elected as a member of the Preston town council, and in 1933–34 served as the borough's first woman mayor, subsequently becoming an alderman. Because Guild stewards were chosen from among the aldermen on the basis of seniority, and because all town councillors played a part in the Guild proceedings, it became impossible to prevent women from participating in the formal business of the Guild Court. At the 1952 Guild, Avice Pimblett was a Guild steward, second in rank to the mayor himself. It was also customary for Guild burgess-ship to be granted to all former mayors who were not already burgesses by hereditary right: Mrs Pimblett herself was made a burgess in 1952, and at the 1972 Guild four women (Doris Dewhurst, Florrie Hoskin, Rita Lytton and Catherine Sharples) were made Guild burgesses, and could then pass their hereditary right on to their sons ... but not to their daughters.

By the late 1980s equal opportunities legislation was in force. This was accompanied by a strong tide of sentiment in favour of admitting women to areas from which they had previously been excluded and, in Preston itself, with the logical argument that if a few women could be burgesses, why should others not be deemed eligible. The small concessions that had already been made were important precedents, and guaranteed that the possibility of admitting women would be debated. In January 1989 the town clerk was requested to investigate the legal position and he soon concluded that there was no bar to the admission of women, since the phrase used to describe hereditary burgess rights—that they could be passed on to 'heirs and successors'—had since 1957 been defined at law as including females as well as males.

It was therefore resolved by the Guild Committee that at the 1992 Guild women should be admitted—the daughters of current Guild members could be added to the Guild Roll, and they would in turn be able to transmit their hereditary rights to their own sons and daughters. For the first time in eight centuries, therefore, the names of daughters as well as sons were read out in the Guild Court at the end of August, as a total of 274 women and girls were admitted as Guild burgesses.

Before the Guild: January to August 1992

As we have seen, the range of events and activities surrounding the Guild had grown steadily over the past century and a half, as the role of the celebrations widened to become more representative of the community as a whole, and also to reflect the changing character of the town. Many of these extra activities were unofficial, and did not appear on Guild programmes, but steadily the official list of events grew and widened in scope. In 1952, although the great majority of events still took place during Guild week itself, some additional ones were included before and after the 'formal' period. Twenty years later, in 1972, there were events during July and August, and quite a few in the period after the Guild during the early months of autumn. But in 1992 the Guild Committee decided to have a year of Guild events, with the major programme beginning at Eastertime and some activities and official events even before that.

The opening of the year was marked by firework displays and other New Year's Eve events, accompanied by an address from the mayor, Miss Mary Rawcliffe, who promised 'a Guild Year to remember'. This ushered in a highly ambitious programme which would carry on until the grand firework display at the opposite end of the year. There had been a great deal of advance publicity for the concerts and other musical events that were being planned, and during 1990 and 1991 much speculation in the columns of the local press about who would be the 'big names'. It appeared that some of the organisers were dropping names with an excessive amount of optimism—among those mentioned were Luciano Pavarotti, Phil Collins, Queen, and Dire Straits, prompting suggestions that the planning was unrealistic. This was denied, but as none of these actually turned up there was perhaps some truth in the claim that the organisers were simply aiming too high.

The first 'spectacular' of Guild Year was the Guild Steam Rally at Riversway, on 2–4 May, with over 250 exhibitors, and the opening of the dock railway for passenger use with a steam train service operating.[7] It was estimated that about 11,500 people attended the weekend event, which made a profit for local charities of £16,000. From then on events were held almost every weekend: an aerial spectacular at Ashton Park, a vintage motorcycle rally, a town criers' competition, a folk fiesta, a 'return of the Vikings' re-enactment at Avenham Park in mid-June, a hobbies fair, and a 'countryside comes to town' event on Moor Park at the end of June. Some of these were regarded as highly successful, but others received much criticism—for example, the last-named had very poor attendance figures despite lovely weather, comment in the *Lancashire Evening Post* blaming high ticket prices and poor publicity.

Similar disappointment was encountered with the Preston Multi-cultural Arts Festival, held at Preston College's Fulwood campus: the organisers had planned it for the Winckley Square annexe but carelessly forgot to obtain an events licence, so the venue was altered at short notice. The weather was very poor, and attendance—perhaps for this reason, perhaps because of the relocation—was much less than had been hoped. The fact that 1992 had one of the wettest summers for decades was a real problem: the 'Canal and Vintage' festival, held at Haslam Park in early August, experienced torrential rain which forced the cancellation of many of the open-air activities, and drastically reduced public attendance. On the other hand, many events were regarded as a great success—the Heineken Music Big Top, in Avenham Park, was attended by over 30,000 people, and the Historic Commercial Vehicle Spectacular on 23 August (for which the weather was kind) was labelled a triumph. Four days later the Lancashire County Fire Brigade held a 'fire-fighting through the ages' event on the Flag Market when the rain was so heavy that cynics suggested the firemen were redundant!

The unsought and unwanted prize for the least successful event went, most unfortunately, to the 'Proud Preston' exhibition which was held on Moor Park from 28 August to 6 September—therefore, throughout Guild week. The idea was derived from the Guild Industries Exhibition, which had been held there during the 1972 Guild, and ultimately from the Trade Exhibition that had been part of the 1952 programme. Both had been highly successful—almost 200,000 people had attended in 1972—and had been used very effectively both to promote Preston's existing industries and to publicise its potential as a site for new employment. In 1992, though, the organisation of the event was handed over to an outside firm, rather than being managed 'in house'. The advance publicity was laden with unsupported claims (for example, that over 350,000 visitors were expected), over 200 stands were booked, and three huge aluminium exhibition halls were brought over from the Netherlands. The weather was dire—which was not the fault of the organisers—but the admission charge of £10 (compared with a mere 30p twenty years before) was their choice. The attendance was pitiful, the exhibitors were furious, many went home early, the Borough Council was landed with a large bill to restore the site, and the promoters went bankrupt. It was indeed a sad and sorry tale.

Elsewhere, there was a very strong emphasis on community events, and many schools were involved in Guild activities. These included important art, music and drama work which could be spread over the months from Easter to the end of the summer term in late July. It was clearly felt that there should be something permanent to record the Guild for posterity, so a number of local schools were involved in planting gardens, or individual trees, or the production of murals, stained glass or commemorative books. The Harris Museum staged a series of special exhibitions and lectures during the eight months before the Guild (and some of them followed on from Guild week itself), and these attracted a total of more than a third of a million visitors. The most popular, not surprisingly, was 'Once Every Preston Guild', which displayed some of the museum's huge collection of Guild artefacts and memorabilia, together with costumes, portraits of Guild mayors, documents, the borough regalia and the Guild Mayor's robes (the latter being borrowed for Guild week and then returned to the exhibition). This attracted a total of almost 150,000 visitors during the year.

These events were of course only part of a much larger and more ambitious programme. As the history of the Guild since the mid-eighteenth century clearly demonstrates, sporting events have been central to the 'fringe' throughout that period. In 1992 the organisers decided to continue that tradition and including a wide range of fixtures in the official calendar. It was generally agreed that the highlight was the inclusion in the Guild programme of the 1992 Milk Race, Britain's largest regular cycling event. Stage 7, a 73-mile run from Southport via Chorley, Bolton, Darwen and Blackburn, finished up at Church Street on 30 May, the finale being eight laps of a town-centre circuit. The weather was excellent and several thousand spectators gathered to watch the event. Other sporting celebrations included a golf trophy competition at Fulwood, a special athletics activities day for schoolchildren, and a national bowling tournament. Musical events were also prominent, including a very successful production of Verdi's *Nabucco* by Preston Opera at the Guild Hall, and culminating in a firework and laser symphony concert in Avenham Park on 29 August. The rain held off but most of the audience were wearing the highly distinctive Guild plastic ponchos, the must-have costume for many during the 1992 Guild.

The Guild Calendar lists a total of 127 events which were part of the official programme between January and the end of August. Some of these reflected the fact that since the 1972 Guild the borough had been substantially enlarged, not only by the addition of Fulwood but also by the inclusion of rural parishes north and east of the town. Therefore, the organisers included events such as Grimsargh Village Guild Festival (for the week beginning 21 June) and Woodplumpton Parish Guild Event. Other events and activities took place outside the borough but were included on the official programme, a reflection of Preston's role as a centre for shopping, entertainment, employment and social activities for a much wider area stretching far beyond its official boundaries. Examples include the opening of a Guild Garden at Priory High School in Penwortham, the Longton Children's Guild Party, and a Guild Arts Week at Carr Hill, Kirkham. The list of events is extraordinarily diverse—from the Old Tyme Music Hall Revue at the Charter Theatre, via the Preston Guild Budgerigar Society Show, to the Thomas the Tank Engine Steam Weekend and the International Caravan Fellowship of Rotarians Guild Rally.

The Borough Council also considered another crucial aspect of community involvement in the Guild—the decoration of streets. As we have seen, this was a major feature of Guilds from the eighteenth century onwards, and by the late nineteenth century highly elaborate and very large decorations were typical—triumphal arches being a special feature. It was decided in 1992 that (no surprise here!) health and safety and traffic management considerations made such highly complex structures too risky. The streets were therefore decorated with garlands, while the town's Christmas lights were adapted for the Guild celebrations. The illuminations were ceremonially switched on by Tom Finney, on 28 August.

The community involvement included a 'best dressed street' competition, a feature that had been part of the official Guild programme since 1922. Initial interest was very limited (just as in 1952 and 1972), but in the end almost fifty streets entered. Judging took place in terrible weather on 29–30 August and the winning street, Marston Moor and Marston Close in Fulwood, received a prize of £300 from Yates's Wine Lodge sponsors of the competition. Mersey Street, the overall winner in 1952 and 1972, kept up its proud Prestonian record and won its area competition. Naturally, too, there were many street parties for the Guild, including places well beyond the boundaries of the borough—the *Lancashire Evening Post* reported them from Lostock Hall, for example. The unremitting rain, high winds and cold caused havoc with decorations and outdoor activities, and many events took place indoors, though at Raleigh Road the dancing took place outdoors in pouring rain before residents went indoors to a hot pot supper in the church hall. Across the borough, the most popular tune played at street parties was said to be 'Bring Me Sunshine'.

Guild week 1992

The proclamation of the Guild has been the start of the formal proceedings as far back as we have records. As was traditional, the announcement was made on the three Saturdays prior to the start of Guild week—historically, this was market day and therefore the most public occasion on which the proclamation could be made. To listen to the proclamation of a Guild in the ancient market place at the heart of the city was to experience a direct link with the medieval past. In 1992, as always on such occasions, large crowds gathered to see the official party, preceded by the regalia of the borough, take its place on the balcony of the Harris building and hear the sergeant at mace proclaim the time-honoured formula: 'OYEZ, OYEZ, OYEZ! All manner of persons here present, whether inhabitants within this Borough or Foreigners, draw near and give your attendance to the reading of the proclamation of a Guild Merchant.' The proclamation announced the Guild, required all burgesses to attend the mayor on the opening day and renew their liberties and privileges, and finished with the grand statement that this was to be 'according to the tenor of the letters patent of our Late Sovereign Lord King Charles the Second and others his Royal Progenitors, Kings and Queens of this Realm, and according to the laudable practice and customs of many Guilds Merchant heretofore held within this Borough, God save the Queen'.

The final proclamation, on 29 August, was attended by a large gathering of dignitaries, including the Bishop of Blackburn, the chairman of the County Council, the members and officers of the Borough Council, ex-mayors, members of parliament, guests from Preston's twin towns of Almelo, Recklinghausen, Nîmes and Kalisz, and many others. The special feature of the event was the arrival of the scrolls of friendship which had been sent in December 1991 and January 1992 to North America, South Africa and Australasia. The idea of sending scrolls, to be signed by exiled Prestonians in these distant parts of the world, had originated in 1952 and was repeated in 1972. The 1992 scrolls (one of which was almost lost en route, stuck in Canadian customs) were augmented by smaller ones sent to each of the twin towns. The Guild Mayor, in his address to the crowd, emphasised the international nature of the Guild celebrations, pointing to the scrolls which reminded us of all those who were proud of their Prestonian heritage, and singling out for special mention the twinning arrangement with Kalisz, Poland's oldest city with a thousand-year history of its own. The later events of Guild week included a special reception, hosted by the Guild mayor, for overseas visitors to the town and for exiled Prestonians who were returning to renew their Guild burgess-ship.

On the following day, Sunday 30 August, the Guild Mayor's church procession was held, the first of the formal public processions of the Guild. The procession brought together many of the voluntary organisations of the town, with representatives of charities, local churches, local government bodies from across Lancashire, the Scouts and Guides, and the armed forces. The Guild Mayor was preceded, according to ancient custom, by the regalia of the borough, and wore the heavy chain of office, the purple robes of office lined and bordered with fur, and the three-cornered Guild Mayoral hat. The weather was variable—though not as appalling as it was on some of the days later in Guild week, when the town was inundated with torrential rain.

The opening of the Guild Court took place on Monday 31 August, with a spectacular procession in which the Guild Mayor was attended by, among many others, the Archbishop of Westminster Cardinal Basil Hume, the Lord Lieutenant (Simon Towneley), the Earl of Derby, Lord Clitheroe, the Bishop of Blackburn, the Bishop of Lancaster, the mayors of the four twin towns and the thirteen other districts in Lancashire, and a glittering array of other important guests. The formal entry to the Guild Hall, to the sound of fanfares of trumpets and preceded by the great standard of the borough, the silver and gold maces, the silver oar and the halberd of the borough, was followed by the opening of the court.

The names of the burgesses were read out. A total of 350 renewed their existing freedom, and 458 new admissions were made, so the list had a grand total of 808 names. After this, the Latin orations were made, by two students—Cathy Hume of Preston College and Alex MacLaren of Cardinal Newman College—with a witty and entertaining reply by the honorary Recorder of the Borough, Judge Anthony Jolly. The Guild Mayor then thanked them for their contributions, and spoke of the problems facing the borough—unemployment and economic downturn, the future shape of local government, and the loss of major industries—but also of the reasons for optimism and the crucial importance of the Guild as a sign of historical continuity in this ancient place. Preston, he said, had resilience and had overcome such problems in the past and would do so again in the future. Following an interval, a religious service was held, conducted by the Reverend Robert Ladds, vicar of Preston, with the assistance of clergy from other denominations. The use of the Guild Hall for these spectacular events was a triumph, for its size and spaciousness provided a perfect setting for a dramatic and intensely moving spectacle whose roots went back in an unbroken line to the twelfth century.

But despite the emphasis on continuity and tradition, there were changes during Guild week itself. In 1992, for the first time since detailed records and eye-witness accounts began in the mid-seventeenth century, there were no formal banquets at the Guild. For generations these were among the highpoints of Guild week, but in 1952 the continuation of rationing had meant that the dinners were much reduced in scale. The banquet at the 1972 Guild was also very modest, although the other social events—especially the balls and dances—were as popular as they had always been. The 1992 Guild organisers decided to dispense with a banquet altogether, and substituted buffet meals at the other events. Perhaps this suited a more egalitarian age—it certainly avoided the headlines (which would surely have appeared) about dignitaries dining lavishly at the expense of hard-pressed ratepayers. But it did mark the end of one of the most characteristic features of Preston Guilds past.

Other changes were evident in the processions which took place during Guild week. Of special significance was the decision, taken in 1990, that the traditional form of the denominational religious processions would be abandoned in favour of an ecumenical event, under the banner 'God Speaks To All'. To have had separate and in a sense competing processions for the different Christian denominations would have gone against the prevailing spirit within the Churches themselves, and would also have sent the wrong message to a wider world. Therefore to set the new tone of harmony and friendship, a monster ecumenical service was held in Avenham Park on Sunday 30 August, the day before the opening of the Guild Court. This event was graced by the presence not only of Cardinal Basil Hume, Archbishop of Westminster, but also of Dr George Carey, the Archbishop of Canterbury, and leaders of the Free Churches. Peter Richardson, the columnist of the *Lancashire Evening Post*, observed that while God might be an Englishman, he certainly wasn't a Prestonian—if he had been he would surely have been kinder and sent some sunshine. For the weather was truly appalling—dripping and drenched worshippers stood in pouring rain, the main pathways, grass and seating areas became flooded, and afterward the area was a quagmire. However, the faithful were undeterred, happy smiles were everywhere apparent, and the huge congregation looked forward to the Churches processions on the following two days.

Because of the sheer scale of the undertaking, and the immense numbers of potential participants, it was agreed almost from the outset that there would have to be two processions—on the Monday of Guild week the churches east of the A6 (London Road–Garstang Road) would form a procession, and on the following day the churches west of the main road would process. The Monday procession involved 58 floats, eleven bands and 3,800 walkers, while on the Tuesday there were 56 floats, nineteen bands and 4,200 walkers. The first day's procession was led by the most senior churchman present for Guild week, Cardinal Basil Hume, accompanied by the Bishop of Blackburn and the Catholic and Anglican bishops of Lancaster. The *Lancashire Evening Post* reported that many participants and spectators found the ecumenical processions intensely moving, and that the celebrations were especially joyful.

The Schools Pageant was on the theme of Preston's history, and was one of the largest ever to have been staged in any Guild. It involved almost 4,000 children, from 57 different schools, and was performed on the Thursday and Friday of Guild week to a combined audience of about 13,000 people. There was much adverse criticism beforehand—as with other events, this focused on the allegedly high cost of tickets, which was said to be preventing parents and grandparents from attending to watch their children. In fact the audience was virtually at capacity. The greatest headache for the organisers related to the venue. The pageant was to have been held in Avenham Park, but because of the terrible weather the site was partly submerged in water and mud. Proposals were made to move the event to PNE's Deepdale ground, but this proved to be impractical, and so Avenham Park it had to be. Special plastic sheeting was laid down, sand was put in a thin layer on top, wooden boardwalks were constructed, and the fates were kind—most of the Thursday afternoon was dry, and on the Friday the weather was *almost* warm and sunny. Afterwards, the audience were full of praise, and a top television producer who was present declared that this was the best pageant he had ever seen.

Another innovation was the Guild Community Procession, held on Thursday 3 September. The original plan had been that there should be an 'Ethnic Minority Communities Procession' on that day, so that the Guild would reflect the multi-cultural and ethnically diverse borough which Preston had become in the previous twenty years. It soon became apparent that, when eventually consulted, the ethnic minorities themselves did not like this idea at all—in effect it would have segregated them from the rest of the Guild events, and there was powerful support from within the minority communities for them to be integrated into the Guild. It was therefore decided that a Communities Procession, representing all sorts of communities, groups, voluntary organisations, and bodies from outside the borough, would be very much better. The procession was a great success—hugely enjoyable for all concerned and in total involving 78 organisations, 82 vehicles and 1,766 walkers. Those present included members of the various Asian communities, Afro-Caribbean residents, the Chinese community and other ethnic groups. Organisations, to name a few chosen randomly, included Preston Muslim Forum, the Samaritans, the National Childbirth Trust, Leyland Cricketers Morris Dancers, and even South Ribble Borough Council!

This event was of special importance in the history of the Guild. It represented a logical continuation of the pattern, first identifiable in 1842, whereby the people of the town have become ever more central to the Guild week events, and it reflects the way in which Preston Guild has readily adapted and responded to changes in Preston itself. It was also apparent that the response of the large crowds who came to watch was particularly enthusiastic, and since 1992 processions and festivals associated with the ethnic communities of the borough have become a standard part of the annual calendar of the town. The impact of the 1992 procession was clearly a very important element in this development.

Of course, the trades processions have been a central feature of Guild week for centuries. For the 1992 Guild the planning of the trades participation began in June 1990, and it was decided that entry fees would be charged (for commercial companies, on a graduated scale according to the number of employees) to defray the costs of hiring the bands that would accompany the marchers and floats. Sponsorship was also sought and eventually, by that means, a considerable profit was made, and distributed to local charities. The procession was held in appalling weather, with torrential rain and high winds, but even so an estimated 250,000 people watched it snake for four miles through the town. There were 123 firms and business organisations, 148 floats, 20 bands and some 1,200 walking participants. In the old days it was possible for trades to produce spectacular floats because the very 'visual' nature of their work—cotton machinery, foundry workers, marching groups of men and women carrying the tools of their trade—but office employment, computerised business and clerical work do not make for particularly impressive visual displays. Therefore many of the floats relied on wit, costumes and lively entertainment, and it was evident that workers themselves had spent much time and effort in achieving really good shows. Whereas in the past the displays had tended to be led by, and reflected the views of, employers, the 1992 Guild trades procession demonstrated the power of the workers! A particular favourite was the Inland Revenue staff float, with employees dressed as thieves in striped T-shirts, carrying large swag bags under the banner 'Stop Organised Crime, Abolish The Inland Revenue'! Plumbs, the household furnishings specialists, had a Roman temple bedecked with draperies, curtains, cushions, luxuriously upholstered chairs, and toga-clad ladies. Others included special vehicles—the fire brigade had a Victorian horse-drawn fire engine, and Dutton Forshaw a series of vintage cars.

At the end of Guild week, on Saturday 5 September, the Guild Court was adjourned for twenty years, to meet again on the first Monday after the Feast of the Decollation of Saint John the Baptist in the year 2012. At the closing ceremonies the Guild Mayor, Harold Parker, admitted new burgesses by gift, as was his right. These were individuals who had no hereditary right to burgess-ship but who were now granted that privilege by the Borough Council, and would henceforth be able to transmit it to their descendants. Those admitted included five stewards of the Guild, four of whom were also former mayors of the borough; eleven other former mayors; Anthony Jolly, the honorary recorder of the borough; Antony Owens, the town clerk and chief executive, who was also clerk of the Guild; Florence Cooke and Tom Finney, for services to the borough; and, in his personal gift, his own brother and grandson. The Guild Mayor himself was then 'generally and gratuitously' admitted as an in-burgess.

After the formal adjournment of the Court there were speeches, in which the two Guild stewards spoke of the invaluable service rendered by the Guild Mayor and Guild Mayoress, and of the Guild spirit which had infected not just the town but also the rural parts of the borough, brought within its boundaries less than twenty years earlier, and of neighbouring districts in South Ribble and Ribble Valley. The Guild Mayor in turn described the personal experience of taking on the role, and the moving sight of tiny children being held up by their parents at the opening Court, to be admitted as burgesses. He read out a message from the Queen, sending warmest wishes to Preston and its people on the occasion of the Guild, and declared that 'The Guild Book is closed. Nothing must prevent it being re-opened in 2012.'

Verdicts

Despite the mammoth effort of three years' planning, and the expenditure of well over £1 million, the Guild of 1992 received more criticism than any of its three twentieth-century predecessors. In part this was because of factors outside the control of the organisers—the national economic recession probably reduced the number of visitors, and of course the dreadful weather, which was unquestionably the worst of any Guild in living memory. But more considered criticism was levelled at the publicity, including the accusation that the Guild had been organised by people who did not fully understand what it was about, and who did not properly appreciate its historic significance to Preston. Television coverage was very limited indeed, and many observers felt that the publicity could have been better directed.

Some events were notably badly attended. Again, the weather undoubtedly played a major part in this, but there was a strong sense that the organisers had overdone things. Previous Guilds—especially 1952 and 1972—indicated that interest did not peak until just before Guild week, in mid-August, which is scarcely unexpected. For example, the 'The Countryside Comes to Town' event at Moor Park was held in excellent weather on a weekend in late June, when plenty of popular interest might have been generated, but the attendance was very poor: the expected crowds never came, and the general verdict was that the publicity was poor and ticket prices far too high. But it is possible that the event was simply too early, and was not associated sufficiently in the popular imagination with Preston (though the aim in this case was to turn the spotlight the rural parts of the borough and on the town's huge rural hinterland). The feeling that there were simply too many events, spread over too long a period of time, was often expressed in the press and in conversation. A full year of Guild events was maybe just too much.

The financial statistics for the Guild were released in 1993, and showed that the cost to the borough was £1.58 million, which included support of £350,000 for non-commercial fringe activities of the sort that are essential to the success of any Guild, and an expenditure of £410,000 on special transport arrangements for the disabled and for children involved in pageants and other events, car parks, illuminations and park and ride facilities. Allowing for inflation, this worked out as significantly cheaper than in 1972, despite the scale of the Guild programme being much expanded. Moreover, the 1992 Guild benefited from vastly increased private and commercial sponsorship, and sale of souvenirs and Guild memorabilia, which helped to offset costs and meant a final net outlay of about £600,000. Despite all the criticism, therefore, the 1992 Guild was not only much larger than any that had gone before, but was also a great deal less costly for the citizens of the borough. Furthermore, approximately £100,000 was raised at a wide variety of events for distribution to local charities. The intangible benefits, in terms of trade and income from almost a million visitors, cannot be measured but must be added to the equation. The 1992 Guild, using these financial and statistical measures, was a triumphant success.

For previous Guilds there was often a specific permanent legacy, in the form of a building or monument opened or started at the time of the Guild itself. In 1761 there was a new Guild Hall, in 1782 and 1862 new town halls, in 1882 the Harris building, and in 1972 the present Guild Hall (though the opening of that was delayed). No comparable commemoration marked the Guild of 1992, apart from the pedestrianisation of the lower end of Friargate in front of the Corn Exchange. And an aspiration of the Borough Council, that Preston would be made a city to mark not only the Guild but also the 40th anniversary of the queen's accession, also came to nothing (Sunderland was honoured instead—though of course Preston only had another ten years to wait for the much-coveted title). So the Guild of 1992 left no permanent mark on the face of the town, and its monument must be sought in the historical record.

As I have noted, this was perhaps the most criticised Guild since the highly controversial celebrations in 1862. There was much carping about the plans and the programme, and heavy condemnation of individual events. To some extent these criticisms were justified. It really is hard to avoid the impression that the plans were over-ambitious, and even unrealistic in some cases. To have a whole year of Guild events was expecting a lot from the people of the town, and there was a real danger that 'Guild fatigue' would set in. The weather, which nobody can control, was clearly to blame for some of the problems, although it did encourage a spirit of resilience in the face of adversity, and the suppliers of Preston Guild waterproof ponchos were heroes of the hour. But the weather alone could not be blamed for all the disappointments and failures. There will always be those who are ready to criticise, and this has been apparent at Guilds since 1822, when the columns of the local press first carried the prognostications of gloom, the warnings that the forthcoming Guild would be a failure, and the grumbles about the cost, the incompetence of the organisers, and the futility of the whole exercise. But in 1992 some of the criticism was merited.

On the other hand, there was very much more that was a resounding success, measured not only by sentimental and optimistic accounts in the press, or the naturally positive views of the organisers, but also by the comments of people 'on the ground' and by the visitor numbers. After the Guild almost everyone concluded that, whatever the predictions, it had all turned out amazingly well. The dire weather, which made so many events a wash-out, also produced that spirit of 'rising to the occasion'—and the fact that a quarter of a million people stood in pouring rain to watch the trades procession suggests that there is a genuine and deep-seated commitment to the Guild which is not going to be diluted or washed away by a small matter of the heavens opening. The town, and tens of thousands of its citizens, had waited twenty years for these events, so the people would be there and make the best of it come hell or (as was sometimes the case) high water.

The 1992 Guild was therefore a tremendous success, held in the face of considerable adversities and thoroughly enjoyed by all who were present. At the end of Guild year, speaking to the crowds in the Flag Market on New Year's Eve, Harold Parker spoke of the importance of feeling pride in Proud Preston. He suggested that the town and its people should be proud of the achievement of the Guild and all that went with it—those feelings and visible indications of community spirit, friendship, tolerance, kindness, and concern for others. Almost four months earlier, at the closing of the Guild Court, he had expressed the view that 'Preston Guild will live on, and we must all pledge ourselves to ensure that we go on to even greater things in the Guild of 2012'.

And now, as I write this, that Guild is a year away. Preston has continued to change and evolve. In 2002 it became a city, in the Queen's golden jubilee year, and for the first time in its history the Guild will be celebrated by the city and its people. Some familiar firms have gone; the university is now one of the largest in Britain; the seemingly endless saga of the Tithebarn project, to redevelop a great swathe of the city centre, shows no sign of reaching any sort of conclusion (the delay and eventual abandonment means that the processions in 2012 won't have to parade round the edge of a gargantuan building site, as might otherwise have happened); and the comments and criticisms, concerns and fears over the next Guild have been voiced for a couple of years in the local press. Twenty years on, we are in another economic recession, this time marked by major reductions in local authority expenditure. The former chief executive a few years ago raised the possibility of making the Guild an annual event (I wrote to protest in outspoken terms!), and more recently questions have been asked about the financing of the Guild.

But ultimately, the Guild goes on, and will continue to go on, because it is an integral part of Preston's long and ancient—and very proud—history. It does not matter whether or not we are, to employ that much-overused phrase beloved of the City Council's press releases, 'the Third City of the North West'. No other place in the British Isles has anything like the Preston Guild. It is unique, and always will be. We should be proud of it.

Guilds and Guild Mayors

1397 (4 June)	William de Ergham
1415 (20 May)	Henry Johnson
1459 (6 May)	Robert de Hoghton
1500 (31 August)	William Marshall
1542 (24 May)	Thomas Tipping
1562 (30 August)	Evan Wall
1582 (30 August)	George Walton
1602 (30 August)	Henry Catterall
1622 (2 September)	William Preston
1642 (29 August)	Edmund Werden
1662 (1 September)	James Hodgkinson
1682 (4 September)	Roger Sudell
1702 (31 August)	Josias Gregson
1722 (3 September)	Edmund Assheton
1742 (30 August)	Henry Farrington
1762 (30 August)	Robert Parker
1782 (2 September)	Richard Atherton
1802 (30 August)	Nicholas Grimshaw
1822 (2 September)	Nicholas Grimshaw
1842 (5 September)	Samuel Horrocks
1862 (1 September)	Robert Townley Parker
1882 (4 September)	Edmund Birley
1902 (1 September)	Frederick, Earl of Derby
1922 (3 September)	Henry Astley-Bell

1952 (1 September)	John James Ward
1972 (4 September)	Joseph Frederick Gray
1992 (31 August)	Harold Parker

As noted in chapter 1, it has long been believed that a Guild was celebrated in 1328 in the mayoralty of Aubred, son of Robert. The document which apparently refers to this Guild is ambiguous, but there must be considerable doubt that it actually relates to the celebration of a Guild in that year. This means that the first accurately dated and documented Guild was that of 1397, and that 27 Guilds have definitely been celebrated in the six centuries between then and 1992. An unknown number must have been held between 1179 (the earliest definite reference to the Guild Merchant) and 1397, when the first accurately documented Guild was celebrated.

Occupation details from the Guild rolls, 1562–1642

Occupation	1562	1582	1602	1622	1642
apothecary	—	—	—	1	2
baker	—	—	2	1	1
barber	—	1	—	2	1
bellfounder	—	—	—	1	—
brewer	—	—	—	—	1
brickmaker	1	3	1	2	1
butcher	4	9	4	8	1
butter-maker	—	—	—	1	—
carpenter	—	6	1	5	—
chandler[1]	—	—	—	—	1
chapman[2]	—	1	—	6	2
cook	—	1	—	—	2
cooper[3]	1	—	—	2	2
cordwainer[4]	2	—	—	—	—
currier[5]	—	—	2	4	2
cutler	—	2	—	1	—
doctor[6]	—	—	1	—	3
draper	5	1	1	6	2
drover	1	—	—	—	—
dyer	—	—	—	1	1
farmer[7]	4	5	2	12	10
feltmaker	—	—	—	—	2
fisherman	1	3	—	—	—
flaxseller	2	2	—	—	—

Occupation	1562	1582	1602	1622	1642
fletcher[8]	1	—	—	—	1
gardener	—	—	—	—	1
girdler[9]	1	—	—	—	—
glassman	—	—	—	—	1
glover	10	15	9	13	5
governor HC[10]	—	—	—	—	1
grocer	—	—	—	—	1
gunsmith	—	—	—	—	1
haberdasher[11]	—	1	—	1	—
hatter[12]	2	—	1	5	2
hosier	—	—	1	—	—
innkeeper	—	1	—	—	—
ironmonger	—	—	—	1	1
joiner	—	—	—	—	1
labourer	6	10	2	10	2
leadbeater	—	1	—	—	—
locksmith	—	—	—	1	1
maltmaker	1	—	—	—	—
mason	1	1	—	—	—
mercer	5	6	1	—	—
miller	1	2	2	5	4
musician	1	—	1	—	3
painter	1	—	—	—	—
parish clerk	—	—	—	—	1
pavier[13]	1	—	—	—	—
pinder[14]	—	1	—	—	—
plasterer	—	—	—	—	3
saddler	2	3	—	3	2
salter[15]	—	—	—	1	—
schoolmaster[16]	1	1	1	2	3
servant	—	2	2	14	12
sexton	—	1	—	—	1
shearman	5	1	—	—	—
shoemaker[17]	7	17	3	12	12
skinner	—	—	—	3	1

Occupation	1562	1582	1602	1622	1642
slater	1	—	—	1	—
smith	1	3	—	5	6
spinner	—	—	—	1	—
spurrier[18]	—	—	—	2	2
tailor	6	10	5	9	9
tanner	—	1	—	2	1
thatcher	—	—	—	—	1
vintner[19]	—	—	—	1	—
watchmater	—	—	—	1	1
weaver[20]	8	12	7	7	11
wright[21]	4	—	—	—	—
Total per year	89	121	47	158	119

Notes

[1] chandler: seller of tallow and candles.

[2] chapman: seller of small wares, pedlar (includes pedlars and badgers).

[3] cooper: maker of barrels and casks.

[4] cordwainer: maker of leather goods.

[5] currier: curer of and dealer in skins and hides.

[6] includes surgeons and chirugeons.

[7] includes yeomen and husbandmen.

[8] fletcher: arrowmaker.

[9] girdler: maker of girdles.

[10] Governor of the House of Correction.

[11] haberdasher: seller of small linen goods.

[12] includes capmakers.

[13] pavier: one who lays paving stones or setts.

[14] pinder: one who rounds up and impounds stray animals.

[15] salter: shopkeeper.

[16] includes usher (assistant master).

[17] includes cobblers (shoemakers).

[18] spurrier: maker of spurs.

[19] vintner: wine-seller.

[20] includes those specifically called linen-weavers (three in total) and woollen-weavers (four in total).

[21] wright: 'maker'—it is ambiguous in this context and perhaps indicates carpenters.

Notes and references

Notes to Chapter 1: The medieval Guild Merchant

1. The information and interpretations in the first half of this chapter were derived mainly from the work of Susan Reynolds (S. Reynolds, *An Introduction to the History of English Medieval Towns* (Oxford University Press, 1977). A broad account of guilds in their urban context is given in C. Platt, *The English Medieval Town* (Secker & Warburg, 1976), while several articles are brought together in R. Holt and G. Rosser (eds), *The Medieval Town: A Reader in English Urban History* (Longman, 1990). A more general overview is given by James Campbell, in 'Power and authority, 600–1300', and S.H. Rigby and Elizabeth Ewan, 'Government, power and authority 1300–1540', in David Palliser (ed.), *The Cambridge Urban History of England vol.1, 600–1540* (Cambridge University Press, 2000).

2. Rural guilds were particularly common in areas of prosperous agricultural activity, such as Devon and Somerset, or East Anglia: there is little evidence of them in north-west England.

3. In the case of Preston, and other north-western towns, there is no evidence of organised links with Europe, but the medieval Guild Rolls of Dublin indicate that formal connections existed between the Anglicised parts of Ireland and some towns in north-west England.

4. Again, this is far better documented (and was much more important) in areas such as Norfolk and Suffolk than in Lancashire. There is little direct evidence of formal religious activities in connection with the Preston Guild Merchant.

5. This is one of the main features of the lists of boroughs in M. Beresford and H.P.R. Finberg, *English Medieval Boroughs: A Handlist* (Newton Abbot, 1973), and the updated and revised list published in *Urban History Yearbook 1981*. The most recent listing of information on medieval boroughs is to be found in the very impressive on-line gazetteer of medieval markets and fairs to 1516, which can be visited at www.history.ac.uk/cmh/gaz/gazweb2.html

6. The Preston borough charters have been transcribed and published on several occasions: Rev. J. Lingard, *The Charters, Granted by Different Sovereigns, to the Burgesses of Preston* (Preston, 1821) was the first major work of this type. The main provisions of the charters are quoted at length in W.A. Abram, *Memorials of the Preston Guilds* (Preston, 1882) [hereafter Abram, *Memorials*]. See also *The Royal Charters of Preston, 1179–1974* (Preston Borough Council, 1979), which is based on Lingard's edition of 1821.

7. All the medieval charters and guild documents of Preston are in Latin: in this book text is given only in translation, unless the Latin is particularly relevant.

8. The charter of King John is the earliest to survive, although it is in very poor condition and almost illegible: Lancashire Archives [LA] CNP/1/2.

9. The story of the supposed charter of Henry I is confused. Clemesha, the most sceptical and original of Preston's earlier historians, was very doubtful of its accuracy: see H.W. Clemesha, *A Bibliography of the History of Preston in Amounderness* (Preston, 1912) [hereafter Clemesha, *Bibliography*]. Other, earlier, historians have been far more willing to believe Walmesley, and have overlooked the evidence of charter recitations.

10 The later medieval and Tudor charters which survive were granted by Richard II (1379), Henry IV (1401), Henry V (1414), Henry VI (1425), and Philip & Mary (1557): LA CNP/1/4–7 and 9. Others are known from Lingard's copies or from references in surviving charters.

11 LA CNP/1/1.

12 M. Bateson, 'The Laws of Breteuil', *English Historical Review* vol.15 no.57 (January 1900) and no.58 (June 1900). The second part of the article includes a detailed discussion of the Preston Custumal, with a transcript of its text. Bateson's conclusions were criticised in her time, but have since been generally accepted.

13 Kuerden's transcript of the supposed 1328 Guild document is given in Abram, *Memorials*, 7–8. In his account of the history of Preston and the Guild, written in about 1682 and published in 1818, Kuerden says that this Guild was held in 1329: *A Brief Description of the Burrough and Town of Preston, and its Government and Guild ... with occasional notes by John Taylor* (Preston, 1818) [hereafter Kuerden, *Description*].

14 Clemesha, *Bibliography*, 75.

15 Abram, *Memorials*, 8.

16 *ibid.*, 9.

17 *ibid.*

18 I wrote that sentence in 1990: over twenty years later, no new evidence has appeared.

19 The Guild Rolls to the end of the seventeenth century are fully transcribed in W.A. Abram, *The Rolls of Burgesses at the Guilds Merchant of the Borough of Preston* (Record Society of Lancashire & Cheshire [RSLC] vol.ix, 1884) [hereafter Abram, *Guild Rolls*]; this volume also has a useful introduction. The Guild Rolls from 1702 to the present have not been published. They, with all the earlier Rolls which survive, are kept among the borough archives at the Lancashire Archives (the Guild records have collection reference CNP/2).

20 Abram, *Memorials*, 15.

21 *ibid.*, 18.

22 By far the best general book on Preston and its development is David Hunt's excellent *A History of Preston* (Carnegie Publishing), which was first published in 1992 in time for the Guild of that year. A new, revised edition appeared in 2009.

23 LA CNP/2/1.

24 Abram, *Guild Rolls*, 1.

25 *ibid.*, xv–xvii.

26 LA CNP/2/2 (1415); CNP/2/2a (1459); CNP/2/3 (1542).

27 It is not impossible that nobody at that Guild was admitted on payment of a fine, but that seems unlikely.

28 Figures calculated from Abram, *Guild Rolls*, 1–19.

29 The evidence which the 1397 Guild Roll provides for migration to Preston is analysed in Alan G. Crosby, 'Migration to Preston in the fourteenth century: the evidence of surnames', *Lancashire Local Historian* no.8 (1993), 6–17.

30 Abram, *Guild Rolls*, 18 and *Memorials*, 19.

31 Abram, *Guild Rolls*, xvii.

32 Abram, *Memorials*, 22.

33 The decision to admit women was made by the Guild Committee of Preston Borough Council on 3 April 1989 (resolution 1705).

34 Lists derived from Abram, *Guild Rolls*, 1–10.

35 See also R. McKinley, *The Surnames of Lancashire* (Leopard's Head Press, English Surnames Series, vol. iv, 1981).

36 See Crosby, 'Migration to Preston', for a detailed analysis of this subject.

Notes to Chapter 2: The Guild from 1542 to 1742

1 The chapter is summarised by Lingard (1821) and in Abram, *Memorials*, 24–6.

2 The Corporation White Book or Minute Book, 1608–1781 (the *Book of Orders for the Town of Preston*, hereafter White Book), is held among the borough archives at Lancashire Archives (reference CNP/3/1/1). It derives its name from its original binding, which was in white kidskin, some of which survives.

3 The electoral history of Preston is considered in detail by W. Proctor, 'Electioneering in Lancashire before Secret Ballot: the Preston election of 1768', *THSLC*, cxi (1959), 93–115.

4 Quoted in Abram, *Memorials*, 61.

5 Quoted in *ibid.*, 81.

6 *ibid.*

7 Almost all Guild orders which relate to the franchise and the conduct of elections were collected and transcribed *c.*1835 in a document now at LA (DDX/123/32).

8 The statistics of burgesses are taken from Abram, *Guild Rolls*, 20–202, and *Memorials*, 71–117.

9 The information concerning trade is extracted from Abram, *Guild Rolls*, 20–122.

10 *ibid.*, 90.

11 *ibid.*, 109.

12 *ibid.*, 93.

13 *ibid.*, 122.

14 *ibid.*, 113.

15 White Book, 3 (23 January 1608/9).

16 Abram, *Guild Rolls*, 90.

17 *ibid.*, 119.

18 *ibid.*, 120.

19 *ibid.*, 123.

20 *ibid.*

21 *ibid.*, 121.

22 *ibid.*, 122.

23 *ibid.*

24 *ibid.*

25 White Book, 218 (1 October 1666).

26 Abram, *Guild Rolls*, 156.

27 *ibid.*, 64.

28 Quoted in Abram, *Memorials*, 32.

29 Abram, *Guild Rolls*, 91.

30 Quoted in Abram, *Memorials*, 33.

31 *ibid.*

32 *ibid.*

33 Abram, *Guild Rolls*, 64–5.

34 *ibid.*, 91.

35 All examples quoted from Abram, *Guild Rolls*, 120–1.

36 P. Whittle, *The History of the Borough of Preston in the County Palatine of Lancaster* (Preston, 1837); of this work Clemesha notes, 'Of very little value except for contemporary matters'.

37 Quoted in Abram, *Memorials*, 41–2.

38 White Book, 207 (10 May 1665).

39 Quoted in Abram, *Memorials*, 80.

40 P. Borsay, 'The English urban renaissance: the development of provincial urban culture *c.*1680–*c.*1760', in P. Borsay (ed.), *The Eighteenth-century Town: A Reader in English Urban History* (Longman, 1990)

41 E. Baines, *Life of Edward Baines* (1851), 14; it is commonly held that the last of all the prosecutions was that in 1772 against Richard Baines. This belief is based on Edward Baines's account, and has been widely published, but the evidence of the minutes of Preston Corporation shows clearly that it is wrong.

42 LA CNP/3/1/4 (Preston Corporation minutes 13 June 1778).

43 *ibid.*, 31 October 1784.
44 Information extracted from Abram, *Guild Rolls*, 15–202.
45 White Book, 554 (30 August 1709).
46 Abram, *Guild Rolls*, 93.
47 *ibid.*
48 White Book, 703 (10 August 1733).
49 Abram, *Guild Rolls*, 93.
50 White Book, 31 (4 May 1632).
51 White Book, 98 (11 October 1651).
52 White Book, 98 (28 February 1652).
53 White Book, 656 (18 December 1724).
54 White Book, 745–7 (various dates 1740–41).

Notes to Chapter 3: Celebrating the Guild up to 1762

1 Kuerden, *Description*, 47.
2 Abram, *Memorials*, 8.
3 Abram, *Guild Rolls*, 1.
4 See Crosby, 'Migration to Preston', 14–15.
5 Abram, *Guild Rolls*, 7.
6 *ibid.*, 1–15.
7 Abram, *Memorials*, 60.
8 *ibid.*, 76–7.
9 *ibid.*, 49–50.
10 *ibid.*, 91.
11 Quoted in Abram, *Memorials*, 25.
12 Kuerden, *Description*, 5–7.
13 White Book, 668 (4 August 1727): nothing more is heard of this project, so presumably there was insufficient public enthusiasm for it to be implemented.
14 *ibid.*, 849 (2 May 1760).
15 *ibid.*, 850 (20 June 1760).
16 *ibid*, 854 (23 April 1761).
17 John Carr was the architect of Lancashire's finest eighteenth-century house, Lytham Hall: had his commission been implemented Preston would have therefore been able to claim work by one of the greatest architects of the day—though the description of the proposed works sounds uncomfortably like a bodged compromise. Perhaps it was as well that it did not go ahead?
18 Abram, *Guild Rolls*, xxiii–xxv.
19 *ibid.*, xxvii–xxix. All other quotations in this section are from the same source.
20 Kuerden, *Description*, 47–8.
21 *ibid.*, 50.
22 *ibid.*, 58–9.
23 *ibid.*, 60–1.
24 *ibid.*, 47.
25 *ibid.*, 79–80.
26 *ibid.*, 62–3.
27 The different oaths are transcribed in full in Kuerden, *Description*, 54–8.
28 *ibid.*, 81–2.
29 *ibid.*, 87–9.
30 The amounts which were paid as fines are recorded in the Guild Rolls from the earliest which survives (1397); these statistics are derived from that source: Abram, *Guild Rolls*, 31–93.
31 White Book, 179 (10 July 1662).
32 *ibid.*, 181 (30 September 1662).
33 *ibid.*, 189 (8 December 1662).

34 *ibid.*, 191 (12 December 1662).

35 A. Hewitson (ed.), *Preston Court Leet Records* (Preston, 1905, hereafter *Court Leet*), 97.

36 Hewitson, *Court Leet*, 103–4.

37 *ibid.*, 111.

38 White Book, 387 (6 August 1683).

39 *ibid.*, 644 (9 July 1723).

40 *ibid.*, 772 (23 June 1743).

Notes to Chapter 4: The Guild from 1762 to 1835

1 See, for example, Marian Roberts, *The Story of Winckley Square, Preston* (2nd edn, ed. Andrew Mather, Preston Historical Society, 2009).

2 LA CNP/3/1/4 (18 June 1782).

3 LA DDX/88/4.

4 LA CNP/3/1/4 (2 July 1801).

5 *ibid.*, 11 September 1801.

6 Abram, *Memorials*, 118–19.

7 LA CNP/3/1/4 (4 October 1802).

8 LA CNP/3/1/5 (29 June 1821).

9 LA CNP/4/2 Preston Improvement Commissioners' minutes 15 July 1822.

10 *ibid.*, 5 August 1822.

11 Abram, *Memorials*, 104–5.

12 LA DDPr/138/93 memoir of Nicholas Grimshaw; Abram, *Memorials*, 110–11.

13 J. Moon, *The Guild Merchant of Preston … An account of the Processions, and public entertainments* (Preston, 1762, hereafter Moon, *Guild Merchant)* 3.

14 Moon, *Guild Merchant*, 7.

15 *ibid.*, 14–15.

16 *ibid.*, 15–16.

17 W. Brockbank and F. Kenworthy (eds), *The Diary of Richard Kay … 1716–1751* (Chetham Society 3rd ser. vol.16, 1968) 54.

18 *Manchester Mercury*, quoted in Abram, *Memorials*, 114.

19 *Manchester Mercury*, quoted in Abram, *Memorials*, 115.

20 I am indebted to Dr Mona Duggan of Ormskirk for drawing my attention to this advertisement.

21 The definitive work on the medals produced to commemorate the Preston Guilds is W.F. Richardson, 'The Guild Medals of Preston and their Background' (unpublished dissertation, Preston 1971).

22 The exception is the official record of the 1992 Guild, a fascinating and exemplary volume compiled by the present author.

23 The work is entitled *The Guild Merchant of Preston; or Preston Guild Companion*. It is described as an 'Exact Representation, on Nineteen Copper Plates, curiously drawn and engraved, of that Ancient Procession … The whole laid down so easy and expressive as to render it a proper help to those Gentlemen and Ladies resorting to Preston'. Abram, *Memorials*, 99–100, quotes the description of the procession given here.

24 Thomas Wilson's poem has been widely quoted. The original is in LA DDX/398/47.

25 I. Wilcockson, *Authentic Records of the Guild Merchant of Preston in the county Palatine of Lancaster, in the year 1822* (Preston, 1822, hereafter Wilcockson, *Authentic Records*), 36–8 quotes an account of the 1802 processions which was published in the *Monthly Magazine*. This is clearly derived from (and in parts lifted straight from) the account in the *Manchester Mercury* which is printed at length in Abram, *Memorials*, 113–14. The material given in this book about the 1802 trades procession is taken from the *Manchester Mercury*.

26 The symbolic significance of the linking of arms by John Horrocks and John Watson was noted at the time: the *Monthly Magazine*, unlike the *Manchester Mercury*, specifically described

them not as colleagues but as 'the two principal and indeed rival manufacturers of the county'. I am grateful to Dr David Hunt, the very eminent historian of Preston, for discussing this question with me.

27 LA DDB/72/356.
28 Wilcockson, *Authentic Records*, 54–9.
29 *Monthly Magazine*, quoted in Wilcockson, *Authentic Records*, 39.
30 Wilcockson, *Authentic Records*, 50–2.
31 *ibid.*, 54.
32 *ibid.*, 61.
33 ibid., 62–5.
34 *Liverpool Kaleidoscope* Guild Supplement, September 1822, quoted in Abram, *Memorials*, 127.
35 LA DDPr/138/2 *A New Song on the Preston Guild*.
36 *Preston Chronicle*, 7 September 1822.

Notes to Chapter 5: The Guild as a social event

1 Quoted in Abram, *Memorials*, 33.
2 White Book, 9 (28 June 1612).
3 Kuerden, *Description*, 48–9.
4 A complete account of the different officials appointed for the Guild is given in Kuerden, *Description*, 63–8.
5 Kuerden, *Description*, 64.
6 *ibid.*, 64–5.
7 P. Clark, *The English Alehouse, 1200–1830* (1983) 135.
8 Kuerden, *Description*, 66.
9 *ibid.*, 67.
10 *ibid.*, 67–8.
11 *ibid.*, 68–70.
12 *ibid.*, 70.
13 *ibid.*, 80.
14 *ibid.*, 81.
15 J. Hunter (ed.), *The Diary of Ralph Thoresby* (1830), quoted in Abram, *Memorials*, 74–5.
16 Moon, *Guild Merchant*, 14–15.
17 *ibid.*, 15.
18 *ibid.*, 16.
19 LA CNP/3/1/4 (11 September 1801).
20 Wilcockson, *Authentic Records*, 74.
21 LA DDPr/138/97 *Summons to Preston Guild*.
22 Wilcockson, *Authentic Records*, 105–6.
23 LA CNP/3/1/5 (2 October 1822).
24 LA DDPr/138/2, *A New Song on the Preston Guild*.
25 Wilcockson, *Authentic Records*, 76.
26 Abram, *Guild Rolls*, 30.
27 Kuerden, *Description*, 59.
28 *ibid.*, 68–9.
29 *ibid.*, 88.
30 Quoted in Abram, *Memorials*, 74–5.
31 Note attached to a copy of *An Epilogue on ye Preston Guild*, quoted in Abram, *Memorials*, 81.
32 Moon, *Guild Merchant*, 14, 16.
33 *ibid.*, 16.
34 Quoted in Abram, *Memorials*, 74.
35 J. Heywood, *An Epilogue spoke by a Comedian the last PRESTON GUILD in Lancashire* (1722).
36 Moon, *Guild Merchant*, 16–17.

37 *Manchester Mercury*, 27 August 1782.

38 *Manchester Mercury*, 17 September 1782.

39 *General Advertiser*, 19 September 1782.

40 Anonymous manuscript describing the 1782 Guild, quoted in *The Kaleidoscope*, 6 August 1802.

41 Memorandum by Nicholas Grimshaw, 7 June 1802, quoted in Abram, *Memorials*, 111.

42 Joseph Shepherd Munden (1758–1832) was a mainstay of performances at Covent Garden from 1790 to 1813, and then at Drury Lane until his retirement in 1824 (on which occasion he played his most celebrated role, Sir Robert Bramble in *The Poor Gentleman*, as he had done at Preston Guild in 1802).

43 Abram, *Memorials*, 115–16.

44 Sophia Dussek (née Corri), a Scottish soprano and composer of Italian descent (1775–1831); Giovanni Battista Cimador, Italian-born and from 1791 London-based composer and music publisher, singer, violinist and pianist (1761–1805).

45 Abram, *Memorials*, 118–19.

46 LA DDPr/138/91/1 *Preston Guild programme 1822*.

47 *The Kaleidoscope* Guild Supplement, 24 September 1822.

48 *ibid.*

49 *Preston Chronicle*, 7 September 1822.

50 Abram, *Memorials*, 132.

51 Wilcockson, *Authentic Records*, 99–100.

52 *ibid.*, 101–2.

53 LA DDPr/138/91/15 Accounts and circular letter re Preston Guild Music Festival.

54 Abram, *Memorials*, 132.

55 Kuerden, *Description*, 80–1.

56 Quoted in Abram, *Memorials*, 81.

57 Moon, *Guild Merchant*, 17.

58 *Manchester Mercury*, 28 September 1802.

59 All descriptions of the 1822 Guild Balls from Wilcockson, *Authentic Records*, 80–92.

60 Wilcockson, *Authentic Records*, 46.

61 *ibid.*, 47–8.

62 *ibid.*, 78.

63 Kuerden, *Description*, 61.

64 Quoted in Abram, *Memorials*, 74.

65 *ibid.*, 81.

66 Moon, *Guild Merchant*, 16–17.

67 *Manchester Mercury*, 17 September 1782.

68 This refers to the open-air public parties at St James's Palace, held to mark the birthday of the sovereign.

69 Wilcockson, *Authentic Records*, 76.

70 *Manchester Mercury*, 10 September 1782 (advertisement); Wilcockson, *Authentic Records*, 76.

71 *The Kaleidoscope*, 3 September 1822.

72 *ibid.*, 24 September 1822.

73 A very full account of the balloon ascent is given in Wilcockson, *Authentic Records*, 94–6.

74 Quoted in Abram, *Memorials*, 74–5.

75 *ibid.*, 87.

76 Moon, *Guild Merchant*, 15.

77 LA DDPr/138/2 *A New Song on Preston Guild*.

78 Original in LA DDX/398/47.

79 *Manchester Mercury*, quoted in Abram, *Memorials*, 115.

80 Quoted in Abram, *Memorials*, 112.

81 LA DDPr/138/96 *Preston Guild of 1842*.

82 *The Kaleidoscope*, 24 September 1822.

83 Richard Assheton, 1st Viscount Cross, *A Family History* (privately published, 1900), quoting Cross family correspondence. I am indebted to the late Marian Roberts for drawing my attention to this reference.

84 LA DDPr/130/9.

85 LA DDX/1554/l; and see A.G. Crosby (ed.), *Benjamin Shaw's Family Records* (RSLC vol.130, 1991).

86 LA DDB1/12/146.

Notes to Chapter 6: The 1842 and 1862 Guilds

1 *Preston Chronicle*, 26 February 1842.

2 *ibid.*, 28 May 1842.

3 *ibid.*, 4 June 1842.

4 Letter to *Preston Chronicle*, 4 June 1842.

5 *Anticipatory Verses on Preston Guild* (1842).

6 *Preston Chronicle*, 11 June 1842.

7 *A New Song on Preston Guild 1842*.

8 It has often been suggested that the decision to hold the 1842 Guild was unanimous, but the very lengthy and detailed report of the debate and vote in the *Preston Chronicle* makes it clear that not only were there significant numbers of Corporation members absent, but that not all those present voted in favour.

9 *Preston Chronicle*, 2 July 1842.

10 R.D. Parker, 'The changing character of Preston Guild Merchant 1762–1862', *Northern History* vol.20 (1984) 108–26 (this ref. from p.121).

11 *ibid.*, 124: this interpretation is derived from Urbanski's thesis on the politics of Preston in 1796–1832.

12 *ibid.*

13 *ibid.*, 121.

14 ibid., 122–3.

15 Preston Corporation, *1842 Guild Committee minutes* (hereafter *1842 Guild Committee*), 18 July 1842. [LA CBP/1].

16 *1842 Guild Committee*, 27 July 1842. [LA CBP/1]

17 Letter from Alfred H. Greenwood, 30 August 1894, in envelope marked *Guild Record 1882* in the Borough archives. [LA CNP/2/13]

18 The shootings in Lune Street are described in several of the published histories of Preston (e.g. Hewitson, 1883). A less 'establishment' perspective is provided by J.E. King, *Richard Marsden and the Preston Chartists, 1837–1848* (University of Lancaster, Centre for North-West Regional Studies Occasional Paper 10, 1981), 29–30.

19 The Roman Catholics had held Guild events of their own since 1802, when a high mass was celebrated in St Mary's Chapel at the same time as the Corporation was attending the civic service. However, these events were unofficial, and not given any recognition by the Guild organisers.

20 Abram, *Memorials*, 137–139; *Preston Chronicle*, 17 September 1842.

21 *Anticipatory Verses on Preston Guild* (1842).

22 *Preston Chronicle*, 17 September 1842.

23 The general opinion among historians today is that the main underlying cause of the Cotton Famine was in fact excessive over-production and stockpiling of cotton cloth, the result of ill-advised management decisions in the industry in the mid- to late 1850s. This stockpiling meant that by 1861–62 the demand for newly produced cloth fell sharply. This existing circumstance was exacerbated in 1863–64 by the drastic reduction in supplies of raw cotton, but the crisis seems to have had earlier—and British—origins.

24 LA CNP/5/1, Preston Corporation 1862 Guild Committee minutes 11 April 1862.

25 *ibid.*, 7 May 1862.

26 *ibid.*, 13 June–14 July 1862 (seven meetings).

27 Abram, *Memorials*, 139.

28 A very detailed description of these processions is given in the *Preston Chronicle*, 17 September 1842.

29 LA CNP/5/1: 5 August 1862.

30 *ibid.*, 9 August 1862.

31 *ibid.*, 11 August 1862.

32 Fulwood did not become part of Preston administratively until 1974.

33 LA CNP/5/1: 12 August 1862.

34 *ibid.*, 18 August 1862.

35 *ibid.*, 20 August 1862.

36 *ibid.*, 27 August 1862.

37 *ibid.*, 9 September 1862.

38 Abram, *Memorials*, 145.

39 Quotation from an anonymous writer in Abram, *Memorials*, 145–6.

40 E. Waugh, *Home-Life of the Lancashire Factory Folk during the Cotton Famine* (1867), 126–8.

41 Abram, *Memorials*, 146–7.

42 *Preston Chronicle*, 17 September 1842.

43 *A New Song on the Jubilee and Sports of Preston Guild, 1842.*

44 LA DDPr/138/102.

45 *Preston Chronicle*, 17 September 1842.

46 Abram, *Memorials*, 139.

47 *Preston Chronicle*, 6 August 1842.

48 *ibid.*

49 LA DDPr/138/97: *Summons to the Preston Guild.*

50 LA CNP/5/1: 14 April 1862.

51 *ibid.*, May–June 1862; Abram, *Memorials*, 148, gives a summary of the overall balance sheet; LA DD Cm/11/3 is the manuscript account for the expenses of the Hallé.

52 Wilcockson, *Authentic Records*, 102–5.

53 Abram, *Memorials*, 146; the event included the placing of a time capsule, one of the very earliest recorded anywhere in Britain. In 1989 I discussed this matter with correspondence with Brian Durrans, then Deputy Keeper at the Museum of Mankind (Ethnography Department of the British Museum) and Britain's top time capsule expert, who was suitably impressed by Preston's pioneering role in this now traditional activity.

54 *ibid.*, 147.

55 LA CNP/5/1: final account and balance sheet.

56 N. Longmate, *The Hungry Mills: the story of the Lancashire cotton famine, 1861–1865* (Aldershot, 1978), 127.

57 LA CNP/5/1: this is the minute of a very long meeting that dealt with all aspects of catering.

58 *ibid.*, 25 July 1862.

59 *Illustrated London News*, 17 September 1842.

60 *ibid.*

61 *Preston Chronicle*, 17 September 1842, quoting a news item in the *Blackburn Standard* of the previous week.

62 *Preston Chronicle*, 17 September 1842.

63 *A New Song on the Preston Guild, 1842.*

64 LA CNP/5/1: 14 July and 28 July 1862.

65 *ibid.*, 15 August 1862.

66 *ibid.*

67 *ibid.*, 11 August 1862.

68 LA DDB1/53/31.

69 LA DDX/438/4.

70 R.A. Arnold, *A History of the Cotton Famine* (1864), 203–4.

71 *The Critic*, October 1862.

72 Anon., *The Distress in Lancashire: a visit to the cotton districts* (1862), quoted in Longmate, *The Hungry Mills*, 127.

Notes to Chapter 7: Preston Guild, 1882–1922

1 A. Hewitson, *History of Preston* (Preston, 1883, hereafter Hewitson, *History*) 101.

2 *Home Words*, vol.xliii (1882).

3 LA SMPr/4/1, All Saints C of E school logbook 24 August 1882.

4 LA SMPr/47/13, St Augustine's Girls' RC school logbook, 2 September 1882.

5 Hewitson, *History*, 107–8.

6 *ibid.*, 108.

7 LA SMPr/4/4, All Saints C of E school logbook, 10 July–1 September 1922.

8 LA SMPr/47/13, St Augustine's Girls' RC school logbook, 3 July–4 August 1922.

9 *Daily Mail*, 8 September 1842.

10 *Preston Chronicle*, 17 September 1842.

11 LA DDX/1089/1/3, Preston and District Power Loom Workers' Union Minutes, 16 May 1882.

12 *ibid.*, 20 June 1882–13 July 1882 (three meetings).

13 *ibid.*, 18 July 1882–14 August 1882 (four meetings).

14 *ibid.*, 22 August 1882.

15 Hewitson, *History*, 105.

16 *ibid.*, 105–6.

17 LA DDX/1089/19/2, Preston and District Textile Trades Federation Minutes, 14 September 1921.

18 *ibid.*, 9 January 1922.

19 *ibid.*, 6 March and 27 March 1922.

20 *ibid.*, 24 April 1922.

21 *ibid.*, 3 July and 10 July 1922.

22 *The Times*, 7 September 1922.

23 Hewitson, *History*, 106.

24 *ibid.*, 103–4.

25 An extensive and interesting correspondence between Charles Hallé, the town clerk and other interested parties survives among the borough archives. It includes letters from Hallé concerning booking performers, and negotiations about the programme (LA CNP/2/13/35–69).

26 Hewitson, *History*, 104, 110.

27 LA CNP/5/2 Preston Corporation 1902 and 1922 Guild Committee Minutes 6 February 1901 and 10 July 1901.

28 Hewitson, *History*, 107.

29 LA DP/376/8, Guild Mayor's Luncheon Menu 1882.

30 *1902 Guild Committee*, 11 June 1902.

31 LA DDX/1089/19/2: 7 August 1922.

32 Hewitson, *History*, 112–13.

33 *ibid.*, 113–14.

34 LA CNP/5/2: 24 July 1902; Full Council in Committee, 31 July 1902.

35 LA CNP/5/2: 7 August 1902.

36 Abram, *Memorials*, 137, 144.

37 *ibid.*, 146–7.

38 Hewitson, *History*, 103–4.

39 LA CNP/5/2: 15 May 1902 (this minute gives useful information concerning the heraldic origins of the Lamb of Preston).

40 LA CNP/5/2: 27 November 1902.

41 F. Billinge (ed.), *Preston Guild 1972: Official Handbook* (hereafter *1972 Official Handbook*) 133.

42 The choice of an outsider would now present major constitutional difficulties. Since the abolition of aldermen under the 1972 Local Government Act the mayor of Preston has to be an elected member of the City Council. For an 'outsider' to be Guild Mayor would require him or her to be elected in the usual way.

43 LA DDX/1471/1.

44 Hewitson, *History*, 114.

45 *The Times*, 7 September 1922.

46 LA CNP/5/2: 12 June 1902 and 7 July 1902.

47 *ibid.*, 19 July 1901 and 19 September 1901.

48 *ibid.*, 7 July 1902.

49 *ibid.*, 24 February 1902 and March 1902.

50 *ibid.*, 5 May 1902.

51 *ibid.*, 23 March 1902.

52 *ibid.*, 5 May 1902.

53 J.H. Spencer, *Preston Gild Merchant 1952: Official Handbook and Programme*, 91.

54 *Anticipatory Verses on Preston Guild* (1842).

55 *Preston Herald*, 8 September 1922.

56 LA CNP/5/2: 22 October 1902.

57 *Daily Mail*, 8 September 1922.

Notes to Chapter 8: The Guilds of 1952 and 1972

1 *Daily Mail*, 10 September 1922.

2 *The Times*, 7 September 1922.

3 LA CBP 1/2 (1941–42), 31 July 1941.

4 LA CBP 1/2 (1945–46), 27 September 1945.

5 LA CBP 1/2 (1946–47), 26 September 1946.

6 LA CBP 1/2 (1950–51: Guild Sub-Committee), 7 November 1950.

7 *1972 Official Handbook*, 133.

8 *ibid.*, 135.

9 Preston Corporation, *Preston Guild Merchant, 1972: Official Record* (hereafter *1972 Official Record*), 113.

10 Spencer, *Preston Gild Merchant 1952*, 95.

11 *1972 Official Handbook*, 141–2.

12 *Preston Guardian*, 13 September 1952.

13 *Prospect of Preston* programme (1972); *Lancashire Evening Post*, 16 September 1972.

14 *Preston Guardian*, 13 September 1952.

15 *Lancashire Evening Post*, 16 September 1972.

16 *Preston Guardian*, 13 September 1952.

17 *1972 Official Record*, 15.

18 *ibid.*, 140–1.

19 *ibid.*, 21–3.

20 *ibid.*, 137–8.

21 Spencer, *Preston Gild Merchant 1952*, 17–38.

22 *1972 Official Record*, 71–144.

23 *ibid.*, 81–3.

24 *ibid.*, 108.

25 *ibid.*, 109.

26 *ibid.*, 121.

27 I am indebted to Messrs E.H. Booth & Sons for the loan of a copy of this menu.

28 *Preston Guardian*, 13 September 1952.

29 *1972 Official Record*, 10, 16, 57–60.

30 *ibid.*, 117–18.

31 *ibid.*, 61–3.

32 *Lancashire Evening Post* and *Preston Guardian* 1952 Guild *Pictorial Souvenir*, 90.

33 *Lancashire Evening Post*, 16 September 1972.

34 1972 *Church of England Procession Official Programme*, 7.

35 *1972 Official Record*, 111–14.

36 *Prospect of Preston* programme (1972) 20.

37 *ibid.*, 21; words by Mrs G. Machell.

38 1952 *Guild Pictorial Souvenir*; *1972 Official Handbook*, 135–6.

39 1952 *Guild Pictorial Souvenir*, 6–14.

40 *1972 Official Record*, 33–5.

41 *ibid.*, 30–2.

42 *Lancashire Daily Post*, 8 September 1922.

43 *1972 Official Record*, 24–6.

Notes to Chapter 9: The Guild of 1992 and a new millennium

1 *Preston Guardian*, 13 September 1952.

2 Most of the content of this chapter is based on my own observations and recollections of the 1992 Guild, including my photographs, and also on the official record of the 1992 Guild which was commissioned by the Borough Council and written by me in 1993: Alan Crosby, *Preston Guild 1992: the official record* (Carnegie Publishing and Preston Borough Council, 1993).

3 For more information on the organisation and planning of the 1992 Guild, and the personalities involved, see Crosby, *Preston Guild, 1992*, 11–15.

4 Crosby, *Preston Guild 1992*, 20–7 discusses the consultancies, the marketing and private sector involvement in full detail.

5 The full list is given in Crosby, *Preston Guild 1992*, 227–8.

6 See Crosby, *Preston Guild 1992*, 16–17; the phrase 'England's greatest carnival' is the sub-title of the present book, and was I think invented by me, so I'm flattered that it was used in this context!

7 The use of the railway was so successful that in 1999 the Ribble Steam Railway was established, having moved from Steamtown in Southport, and from 2005 a regular steam-hauled passenger service has operated.

Picture acknowledgements

The following images are reproduced by kind permission of their owners, custodians or copyright holders: Preston City Council and the Harris Museum and Art Galley (nos 1, 3, 4, 15, 16, 19, 20, 27–28, 30, 31, 44, 45, 47–48, 50–52, 55, 56 and 58); David Kidson (Winter & Kidson Multimedia) and the Harris Museum and Art Gallery (nos 23–26); Preston City Council and Lancashire Archives (nos 6–14, 17); the Lancashire Evening Post and Lancashire Archives (nos 21, 33–38, 40, 42 and 43). Many thanks to Andrew Southworth (nos 5, 32, 41, 46, 53–54) and Meg and Stephen Davies (nos 2, 49, 55 and 57). The 1922 Guild Medal (no. 29) belongs to the publisher.

Index